Rethinking the Law of Armed Conflict in an Age of Terrorism

Rethinking the Law of Armed Conflict in an Age of Terrorism

Christopher A. Ford
and
Amichai Cohen

LEXINGTON BOOKS
Lanham • Boulder • New York • Toronto • Plymouth, UK

A portion of Chapter 3 was originally published as "Debate: Israel's Policy of Targeted Killing" by Steven R. David. *Ethics and International Affairs*, Vol. 17, No. 3 (2003), pp. 111–26. © 2003 Carnegie Council for Ethics in International Affairs. Reprinted with the permission of Cambridge University Press.

Published by Lexington Books
A wholly owned subsidiary of The Rowman & Littlefield Publishing Group, Inc.
4501 Forbes Boulevard, Suite 200, Lanham, Maryland 20706
www.rowman.com

Estover Road, Plymouth PL6 7PY, United Kingdom

British Library Cataloguing in Publication Information Available

Library of Congress Cataloging-in-Publication Data

Rethinking the law of armed conflict in an age of terrorism / edited by Christopher A. Ford and Amichai Cohen.
p. cm.
Summary: "Ten years after the terrorist attacks of September 11, 2001, Rethinking the Law of Armed Conflict in an Age of Terrorism, edited by Christopher Ford and Amichai Cohen, brings together a range of interdisciplinary experts to examine the problematic encounter between international law and challenges presented by conflicts between developed states and nonstate actors, such as international terrorist groups. Through examinations of the counter-terrorist experiences of the United States, Israel, and Colombia--coupled with legal and historical analyses of trends in international humanitarian law--the authors place post-9/11 practice in the context of the international legal community's broader struggle over the substantive content of international rules constraining state behavior in irregular wars and explore trends in the development of these rules"—Provided by publisher.
ISBN 978-0-7391-6653-6 (hardback) — ISBN 978-0-7391-6654-3 (electronic)
1. Terrorism (International law) 2. Terrorism—Prevention—Law and legislation. 3. Combatants and noncombatants (International law) 4. Terrorism—Prevention—Law and legislation—Israel. I. Ford, Christopher A., 1967- II. Cohen, Amichai.
KZ7220.R48 2012
341.6—dc23 2011039162

∞™ The paper used in this publication meets the minimum requirements of American National Standard for Information Sciences—Permanence of Paper for Printed Library Materials, ANSI/NISO Z39.48-1992.

Printed in the United States of America

From Dr. Ford

To Stella-Grace and Schuyler, my dear SGs:
"More handy than gold . . . /
Stronger than a solid castle, /
In all perils they stand firm."

From Dr. Cohen

To SMADAR
Proverbs 31:10

Jetsun Milarepa
One Hundred Thousand Songs
(C.C. Chang, trans.)

Contents

Preface and Acknowledgments

This volume is the outgrowth of a two-day conference, sponsored by the Jerusalem Center for Public Affairs and Hudson Institute, which took place in Washington, D.C., in December 2009. For the 10th anniversary of the terrorist attacks of September 2001, our participants have revised and expanded the talks they gave and papers they presented at that earlier event. We are grateful to the Jerusalem Center and to Hudson for their encouragement and continued support in preparing this book.

Dr. Cohen wishes to thank Dean Claudio Grossman, of the Washington College of Law at American University, for inviting him to stay in Washington during academic year 2009–10, and for the generous financial support Dr. Cohen received during that year. Both editors thank Lenore Lautigar of Lexington Books for her patience and encouragement.

We would like to thank the Jerusalem Center for Public Affairs for its financial suppport in the publication of this book.

Christopher Ford
Washington, D.C.

Amichai Cohen
Modi'in, Israel

Introduction

Rethinking Armed Conflict in an Age of Terrorism

Christopher A. Ford

Americans have grown accustomed to thinking that the world changed in some important way on September 11, 2001, when *al Qaeda* terrorists slammed hijacked commercial airliners into the World Trade Center Towers in New York and into the Pentagon—and a fourth aircraft merely into the ground, rather than the U.S. Capitol or the White House—causing some 3,000 deaths. They are not wrong to think this, but most Americans usually give less thought to precisely *how* the world has changed, and to what degree. Nor, indeed, is it well understood that some of the things that seemed so novel about counterterrorist conflict in the new century actually made their appearance—albeit sometimes in attenuated forms—somewhat earlier, both for the United States and elsewhere, particularly Israel.

The basic post-9/11 intuition is sound, for the world is indeed not the same as it was before the attacks. We will fail to see important things about these changes, however, if we do not set aside our parochialism and understand them in their broader perspective. Though "9/11" helped to crystallize many of these changes, to sharpen the challenges presented, and to highlight the dilemmas involved, and though it forced Americans to consider them urgently and explicitly as never before, the dynamics involved have been not specifically *American* but indeed *global.*

This volume represents the work of a group of interdisciplinary experts from the United States, Israel, and Colombia, brought together by Hudson Institute and the Jerusalem Center for Public Affairs to offer readers their insights into how these broad dynamics have changed—or perhaps *should* change—how we think about the law of armed conflict (LOAC) in this age in which counterterrorist struggles across multiple national frontiers against non-state adversaries have become such a common type of conflict. These scholars do not entirely agree upon what has changed, from the perspective of international legality, and where the strange trajectory of modern conflict is taking us. They do, however, offer valuable perspectives and insights that help illuminate this important topic now that a full decade has passed since that grim autumn morning in New York and Washington, D.C.

Ariel Zemach begins the essays in this volume with a chapter that offers a new perspective upon what has come before. Specifically, he addresses the indeterminacy—albeit apparently the *unintentional* indeterminacy—of international law in the wake of the First Additional Protocol to the Geneva Conventions when it comes to irregular combatants.

That this ambiguity was not intended is both ironic and clear from the intentions of the drafters of Additional Protocol I in the mid-1970s, who seem to have had the anti-imperialist aim of introducing "just war" concepts into the corpus of the *jus in bello* by having the law essentially *side* with irregular combatants engaged in struggles against unjust regimes such as *apartheid*-era South Africa or remnant European colonial administrations in the developing world. This was to be accomplished, *inter alia,* by declaring such struggles to be international armed conflicts—with the effect that state belligerents would have to give their guerrilla adversaries prisoner-of-war (POW) status and otherwise restrain their behavior in fighting such irregulars. The Protocol, in its Articles 1(4) and 44(3), also would have somewhat relaxed the prior duty of guerilla combatants to distinguish themselves from the civilian population, in part by designating them as combatants based more upon their *status* as belligerents than upon their specific actions at any particular point in time.

As Zemach recounts, however, the irony comes in the way this effort seems to have redounded *against* irregular fighters. Additional Protocol I *succeeded* only so far as it eroded existing customary norms that had hitherto provided at least limited protections to guerrilla fighters under longstanding principles of distinguishing between combatants and civilians. Yet because it was not ubiquitously adopted, and because major players in the international system specifically objected to it in these very particulars, the Protocol *failed* to *replace* those older customary rules with the new, even more guerrilla-friendly norms it tried to offer.

The result, Zemach suggests, was a legal system that became, in the aggregate, *less* protective of irregular combatants, even as the groundwork was being laid for the emergence of nontraditional state-on-non-state irregular conflicts as an ever more prevalent part of the global environment. Zemach argues, for instance, that under previous standards developed under the Hague Conventions, state belligerents were bound to a sort of "package deal" whereby if a guerrilla could be attacked he must also perforce be given POW status if captured, but he was not to be considered a combatant at all—and was thus a civilian immunized against lawful attack—unless actually taking part in hostilities. Additional Protocol I's emphasis on *status*-based combatant categorization, however, has served to undermine this Hague standard as a norm of customary international law, yet without the Protocol's rules having *themselves* become a replacement norm.

Accordingly, it is *less* clear than before what rules, if any, apply to states fighting against such irregular adversaries. This has the result, Zemach suggests, that this *gap* in the law must be filled according to the "freedom principle" of international jurisprudence, best known from the famous 1927 *Lotus* decision of the Permanent Court of International Justice. In the absence of a clear rule to the contrary, this doctrine indicates, sovereign states may act as they wish—and so, perhaps, may they when facing irregular combatants.

In Zemach's account, in the narrow class of circumstances where individuals would be classified as combatants under Additional Protocol I but would *not* be considered combatants under the Hague Conventions—that is, in cases involving guerrillas not immediately engaged in hostilities—the *Lotus* principle would suggest that their state adversary may, lawfully, both *attack* them at will and *decline* to give them POW status if they are captured. And this, of course, is what some countries have indeed chosen to do in the years since the Protocol's emergence in 1977.

Thus, perhaps, is the road to hell paved. The drafters of the First Additional Protocol aimed to help irregular forces fighting against established state powers, but if Zemach is right, the Protocol has made it easier for such powers to act lawfully against irregular combatants with more leeway than ever. Zemach's analysis thus provides a fascinating "backstory" for the other authors' accounts of international law and practice in the counterterrorist wars of the last decade or so.

Jeremy Rabkin follows Zemach's analysis with his own, even more critical account of the First Additional Protocol—and, indeed, a scathing review of the entire modern project of developing new norms of international humanitarian law (IHL). In Rabkin's eyes, this effort is not as counterproductive as Zemach describes it as being, from the perspective of its drafters' intent to privilege guerrilla combatants in their struggles with state adversaries. It has been, for Rabkin, all *too* productive in producing a legal environment that favors terrorist groups against liberal democracies.

To Rabkin, the modern IHL project is a misbegotten one, the product of a sensibility and a political agenda the explicit aim of which was to depart from time-tested rules—ones developed with an eye to balancing the realities and responsibilities of warfare with the needs of humanity—in order to create *new* norms restricting the ability of Western powers to resist *anti*-Western irregulars during the era of decolonization. IHL is not, he thinks, the product of a natural and necessary evolution based upon the dictates, and representing the collective conscience, of "humanity." It is, rather, a blatantly *political* project which in effect seeks to use the law as a *weapon* of war by privileging one type of combatant over another.

According to Rabkin, the basic mischief of this project has been aided and abetted over time by organizations such as the International Committee of the Red Cross (ICRC) and Human Rights Watch, as such groups have changed over time from neutral providers of humanitarian services in time of war to institutions with more purely policy- and legal-advocacy roles that have given them fundraising and media-placement incentives to embrace and assist anti-Western positions. The final ingredient in the recipe that has produced the modern IHL project, Rabkin argues, is simple neglect or abdication by some Western governments themselves, particularly in Europe. As their own post-Cold War situations have relieved them of any perceived need to be concerned with how future wars might actually be fought and won, he contends, some such governments have with this shift jettisoned any concern for thinking responsibly about the laws of war, now finding it easier to win acclaim for embracing the positions of IHL advocates than to think thoughtfully and constructively about how to craft sensible legal norms.

Rabkin recognizes that the IHL genie cannot, as it were, be put entirely back in the bottle. Nonetheless, he urges Western governments to remain alive—and indeed to call attention—to the contingency, indeterminacy, and nuanced nature of the laws of war, as well as to the still fundamentally *contested* character of agenda-driven IHL interpretations whose advocates tend to portray them as clear and unquestionable verities. He also exhorts Western governments not to cede to international institutions the interpretive authority to pronounce upon the "proper" balance between military necessity and humanitarian obligations. To do this, Rabkin feels, is tantamount to ceding the capacity for self-defense itself.

In the third essay, Steven David offers his own perspective upon the development of legal norms in Zemach's ambiguous post-1977 era of neither-Geneva-nor-the-Hague warmaking, with an account of Israel's recent experience in trying to develop one particular way to fight irregular adversaries both effectively and humanely: targeted killing. To be sure, Israel appears to have engaged in some forms of targeted killing for many years in special cases, probably most famously in its campaign to track down and eliminate the "Black September" Palestinian perpetrators of the massacre of Israeli athletes at the 1972 Summer Olympics in Munich. This policy continued through the 1990s, being seen, for example, in the unsuccessful Israeli attempt on the life of Hamas leader Khalid Meshal with a neurotoxin in Amman, Jordan, in September 1997.

The modern phase of Israeli targeted killing operations, however, really emerged during the Palestinian uprisings of the so-called Second Intifada in 2000. Where previous Israeli attempts to kill high-ranking terrorist adversaries had been at least notionally covert—and thus, theoretically perhaps, nothing more than a continuation of the sort of secret high jinks in which states have, for better or worse, engaged for hundreds of years—the new targeted killing policy was distinguished by its essential *openness*. Conducted less frequently with spies and in secret than relatively openly and with more stereotypically "military" tools such as helicopter gunships and precision-guided weapons, these new killings have emerged in Israeli practice as an essentially acknowledged alternative to, or perhaps an *aspect of*, ordinary warfare.

David's essay explores Israel's experience of this new mode of targeted killing from both a policy and a legal perspective, analyzing it not simply in military terms (e.g., its effectiveness in disrupting or deterring terrorist operations) but as an Israeli response to the novel challenges of the "lawfare" aspects of modern irregular conflict in which terrorist combatants seek to conceal themselves amongst a civilian population and to reap propaganda and political benefits from state counterstrikes that cause injury or death to their human shields.

Through this prism, David sees targeted killing operations as a way to economize on civilian damage, thus seeking fidelity—in this nontraditional sort of war—to the very LOAC principles that terrorist concealment strategies seek to exploit against a state adversary. As an alternative to the unattractive options of either *not* fighting back against terrorist adversaries or pursuing them with traditional firepower techniques bound to cause terrible casualties among civilians, David suggests that targeted killing has emerged as a morally and legally defensible model for modern warfare: a military tool for attacking terrorist enemies while ensuring maximal compliance with international law.

His analysis, however, is not unequivocal. As a *policy* choice, David does see some dangers lurking in Israel's targeted killing strategy—and, by implication, in the now even more famous American fondness for using drone aircraft in this same regard against terrorist targets in Afghanistan, Iraq, Pakistan, and Yemen. In particular, his essay discusses the potential implications should targeted killing be perceived as undermining longstanding international norms against assassination. Legally speaking, he correctly stresses that these two categories are separate ones, with targeted killing being distinguishable from assassination by its use against combatant adversaries rather than, say, against the political leader of another state in peacetime. Nonetheless, both types of killing appear superficially similar enough that whatever the lawyers say, one might worry that widespread acceptance of targeted killing could make assassination seem less taboo.

David, however, points out that two factors may help counterbalance this "erosion" effect. First, it is not clear that targeted killings against *non-state* combatants will undermine existing rules with respect to how *states* treat each other's leaders. Indeed, as noted earlier, it is to a great extent precisely the *point* of targeted killing to move against irregular adversaries in ways maximally compliant with existing international law. Because it actually represents an attempt at state *fidelity* to the ideal of law-governed conduct, targeted killing may not be too corrosive to legal compliance by other *states*. Meanwhile, the *non*-state terrorist targets of such policies are generally themselves contemptuous of legal restraint in any event, and are unlikely to conform to LOAC standards whether or not targeted killing is employed against them.

Second, the modern Israeli approach to targeted killings stresses *military*-style tools, is generally acknowledged, and occurs in comparatively open circumstances and in time of a clear conflict. This may help insulate it from undercutting traditional norms against treachery, and help to prevent such attacks from being too much confused with assassination. David emphasizes that Israel has *not* always cleanly preserved the apparent distinction between its targeted killings and assassination—for instance, in having hit teams pose as foreign tourists in Dubai or Amman—but he makes clear that much of modern Israeli practice can indeed be defended on these grounds.

Finally, David's account of the Israeli experience notes that Israeli practice has sometimes tended to get mixed up with "retribution" motives, rather than remaining tied to more traditional LOAC concepts such as military necessity. These are different frameworks, with different legal implications. (Retribution might justify killing someone guilty of a past attack even if there were clearly no likelihood of him ever attacking again, but this could be problematic in terms of military necessity.) In this sense, too, David's description of Israeli practice suggests a policy struggling with itself, and perhaps a new approach to warfare that has as yet only incompletely emerged.

All in all, David offers a mixed review of Israel's experience with targeted killings, acknowledging some drawbacks but still defending the policy as a moral tool that seeks to achieve military results at minimum cost to civilians. It is, he contends, the "least bad option" for a state facing a conflict with terrorist adversaries, and is indeed *less* humane to one's irregular opponents *only* than the alternative of not attacking terrorist adversaries at all—an option that neither Israeli nor American leaders felt able to rely upon once terrorist attacks had reached a particularly horrific intensity.

In David's description, targeted killing thus emerges as a strategy that has evolved in *support* of LOAC goals, seeking a way to serve LOAC ends in circumstances that do not cleanly fit the mold of traditional conflict, and against enemies who seek to exploit the law as a *de facto* weapon of war by deliberately hiding among innocents. David offers some suggestions about how the Israeli approach could be changed—for example, by using targeted killing only against targets clearly somehow in the enemy's combatant chain of command, and bringing the policy, as it were, more fully into the open by subjecting it more to the hurly-burly of democratic accountability—but at the end of the day he defends targeted killing as the best available option in trying circumstances.

Yuval Shany picks up the baton next, though now in order to offer a more cautionary note, pointing out that in modern democracies, terrorist conflicts have often resulted in a dramatic and worrying empowerment of the executive branch of government. He warns that the executive branch is the one most likely to abuse such authority—especially because this very empowerment erodes *other* branches' ability to provide necessary corrections—and that what purports to be quite reasonably act-consequential responses to terrorist outrages can often have worrisome rule-consequentialist outcomes, distorting government's proper functioning and imperiling citizens' rights and freedoms.

Shany urges readers to evaluate counterterrorism (CT) policies not simply on their own merits, as specific separate decisions, but also with an eye to their second-order consequences—such as their impact upon how political and legal institutions work, or the balances struck *within* systems of governance. From this perspective, he sees CT decisions driven by the perceived exigencies of modern terrorism threats leading to *imbalances* within democratic governments, in which the executive branch acquires too much power and exercises it beyond the reach of potential institutional corrections. In response to such problems, Shany suggests the need for "absolute procedural and substantive norms" that would serve to limit government power no matter *which* branch asserts it.

In Shany's view, executive overreach is visible both in post-9/11 America and in Israel. In response to domestic and international criticism, executive authorities in both countries have engaged in "reactive institutional reform," but they have tended therein to focus upon review mechanisms *within* the executive—seemingly to take advantage of the political legitimacy benefits of being seen to *have* an oversight system while yet limiting its reach and effectiveness.

Even where courts choose to involve themselves, Shany worries that they generally tend to align themselves with the executive, and may ultimately tend only to legitimate, rather than also actually to *constrain,* executive power. Nor, he suggests, can political remedies form a reliable corrective, inasmuch as he feels that political bodies frequently defer to security services' expertise, and may be biased to favor task-oriented executive discretion in foiling terrorist attacks over taking steps to ensure the protection of detainees' rights. All in all, therefore, Shany feels there to remain a real risk that executive discretion will be abused and rules "chronically misapplied." This, he observes, "raises the problem of *Quis custōdiet ipsōs custōdēs*": who will guard the guardians?

To help counter this, Shany argues for reestablishing real supervision of the executive branch. One possibility in this regard, he writes, is to turn more to *international* supervision. Such procedures and organs raise their own problems, including legitimacy concerns related to perceived bias and politicization of the sort discussed in more depth by Elizabeth Samson in her own contribution to this volume assessing the impact of Richard Goldstone's report to the United Nations on Israel's "Operation Cast Lead" in Gaza. (As Christopher Ford points out later in this volume, moreover, the use of force in intelligence-driven CT operations in far-flung corners of the world—such as U.S. drone strikes in Yemen or the wilds of Pakistan—may also prove in some ways structurally resistant to outsider second-guessing.) Shany notes, however, that it is also possible for international investigations—or the prospect thereof—to spur more serious *national* inquiries, suggesting that the European Court of Human Rights has had some such "shadow" effect in the United Kingdom.

As an alternative to such international supervision, Shany offers the possibility of "normative elaboration of criteria for derogating from ordinary monitoring procedures." By this he means that special standards would be articulated for when to invoke "war" versus "peace" as the operative paradigm—a standard that might, through the prism of Steven David's analysis, help distinguish targeted killings from mere extrajudicial executions—or what sorts of circumstances would justify imposing a state of emergency. States wishing to shift into a paradigm that entails fewer substantive and procedural restrictions on executive power, in other words, would be expected, in effect, to submit this decision itself to special scrutiny. By developing or clarifying norms for such shifts, Shany hopes to ensure that such paradigm shifting occurs only under well-justified circumstances. He also suggests that decisions interfering with the right to life, such as targeted killings, be subjected to special procedural requirements for *ex ante* informational certainty, as well as *ex post* investigation for purposes of accountability.

Finally, Shany offers the idea of moving from "balancing" norms—in which institutions of government are expected to play corrective roles vis-à-vis each other—to a system more focused upon *absolute* norms designed to minimize second-order abuse-of-discretion and other rule-consequentialist problems under the pressure of events in CT conflicts. As recounted in Amichai

Cohen's examination herein of terrorism-related litigation in the United States and Israel, some such trend—focused upon due-process protections for detainees rather than substantive constraints upon executive power *per se*—may already be underway. Shany emphasizes, however, that approaching the question of absolute norms seriously would involve much broader study of the rules and interrelationships involved in how a government functions than courts are accustomed to providing in case-by-case jurisprudence.

John Shenefield's chapter on the Foreign Intelligence Surveillance Act (FISA) in the United States provides a different window upon the challenges of reconciling expedient action with oversight. FISA itself, of course, was an effort in 1978 to place the field of domestic electronic surveillance within an explicitly statutory framework—and to subject its operational particulars, moreover, to new institutions of judicial review—after years of essentially untrammeled executive discretion. The development, adjustment, and contestation of these rules in the intervening years thus provides a fascinating case study of maintaining and adjusting a framework for regularity and accountability—in fits and starts through legislative amendments and other processes over the years—as the telecommunications field and the nature of U.S. national security threats have changed.

One important message of Shenefield's essay would seem to be that the process of FISA's evolution has today fallen behind the times and that the statute would benefit from an overhaul. Some of its distinctions, he writes, are arbitrary "and bear little if any relationship to expectations of privacy or the imperatives of collection." One should perhaps not expect too much conceptual or structural elegance from statutory products of legislative bargaining, of course, and Shenefield suggests that we should be happy that today's cobbled-together legislative "sausage" of FISA works as well as it does. Nevertheless, he urges the law's repair and rationalization.

Shenefield describes an important theme in FISA's development over the decades as being its gradual, though only partial, evolution from a conceptual scheme emphasizing the specific *premises* to be monitored to a system more focused upon the *persons* in question. This process is by no means complete, however, and FISA today embodies a hybrid, patchwork approach in which both location (e.g., whether or not the target is in the United States) and person (e.g., whether or not the target is a "U.S. person," or an "agent of a foreign power") are critical variables—as well, to some extent, as the *means* of intelligence collection involved, and where it takes place.

This, Shenefield contends, is needlessly complex. He urges that this complicated matrix be simplified into a principally individual system, keyed to the status of the particular person targeted as a U.S. person (or otherwise). FISA's other distinctions, he argues, are no longer appropriate: method-specific rules are doomed always to be at least one step behind a rapidly changing technological world, "foreign power" concepts are unworkable in the face of today's terrorist threats, and physical location is either perilously indeterminate or simply irrelevant in today's global information pool. FISA, he writes, has already started to move haltingly in this direction through *ad hoc* legislative tweaks, but a wholesale scrub is needed in order to create a clean scheme that reflects our current understanding both of evolving threats and modern privacy requirements.

Shenefield also uses the saga of pre- and post-9/11 struggles over the issue of the famously misconstrued FISA "wall" between intelligence and law enforcement—and over the "purpose" test long applied in this regard—to illustrate the tenacity of conceptual, cultural, and bureaucratic inertia in approaching domestic electronic surveillance issues within the U.S. system. FISA's story, it would appear, is only *partly* about the specific provisions of a specific portion of the U.S. code. Also of importance are the assumptions and attitudes that surround the system and permeate actors' interpretations of their operational legal reality, and the political and institutional "teething pains" that can accompany shifts in the basic legal frameworks governing a particular area of activity.

Shenefield argues that U.S. confusions over the infamous "wall" and "purpose test" suggest that "bureaucratically, [and] culturally—there is work probably still to be done" even in working through the implications of the *existing* electronic surveillance framework. In his view, this makes systematic FISA reform more important, for such work would be greatly aided by the articulation of a clean, rationalized rule such as the individual-focused concept he promotes. (Shenefield also makes several more specific suggestions with respect to the details of current FISA debates, concerning roving wiretaps, "business records" access, and "lone wolf" surveillance.)

All in all, Shenefield's account offers FISA as what is, in effect, another example of legal regimes struggling to adopt to the "new normal" of a world presenting challenges not quite like those in reaction to which its rules were formulated years earlier. FISA's is not just a post-9/11 story arc, of course. Indeed, its history has been one of gradual legislative adjustment—and, more recently, judicial clarification—for some decades. That all this has, *selon* Shenefield, worked at all is testimony to the relative effectiveness of this ongoing, *ad hoc* adjustment process. That it yet needs, in his view, a more comprehensive overhaul, however, may also indicate that sometimes piecemeal alteration is inadequate, and that wholesale conceptual reframing may sometimes still be required. In this respect, the FISA saga helps provide additional perspective upon this volume's other essays about how the legal system has struggled with modern terrorism.

The FISA story tracks much broader LOAC-related debates in the U.S. context between "absolutist" arguments about inherent executive authority and more conventionally rule-bound constructions of the president's authority with regard to national security. Such inherent-authority arguments arose quite sharply in the surveillance arena, with respect both to the National Security Agency's Terrorist Surveillance Program (TSP) after 9/11, and to the Bush Administration's suggestion in legal papers that FISA itself is unconstitutional if it denies an inherent presidential right to freely monitor the nation's enemies in wartime—even if these enemies are shadowy non-state actor terrorists and, in some small proportion, Americans operating domestically besides.

As Shenefield notes, the positions suggested by such debates are, in theory, at opposite ends of the spectrum of constitutional theory. "Theory," however, "here as in so many other cases, gets mugged by harsh reality." The FISA debates, as they have actually played out, represent a basically non-absolutist answer, as the branches have in practice fumbled their way forward—both sides finding that they "must adjust to each other so that both can function as a shared responsibility."

As suggested by Shenefield's invocation of Corwin's interbranch "invitation to struggle" for primacy in foreign affairs—and also by the dynamics discussed by Ford's account of "bargaining in the shadow" of a showdown or constitutional crisis that all participants wish to avoid—such a way of feeling out solutions offers more a *process* answer than a substantive "package" of responses. In Shenefield's account, resolution to the TSP controversy came not through a binary choice between alternatives, of the sort one might expect in criminal or civil litigation, but through a more *political* process. Ultimately, Congress endorsed (and thus legitimated) executive surveillance of communications in which the target was merely "reasonably believed" to be located outside the United States. TSP acquired more reviews and accountability, but it continued nonetheless, and now with a Congressional imprimatur. As with the combatant detention and other war-paradigm issues discussed later in this volume in Ford's chapter, the TSP story thus illustrates the development of a "new normal" rule as the result of bargained, but limited, retrenchment from a paradigm of absolutist executive assertion. In Shenefield's characterization, such solutions may prevent conformity to "doctrinal purity," but can often prove workable.

With FISA, therefore, Shenefield calls for a similar broad "compromise in which the president asks Congress to share responsibility for simplifying and clarifying this legal regime" in ways that would modernize and streamline a system that is not wrongheadedly designed at the most basic level, but which should now be made less "cumbersome, slow, and laborious," "hideously complex," and "resource-intensive." As noted, he also suggests the importance of such streamlining as what might be termed a *performative act:* not merely *having* improved rules, but also articulating the framework clearly enough—and making a statement about its advent having sufficient political and conceptual power–that bureaucratic and institutional players will actually realign their mindsets and operational practices appropriately. With such a process, undertaken in the open and with the involvement of multiple branches of government, Shenefield suggests we can save FISA from becoming "obsolete," and build a system for regulating domestic electronic surveillance that will be sustainable for many years to come.

Having in mind such processes of interbranch bargaining or conflict, Amichai Cohen's study of terrorism-related litigation in the United States and Israel provides a valuable perspective—and its own sort of analytical corrective. He rejects the idea of there being a crisp distinction between (a) a "law" paradigm and (b) a supposed "war" paradigm in which there is relatively little constraint upon government behavior, no role for the courts, and less protection for civilians. Instead, Cohen argues that these issues have always existed more on a continuum than as a binary choice between such alternative frameworks.

Moreover, Cohen suggests that the evolution of criminal jurisdiction over combatant treatment cases will have little real impact in the ongoing Israeli and American struggles against terrorism, and perhaps may ultimately serve more to legitimate than to restrain executive power. Indeed, he makes the point that judging from terrorism-related case law in the United States and Israel to date—principally with regard to issues of detainee treatment—what seems to have mattered most to courts are not abstract paradigmatic questions of whether to apply a "war" framework or a more civilian "legal" one, but rather whether or not the events in question have occurred in territory under the *de facto* control of the state. This dichotomy between control and no control, he suggests, is a very significant factor in such jurisprudence, and may even help explain the "war" versus "law" distinction itself.

After all, in traditional "war," hostilities occur in contested areas not usually fully under the control of either side, so there is some logic in *restricting* the applicability of normal civilian law, which may be seen as a framework for regulating affairs in your "own" space. Where a state does effectively control a territory, however, there is a stronger case for having civilian law serve as its default system, setting rules for its conduct there—even if some hostilities are nonetheless occurring in that area as part of a more nontraditional conflict.

According to Cohen, most government lawyers have argued the existence of a stark, paradigmatic war/law dichotomy in order not specifically to preclude the applicability of law *per se* but rather, and more narrowly, simply to keep the *courts* from telling the government what to do. (Courts are traditionally expected to stay out of "war" matters.) Yet, led by the Israeli Supreme Court, many courts *have* stepped into the business of pronouncing upon government actions in modern CT conflicts. Cohen emphasizes, however, that this involvement has usually come in circumstances where the government has been in clear territorial control of the location where the facts of the case took place (e.g., pre-pullout Gaza, the West Bank, or Guantánamo Bay), and has usually taken the form *only* of insisting upon due process protections against executive efforts to bypass the court system entirely.

For this reason, Cohen discounts the conventional account of judicial systems, confronted by executive overreaching, that have opted suddenly to assert new powers in regulating "war" functions for the first time. Territorial control, he suggests, has long been a critical factor in allowing courts a role in checking unilateral executive power, and ensuring due-process rights is a very traditional—indeed *core*—judicial function that does not necessarily imply providing any substantive protection to detainee defendants. Nor, he stresses, is there much sign of courts' willingness to intervene in matters that are not in some sense "criminal" and do not involve due-process issues. In this respect, there is little that is really "new" about contemporary CT cases.

Cohen, then, essentially admonishes us to ignore those who prophesy doom as a result of judicial activism in giving terrorist detainees legal rights. In fact, as noted, he speculates that the net effect of such judicial involvement is not necessarily to detainees' benefit at all. So far, Cohen suggests, the courts may have done more to provide legitimacy to what the government *still* ends up being able to do (e.g., imprison enemy combatants indefinitely) than they have actually to *restrain* executive power. Seen through this prism, Israeli and American CT litigation thus seems to be yet another arena in which the system has been feeling its way forward—if perhaps not toward a wholly *new* legal paradigm to apply to modern irregular conflicts, then at least toward an *adjusted* one in which longstanding principles are applied in less familiar ways in response to nontraditional security challenges. Things have not been refashioned afresh, as it were, but neither do they remain the same.

As we have seen, in response to the challenge of "guarding the guardians" and protecting the legal system against executive overreaching, Yuval Shany suggested that *international* oversight might in some circumstances provide a complement to purely national correctives such as litigation or legislative intervention. Elizabeth Samson's contribution to this volume, however, describes an example of such an attempt at international oversight which seems not to have gone particularly well—and indeed which has now been rather humiliatingly retracted, at least in part, by its principal author.

Former South African Supreme Court Justice Richard Goldstone headed a United Nations mission to inquire into allegations of war crimes during Israel's "Cast Lead" campaign in Gaza in 2008–09. As Samson observes, this mission had great importance—or at least *potential* importance—because this area of the LOAC is widely said to be in flux: there is a widespread perception that traditional legal paradigms may be in some way poorly suited to modern irregular conflicts.

In today's "new era of armed conflict," the dominant mode of war seems to be one in which state combatants are engaged against *non-state* ones, a type of conflict that raises questions about whether new rules are needed. Some have called for a reexamination of the international norms of armed conflict, arguing the need to modify or replace existing rules, and feeling that some new approach is needed. Others insist that one or another body of existing law actually applies perfectly well, although opinions differ about *which* one is the right answer. As fascinatingly recounted in Juan Carlos Gómez's contribution to this volume, some even seem to take an *ad hoc* approach—applying different bodies of existing law on a shifting basis, depending upon immediate operational circumstances.

In any event, the Goldstone Report represented a significant opportunity to contribute to such legal debates. It offered a chance to demonstrate that existing law, or some component thereof, made practical, moral, and legal sense as a way to regulate modern CT conflict and hold belligerents properly accountable for their actions. It also offered an opportunity to vindicate the international inquiry as a means of addressing such issues. Unfortunately for Goldstone, his particular effort did not live up to this promise.

In Samson's critique—one that has been strengthened by Goldstone's own public admission that if he knew then what he knows now, he would have produced a very different report—Goldstone's response to the challenges of applying the framework of international law to modern irregular warfare was a notably *bad* answer to the challenges it tried to address, an ill-supported and almost mischievous contribution to the ongoing process of contested legal *becoming* that is modern international law. Both the report's fiercely controversial issuance and Goldstone's subsequent personal retraction of its most significant conclusions have arguably left the field in more flux than ever.

The answer Samson herself suggests to the challenges of irregular conflict is not to forsake but rather to turn *back* to the animating principles of the LOAC—military necessity, distinction between combatants and noncombatants, proportionality of force, humanity, and the avoidance of unnecessary suffering—in order to use them as inspiration in adapting the legal framework to modern circumstances. A key problem for law-abiding state participants in contemporary conflicts, however, is the fact that the idea of rules applying "between combatants" is imperiled because one side ignores or actually seeks to take *advantage* of the LOAC's admirable distinction between combatants and noncombatants.

Irregular fighters who conceal themselves amongst the population, and who conduct military operations based out of civilian centers sure to suffer tremendously from state-party counterstrikes, seek to make a law-abiding state's desire to *preserve* the law's admirable distinction between combatants and noncombatants into a weapon of asymmetric warfare wielded *against* that state. This weapon, moreover, is likely to be effective in direct proportion to the degree to which the state wishes to *uphold* the LOAC value of distinction, with the effect that this irregular tactic deliberately imperils the entire LOAC edifice by pitting its elements (e.g., necessity and distinction) against each other, at the expense of innocent noncombatants.

Such, Samson suggests, was precisely the "legal" strategy of Hamas during Israel's Operation Cast Lead, and this fundamental challenge is what Goldstone most notably failed to grasp, let alone help the law address. Civilian casualties are to a great extent inevitable in all war, of course, but when at least one side *deliberately* endangers civilians by conducting military operations from their midst, one might expect objective outside observers to give *this* belligerent a healthy share of blame for the foreseeable results when its opponent—following the LOAC principle of military necessity—strikes at these combatants. Indeed, since such tactics *intentionally* imperil civilians while the actions of the counterstriking state do so only *derivatively,* one might suppose it a sensible, if rebuttable, presumption to deem the resulting casualties a "war crime" by the civilian-collocated terrorist rather than the combatant.

Yet this is precisely what Goldstone did not do. Indeed, as both Samson and Ford make clear in their respective essays, Goldstone seems to have adopted a presumption that went precisely the other way, adopting a logical syllogism whereby Israel was presumed to have *intended* any civilian casualties that cannot conclusively be proven to have been unintentional. In his now-famous retraction,[1] in fact, Goldstone essentially admits this, describing himself as having concluded that Israel deliberately targeted civilians simply because civilian deaths had occurred and Goldstone "had no evidence on which to draw any other reasonable conclusion." This would be a somewhat surprising logic in any war—for he basically reached a conclusion of war crimes essentially in the *absence* of any information one way or the other about the relevant belligerent's actual intentions vis-à-vis civilians or efforts to minimize civilian casualties—but it is positively extraordinary in a conflict in which, as his own report acknowledged, Israel's Hamas opponents mounted military operations (e.g., rocket attacks) from heavily populated civilian areas.

Samson is surely right that the Goldstone Report, between its troubling logic and its author's subsequent recantation of its most noteworthy conclusions, failed to contribute constructively to the development of international law—and may have made the law seem more unequal than ever to modern challenges—at a time when the LOAC's adequacy and coherence is being increasingly questioned. An opportunity missed indeed.

In his own chapter, Juan Carlos Gómez offers a very different window into these dilemmas. He provides an insider's account of how one country—Colombia—has practiced counterterrorist war in a highly self-aware process through which in its day-to-day military and security force operations the country applies *both* the more conflict-focused IHL *and* the more "civilian" human rights law (HR) paradigms on a shifting basis, adopting each in turn based upon assessments of the specific circumstances of the moment.

As with several of the other authors, Gómez feels modern warfare to have been going through an important shift, moving from more traditional, industrial-scale conceptions of warmaking to "small, nebulous, and [often] covert" conflicts with enemies who look and act a bit like the criminals who are the targets of civilian law enforcement but who are real combatant adversaries nonetheless. *This* battlefield, Gómez notes, is a different one than international lawyers are used to conceptualizing, for such wars "in the midst of the people"—in this case, Colombia's *own* people—present special challenges for governments that care about protecting the "hard-won freedoms and rights" of the citizenry and minimizing civilian suffering. (Governments that *don't* care so much about such things, or about legal compliance in the first place, will be less troubled and challenged by modern irregular warfare, of course.)

As Gómez characterizes it, this new conflict environment is not one in which—as is sometimes casually assumed—civilian norms are entirely *displaced*. Rather, while these conflicts bring forth a genuine mode of "warfare," it is a type that is to some extent yet *coextensive* with the civilian world. Law-abiding leaders must figure out how to arrange this cohabitation, devising an approach that is simultaneously militarily effective, humane, and sustainable for potentially quite long periods of time. This is a qualitatively new challenge for modern democracies.

Most discussions of these issues, including those appearing elsewhere in this volume, analyze the question principally through the prism of the U.S. or Israeli experience. Gómez, however, offers an invaluable additional account: of Colombian practice in its long—and remarkably successful—campaign against the guerrilla fighters and terrorist drug traffickers of the Revolutionary Armed Forces of Colombia (FARC).

According to Gómez, in Colombian government practice, observance of the law is deemed to be a critical priority, and "no action of defense or security" can be undertaken outside of legal parameters. He suggests that an "ideal" answer in the quest for a legal framework for governing irregular conflicts might someday be found in the reformulation of international rules in order to provide tailor-made standards customized specifically with an eye to the peculiarities of modern counterterrorism. Broad international agreement upon such standards, however—which Gómez feels would be needed before they could become a tenable fountainhead for security planning—has not yet been forthcoming.

In the absence of such a supervening set of rules—and facing an acute tension between the need to fight in order to ensure the survival of the state and the need to *restrain* the conduct of the security services in order to preserve the *legitimacy* of that state—Colombia has apparently decided to decide the issue on a case-by-case basis. In a conspicuous contrast to most accounts by other Western lawyers, who tend implicitly or explicitly to assume that one single paradigm or another applies to all the circumstances of modern CT war but who disagree about which one provides the right answer, Gómez's account of Colombian operational legal practice stresses the potential applicability, and contingency, of both frameworks.

In effect, Gómez's account suggests that Colombia feels that *both* IHL and the LOAC coexist to some extent in the same legal-conceptual space, and that neither model can be said to fade away on a blanket basis through some process of paradigmatic succession or phase-transformation. Instead, Gómez postulates a continuum of transition between a "normality" of an environment threatened principally by *criminal* violence and a "conflict" zone of higher-intensity and more "military" operations.

Politically, he recounts, Colombia has never recognized the official existence of an armed conflict, but its security services nonetheless choose to treat IHL as "a necessary reality"—and apparently as something of a default case where officials are not entirely sure which set of rules is most appropriate. Yet since much contemporary CT work occurs in what Gómez terms the "Gray Zone" in the middle of his postulated continuum, HR rules remain important, and always at least potentially applicable.

In Colombia, the job of ascertaining which legal framework should apply to any particular operation—that is, in effect, whether a proposed action is "police" or "military" work—is in large part the job of the Operational Legal Advisors (or AJOs in their Spanish acronym), working closely with intelligence agencies in order to identify and, critically, to *characterize* specific threats as being within the ambit of either IHL or HR rules. These decisions, and operational guidelines based upon the rules thereby invoked, are provided to security units in the form of mission-specific Rules of Engagement (ROEs), with actual choices being subjected to After Action Reviews (AARs) of both military and police operations. Such a basic institutional framework is not uncommon in law-abiding democracies, but in Gómez's account Colombia seems to distinguish itself by its legal-operational flexibility, with security forces conducting both "military" and "police" work in the same territory, in quick and shifting succession, according to day-by-day and target-by-target assessments. Gómez suggests the Colombian model as one that may hold promise for other states faced with analogously severe CT challenges on their own territory.

Christopher Ford's essay focuses in particular upon American practice in the post-9/11 era, and follows some of the other authors in describing the development of new or modified approaches in response to the "new normal" presented by modern CT warfare. He stresses, however, that much of what is taken as being new in U.S. practice in fact had important antecedents in *pre*-9/11 practice, and that much of what was depicted in some quarters as outrageous Bush Administration overreaching has, in fact, quietly been ratified both by continuity in Obama Administration practice and by a considerable degree of Congressional and judicial legitimization. This story arc suggests that the process of adapting to modern warfare's "new normal" has been far less spasmodic and idiosyncratic than is sometimes supposed: it seems, in fact, to represent a broader evolutionary process.

In Ford's characterization, early Bush administration invocations of sweeping "war-paradigm" powers were succeeded by a period of readjustment, interbranch bargaining, and judicial tweaking, eventually producing modified standards that differ somewhat—but not usually dramatically—from the powers originally claimed. In particular, these adjustments tend to have occurred in ways that seem designed to adapt the "war" paradigm to the peculiar circumstances of modern irregular war that make unqualified application of "war-paradigm" thinking seem somewhat problematic, such as the conflict's potential endlessness, and the transboundary character of the contemporary CT battlespace.

It may well be, as Samson suggests, that the LOAC's guiding principles of necessity, proportion, distinction, and humanity can indeed be coherently served in such modern conflict environments. David's analysis of targeted killing, for instance, indicates such policies can be quite clearly conceptualized as lawful and moral responses to the dilemmas of modern war, and as attempts to be *faithful* to LOAC principles. Ford agrees, but notes that the nonreciprocal nature of the LOAC in modern irregular conflicts, the informational ambiguity of operational decisions in circumstances in which traditional "lines" do not exist and adversaries are distinguishable from innocents in some cases only by their fleeting actions of the present moment, and the non-territoriality of the battlespace make such conflicts more difficult to oversee in any systematic and objective way by nonparticipant observers.

These dynamics, Ford argues, may be producing a creeping decentralization and *interiorization* of legal restraint—a process encouraged by the degree to which, as Samson notes in her essay, assessments of the legality of an operational decision depend so much upon questions of good faith and reasonable judgment based upon the information available at the time. Through this lens, Ford suggests, the most important way to incorporate LOAC-inspired restraint into the decentralized and highly irregular conflicts of our "new normal" is not through international inquiries, *post hoc* investigation, or even lawyering *per se* at all, but instead through the training regimens and cultivated ethical self-conceptions of individual participants.

With traditional Geneva-era ideals of reciprocity having been eroded both as a legal requirement and as an incentive for state participants to care about the law—inasmuch as states in modern CT conflicts cannot expect their irregular adversaries to care a whit about conforming to the law *themselves,* whether or not state forces comply—and with compliance relying heavily enough upon intentionality in ambiguous factual circumstances as to make these matters awkwardly resistant to outside intelligibility—Ford suggests that the LOAC may be coming to resemble "virtue ethics" as much as it does a crisp, exogenous system of behavior-constraining rules. Such a conception of restraint, strongly focused upon intentionality and the good faith and moral self-identity of each participant, but both inherently somewhat flexible and resistant to the bright-line constructions and binary categorizations of ordinary law, may look rather unlike the legality to which many international lawyers have aspired through generations of efforts at codification and the creation of institutions such as the International Criminal Court. Ford urges, however, that we not dismiss such a framework out of hand: it may turn out to be more relevant, and more appropriate—and to have deeper roots in the Western legal tradition—than one might think.

In the concluding essay of this volume, Amichai Cohen resurveys the broad range of issues discussed by the authors and builds upon their insights to identify important themes in the development of international legality in the face of modern CT and irregular-warfare challenges. His analysis looks at two facets of the intersection of law and national security: (1) the "internal" law of national security, by which he means the allocation of authorities and responsibilities for security affairs within a government (including what Cohen terms hierarchical, functional, spatial, and temporal aspects of the law); and (2) the "external" law of national security, which refers to how national security is balanced against *non*-national security equities such as human rights. In both facets, Cohen calls for further study and consideration of the proper role of international law in these matters, as well as of possible additional changes in the roles of different domestic institutions and branches, the meaning of individual rights, and the role of courts in preserving domestic legal systems.

For the most part, the story told in this volume is of indeterminacy, contestation, and change, but as Cohen details, there are also important themes herein of continuity and evolution. The law of armed conflict has indeed faced some rethinking in the face of modern CT conflict, and cannot be said to be where it was on September 10, 2001—or 1976, for that matter. Yet it would be wrong to describe us as now inhabiting an entirely new legal world, and much of the analysis herein tends to confound the legal stereotypes often used to depict the post-9/11 LOAC. The law is to some degree in flux, but it does not appear to have become entirely irrelevant or obsolete; there has been an accretion of executive power, but not without check, adjustment, retrenchment, interbranch legitimization, and even some articulation of absolute due-process norms in the face of executive assertion; novel practices have evolved in an effort to allow security services to serve LOAC principles, notwithstanding these modern challenges; and the ideal of law-derived operational restraint seems to remain quite healthy. The truth, as so often, is more complicated and nuanced than the polemic. The essays herein seek to tell some of this story.

NOTE

1. Richard Goldstone, "Reconsidering the Goldstone Report on Israel and war crimes," *Washington Post,* April 1, 2011. http://www.washingtonpost.com/opinions/reconsidering-the-goldstone-report-on-israel-and-war-crimes/2011/04/01/AFg111JC_story.html>.

Chapter 1

The Law That Turned Against Its Drafters

Guerrilla-Combatants and the First Additional Protocol to the Geneva Conventions

Ariel Zemach

The First Additional Protocol to the Geneva Conventions[1] (Protocol) introduces a new legal regime governing certain types of conflicts between a state and a non-state actor. The cornerstone of this regime is Article 1(4) of the Protocol, which categorizes "conflicts in which peoples are fighting against colonial domination and alien occupation and against racist regimes in the exercise of their right of self-determination" as international armed conflicts.[2] The provision's use of emotionally loaded terms like *colonial domination*, *alien occupation*, and *racist regimes* clearly demonstrates that the purpose of its drafters was to assist those engaged in one of the types of *just war* described in the provision. This intention is also demonstrated by the legislative history of the Protocol.[3] Indeed, commentators have observed that the Protocol's introduction of the notion of *just war* to humanitarian law undermines a fundamental principle of international law concerning the separation of *jus ad bellum* from *jus in bello*.[4]

The attempt to increase humanitarian protections for guerrillas fighting a *just war* largely concerned the expansion of the category of guerrillas entitled to prisoner-of-war (POW) status. The drafters of Article 1(4) thought it necessary to categorize the situations described in this provision as *international* armed conflicts, rather than as *non-international* armed conflicts, because only combatants participating in the former are entitled to POW status.[5] Article 1(4) is complemented by Articles 43 and 44 of the Protocol which, *inter alia,* aim to ensure that guerrillas are able to meet the conditions for entitlement to POW status.[6]

I argue, however, that, notwithstanding the intentions of its drafters, the Protocol does guerrilla fighters a disservice. In terms of its impact on customary law, in fact, the Protocol operates only to the detriment of guerrilla fighters.

This chapter explores the effect of the Protocol's provisions on customary international law, both with regard to the question of entitlement to POW status and with regard to the application of the principle of distinction in the conduct of warfare. The latter principle holds that "the parties to the conflict must at all times distinguish between civilians and combatants. Attacks may only be directed against combatants. Attacks must not be directed against civilians."[7] This protection is afforded to civilians "unless and for such time as they take a direct part in hostilities."[8]

At the heart of my argument lies the proposition that state practice may have a destructive effect on customary norms that exceeds its constitutive effect. In other words, state practice inconsistent with a preexisting rule of customary law, which does not meet the threshold for the creation of a *new* rule of customary law, may nevertheless *undermine* the customary status of the preexisting rule. This, I suggest, is precisely what has happened with the Protocol. While the Protocol's provisions regarding guerrilla insurgency failed to acquire a status of customary norms, they nonetheless undermined the customary status of preexisting rules.

The implications of this are twofold and—from the perspective of the Protocol's drafters, who intended to give additional protections to groups fighting against state adversaries in irregular conflicts—sadly ironic. First, the Protocol failed to expand the category of guerrillas entitled to POW status under customary law. Second, the Protocol eroded much of the protection against attack previously afforded to guerrillas under the customary law principle of distinction. Hence, from the perspective of guerrilla fighters, the Protocol had *only* adverse consequences in terms of its influence on the state of customary international law.

I. COMBATANT STATUS AND ENTITLEMENT TO POW TREATMENT: HAGUE VERSUS THE PROTOCOL

International humanitarian instruments differ in how they delineate the boundaries of the category of combatants in an international armed conflict. According to Article 1 of the Hague Regulations Respecting the Laws and Customs of War on Land (Hague Regulations),[9] individuals who are not members of the regular armed forces of a state are considered combatants if (1) they are members of an armed group otherwise belonging to a state, and (2) they fulfill all of the following conditions:

(a) being under responsible command;
(b) wearing a fixed distinctive sign recognizable at a distance;
(c) carrying arms openly; and
(d) conducting their operations in accordance with the laws and customs of war.[10]

The same definition of *combatants* may be inferred from the categories of persons who have the right to prisoner of war status pursuant to Article 4 of the Third Geneva Convention Relative to the Treatment of Prisoners of War[11] (Third Geneva Convention).

There is little doubt that Article 1 of the Hague Regulations reflected customary law at the time the Protocol was adopted by the 1977 Geneva Diplomatic Conference[12] (hereafter Diplomatic Conference). Opinions vary, however, on precisely what this traditional customary rule entailed—and, specifically, about whether the definition of combatants contained in the Hague Regulations is confined to the question of entitlement to POW status or whether it also pertains to the application of the principle of distinction in the conduct of warfare, which generally allows attacks against combatants and proscribes such attacks when directed against civilians not taking direct part in hostilities.

By way of comparison to this traditional rule, a different definition of *combatants* is provided by Article 43 of the Protocol. The Protocol delineates the category of combatants by reference to the term *armed forces*, which is defined by Article 43(1) of the Protocol as follows:

> The armed forces of a Party to a conflict consist of all organized armed forces, groups and units which are under a command responsible to that Party for the conduct of its subordinates, even if that Party is represented by a government or an authority not recognized by an adverse Party. Such armed forces shall be subject to an internal disciplinary system which, *inter alia*, shall enforce compliance with the rules of international law applicable in armed conflict. [13]

Article 43(2) of the Protocol proceeds to provide that all members of such armed forces are combatants (with two exceptions: medical and religious personnel).[14]

> All commentators agree that the definition of *combatants* contained in the Protocol fulfills two functions. First, it delineates the boundaries of the category of individuals entitled to POW status: only combatants qualify for POW status.[15] Second, in accordance with the principle of distinction, only combatants may be attacked on the basis of their status, even when not taking direct part in hostilities.[16]

As noted, Article 43(1) of the Protocol provides that armed forces "shall be subject to an internal disciplinary system which, *inter alia,* shall enforce compliance with the rules of international law applicable in armed conflict."[17] The International Committee of the Red Cross (ICRC) therefore concluded in its official *Commentary on the Additional Protocol* that compliance with the law of war at the *group level* is a constitutive element of the definition of "*armed forces*" contained in Article 43. According to the ICRC's *Commentary,* "armed forces as such must submit to the rules of international law applicable in armed conflict, this being a constitutive condition for the recognition of such forces, within the meaning of Article 43 (*Armed forces*)."[18] The *Commentary* elaborates that the rules of the law of war "must be complied with by the armed forces as such, at the risk of disqualification . . . for if the status of the group is contested, it will be the individuals who will be deprived of combatant or prisoner-of-war status."[19] Several commentators subscribe to this view.[20] Similarly, the British military's Manual of the Law of Armed Conflicts states with regard to Article 43 of the Protocol:

> Any force, group, or unit which in the course of its operations systematically fails to obey the law runs the risk of being regarded as not being subject to an effective disciplinary system and therefore not being a legally recognizable armed force under international law. The members of such a force would not be entitled to combatant status and would be liable to trial and punishment in the same way as other non-combatants who participate directly in hostilities. [21]

However, it seems that the ICRC has abandoned this view. More recent ICRC commentaries seem to maintain that, while Article 43 requires armed forces to respect and enforce the law of war at the group level, such a requirement is not a constitutive element of the definition of armed forces.[22] I subscribe to the latter position. The Protocol's definition of combatants eliminates any distinction between state regular armed forces and other armed groups party to an international armed conflict. According to Article 43 of the Protocol, "all armed forces are 'regular,' whether they are established by a State in pursuance of appropriate laws, or by another Party to the Conflict using its own methods, or even if they have risen spontaneously."[23] In the words of the ICRC's *Commentary on Customary International Humanitarian Law,*

> [t]he definition in Article 43 of Additional Protocol I is now generally applied to all forms of armed groups who belong to a party to an armed conflict to determine whether they constitute armed forces. It is therefore no longer necessary to distinguish between regular and irregular armed forces. All those fulfilling the conditions in Article 43 of Additional Protocol I are armed forces. [24]

Hence, viewing compliance with the law of war at the group level as an essential element of the Protocol's definition of armed forces would lead to peculiar results: a state army that does not respect the laws of war (e.g., the Iraqi army during the First Gulf War, which, as a matter of policy, resorted to the use of *human shields* and launched extensive rocket attacks against civilian populations in Israel and Saudi Arabia) would not be considered an armed force at all, and none of the soldiers of such army would be considered combatants. The prospect of such an absurd result—a state army with no combatants—suffices to preclude the construction of Article 43 presented in the earlier ICRC Commentary. Indeed, no state engaged in a traditional inter-state war has ever considered the army of the opposing state to be comprised in its entirety of civilians.

Article 44(1) of the Protocol provides that "[a]ny combatant, as defined in Article 43, who falls into the power of an adverse Party shall be a prisoner of war."[25] Article 44 then proceeds to pronounce the exceptions to the rule granting combatants POW status. Whereas "as regards members of regular armed forces, the Protocol does not change the situation provided for in the Third Convention,"[26] the Protocol expands the category of guerrilla fighters who are entitled to POW status, far beyond the standards set forth in the Hague Regulations of 1907 or the Third Geneva Convention of 1949.

The Protocol's expansion of the category of fighters entitled to POW status is threefold:

(a) First, the Protocol provides that members of armed groups that are not affiliated to a state in any way may also be entitled to POW status, when taking part in an armed conflict of the type described in Article 1(4) (e.g., a struggle against *alien occupation*).[27]

(b) In deviance from the Hague Regulations and the Third Geneva Convention, the requirement that guerrilla fighters individually abide by the laws of war is no longer a condition for entitlement to POW status.[28]

(c) Finally, the Protocol also considerably relaxes the requirement, contained in the Hague Regulations and in the Third Geneva Convention, that guerilla fighters distinguish themselves from the civilian population (i.e., wear uniforms or display other distinctive signs, and carry arms openly) as a condition for entitlement to POW status.

This last factor deserves special note. Article 44(3) of the Protocol "allows a guerilla combatant to wear purely civilian dress, if the nature of the hostilities requires it"[29]—that is, where "a guerrilla fighter could not distinguish himself from the civilian population throughout his military operations and still retain any chance of success."[30] Under such factual circumstances, the obligation of a guerrilla combatant to carry arms openly is also narrowed by the Protocol, so that it only applies: "(a) during each military engagement; and (b) during such time as he [the combatant] is visible to the adversary while he is engaged in a military deployment preceding the launching of an attack in which he is to participate."[31] Only a guerrilla combatant who violates this narrow requirement—and who is captured while committing such violation—is denied POW status.[32] This was said to represent "a major development in the law."[33] The Protocol aimed to remove "the 'presumption of illegality,' of which guerilla fighters have complained."[34]

II. HAVE THE PROTOCOL'S PROVISIONS ON GUERRILLAS BECOME A *DEAD LETTER*?

Article 96(3) of the Protocol provides that

> The authority representing a people engaged against a High Contracting Party in an armed conflict of the type referred to in Article 1, paragraph 4, may undertake to apply the Conventions and this Protocol in relation to that conflict by means of a unilateral declaration addressed to the depositary. Such declaration shall, upon its receipt by the depositary, have in relation to that conflict the following effects:
>
> a) the Conventions and this Protocol are brought into force for the said authority as a Party to the conflict with immediate effect;
> b) the said authority assumes the same rights and obligations as those which have been assumed by a High Contracting Party to the Conventions and this Protocol; and
> c) the Conventions and this Protocol are equally binding upon all Parties to the conflict.[35]

In the absence of such a declaration (hereinafter Article 96 declaration), the Geneva Conventions and the Protocol have no application to the situations described in Article 1(4) of the Protocol. Members of the armed forces of a national liberation movement (NLM) are not afforded the protection of those treaties, in other words, unless the movement formally accepts all the obligations contained in the Geneva Conventions and the Protocol in the same way as the state parties.

The language of Article 1(4) and Article 96(3) clearly indicates that the submission of an Article 96 declaration is not constitutive of the existence of an armed conflict. On the contrary, the existence of an armed conflict is a precondition for the application of Article 96(3).[36] The prevailing view is that a conflict between a state and a non-state actor qualifies as an armed conflict where hostilities meet a certain threshold in terms of the scale of the violence, its duration and the level of organization of the rival parties.[37] Those criteria, enunciated by the International Criminal Tribunal for the Former Yugoslavia (ICTY) in the context of internal armed conflict,[38] also seem to apply to hostilities between an occupant and guerrilla forces of the type addressed in Article 1(4) of the Protocol.[39]

To date, no NLM has ever made an Article 96 declaration. Theodor Meron speculates that NLMs have refrained from submitting such declaration "perhaps because they would have had difficulty accepting and carrying out all the obligations stated in the Protocol."[40] In my own view, NLMs have been reluctant to submit an Article 96 declaration because they prefer to portray hostilities that are essentially armed conflicts as law enforcement situations, given the broad liberties to exercise lethal force afforded to a state under the law of war.[41] In view of the reluctance on the part of NLMs to submit an Article 96 declaration, George Aldrich asserts that "in effect, [Article 1(4)] is a dead letter."[42] Similarly, Meron submits it is improbable that the protections afforded by the Protocol to guerrillas fighting an alien occupation will ever be given an effect.[43]

I argue, however, that the Protocol's provisions significantly affect the legal regime applicable to an armed conflict between an occupant and guerrilla forces, even in the absence of an Article 96 declaration. As I show below, such a conflict between an occupying state and guerrilla forces is properly categorized as an *international* armed conflict regardless of Article 1(4) of the Protocol. It is therefore governed by the customary law of international armed conflict, which, in turn, is greatly influenced by the Protocol's provisions, including the ones concerning guerrilla fighters' combatant status and POW entitlement.

It is important to observe that Article 96(3) of the Protocol does not represent an impediment to the development of *customary rules* that confer upon guerrilla fighters the privileges and protections afforded to combatants under the Protocol, regardless of whether the NLM submitted an Article 96 declaration. Addressing the function of an Article 96 declaration, the ICRC Commentary on the Protocol observes:

> . . . the status recognized to liberation movements indeed gives them, as it gives States, the right to choose whether or not to submit to international humanitarian law, insofar as it goes beyond customary law.[44]

It seems, then, that the purpose of Article 96(3) is to put NLMs on par with states. Article 96(3) establishes an exception to the rule of nonreciprocity in the application of humanitarian law.[45] The drafters of the Protocol took the view that "the Protocol and the Conventions must apply equally to both sides if they are to apply to the conflict at all."[46] Only those who undertake the obligations contained in those treaties may enjoy the privileges they afford. While only states may become formal parties to the Protocol, NLMs may acquire a status equivalent to that of parties by submitting an Article 96 declaration.

The drafters of Article 96 thus intended to allow guerrilla movements a choice whether or not to accept the *non-customary* rules applicable to an international armed conflict (contained in the Protocol and Geneva Conventions), just as states are afforded such choice. Significantly, however, NLMs are bound by the rules of *customary* humanitarian law regardless of whether they submitted an Article 96 declaration, and the reciprocity principle embodied in Article 96 is therefore consonant with affording guerrillas the privileges and protections contained in customary norms. Hence, the absence of an Article 96 declaration only precludes the application of the *non-customary* rules of humanitarian law to a conflict of the type described in Article 1(4).

III. DO THE PROTOCOL'S RULES REGARDING THE ENTITLEMENT OF GUERRILLAS TO POW STATUS REFLECT CUSTOMARY LAW?

As described above, Article 44(3) of the Protocol significantly eroded the requirement that guerrilla combatants distinguish themselves from the civilian population as a condition for entitlement to POW status. Has this provision acquired the status of customary international law? This question seems to be intertwined with the question of whether Article 1(4) of the Protocol acquired such status, for, as also noted earlier, the legislative history of the Protocol clearly demonstrates that both Article 1(4) and Article 44(3) are part of a single effort to confer upon guerrilla fighters, engaged in an armed conflict of the type described in Article 1(4), the status of privileged combatants and thereby entitlement to POW status. Indeed, many states parties to the Protocol consider the purview of Article 44(3) to be basically confined to the situations described in Article 1(4).[47]

Article 44(3) generated much controversy at the Diplomatic Conference leading to the adoption of the Additional Protocols.[48] It was widely criticized for undermining the humanitarian protections afforded to civilians. As noted by one commentator, the requirements, contained in the Hague Regulations and the Third Geneva Convention, that combatants wear fixed distinctive sign and carry arms openly

> can be viewed as indispensable preconditions for compliance with the cardinal humanitarian principle of *jus in bello:* the requirement that combatants distinguish between civilian and military targets. If combatants do not clearly distinguish themselves from civilians by wearing some "distinctive sign" and carrying their arms openly, the adversary will not be able to know whom it should be targeting, and will therefore have an overwhelming incentive to target its opponents without much attention to the combatant/civilian distinction.[49]

Article 44(3) was eventually adopted by the Diplomatic Conference by 73 votes in favor, one vote against (Israel), and 21 abstentions.[50] Among the abstaining states were most Western democracies. Most Western states reacted negatively to Article 1(4) as well.[51] This response was

> primarily out of concern either that it could import into humanitarian law the dangerous concept of the just war and might lead to other provisions limiting protections of the law to those engaged in "just wars," or that it could be construed to justify external intervention in such wars.[52]

In the aftermath of the Conference, the U.S. administration of President Ronald Reagan cautioned that this provision is harmful also

> because it would grant those fighting for such movements immunity from prosecution for belligerent acts, and because treating as soldiers members of groups like the [Palestinian Liberation Organization] that often use terrorist tactics undesirably enhances their stature, "to the detriment of the civilized world community."[53]

Indeed, the United States, which supported the adoption of Article 44(3) at the Diplomatic Conference, shortly afterwards revised its position drastically, and refused to ratify the Protocol. Pointing mainly to Article 1(4) and Article 44(3) of the Protocol,[54] the United States asserted that this instrument is "fundamentally and irreconcilably flawed."[55]

This controversy has important implications for the question of the status of these provisions of the Protocol as customary international law. It led Christopher Greenwood to conclude in 1991, for example, that "Article 1(4) went well beyond customary law . . . and has not met the criteria for being absorbed into customary law since its inclusion in Protocol I."[56] Similarly, the United States has declared that Article 44(3) "clearly does not reflect customary law."[57]

This is a question worth further examination, for not all commentators agree. One cannot overlook the fact that since those statements were made the number of states parties to the Protocol has increased considerably. Most of the states that did not support the adoption of Article 1(4) and Article 44(3) at the Diplomatic Conference have subsequently ratified the Protocol.[58] There are currently 168 states parties to the Protocol,[59] among them all of the permanent members of the U.N. Security Council except for the United States. Hence, Meron has asserted that "the number and the quality of the ratifying states enhance the character of the Protocol as an instrument largely declaratory of customary law."[60] In its recent Direct Participation Report, the ICRC nevertheless seems to have taken the view (without providing any reasoning) that Article 1(4) and, by extension, Article 44(3) have *not* yet attained the status of customary law.[61] I subscribe to this view for several reasons.

First, in view of the United States' preeminence as a military power and its unique position in the international community, it seems that an adamant objection on the part of the United States to a conventional rule of humanitarian law presents a significant obstacle to its development into customary law.[62] Second, the states abstaining in the vote on the adoption of Article 44(3) at the Diplomatic Conference made, on that occasion, declarations which, in fact, demonstrate adamant *rejection* of the rule that relaxes the duty of guerrilla-combatants to distinguish themselves from the civilian population.[63] For example, Spain's abstention was accompanied by the following declaration:

> The text presented does not guarantee the safety of the civilian population, which is the essential aim of the instruments under consideration. In the view of this delegation, the terms in which the article is drafted could favour the development of the new phenomenon known as urban guerrilla warfare and, therefore, a certain form of terrorism, thus constituting a grave danger to the security of States and a step on the road to international subversion. [64]

Similarly, Ireland declared, upon abstaining in the vote on Article 44(3), that "the protection of the civilian population demanded by humanitarian principles is eroded by Article 44 to an unacceptable extent."[65]

Such declarations seem to suggest that the subsequent ratification of the Protocol by most of the abstaining states reflected a judgment on the part of those states that, overall, the benefits of the Protocol from a humanitarian perspective outweighed the flaws of Article 1(4) and Article 44(3), rather than a view that accepts those latter provisions as part of customary law. This conclusion is supported by the fact that the military manuals published by several states that ratified the Protocol nevertheless define combatants entitled to POW status by reference to the terms of the Third Geneva Convention, rather than by reference to the terms of the Protocol.[66]

Third, there has not been, so far, any state practice on the ground applying the provisions of the Protocol regarding entitlement of guerrilla-combatants to POW status. As noted by Theodore Meron, "there is no recorded case of combatant and POW privileges being granted to members of such movements as a result of the Protocol."[67] This is not necessarily attributable to state rejection of Articles 1(4) and 44(3), for as we have seen, no NLM has ever submitted an Article 96(3) declaration in the first place—which is required in order to trigger the application of the Protocol to armed conflicts of the type described in Article 1(4). Nevertheless, while customary law can be developed as a result of state practice other than actions on the ground,[68] the absence of such actions should elicit in us a greater degree of caution in determining that a norm of customary law has indeed evolved.

All in all, therefore, it does not seem to me that the Protocol's provisions regarding entitlement of guerrilla fighters to POW status reflect a rule of customary international law. But what about the Protocol's definition of *combatants* as applied to the *principle of distinction* in the conduct of warfare? Under the terms of the Protocol, as we have seen, all full-fledged members of a guerrilla organization that is a party to an international armed conflict are considered combatants, and may therefore be targeted on the basis of their status even when not taking direct part in the hostilities. Does this rule reflect customary international law?

My inquiry in this respect is threefold. We saw that Article 1(4) of the Protocol has *not* obtained the status of customary law. The Protocol applies only to international armed conflicts. The first question therefore concerns the proper categorization of an armed conflict between an occupying power and guerrilla forces, regardless of Article 1(4). Does customary international law consider such a conflict an international armed conflict or a non-international armed conflict? It is important to observe here that the customary definition of combatants in a non-international armed conflict resembles the one contained in the Protocol.[69]

In the following pages, my inquiry will demonstrate that an armed conflict between an occupier and guerrilla forces is properly categorized as an *international* armed conflict. This conclusion, in turn, raises two more questions. First, did the definition of combatants contained in Article 43 of the Protocol, as regards the application of the principle of distinction, depart from a preexisting rule of customary international law? And second, if so, has it subsequently obtained the status of customary international law, replacing the old customary rule?

IV. CATEGORIZING AN ARMED CONFLICT BETWEEN AN OCCUPIER AND GUERRILLAS

The application of the law of war depends on the existence of either an international armed conflict or a non-international armed conflict.[70] Yet large-scale hostilities between a state and a non-state entity, which transcend the territory of the state involved—e.g., the recent conflict between Israel and Hamas in Gaza, or the conflict between the United States and *al-Qaeda*—do not fall neatly within the customary definitions of either an international *or* a non-international armed conflict.

The conduct of parties to a non-international armed conflict is regulated under Common Article 3 of the Geneva Conventions,[71] as well as under the Second Additional Protocol to the Geneva Conventions[72] (Protocol II). The definitions of a non-international armed conflict contained in those treaties refer to a conflict occurring *within* the territory of a state party.[73] Some commentators thus argue that a conflict between a state and a non-state actor, which transcends the territory of the state party to the conflict, cannot be regarded as a non-international armed conflict.[74] Considering such conflict an international armed conflict is also problematic, however, since, according to the prevailing definition of an international armed conflict, such conflict is waged between two or more states.[75]

The bulk of authority nevertheless favors the view that large-scale hostilities between a state and a non-state entity, which transcend state borders, should be considered an armed conflict of at least some sort.[76] To that end, both courts and commentators have stretched the customary definition of either an international armed conflict (beyond interstate conflicts) or a non-international armed conflict (beyond conflict occurring strictly *within* the territory of a particular state) to encompass such hostilities.

In *Hamdan v. Rumsfeld,*[77] the U.S. Supreme Court concluded that the conflict between the United States and *al-Qaeda* was a non-international armed conflict, to which Common Article 3 of the Geneva Conventions applied.[78] In *Hamdan,* the Court examined, *inter alia,* which humanitarian law provisions applied to the legal proceedings initiated against Salim Ahmed Hamdan, a suspected al-Qaeda operative captured in Afghanistan.[79] Observing that Common Article 3 speaks of a "conflict not of an international character,"[80] the Court opined that this term "is used here in contradistinction to a conflict between nations,"[81] and thus encompasses all large-scale hostilities between a state and a non-state actor.[82]

It seems that the main concern of the U.S. Supreme Court was to ensure that Hamdan, assuming he was not entitled to a prisoner-of-war status, nonetheless received the minimum of humanitarian law protections granted under Common Article 3. The Court subscribed to the position of the International Committee of the Red Cross that "nobody in enemy hands can be outside the law,"[83] and hence joined its conclusion that the scope of application of Common Article 3 "must be as wide as possible."[84] This concern seems irrelevant, however, in the context of hostilities between an occupier and a local guerrilla organization. Common Article 2 of the Geneva Conventions provides a population under occupation with a wide range of humanitarian protections, regardless of the existence of armed conflict.[85] The protections afforded under Common Article 2, in fact, exceed those secured under Common Article 3.[86] Hence, the application of Common Article 3 would not add to the protections enjoyed by the local population of an occupied territory, whether civilians or guerrillas.

Hamdan did not concern a conflict between an occupier and guerrilla forces.[87] Such a conflict was addressed, however, by the Israeli Supreme Court in *Public Committee Against Torture in Israel v. Government of Israel* (a.k.a. the *Targeted Killing Case*).[88] Examining whether the Israeli policy of undertaking targeted killings of suspected Palestinian terrorists, carried out in the course of the uprising known as the al-Aqsa Intifada, was lawful under international law, the Court first observed that hostilities between Israel and Palestinian armed groups amounted to an armed conflict.[89] It then proceeded to conclude—without providing any reasoning—that an armed conflict between an occupier and guerrilla forces should be categorized as an international, rather than a non-international, armed conflict.[90] The author agrees with this conclusion for the following reasons.

While a violent conflict within an occupied territory may share many of the characteristics of a non-international armed conflict,[91] classifying it as such seems inconsistent with the present rules of international law.[92] The structure of international humanitarian instruments suggests that a state of occupation is closely associated with an international armed conflict. The Geneva Conventions and the Additional Protocols to the Geneva Conventions distinguish between two bodies of law: (a) the norms that regulate international armed conflicts *and* situations of occupation, and (b) the norms that regulate non-international armed conflicts.[93] The humanitarian provisions concerning the protection accorded to civilians in an occupied territory are all part of the former. By contrast, the norms of non-international armed conflict are not intertwined in any way with the law of occupation.

This structure is also maintained in the Rome Statute of the International Criminal Court (Rome Statute).[94] The Preparatory Commission for the International Criminal Court thus noted that war crimes committed by an occupier are considered conduct that "took place in the context of and was associated with an international armed conflict."[95] The Rome Statute further provides, for example, that the provision prohibiting an occupier from settling its own population within the occupied territory and from forcibly dislocating all or parts of the local population is part of "the laws and customs applicable in international armed conflict."[96]

The International Criminal Tribunal for the Former Yugoslavia (ICTY) recognized that an armed conflict involving more than two parties may have both internal and international aspects.[97] For instance, where the armed forces of a state intervene in hostilities between government forces and opposition groups in another state, the armed conflict can be characterized "as both internal and international, or alternatively, as an internal conflict alongside an international one."[98] As noted by Lindsay Moir, this approach represents a "theory of pairings, enabling the application of different legal regimes between various parties according to their relationship with each other."[99] However, this chapter concerns hostilities that are essentially confined to two parties: an occupier and guerrilla forces within the occupied territory. Furthermore, in some cases, such as the al-Aqsa Intifada, the hostilities within the occupied territory take place while there is a state of peace between the states parties to the initial international conflict that led to the occupation.[100] It seems that an armed conflict with only two parties cannot be regarded both international and non-international.

In view of the close relationship between the law of occupation and the law of international armed conflict, it is hard to see how hostilities between an occupant and guerrilla forces can be classified as a non-international armed conflict. It seems, then, that an armed conflict between an occupier and guerrilla forces is properly categorized as an international armed conflict, regardless of Article 1(4) of the Protocol.[101]

V. THE FUNCTION OF ARTICLE 1 OF THE HAGUE REGULATIONS

Did the Protocol's definition of combatants—as applied to the principle of distinction, in that combatants may be targeted but noncombatants cannot—depart from the preexisting customary law of international armed conflicts? To answer this requires examining the function of Article 1 of the Hague Regulations. According to one view, the definition of combatants contained in Article 1 of the Hague Regulations does not concern the principle of distinction in the conduct of warfare. Rather, it only concerns the question of entitlement to POW status. According to this view, the definition of combatants that may be attacked under the principle of distinction, contained in Article 43 of the Protocol, did not depart from preexisting customary law. Such customary law was established by state practice unrelated to Article 1 of the Hague Regulations. The ICRC has taken this approach in its recent *Interpretive Guide on the Notion of Direct Participation in Hostilities,* which states:

> According to Additional Protocol I, the armed forces of a party to the conflict comprise all organized armed forces, groups and units which are under a

> command responsible to that party for the conduct of its subordinates. At first glance, this broad and functional concept of armed forces seems wider than that underlying the Hague Regulations and the Geneva Conventions. Although these treaties do not expressly define armed forces, they require that members of militia and volunteer corps . . . fulfill four requirements:
>
> (a) responsible command;
> (b) fixed distinctive sign recognizable at a distance;
> (c) carrying arms openly; and
> (d) operating in accordance with the laws and customs of war.
>
> Strictly speaking, however, these requirements constitute conditions for the post-capture entitlement of irregular armed forces to combatant privilege and prisoner-of-war status and are not constitutive elements of the armed forces of a party to a conflict.
>
> Thus, while members of irregular armed forces failing to fulfill the four requirements may not be entitled to combatant privilege and prisoner-of-war status after capture, it does not follow that any such person must necessarily be excluded from the category of armed forces and regarded as a civilian for the purposes of the conduct of hostilities. [102]

According to this approach, there are *two* customary definitions of the term *combatant* in international armed conflict, which serve different purposes. The first, embodied in Article 43 of the Protocol, concerns the application of the principle of distinction; the second, embodied in Article 1 of the Hague Regulations and in Article 4 of the Third Geneva Convention, concerns entitlement to POW status. Persons who fall within the first definition but not within the second are often referred to as *unprivileged combatants* or *unlawful combatants*.[103] They are considered legitimate objects of attack at all times, but they are not entitled to POW status.

This position was taken by the U.S. administration of President George W. Bush in the wake of the terrorist attacks of September 11, 2001. The administration maintained that the hostilities between the United States and *al-Qaeda* should be deemed an international armed conflict,[104] and U.S. officials categorized *al-Qaeda* members as unlawful combatants.[105] Hence, the administration claimed that *al-Qaeda* members could be considered legitimate objects of attack just like more traditional combatants, except that they were not entitled to POW status if captured.[106] The United States thus contested the claim that anyone who does not qualify for POW status is automatically a civilian.[107]

According to another view, however, the definition of combatants contained in Article 1 of the Hague Regulations, which reflects customary law, pertains both to the question of entitlement to POW status *and* to the application of the principle of distinction. By this interpretation, those two aspects of a combatant status are inseparable. The status of combatant in an international armed conflict is thus a package deal: a combatant enjoys immunity for violence within the law of war, and is liable to be the object of such violence. Hence, the Hague Regulations allow for only two categories: lawful combatants and civilians. Anyone engaged in combat who does not qualify for POW status—in other words, anyone who is not a lawful combatant—is a civilian. (I shall hereafter term this approach *the two-category approach.*)

This two-category approach was endorsed by the Israeli Supreme Court in the *Targeted Killing Case.*[108] Concluding that the hostilities characterizing the al-Aqsa Intifada amounted to an international armed conflict, the Court proceeded to examine the status of Palestinians taking part in the hostilities.[109] The Court observed that the customary definition of combatants in international armed conflicts is provided by Article 1 of the Hague Regulations. It then determined that members of Palestinian terrorist organizations do not meet all of the cumulative conditions for inclusion in the category of combatants, stipulated in the Hague Regulations, because they do not wear a fixed distinctive sign recognizable at a distance, and, moreover, they do not refrain from targeting civilians and therefore do not meet the requirement that their operations be "in accordance with the laws and customs of war."[110] The Court thus concluded that members of Palestinian terrorist organizations cannot be considered combatants, and must therefore be considered civilians.[111] In rejecting the Israeli government's argument that the Court should recognize an unlawful-combatant category under international law, the Court concluded that "the data before us is not sufficient to recognize this third category."[112] The Court's judgment is premised on the Court's construction of *customary* humanitarian law.[113] The absence of the Protocol's definition of combatants from the Court's analysis therefore indicates that the Court did not consider that definition to have obtained the status of customary law.

The law of war prohibits attacks directed at civilians "unless and for such time as they take a direct part in hostilities."[114] Applying this rule, the Court broadly interpreted the circumstances under which a member of a terrorist organization should be viewed as directly participating in hostilities and thus subject to targeting.[115] Nevertheless, the liberties to target civilian fighters afforded to the state under the Court's construction of the law of war are far narrower than the permission to attack *combatants* afforded to parties to an armed conflict under the law of war's principle of distinction.[116] The central feature of the law of war—the permission to target combatants on the basis of their status—was thus taken from it, simply because under the Court's construction of the law of war, an armed conflict between a state and a terrorist group is one in which only one party to the conflict has combatants.

The two-category approach adopted by the Israeli Court has for this reason been vastly criticized in the literature. David Kretzmer observed, for instance, that

> [w]hen the armed conflict is essentially between a state and the terrorist group, the theory that the terrorists are civilians simply does not make sense. An armed conflict model of law . . . cannot be applicable if only one party to the conflict has combatants.[117]

Curtis Bradley further observes that the Israeli Court's construction of the law of war "may create perverse incentives." "One of the central purposes of the laws of war," he writes, "is to encourage fighters both to distinguish themselves from civilians and to avoid attacking civilians."[118] Yet under the approach taken by the Israeli Court, "a nation engaged in an armed conflict has *less* ability to target and detain fighters who fail to wear uniforms or who purposefully target civilians than if those fighters observe the principles of distinction."[119] This approach thus "seems to reward the very conduct that the laws of war are designed to prevent."[120]

I subscribe, however, to the view, taken by the Israeli Court, that the definition of combatants contained in Article 1 of the Hague Regulations is *not* confined to the issue of POW status, but also concerns the application of the principle of distinction. Article 1 of the Hague Regulations provides that "the laws, rights and duties of war"[121] apply to persons who qualify as *belligerents* (i.e., combatants) under this provision.[122] Hence, combatants do not merely enjoy entitlement to POW status (i.e., *war rights*). Combatants are also, more generally, those to whom the laws of war are applicable. The laws of war obviously extend beyond entitlement to POW status. Individuals designated by Article 1 of the Hague Regulations as subjects of the laws of war are included within the sphere of permissible violence. Such inclusion is twofold: such persons are not only afforded the right to kill under the law of war (*war rights*), but are also liable to be the object of attacks.

Moreover, the Hague Regulations do not contain an explicit prohibition against attacks directed at civilians. Yet it is unlikely that this issue is not addressed in any way by the Hague Regulations, especially in view of the Regulations' prohibition of lesser transgressions such as wanton destruction of property.[123] It seems, then, that the prohibition against attacking civilians is embodied in the definition of combatants contained in Article 1 of the Hague Regulations.

Finally, Article 50(1) of the Protocol, which defines the term *civilians* in relation to the principle of distinction, refers to persons entitled to POW status under Article 4 of the Third Geneva Convention as one of the groups excluded from the category of civilians.[124] (Another group which

Article 50(1) excludes from the category of civilians is persons considered combatants under Article 43 of the Protocol.[125] This latter group in fact covers the entire category of persons entitled to POW status under the Third Geneva Convention.[126]) This linkage between Article 4 of the Third Geneva Convention and the principle of distinction in the conduct of warfare is a further indication that the definition of *belligerents* in Article 1 of the Hague Regulations is not confined to the question of POW status.[127]

It seems, then, that Article 1 of the Hague Regulations is inconsistent with the Protocol not only with regard to the question of entitlement to POW status, but also with regard to the application of the principle of distinction. The Protocol represents a considerable expansion of the category of combatants pronounced in the Hague Regulations both with regard to the question of entitlement to POW status and with regard to the application of the principle of distinction. Article 1 of the Hague Regulations, as we have seen, clearly represented a norm of customary law at the time of the adoption of the Protocol by the Diplomatic Conference, a norm from which the Protocol departed.

VI. HAS THE PROTOCOL'S DEFINITION OF COMBATANTS BECOME CUSTOMARY LAW?

Has the Protocol's definition of combatants, *as applied to the principle of distinction,* subsequently acquired the status of customary international law, replacing the preexisting customary rule embodied in the Hague Regulations? The Israeli Supreme Court has answered this question in the negative.[128] I share this view.

Clearly, the objection on the part of several states to the legal regime established under Articles 43–44 of the Protocol merely concerned the expansion of the category of individuals entitled to POW status. It did not concern the expansion of the sphere of legitimate objects of attack that resulted from the Protocol's definition of *combatants.*[129] The language of the Protocol suggests, however, that the two aspects of the combatant status—liability to be attacked and entitlement to POW status—are inseparable. The drafters of the Protocol viewed the status of *combatant* in an international armed conflict as a package deal: a combatant enjoys immunity for violence within the law of war, and is liable to be the object of such violence.[130]

Furthermore, as we have seen, the legislative history of the Protocol clearly indicates that the sole purpose of its drafters in expanding the category of combatants beyond that pronounced in the Hague Regulations was to expand the category of guerrillas entitled to POW status. The expansion of the category of individuals liable to be attacked was only a byproduct, a price to be paid in order to achieve that aim. Given the language of the Protocol and its legislative history, it is hardly arguable that the Protocol created a new rule of customary international law with respect to one aspect of a combatant status but not with respect to the other.

I argue, however, that while Article 43 and Article 44 of the Protocol, as applied to guerrillas, did *not* gain the status of customary rules, those provisions nevertheless have had a significant impact upon the state of customary international law. The Protocol, I argue, has *undermined* the customary status of Article 1 of the Hague Regulations.

VII. THE DESTRUCTION OF CUSTOMARY NORMS

Both treaty rules and customary rules may die without being replaced by other rules. Treaty provisions may fall into desuetude.[131] More importantly for the purpose of this chapter, state practice may have a destructive effect on customary norms which exceeds its constitutive effect. In other words, state practice inconsistent with a preexisting rule of customary law, but which does not meet the threshold for the creation of a *new* rule of customary law (i.e., to replace the one it contradicts), may nevertheless suffice to render the status of the preexisting customary rule uncertain. Such uncertainty amounts to the abolition of the preexisting rule. Drawing upon the consent-based nature of international legal rules,[132] Michael Glennon explains:

> Where a rule of international law has been repeatedly disregarded by a significant number of states over a long period of time there is no longer reason to believe that states feel obliged to comply with that rule. Of course, differences of opinion can easily arise as to whether a given norm qualifies as law, because it is difficult to identify the precise moment at which the balance tips. But at some point state practice that is inconsistent with a norm is simply too thick to justify the conclusion that states really accept the norm as obligatory; at some point, "noncompliance shades into nonlaw." At this point, as I have argued elsewhere, the reason for the rule's demise is often that the status of the rule is uncertain, and the 'freedom principle' causes disputes over application of the rule to be decided in favor of the state proposing to act. [133]

Clearly, the requirement of state consent as a condition for the application of customary international law is not stringent. Hence,

> a state that does not share the community's sense that a particular norm is a rule of customary international law cannot, based on that fact alone, claim to be exempt from the rule. Rather, [under the persistent objector doctrine,] the state must make its objections widely known, must do so before the practice solidifies

> into a rule of customary international law, and must make the objection on a consistent basis.[134]

Nonetheless, the consent-based structure of international law allows "a significant number of states"[135] to *abolish* a customary rule through engaging "over a long period of time" in practice that is inconsistent with such rule.

Glennon thus concludes that inconsistency between state practice and a preexisting rule of international law

> can be considered to have created a *non liquet,* to have thrown the law into a state of confusion where legal rules are not clear and where no authoritative answer is possible. . . . The "default position" of international law has long been that when no restriction can be authoritatively established, a state is seen as free to act.[136]

Other commentators share this view.[137]

It seems that Glennon's use of the term *non-liquet* is not entirely accurate. The doctrine of *non-liquet* assumes that international law is incomplete. It concerns situations in which no rule of international law provides an answer to the legal question at hand, and the judge therefore cannot determine the case on the basis of international law.[138] By contrast, Glennon actually adheres to a theory which assumes the *completeness* of international law. According to this theory, gaps in international law are always filled by the *freedom principle*—explicated by the Permanent Court of International Justice in the *Lotus Case*[139]—according to which "when no restriction can be authoritatively established, a state is seen as free to act."[140] This catchall, permissive rule steps in whenever international law does not otherwise provide a clear answer to the legal question at hand. Hence, by resorting to this principle where no rule is otherwise discernable, an international judge may *always* determine a case on the basis of international law.[141]

While the notion of *non-liquet* has been generally rejected by both courts and commentators,[142] the reasons for such rejection do not affect the soundness of Glennon's approach concerning the *freedom principle.* Commenting on the objections to a finding of *non-liquet,* Jose Alvarez observes that

> [i]t remains anathema for judges (or international law scholars) to proclaim that there is no law. A declaration of *non-liquet* would be in the views of most a defeat for the dispute settlement system as well as for the general hopes of constructing a rule-oriented regime not dependent on power.[143]

Similarly, Weil observes that "[j]udges, especially, are reluctant to find that they have no solution to the problem before them. The more scholarly reason [for the rejection of *non-liquet*] usually put forward is the social need for the settlement of disputes."[144] According to Weil, "the principle of freedom to choose the means of settlement of international disputes, as well as the prominence given by the parties in a specific case to judicial settlement," would be defeated "if an international tribunal were to pronounce a *non liquet* when it cannot find in the law a solution to the problem before it."[145] These objections to a finding of *non-liquet*—which seem to apply only to contentious cases, and not to advisory opinions issued by the International Court of Justice[146]—do not undercut an approach that allows use of the freedom principle to resolve any case that is not governed by a specific customary or conventional rule.

Let us therefore apply this approach to the Protocol's impact upon customary international law. I argue that while the Protocol's provisions regarding guerrilla insurgency *failed* to acquire a status of customary norms, they nevertheless *undermined* the customary status of preexisting rules. The Protocol is a *law-making treaty*—as opposed to a *treaty-contract*[147]—and it is one to which the vast majority of states are parties. As observed by Ian Brownlie, law-making treaties

> are in principle binding only on parties, but the number of parties, the explicit acceptance of rules of law, and, in some cases, the declaratory nature of the provisions produce a strong law-creating effect at least as great as the general practice considered sufficient to support a customary rule.[148]

While provisions contained in a law-making treaty do not always acquire the status of customary international law, they may yet represent state practice inconsistent with a preexisting customary norm—practice that "is simply too thick to justify the conclusion that states really accept the norm as obligatory."[149] This applies to the Protocol's provisions regarding the definition of combatants and qualifications for POW status. Inconsistency between those provisions, on the one hand, and the definition of combatants contained in the Hague Regulations, on the other hand, suffices to render the Hague rule's customary status uncertain, thereby triggering the application of the freedom principle.

In addition to his argument predicated on the consent-based nature of international law, it should be noted, Glennon presents a broader theory concerning the identification of legal norms in general. He submits that a norm is obligatory if the expected costs of violating it generally outweigh the benefits of such violation. In the context of international law, a norm

> is obligatory because the costs of violation outweigh the benefits for nearly all states nearly all of the time, so violations are rare. . . . If the costs of violation do not outweigh the benefits and the rule is breached by a significant number of

> states a significant number of times over a significant period of time, the norm in question may still have an effect on state behavior, just as social norms affect individual behavior, but it is not a rule of international law.[150]

Similarly, Andrew Guzman submits that a norm qualifies as international customary law only if the expected reactions of other states to a violation of that norm generate incentives to abide by that norm.[151] According to Guzman, "in a world of rational states customary international law is relevant only when it has some impact on payoffs."[152] Hence, "we model customary international law as a set of rules the violation of which will generate costs."[153] Guzman elaborates:

> Given that the rules in question arise without explicit agreement, it seems sensible to limit the definition to legal rules that have some effect. . . . [Customary law] can only affect behavior if there is some sanction associated with noncompliance. The two sanctions of greatest interest can be labeled direct sanctions and reputational sanctions. Direct sanctions are specific punishments meted out by other states in response to a violation. . . . Reputational sanctions give states a separate reason to comply with the rules of international law in general and customary international law in particular. A refusal to comply with international obligations today signals to other countries a willingness to violate the law. Other states then use this information to decide how to interact with the violating state in the future.[154]

This approach seems to support the view that the Protocol undermined the customary status of Article 1 of the Hague Regulations. As the vast majority of states are parties to the Protocol, it seems that state conduct which the Protocol allows would not generally be expected to generate substantial costs in terms of direct or reputational sanctions, even where such conduct is inconsonant with the Hague Regulations. It is not likely that such conduct will "signal to other countries a willingness to violate the law."[155] This suggests that the Hague approach to combatant status has indeed eroded.

The Israeli Court has concluded that the definition of combatants contained in Article 1 of the Hague Regulations reflects customary law, notwithstanding its inconsistency with the Protocol's definition of combatants. I argue, however, that the Court's approach leads to peculiar results, for a customary rule containing one definition of *combatants* cannot coexist with a conventional rule providing another definition. The customary prohibition against attacking civilians is a *peremptory norm* of international law.[156] A treaty rule that derogates from this customary prohibition—in other words, a treaty provision which classifies as combatants those who are actually considered civilians under customary law—should thus be considered void.[157]

The approach taken by the Israeli Supreme Court means, then, that a provision of the Protocol—Article 43, as applied to guerrilla combatants—is void, because it conflicts with a peremptory rule of international law. Hence, a state party to the Protocol, which engages in an armed conflict of the type described in Article 1(4), would be violating international humanitarian law when attacking persons that are defined as legitimate objects of attack under the Protocol. (This would be true regardless of whether or not the non-state actor submits an Article 96 declaration.) This result seems at the very least counterintuitive, particularly because of the status of the Protocol as *a law-making treaty* to which the vast majority of the states are parties.

Another problematic implication of the approach taken by the Israeli Supreme Court concerns the application of the principle of distinction in the context of international criminal law (ICL). Article 8(2)(b)(i) of the Rome Statute proscribes "intentionally directing attacks . . . against individual civilians not taking direct part in hostilities." Such attacks are a war crime.[158] This definition of crime, as most definitions of war crimes contained in the Rome Statute, is widely considered to be reflective of customary international law.[159] As all agree that civilians are those who are not categorized as combatants, it is the customary definition of combatants that determines the scope of the criminal prohibition against attacking civilians.[160] Hence, according to the approach taken by the Israeli Supreme Court, attacks that are entirely permissible under the Protocol (in view of the Protocol's relatively broad definition of combatants) are nonetheless considered war crimes under ICL.

This bizarre result—a law-making treaty permitting a conduct that is considered a war crime under customary international law—stands in sharp contrast with the prevailing view of ICL as being confined to "the most serious crimes of concern to the international community as a whole."[161] It trivializes international criminal prohibitions, and adversely reflects on the integrity of the Protocol in its entirety. Most importantly, however, such a situation raises serious fair notice concerns.

The fair notice principle entails the requirement that criminal norms be clear.[162] (It is obviously unjust to punish someone for violating a rule that cannot be understood.) This requirement is not fulfilled, however, where customary international criminal law proscribes conduct that the Protocol allows. Simply put, individuals looking for notice could not be expected to know that the definition of combatants, which pertains to the criminal prohibition on attacks against civilians, is *not,* in fact, the one clearly offered for this purpose in the recent and much-publicized purportedly law-making Protocol of 1977 but, rather, the narrower and much older definition of combatants contained in Article 1 of the Hague Regulations of 1907. This clearly presents fair notice problems. Subscribing to the view that international criminal prohibitions must reflect clear, self-evident norms, the British military court in Germany stated, "[i]t is quite obvious that no sailor and no soldier can carry with him a library of international law, or have immediate access to a professor in that subject who can tell him whether or not a particular command is a lawful one."[163] In this case, in fact, it is likely that even access to such a library or professor would not alleviate the fair notice difficulty that arises here.

But even if the Rome Statute *did* clearly state that the international criminal prohibition on attacking civilians relies on the narrower definition of combatants contained in the Hague Regulations, serious fair notice concerns would still arise precisely because the Protocol publicizes a contradictory standard. Fairness requires more than individuals' *knowledge* of the content of a criminal prohibition. It also requires, more generally, that individuals be aware of the dissonance between their behavior and the law. Such awareness is undermined where a conduct subject to international criminal prohibition is allowed by another provision of international law applicable to the individual. (The natural inhibition of a reasonable person against violating a criminal prohibition weakens in such cases of mixed signals.) The warning sign of unlawfulness, presented by the criminal prohibition, fades. Hence, Michael Moore has observed, for example, that inconsistency between a criminal prohibition and another statutory provision violates the fair notice principle and therefore makes the criminal prohibition *void-for-vagueness*" under the U.S. Constitution's due process clause.[164] There is no reason to think this should not be true in the context of international law as well. In this case, it is clearly too much to expect individuals to realize that the Protocol's definition of combatants is void because it derogates from a peremptory norm of international law.

In conclusion, it seems that the definition of combatants contained in Article 1 of the Hague Regulations pertains both to the application of the principle of distinction *and* to the question of entitlement to POW status. The Protocol, which departs from this definition, renders its customary status uncertain in both contexts. This ambiguity, in turn, brings the freedom principle into play.

The assumption—implicit in the Israeli Supreme Court's judgment in the *Targeted Killing Case*—that Article 43 of the Protocol did not gain the status of customary law has led the Israeli court, without further analysis, to the conclusion that it is the definition of combatants contained in the Hague Regulations that reflects customary law. I submit that the Court erred in disregarding the capacity of a law-making treaty inconsistent with a preexisting customary rule to render the latter's status uncertain, thus triggering the application of the freedom principle.

It is important to delineate the purview of the freedom principle both with regard to the application of the principle of distinction and with regard to the question of entitlement to POW status. Obviously, most individuals considered civilians under the Hague Regulations would also be classified as such under the Protocol. Customary humanitarian law prohibits attacks against such individuals, unless and for such time as they take direct part in hostilities. Hence, the freedom principle (the *Lotus Doctrine*) has no relevance to such cases, as there is no uncertainty about the law. This principle does come into action, however, where attacks proscribed under the Hague Regulations are permissible under the Protocol—which is the case where individuals are classified as combatants under the Protocol but not under the Hague Regulations. In such cases, on account of the freedom principle, a state may freely attack such persons subject only to the limitations the law of war places on attacks against combatants (e.g., prohibition on the use of certain types of weapons).

To be sure, Article 50(1) of the Protocol provides that "in case of doubt whether a person is a civilian, that person shall be considered to be a civilian."[165] This provision seems to reflect customary law. However, this provision concerns situations in which the circumstances pertaining to the classification of a person as civilian/combatant are unclear.[166] It does not concern situations in which *the law itself* is unclear.

Similarly, the freedom principle applies in addressing the question of entitlement to POW status where detainees qualify for such status under the terms of the Protocol but *not* under the terms of the Hague Regulations and the Third Geneva Convention. In such cases, the freedom principle allows the detaining state to deny the detainees POW status. The freedom principle, however, has no application where the detained persons meet the more stringent qualifications for POW status stipulated by the Hague Regulations and Third Geneva Convention.

The ironic result of this, therefore, is that the Protocol—a treaty designed to give greater protections to irregular combatants fighting state adversaries—is an instrument that seems to have turned against its drafters, or at least against those whom these drafters intended to help. As a result of the Protocol's inconsistency with Hague norms regarding combatant status, the Protocol has *undermined* the customary status of the latter without replacing them with new customary norms. The resulting uncertainty about which standard obtains has, in turn, left states *less* constrained than before in fighting such guerrilla adversaries.

Consequently, persons who qualify as combatants under the Protocol but not under the Hague Regulations may now be attacked, whereas before they were afforded a relatively broad protection. At the same time, detainees who qualify for POW status under the terms of the Protocol but *not* under the terms of the Hague Regulations and the Third Geneva Convention may now be denied such treatment notwithstanding the Protocol's effort to give it to them. Guerrilla fighters, one suspects, may not thank the Protocols' drafters for all this assistance.

NOTES

1. Protocol Additional to the Geneva Conventions of 12 August 1949, and Relating to the Protection of Victims of International Armed Conflicts, Protocol I, June 8, 1977, 1125 U.N.T.S. 3., art. 69(1) [hereinafter Protocol].

2. *Id.*, art. 1(4).

3. The last Resolution adopted by the United Nations General Assembly prior to the opening of the Diplomatic Conference which drafted the Protocol was Resolution 3103 (XXVIII) of 12 December 1973, entitled "Basic Principles of the Legal Status of the Combatants Struggling Against Colonial and Alien Domination and Racist Regimes." The Resolution stated that it is necessary to draft "additional instruments and norms envisaging, *inter alia,* the increase of the protection of persons struggling for freedom against colonial and alien domination and racist regimes." The Resolution proceeds to state that combatants engaged in such struggles should enjoy prisoner-of-war status. *See also*, e.g., Johan D. van der Vyver, "Legal Ramifications of the War in Gaza," *Florida Journal of International Law,* vol. 21 (2009), at 403, 412.

4. Richard D. Rosen, "Targeting Enemy Forces in the War on Terror: Preserving Civilian Immunity," *Vanderbilt Journal of Transnational* Law, vol. 42 (2009), at 683, 722 (observing that Article 1(4) "collapses the concept of *jus ad bellum* into *jus in bello,* making application of international humanitarian principles dependent upon the justness of one's cause.")

5. Guerrilla combatants who participate in non-international armed conflicts are not entitled to Prisoner of War status. As noted by the ICRC, the law of non-international armed conflicts "does not prevent bringing to justice a member of an insurgent armed group for the act of taking up arms. It does not confer upon him either combatant or prisoner-of-war status." International Committee of the Red Cross, *on the Additional Protocols of June 1977 to the Geneva Conventions of 12 August 1949* (Yves Sandoz, Christophe Swinarski, & Bruno Zimmermann eds.) (1987), at 1344 [hereinafter *ICRC Commentary on the Additional Protocols*].

6. Michael A. Newton, "Exceptional Engagement: Protocol I and a World United Against Terrorism," *Texas International Law Journal,* vol. 45 (2009), at 323, 345–346; Robert D. Sloane, "Prologue to a Voluntarist War Convention," *Michigan Law Review,* vol. 106 (2007), at 443, 465.

7. Jean-Marie Henckaerts & Louise Doswald-Beck, *Customary International Humanitarian Law, Volume 1: Rules* (ICRC, 2005) at 3 [hereinafter *ICRC*

Commentary on Customary International Humanitarian Law—Rules]; Protocol, *supra,* at Arts. 48 & 51(2).

8. *ICRC Commentary on Customary International Humanitarian Law—Rules, supra,* at 19; Protocol, *supra* note 1, art. 51(3).

9. Regulations Annexed to the Hague Convention Respecting the Laws and Customs of War on Land (October 18, 1907), 36 Stat. 2295, T.I.A.S. No. 539, at Art. 1 [hereinafter Hague Regulations].

10. *Id.*

11. Geneva Convention Relative to the Treatment of Prisoners of War (August 12, 1949) at Art. 4(A)(2), 6 U.S.T. 3316, 75 U.N.T.S. 135 [hereinafter Third Geneva Convention]; *see also* David Kretzmer, "Targeted Killing of Suspected Terrorists: Extra-Judicial Executions or Legitimate Means of Defense?," *European Journal of International Law,* vol. 16 (2005) [hereinafter Kretzmer I], at 171, 191.

12. HCJ 393/82 *A Cooperative Society Lawfully Registered in the Judea and Samaria Region v. Commander of the IDF Forces in the Judea and Samaria Region* (English excerpt in 14 ISR. Y. B. HUM. RTS. 301 (1984)) (the Court observed that "the Hague Regulations are generally regarded as declaratory of customary international law.").

13. Protocol, *supra,* at Art. 43(1).

14. *Id.,* at Art. 43(2) ("Members of the armed forces of a Party to the conflict (other than medical personnel and chaplains covered by Article 33 of the Third Convention) are combatants, that is to say, they have the right to participate directly in hostilities.").

15. *Id.,* at Art. 44(1).

16. As noted by the ICRC, "[t]he Conference considered that all ambiguity should be removed and that it should be explicitly stated that all members of the armed forces . . . can participate directly in hostilities, i.e., *attack and be attacked.*" *ICRC Commentary on the Additional Protocols, supra,* at 515.

17. Protocol, *supra,* at Art. 43(1).

18. *ICRC Commentary on the Additional Protocols, supra,* at 525.

19. *Id.,* at 522–3.

20. Theodor Meron, "The Time has Come for the United States to Ratify Geneva Protocol I," *American Journal of International Law,* vol. 88 (1994), at 678, 683; Sean Watts, "Reciprocity and the Law of War," *Harvard International Law Journal,* vol. 50 (2009), at 365, 428–9; George H. Aldrich, "Prospects for United States Ratification of Additional Protocol I to the 1949 Geneva Conventions," *American Journal of International Law,* vol. 85 (1991), at 1, 8.

21. U.K. Ministry of Defense, *The Manual of the Law of Armed Conflict* (Oxford: Oxford University Press, 2004), at 39 [hereinafter *British Manual of the Law of Armed Conflict*].

22. International Committee of the Red Cross, *Interpretive Guide on the Notion of Direct Participation in Hostilities Under International Humanitarian Law* (ICRC, May 2009), available at: <http://www.icrc.org/Web/Eng/siteeng0.nsf/htmlall/p0990/$File/ICRC_002_0990.PDF> [hereinafter *ICRC Direct Participation Report*]

at 21. In this document, the ICRC observes that "according to Additional Protocol I, the armed forces of a party to the conflict comprise all organized armed forces, groups and units which are under a command responsible to that party for the conduct of its subordinates." The ICRC does not mention any requirement that the armed group respect and enforce humanitarian law as an element of the definition of "armed forces." *See also ICRC Commentary on Customary International Humanitarian Law—Rules, supra,* at 14 (*noting,* in reliance upon Article 43(1) of the Protocol, that "[t]he armed forces of a party to the conflict consist of all organized armed forces, groups and units which are under a command responsible to that party for the conduct of its subordinates").

23. *ICRC Commentary on the Additional Protocols, supra* at 512.

24. *ICRC Commentary on Customary International Humanitarian Law—Rules, supra,* at 16.

25. Protocol, *supra,* at Art. 44(1).

26. *ICRC Commentary on the Additional Protocols, supra,* at 526.

27. Protocol, *supra,* at Arts. 1(4) & 43–44.

28. Commenting on Article 43 of the Protocol, the ICRC observed:

> "This means that violation by a combatant of the rules of international law applicable in armed conflict, does not deprive such a combatant of his right to be treated as a prisoner of war. However, under the Hague Regulations, this did not apply to members of militias and volunteer corps, unless they gave evidence in the field that they did indeed fulfill the conditions listed in Article 1 of the Regulations. Thus they had to prove that they acted in accordance with the laws and customs of war in their operations. Article 4A(2) of the Third Convention does not seem to have modified this situation with regard to members of resistance movements, so that the paragraph under consideration here actually constitutes an amendment to that article on this point. In fact, this paragraph is perfectly clear and abolishes any distinction; whether it concerns a guerrilla fighter or a uniformed soldier of the regular army, if such a combatant has violated the rules of international law applicable in armed conflict, that fact by itself shall not deprive him of his status."

ICRC Commentary on the Additional Protocols, supra, at 525–6.

29. *Id.,* at 516.

30. *Id.,* at 529.

31. Protocol, *supra,* at Art. 44(3).

32. *Id.,* at Art. 44(4); *ICRC Commentary on the Additional Protocols, supra,* at 538 & 540.

33. *Id.* at 536; *see also* Newton, *supra,* at 345 (observing that the Protocol presented "fundamental modifications to the well-established law of combatant immunity"); Watts, *supra,* at 426.

34. *ICRC Commentary on the Additional Protocols, supra,* at 515.

35. Protocol, *supra,* at Art. 96(3).

36. *ICRC Commentary on the Additional Protocols, supra,* at 1091 ("The declaration laid down in this paragraph is only possible if an armed conflict is conducted against a Party to the Protocol.").

37. *Prosecutor v. Tadic,* Case No. IT-94–1-AR72, Appeal on Jurisdiction, ¶ 67 (October 2, 1995), *published in* 105 I.L.R. 419 [hereinafter *Prosecutor v. Tadic—Jurisdiction*]; *Prosecutor v. Tadic,* Case No. IT-94–1-T, Judgment, ¶ 562 (May 7, 1997), *published in* 112 I.L.R. 1 [hereinafter *Prosecutor v. Tadic—Judgment*].

38. *Prosecutor v. Tadic, supra.*

39. *British Manual of the Law of Armed Conflict, supra,* at 30. The British manual observes that one of the conditions for the applicability of Article 1(4) of the Protocol is that "there must be an armed conflict. The threshold of violence required to render the situation an armed conflict is the same as that required for internal armed conflicts." *See also* HCJ 769/02 Public Committee Against Torture in Israel v. Government of Israel [2006] (2) IsrLR 459, 464, available at <http://elyon1.court.gov.il/files_eng/02/690/007/e16/02007690.e16.pdf> [hereinafter *Targeted Killing Case*] (observing, relying upon an analysis of the scale of the violence and its level of organization, that hostilities between Israel and Palestinian armed groups in the occupied Palestinian territories amounted to an armed conflict).

40. Meron, *supra,* at 681.

41. David Kretzmer has shown that in cases of hostilities between a state and a non-state entity, it is the *former* that has a significant interest in characterizing the situation as an armed conflict, because the permission to exercise violence afforded to a state under the law of war's principles of distinction and proportionality is much broader than that granted to a state under the legal regime governing law enforcement situations. David Kretzmer, "Rethinking the Application of IHL in Non-International Armed Conflicts," *Israeli Law Review,* vol. 42 (2009) [hereinafter Kretzmer II], at 8, 23–31.

42. Aldrich, *supra,* at 7.

43. Meron, *supra,* at 681; *see also* Sloane, *supra,* at 467 ("Experience effectively 'resolved' the disputes prompted by Articles 1(4), 43, 44, and 96(3) by showing that they would remain academic.").

44. *ICRC Commentary on the Additional Protocols, supra,* at 1089–90.

45. Addressing the principle of nonreciprocity in the application of humanitarian law, the ICRC has observed that "[t]he obligation to respect and ensure respect for international humanitarian law does not depend on reciprocity." *ICRC Commentary on Customary International Humanitarian Law—Rules, supra,* at 498.

46. Aldrich, *supra,* at 6.

47. Jean-Marie Henckaerts & Louise Doswald-Beck, *Customary International Humanitarian Law, Volume 2: Practice* (ICRC, 2005) at 3 [hereinafter *ICRC Commentary on Customary International Humanitarian Law—Practice*], at 2551 ("Upon signature and/or ratification of Additional Protocol I, Australia, Belgium, Canada, France, Germany, Ireland, South Korea and UK stated that the situation described in the second sentence of Article 44(3) of Additional Protocol I could exist only in occupied territories or in armed conflicts covered by Article 1(4) of Additional Protocol I (wars of national liberation).").

48. *ICRC Commentary on Customary International Humanitarian Law—Rules, supra,* at 387.

49. Nathaniel Berman, "Privileging Combat? Contemporary Conflict and the Legal Construction of War," *Columbia Journal of Transnational Law,* vol. 43 (2004), at 1, 43. Also see, Rosen, *supra,* at 687 ("The Protocol also virtually eliminates the requirement that combatants distinguish themselves from the civilian population, thus degrading an essential element of civilian immunity—the ability to discriminate between combatants and civilians.").

50. CDDH, Official Records, Vol. VI, CDDH/SR.40 (May 26, 1977), at 121.

51. Aldrich, *supra,* at 5.

52. *Id.*

53. *Id.*

54. *Id.,* at 2–5.

55. Letter of Transmittal from President Ronald Reagan, *Protocol II Additional to the 1949 Geneva Conventions, and Relating to the Protection of Victims of Non-International Armed Conflicts,* S. Treaty Doc. NO. 2, 100TH Congress, 1st Session (1987), at III, *reprinted in American Journal of International Law,* vol. 81 (1987), at 910.

56. Christopher J. Greenwood, "Customary Law Status of the 1977 Additional Protocols," in *Humanitarian Law of Armed Conflict: Challenges Ahead: Essays in Honour of Frits Kalshoven* (Astrid J. M. Delissen & Gerard J. Tanja eds.) (The Hague: Martinus Nijhoff, 1991), at 93, 112.

57. *ICRC Commentary on Customary International Humanitarian Law—Practice, supra,* at 2560.

58. *ICRC Commentary on Customary International Humanitarian Law—Rules, supra,* at 387–88.

59. ICRC, *International Humanitarian Law—State Parties/Signatories,* available at <http:// www.icrc.org/ihl.nsf/WebSign?ReadForm&id=470&ps=P#ratif>.

60. Meron, *supra,* at 681.

61. *ICRC Direct Participation Report, supra,* at 24, n. 25 ("*For States party to Additional Protocol I,* the law governing international armed conflicts also applies to armed conflicts between States and national liberation movements within the meaning of Article 1(4) of Additional Protocol I.") (emphasis added). In the view of the ICRC, large-scale hostilities between a national liberation movement and a state that is not a party to the Protocol are considered a non-international armed conflict. *Id.,* at 24. Hence, the ICRC does not consider Article 1(4) of the Protocol to have obtained the status of customary law.

62. Andrew T. Guzman, "Saving Customary International Law," *Michigan Journal of International Law,* vol. 27 (2005), at 115, 150 ("Formally, of course, all states have equal rights under international law, and no single state or small group of states is able to create or change customary international law on its own. In practice, there is no doubt that analysis of customary international law rules inevitably gives greater weight to more powerful and more affected states. Whether this is desirable or not, it is hard to imagine any other outcome.").

63. *ICRC Commentary on Customary International Humanitarian Law—Practice, supra,* at 2556–59.

64. *Id.,* at 2559.

65. *Id.*, at 2557–58.

66. According to the ICRC, France's *Law of Armed Conflict Manual* defines combatants with reference to Article 4(A) of Geneva Convention III, while the equivalent Italian document defines *lawful combatants* as: "(a) members of the armed forces; [and] (b) members of militia, of volunteer corps, of resistance movements, who belong to a Party to the conflict, operating outside or inside their own territory, even if this territory is occupied, provided they fulfill the following conditions: (1) being under a Head responsible for his own subordinates; (2) wear a uniform or a fixed distinctive sign recognizable from a distance; (3) carry arms openly; [and] (4) abide by the laws and customs of war" *Id.* at 80–81. Belgium's *Law of War Manual* defines armed forces as comprising: "All members of organized armed forces . . . Members of organized resistance movements are also considered to be combatants provided they: (a) are subject to internal discipline; (b) wear a fixed distinctive sign recognizable from a distance; (c) carry arms openly; [and] (d) comply with the laws and customs of war." *Id.* at 89. For its part, Russia's *Military Manual* "provides that members of organized resistance movements enjoy POW status upon capture provided they fulfill the conditions set out in Article 4(A)(2) of Geneva Convention III." *Id.* at 2553–54.

67. Meron, *supra*, at 681.

68. Michael Akehurst, "Custom as a Source of International Law," *British Yearbook of International Law*, vol. 47 (1976), at 1, 2, 5–6; Bruno Simma & Philip Alston, "The Sources of Human Rights Law: Custom, *Jus Cogens*, and General Principles," *Australian Yearbook of International* Law, vol. 12 (1992), at 82, 89–90 ("Rules or principles proclaimed, for instance, by the General Assembly . . . are taken not only as starting points for the possible development of customary law in the event that State practice happens to lock on to these proclamations, but as a law-making process which is more or less complete in itself, even in the face of contrasting 'external' facts."); Guzman, *supra*, at 152 ("The majority view is that the practice requirement can indeed be satisfied with reference to statements and claims made by states.").

69. There is no doubt that in applying the principle of distinction in non-international armed conflict, all full-fledged members of the armed forces of parties to the conflict are considered combatants, regardless of whether they distinguish themselves from the civilian population and abide by the laws of war. *See ICRC Direct Participation Report, supra*, at 27; Orna Ben-Naftali & Keren Michaeli, "'We Must Not Make a Scarecrow of the Law': A Legal Analysis of the Israeli Policy of Targeted Killings," *Cornell International Law Journal*, vol. 36 (2003), at 233, 271; Kretzmer I, *supra*, at 197–98. Indeed, the U.S. Supreme Court considers large-scale hostilities between the United States and a transnational terrorist organization—*al-Qaeda*—to be a non-international armed conflict, and therefore regards members of this organization as combatants. *Hamdan v. Rumsfeld*, 548 U.S. 557, 629–32 (2006). Guerrilla combatants who participate in non-international armed conflicts, however, are not entitled to prisoner -of -war status.

70. *Prosecutor v. Tadic—Jurisdiction*, *supra*, at ¶ 67.

71. Geneva Convention Relative to the Protection of Civilian Persons in Time of War, Aug. 12, 1949, 6 U.S.T. 3516, 75 U.N.T.S. 287, 318–38, art. 3 [hereinafter Fourth Geneva Convention].

72. *See* Protocol Additional (II) to the Geneva Conventions of 12 August 1949, and relating to the Protection of Victims of Non-International Armed Conflicts, opened for signature Dec. 12, 1977, 1125 U.N.T.S. 609 (entered into force Dec. 7, 1978), Art. 1(1). [hereinafter Protocol II].

73. Fourth Geneva Convention, *supra,* at Art. 3; Protocol II, *supra,* at Art. 1.

74. *See* Berman, *supra,* at 32 (citing the language of Common Article 3 and observing that *al-Qaeda*'s attacks on September 11, 2001, "seemed too trans-border in nature to be non-international"); Roy S. Schondorf, "Extra-State Armed Conflicts: Is There a Need for a New Legal Regime?," *New York University Journal of International Law and Politics,* vol. 37 (2004), at 32, 35 (arguing that the law of non-international armed conflict only concerns purely internal conflicts); Natasha Balendra, "Defining Armed Conflict," *Cardozo Law Review,* vol. 29 (2008), at 2461, 2472.

75. *ICRC Commentary, The Geneva Convention for the Amelioration of the Wounded and Sick in Armed Forces in the Field* (Jean S. Pictet, ed.) (ICRC, 1952) [hereinafter Commentary of the First Convention], at 32; U.N. Commission on Human Rights, *Question of the Violation of Human Rights in the Occupied Arab Territories, Including Palestine—Report of the Human Rights Inquiry Commission Established Pursuant to Commission Resolution S-5/1 of 19 October 2000,* U.N. ESCOR, 57th Sess., U.N. Doc. E/CN.4/2001/121 (2001), at 12 (observing with regard to the Israeli-Palestinian conflict that "[c]learly, there is no international armed conflict in the region, as Palestine, despite widespread recognition, still falls short of the accepted criteria of statehood"); Gabor Rona, "Interesting Times for International Humanitarian Law: Challenges From the 'War on Terror,'" *Fletcher Forum on World Affairs,* vol. 27, (2003), at 55, 58; Derek Jinks, "September 11 and the Laws of War," *Yale Journal of International Law,* vol. 28 (2003), at 1, 20; Chris Downes, "'Targeted Killing' in an Age of Terror: The Legality of the Yemen Strike," *Journal of Conflict and Security Law,* vol. 9 (2004), at 277, 283; Balendra, *supra,* at 2472.

76. *See, e.g., Hamdan v. Rumsfeld,* 126 S. Ct. 2749, 2795–96 (2006) (concluding that the conflict between the United States and *al-Qaeda* was a *non*-international armed conflict); *Targeted Killing Case, supra,* at 464 (observing that hostilities between Israel and Palestinian armed groups amount to an international armed conflict); *see also* William H. Taft IV, "The Law of Armed Conflict After 9/11: Some Salient Features," *Yale Journal of International Law,* vol. 28 (2003), at 319, 320 ("The law of armed conflict provides the most appropriate legal framework for regulating the use of force in the war on terrorism."); Jinks, *supra,* at 9 ("I argue that the laws of war applicable in non-international armed conflict govern the September 11 attacks and that the attacks violated these laws."); Ben-Naftali & Michaeli, *supra,* at 259 (arguing that the hostilities between Israel and Palestinian armed groups amount to a non-international armed conflict); Amos Guiora, "Targeted Killing as Active Self-Defense," *Case Western Reserve Journal of International Law,* vol. 36 (2004), at 319, 328; Norman G. Printer, "The Use of Force Against Non-State Actors Under

International Law: An Analysis of the U.S. Predator Strike in Yemen," *UCLA Journal of International Law and Foreign Affairs,* vol. 8 (2003), at 331, 359 (applying the law of war to U.S. military operations against *al-Qaeda* members); Downes, *supra,* at 281–84 (arguing that hostilities between *al-Qaeda* and the United States constitute a non-international armed conflict).

77. *Hamdan v. Rumsfeld, supra.*

78. *Id.,* at 2795–96.

79. *Id.*

80. Fourth Geneva Convention, *supra,* at Art. 3.

81. *Hamdan v. Rumsfeld, supra,* at 2795.

82. *Id.,* at 2796.

83. *Id.,* at 2796 n. 63.

84. *Id.,* at 2796; *see also* ICRC, *Commentary: Geneva Convention Relative to the Treatment of Prisoners of War* (ICRC, 1960), at 36 [hereinafter Commentary on the Third Convention].

85. Fourth Geneva Convention, *supra,* at Art. 2 ("The Convention shall also apply to all cases of partial or total occupation of the territory of a High Contracting Party, even if the said occupation meets with no armed resistance."); *see also* Fourth Geneva Convention, *supra,* at Art. 6.

86. *Hamdan v. Rumsfeld, supra,* at 2796; *cf.* Fourth Geneva Convention, *supra,* at Arts. 71–74 (containing fair trial guarantees applicable within an occupied territory).

87. The Court did not determine that the status of the United States in Afghanistan was that of an occupant. *See generally, Hamdan v. Rumsfeld, supra.* Hamdan was captured during the initial U.S. invasion of Afghanistan, and it seems that this invasion did not result in a state of occupation. *See* Adam Roberts, "Transformative Military Occupation: Applying the Laws of War and Human Rights," *American Journal of International Law,* vol. 100 (2006), at 580, 604 (stating that "the establishment of a foreign military occupation regime was not necessary in Afghanistan. After the fall of the Taliban and the accession to power of the Afghan Interim Authority on December 22, 2001, the coalition's role was essentially to aid the government.").

88. *Targeted Killing Case, supra.*

89. *Id.* at 464.

90. *Id.*

91. Addressing the applicability of the law of war to situations of belligerent occupation, Kenneth Watkin observes that

> "[c]riteria not that dissimilar to those used to identify non-international armed conflicts might be employed, including the nature of the opposing force (i.e., Is the group organized to conduct hostilities?), the level of violence used by the group, and the degree of freedom of the group in terms of operating outside the occupying power's control."

Kenneth Watkin, "Controlling the Use of Force: A Role for Human Rights Norms in Contemporary Armed Conflict," *American Journal of International Law,* vol. 98 (2004), at 1, 28.

92. Some commentators classified the al-Aqsa Intifada as a non-international armed conflict. *See* Kretzmer I, *supra*, at 210; Ben-Naftali & Michaeli, *supra*, at 256; *see also* U.N. Inquiry Commission Report, *supra*, at 12–13. I submit, however, that such a view is erroneous.

93. Common Article 3 of the Geneva Conventions regulates the conduct of parties to non-international armed conflicts. The other provisions of the Fourth Geneva Convention regulate the conduct of parties to an international armed conflict as well as the conduct of an occupant. *See* Fourth Geneva Convention, *supra*, at Arts. 2 & 3; *see also* Jinks, *supra*, at 11–12 (noting that the *grave breaches* regime established under the Geneva Conventions for the punishment of international crimes does not apply to non-international armed conflicts). The First Additional Protocol to the Geneva Conventions regulates the conduct of parties to an international armed conflict as well as the conduct of an occupant. *See* Protocol, *supra*. The Second Additional Protocol to the Geneva Conventions, in turn, regulates the conduct of parties to a non-international armed conflict. *See* Protocol II, *supra*.

94. Articles 8(2)(a) and 8(2)(b) of the Rome Statute regulate the conduct of parties to an international armed conflict as well as the conduct of an occupant, while Articles 8(2)(c) and 8(2)(d) of the Statute regulate the conduct of parties to a non-international armed conflict. Rome Statute of the International Criminal Court, U.N. Doc. A/CONF/183/9 (July 17, 1998) [hereinafter Rome Statute] at Art. 8(2)(a)-(d), *reprinted in International Legal Materials*, vol. 37 (1998), at 999.

95. *Commentary, The International Criminal Court: Elements of Crimes and Rules of Procedure and Evidence* (Roy S. Lee ed.) (Ardsley: Transnational Publishers, 2001), at 113, 115.

96. Rome Statute, *supra*, at Art. 8(2)(b)(viii).

97. *Prosecutor v. Tadic—Jurisdiction, supra*, at ¶ 72.

98. *Id.*

99. Lindsay Moir, *The Law of Internal Armed Conflict* (Cambridge: Cambridge University Press, 2002), at 47.

100. Prior to the Israeli occupation of the West Bank and the Gaza Strip, those areas were controlled by Jordan and Egypt respectively. Israel concluded peace agreements with both Egypt and Jordan prior to the eruption of the al-Aqsa Intifada.

101. Other commentators share this conclusion. *See*, e.g., Antonio Cassese, "Expert Opinion on Whether Israel's Targeted Killings of Palestinian Terrorists is Consonant with International Humanitarian Law" (June 13, 2003), in HCJ Petition 769/02, available at <http://www.stoptorture.org.il/eng/search.asp> (asserting that the law applicable to the al-Aqsa Intifada "is the body of international customary and treaty rules relating to international armed conflicts, in particular to *occupatio bellica* of foreign territory").

102. *ICRC Direct Participation Report*, *supra*, at 21–22.

103. Curtis A. Bradley, "The United States, Israel and Unlawful Combatants," *Green Bag 2d*, vol. 12 (2009) at 397, 399.

104. Hamdan, 548 U.S. at 630–31 ("the Government asserts that Common Article 3 does not apply to Hamdan because the conflict with al-Qaeda, being 'international in

scope,' does not qualify as a 'conflict not of an international character'"). As noted above, however, the Court rejected the Government's view and categorized the conflict as a non-international armed conflict.

105. Bradley, *supra*, at 399.

106. *Id.*

107. *Id.*

108. Targeted Killing Case, *supra*.

109. *Id.*, at 486–90.

110. *Id.*, at 485.

111. *Id.*, at 486–88.

112. *Id.*

113. *Id.*, at 464.

114. Protocol, *supra*, at Art. 51(3) (providing that civilians "shall not be the object of attack . . . unless and for such time as they take a direct part in hostilities"). This rule is now considered a customary norm of international humanitarian law.

115. The Court reasoned that this concept includes not only persons who carry out terrorist attacks but also those who recruit them and provide them with weapons as well as those who plan and direct the attacks. Targeted Killing Case, *supra*, at 496–99. The Court further concluded that persons involved in ongoing terrorist activities are subject to targeting even during the time in between hostile acts. *Id.* at 499–500.

116. *See generally*, Amichai Cohen & Yuval Shany, "A Development of Modest Proportions: The Application of the Principle of Proportionality in the Targeted Killings Case," *Journal of International Criminal Justice*, vol. 5 (2007), at 310. The Court concluded that the law of war permits the targeted killing of civilians who are, at the time, directly participating in hostilities only where the following cumulative requirements are fulfilled. First, reliable and verified information is needed regarding the identity and activity of the civilian who is allegedly taking part in the hostilities, which places a heavy burden of proof on the attacking army. Second, even a civilian who is taking a direct part in hostilities cannot be attacked if less harmful means, such as arrest, interrogation, and trial, can be employed. Third, after each targeted killing, a retroactive, thorough and independent investigation must be conducted regarding the precision of the identification of the target and the circumstances of the attack. And fourth, any collateral damage inflicted must withstand the proportionality test. *Id.*, at 500–02. Clearly, the second and third requirements do not pertain to attacks against *combatants* carried out in pursuance with the law of war's principle of distinction. Under the law of war's principle of distinction, it is not incumbent on the army of either of the warring parties to afford enemy combatants a meaningful opportunity to surrender, and thereby prevent an attack, so long as the latter do not actively indicate their desire to do so. Kretzmer I, *supra*, at 191.

117. Kretzmer I, *supra*, at 194; *see also* Bradley, *supra*, at 402. Curtis Bradley elaborates that:

> "[T]he conception of 'civilians' in the Geneva Conventions does not fit well with the reality of an armed conflict with a terrorist organization. While the Conventions envision

> that civilians might sometimes take part in hostilities, they envision that this combatancy is a temporary deviation for these individuals, and that there is some separate group of full-time fighters. For a terrorist organization engaged in an armed conflict with a nation, however, the involvement of the members of such an organization in hostilities is not some temporary deviation from their normal circumstances. . . . Nor is there any separate set of full-time fighters—the members of the terrorist organization are themselves the full-time fighters."

Bradley, *supra,* at 402.

118. *Id.,* at 401.

119. *Id.*

120. *Id.,* at 401–02.

121. Hague Regulations, *supra,* at Art. 1.

122. *Id.*

123. *Id.,* at Art. 23(g).

124. Protocol, *supra,* at Art. 50(1).

125. *Id.*

126. *ICRC Commentary on the Additional Protocols, supra,* at 611 ("Article 50(1) also refers to Article 43 of the Protocol, which contains a new definition of armed forces covering the different categories of Article 4 of the Third Convention.").

127. Note that Article 4 of the Third Geneva Convention is essentially predicated on the language of Article 1 of the Hague Regulations.

128. According to the Court, the data regarding state practice presented to the Court was insufficient to conclude that any customary rule that departs from the rules contained in Article 1 of the Hague Regulations has emerged.

129. Unlike Article 44 of the Protocol, Article 43—which defines *combatants*—was adopted by consensus at the Diplomatic Conference. *ICRC Commentary on Customary International Humanitarian Law—Practice, supra,* at 87.

130. As noted earlier, Article 50 of the Protocol explicitly recognizes the linkage between the question of entitlement to POW status and the definition of civilians protected against attacks. *See also ICRC Commentary on the Additional Protocols, supra,* at 515 ("The Conference considered that all ambiguity should be removed and that it should be explicitly stated that all members of the armed forces . . . can participate directly in hostilities, i.e., *attack and be attacked.*").

131. Michael J. Glennon, "How International Rules Die," *Georgia Law Journal,* vol. 93 (2005) [hereinafter Glennon I], at 939, 957; D.P. O'Connell, *International Law* (London: Stevens, 1965), at 284; Georg Schwarzenberger, *A Manual of International Law* (New York: Praeger, 1967), at 167; Arthur M. Weisburd, "Customary International Law: The Problem of Treaties," *Vanderbilt Journal of Transnational Law,* vol. 21 (1988), at 1, 22.

132. *See* Glennon I, *supra,* at 941 ("The prevailing theory of validity in international law is familiar. At its core is the classic positivist idea that states are obliged to follow only those rules to which they assent. They assent through words, or treaties, and deeds, or custom. If it has not consented to a given rule, a state is free to disregard the rule.").

133. *Id.*, at 960.

134. Guzman, *supra*, at 143–43.

135. Glennon I, *supra*, at 960.

136. Michael J. Glennon, "The UN Security Council in a Unipolar World," *Virginia Journal of International Law*, vol. 44 (2003) [hereinafter Glennon II], at 91, 98.

137. Charles Pierson, "Preemptive Self-Defense in an Age of Weapons of Mass Destruction: Operation Iraqi Freedom," *Denver Journal of International Law & Policy*, vol. 33 (2004), at 150, 172 ("A *non liquet* ('it is not clear') occurs when the legal norms in an area of the law are so internally contradictory or confused that we cannot articulate the law. Under the rule in *The S.S. Lotus* states may do as they please unless a restriction has been established by treaty or customary law.").

138. Daniel Bodansky, "*Non Liquet* and the Incompleteness of International Law," in *International Law, The International Court of Justice and Nuclear Weapons* (Laurence Boisson de Chazournes & Philippe Sands eds.) (Cambridge: Cambridge University Press, 1999), at 153, 154 ("Today, *non liquet* refers to an insufficiency in the law: specifically, a finding by a court that the law does not permit a conclusion one way or the other concerning the issue in question.").

139. *Case of the SS Lotus*, PCIJ Series A, No. 10 (1927), at 18–19.

140. Glennon II, *supra*, at 98.

141. For an elaboration on this approach, *see* Prosper Weil, "'The Court Cannot Conclude Definitively . . . ' *Non Liquet* Revisited," *Columbia Journal of Transnational Law*, vol. 36 (1997), at 109, 112–13.

142. Hersch Lauterpacht, *The Function of Law in the International Community* (Oxford: Oxford University Press, 1933), at 61–62 (maintaining that "the question whether the judge is at liberty to refuse to give a decision on the ground of the supposed absence of a rule of law applicable to the individual case . . . has been answered, with decisive determination, in the negative . . . by the very fact of the establishment of a community under reign of law"); Jose Alvarez, "The Internationalization of U.S. Law," *Columbia Journal of Transnational Law*, vol. 47 (2009), at 537, 555 (pointing to the "general principle that international adjudicators should avoid determinations of *non-liquet*, i.e., that no law applies to resolve a dispute"); Weil, *supra*, at 110 ("The allergy of international tribunals, in particular the I.C.J., and scholars alike to *non liquet* is a well-known phenomenon. The view prevailing among writers is that there is no room for *non liquet* in international adjudication because there are no lacunae in international law.").

143. Alvarez, *supra*, at 555.

144. Weil, *supra*, at 114.

145. *Id.*, at 115–16.

146. *Id.*, at 117.

147. Akbar Rasulov, "Revisiting State Succession to Humanitarian Treaties: Is there a Case for Automaticity?" *European Journal of International Law*, vol. 14 (2003), at 141, 159 (observing that humanitarian treaties are a subclass of law-making treaties). For the distinction between law-making treaties and treaty-contracts, *see* Ian Brownlie, *Principles of Public International Law* (5th ed.) (Oxford: Oxford University Press,

1998), at 11–13; Timothy Hillier, *Principles of Public International Law* (2nd ed.) (London: Routledge-Cavendish, 1999), at 17.

148. Brownlie, *supra,* at 12.

149. Glennon I, *supra,* at 960. One could argue, however, that the holding of the International Court of Justice in the *North Sea Continental Shelf Case* stands in contrast with the proposition that a law-making treaty may undermine the customary status of a pre-existing rule without establishing a new customary rule. That case involved a dispute between Germany on the one hand and Denmark and the Netherlands on the other hand over the continental shelf. The ICJ determined that Article 6 of the Geneva Convention of 1958 on the Continental Shelf—a law-making treaty—which lays down the equidistance rule for apportionment of a common continental shelf, has not acquired the status of customary law. *North Sea Continental Shelf Case,* ICJ Reports (1969) 3, 41. The Court then proceeded to hold that the delimitation, as between the parties, of the continental shelf has to be made on the basis of *equitable principles. Id.,* at 47. It seems that the Court regarded resort to equitable principles as reflecting an existing rule of customary international law inconsistent with the treaty rule. *Id.* at 13; *see also* Akehurst, *supra,* at 17. The Court did not consider the possibility that a provision contained in a law-making treaty that does not acquire the status of customary law may yet have the effect of undermining the status of a pre-existing customary rule.

Yet it seems that there is a good reason to distinguish the *Continental Shelf Case* from the issue addressed here. In the *Continental Shelf Case,* the parties requested the Court to resolve a controversy between them "concerning the delimitation, as between them, of the continental shelf in the North Sea." *North Sea Continental Shelf Case, supra,* at 5–6. Obviously, in the absence of a specific rule of international law pertaining to this question, the resolution requested by the parties could not be had by resorting to the freedom principle. The *Lotus Doctrine* was thus of no relevance to the question before the Court. Hence, resort to equitable principles was the only avenue open to the Court in order to avoid a finding of *non-liquet.* The Court's approach may thus be attributed to its reluctance to hand down a holding of *non-liquet,* given the general prohibition on such holdings in contentious cases.

150. Glennon I, *supra,* at 953.

151. Guzman, *supra,* at 133–140.

152. *Id.,* at 133.

153. *Id.,* at 156.

154. *Id.* at 133–35.

155. *Id.*

156. *See,* e.g., *Prosecutor v. Galic,* Case No. IT-98–29-T, Judgment and Opinion, ¶ 98 (December 5, 2003), available at <http:// www.icty.org/x/cases/galic/tjug/en/gal-tj031205e.pdf> (comment by International Criminal Tribunal for the Former Yugoslavia that the humanitarian law prohibition of attacks against civilians constitutes "a peremptory norm of customary international law"); Christopher C. Joyner, "Arresting Impunity: The Case for Universal Jurisdiction in Bringing War

Criminals to Accountability," *Law & Contemporary Problems*, vol. 59 (1996), at 153, 169 ("[I]f an international agreement that advocated perpetration of war crimes were consummated between states, its lawfulness would be rendered null and void on grounds of *jus cogens*, that is, that its provisions violated peremptory norms protecting the customary legal protections of innocent civilians under international humanitarian law.").

157. Vienna Convention on the Law of Treaties, May 23, 1969, 1155 U.N.T.S. 331, at Arts. 53 & 64 (providing, respectively, that "[a] treaty is void if, at the time of its conclusion, it conflicts with a peremptory norm of general international law," and that "[i]f a new peremptory norm of general international law emerges, any existing treaty which is in conflict with that norm becomes void and terminates."); *see also* Joyner, *supra*.

158. Rome Statute, *supra*, at Art. 8(2)(b)(i).

159. Antonio Cassese, Paola Gaeta, & John R.W.D. Jones, *The Rome Statute of the International Criminal Court: A Commentary*, Vol. II (Oxford: Oxford University Press, 2002), at 1893–94.

160. Neither the Rome Statute itself nor the elements of crimes stipulated by the Preparatory Committee for the International Criminal Court contain a definition of *combatants*. Knut Dormann, Louise Doswald-Beck, & Robert Kolb, *Elements of War Crimes Under the Rome Statute of the International Criminal Court: Sources and Commentaries* (ICRC, 2005), at 130. (In its commentary on the elements of the criminal prohibition against attacking civilians, the ICRC refers to the definitions of civilians and combatants contained in the Protocol, ignoring the definition of combatants contained in Article 1 of the Hague Regulations. This can be explained by the fact that, in the view of the ICRC, Article 1 of the Hague Regulations does not concern the principle of distinction. I argued above, however, that this view seems to be erroneous.)

161. Rome Statute, *supra*, at Preamble & Art. 1.

162. Andrew Ashworth, *Principles of Criminal Law* (Oxford University Press, 1991), at 59. International criminal tribunals have addressed the application of this requirement in international law when trying violators of customary, non-codified international criminal norms. *See* Judicial Decisions: International Military Tribunal (Nuremberg), Judgment and Sentences *(1946), reprinted in American Journal of International Law*, vol. 41 (1947), at 172; *see also Decision on the Defense Motion on Jurisdiction* (Prosecutor v. Dusko Tadic), 1995 ICT Trial Chamber, Case No. IT-94–1-T. (Aug. 10).

163. *In re Eck and Others (The Peleus)*, 13 I.L.R. 248, 249 (British Military Court, Hamburg 1945).

164. Michael S. Moore, *Act and Crime: The Philosophy of Action and Its Implications for Criminal Law* (Oxford: Oxford University Press, 1993), at 241 ("The void-for-vagueness doctrine requires legislatures to frame acts with sufficient clarity that they can be understood by those to whom they are directed. Such failure of understanding can occur not only because of vagueness in some statutory predicate, but also because of . . . inconsistency between this statutory provision and some other . . .

Any of these inabilities to understand makes a criminal statute 'void for vagueness' under the due process clause.").

165. Protocol, *supra,* at Art. 50(1).

166. *ICRC Commentary on the Additional Protocols, supra,* at 612 (observing that this provision concerns persons "whose status seems doubtful because of the circumstances. They should be considered to be civilians until further information is available, and should therefore not be attacked.").

Chapter 2

The Strange Pretensions of Contemporary Humanitarian Law

Jeremy Rabkin

Military commanders have recognized *laws of war*—or, as they were often and more aptly termed, *customs of war*—for many centuries. It was not until 1899 that an effort was made to reduce these norms of warfare to a written and formally agreed upon international code. Subsequent experience does not inspire great confidence in this effort.

Among other things, all the powers participating in The Hague Peace Conference of 1899 (including Germany, Britain, France, Russia, the United States, and a host of smaller nations), however, subscribed to a declaration against the use of asphyxiating gases in warfare.[1] But Germany resorted to poison gas attacks in the first year of the First World War. Thereafter, all the major combatants felt free to take up this terrible new weapon and it became a standard feature of trench warfare in that conflict.

What aroused far more indignation at the time was the German practice of submarine attacks on merchant vessels to prevent supplies reaching Britain and France during the war. Rules to limit submarine attacks—by requiring advance warning to targeted ships and time for passengers and crew to reach "a place of safety"—were agreed upon at a London conference in 1936.[2] Germany, Japan, Britain, and the United States were among the 50 signatories.

On the outbreak of war in 1939, however, Germany disregarded this agreement and reverted to submarine attacks, without warning, on civilian shipping. Britain then felt free to unloose submarine attacks on German and Italian shipping in the Mediterranean. The U.S. Navy deployed similar submarine attacks against Japanese shipping in the Pacific War, with most decisive effects.

What is new in today's world is not the effort to persevere in attempts to restrain the violence of war. Even after the extreme brutalities of the Second World War, new efforts were made to codify restraints in the Geneva Conventions of 1949. The range and specificity of contemporary norms is somewhat new. But the most remarkable novelty is the notion that such restraints can be insisted upon, even when one side ignores them, and even when noncompliant fighters gain systematic advantage from their disregard of the agreed-upon standards.

The change in expectations is reflected in the new terminology. For centuries, rules of restraint were called *laws or customs of war*. And *war* was understood to describe only full conflicts between independent states, the professional armies of which could be expected to meet current adversaries in a future conflict, where today's restraint would be recalled and reciprocated in some future battle.[3]

Today, the rules supposed to govern the conduct of warfare are more commonly called *international humanitarian law*. This terminology suggests that humanity has somehow generated its own law for its own ends. Those who violate this law are guilty of *crimes against humanity*. And *humanity* is, of course, a higher authority than any one state.

There is, of course, a distinguished intellectual pedigree to claims for legal authority transcending the current preferences of particular states. In earlier times, serious people talked quite seriously about the law of God or the law of Nature (or as the American Declaration of Independence has it, "the laws of Nature and Nature's God"). But serious people also had quite serious disagreements about the content and application of such higher law. How likely is it that, after disavowing theology and metaphysics and simply invoking humanity, we will find that we all agree on this higher law?

I will elaborate four general claims in what follows. First: the seeming premise of today's international humanitarian law—that this law binds the conduct of military operations, regardless of circumstances or consequences—is not the culmination of a time-honored tradition, as sometimes portrayed, but is, in fact, a recent and radical innovation. Second: the current standards—or what are often taken to be such standards—were, to a large extent, the product of efforts by anti-Western governments and movements, seeking to change previously accepted standards to their own advantage. Third: advocacy organizations such as the International Red Cross, Human Rights Watch, and Amnesty International have strong incentives to embrace an anti-Western view of the relevant standards, albeit one disguised as a neutral or internationalist view. Fourth: many Western governments now give credibility to such efforts, because they no longer expect to engage in actual military operations of their own.

It does not follow from this analysis that we must now repudiate all efforts to restrain the violence of war. But it surely follows that the United States and its actual allies have a stake in resisting the imposition of supposed international consensus rules, as they come to be interpreted by international authorities in disregard of experience in actual current conflicts. Law that privileges our enemies can be worse than lawlessness.

I. THE TRADITIONAL LAW OF WAR WAS ALWAYS CONTINGENT

If humanitarian law takes precedence over all tactical or strategic considerations of warring armies, it should not matter who the combatants are or what they are fighting for. If a military measure violated humanitarian standards, it would simply be unlawful and therefore always unacceptable.

In the past, however, even moralists did not embrace such an absolutist view. In the 16th Century, Catholic commentators in the *just war* tradition excused even rape and pillage, if committed by an army fighting for a just cause.[4] The idea that emerged in the 18th Century, that war should generally be fought with restraint, was more plausible when war was presumed to be fought for limited aims—fought, that is, by states focused on gaining marginal advantages over rivals, rather than fighting for some high-minded principle or over the very survival of one or more countries as independent entities. In the world wars of the 20th Century, even Western democracies put aside previous humanitarian scruples, embracing such tactics as food blockades and bombing of cities.

The culminating tactic of the Second World War, the American use of atomic bombs on Japanese cities, has certainly been criticized. But the more telling point is that the decision has many serious defenders even today—defenders who judge the act in the context of a terrible war, which would probably have continued through more terrible battles if not for the sudden, shocking use of the atomic bombs in August of 1945.

Perhaps most telling is that, even today, there is no consensus among moralists on the propriety of threatening nuclear retaliation as a deterrent. If inflicting mass suffering on civilians were always improper, then resort to nuclear weapons might seem always to be wrong. In the mid-1980s, when American Catholic bishops drafted a statement based on this reasoning, Pope John Paul II insisted that the statement be recast. It was not, in his view, an ethical stance to assure potential nuclear aggressors that they would face no like retaliation for using their weapons.[5] A decade later, when the International Court of Justice was asked to deliver an advisory opinion on the question, it could not muster a majority for the proposition that it would always be wrong to threaten use of nuclear weapons to deter a nuclear or other attack that threatened a country's existence.[6]

The moral issue remains, at the least, very challenging, and the complications are not limited to the most extreme case. It is not obviously moral to assure potential aggressors or potential perpetrators of terrible violence that if they target moral states, they need never fear retaliation. To think that way is to insist that it is better to let evil triumph than to resist it by questionable means.

The traditional law of war had a direct answer to such dilemmas: belligerent reprisal. What would otherwise be unlawful could be considered a permissible practice if necessary (or reasonably calculated) to force the enemy to refrain from the same practice. So, during the American Civil War, President Lincoln openly threatened to execute Confederate prisoners if Confederate troops did not cease their practice of massacring captured black troops of the Union army.[7]

Where reciprocal restraint could not be expected, military commanders did not think it proper to impose much constraint on their own forces. The American army did not, for example, exercise much restraint in wars against Indian tribes on the frontier in the Nineteenth Century. Nor did the British army exercise much restraint in suppressing tribal raids on India's Northwest Frontier in the same period.[8]

When the Hague Peace Conference sought to codify rules in a formal treaty, therefore, it included a broad escape clause. The rules would only apply "between contracting Powers [that is, signatories to the treaty setting out these standards] and then only if all the belligerents are parties to the Convention." (Article 2) Even the possibility that one side would gain some marginal advantage from unrestrained allies was enough to invalidate the rules. The Hague rules would apply only in wars where all participants adhered to them.

The major powers at the time were quite serious about these restrictions on the reach of their agreement. In the first years following the 1899 Peace Conference, they all had occasions to demonstrate their understanding of what they had embraced. Britain fought a brutal war against Dutch farmers (the so-called *Boers*) in South Africa. In the course of that conflict, the British army tried to deprive guerrilla fighters of civilian support by confining civilians in detention centers. British authorities called them *concentration camps* and a later generation of Germans borrowed the term in full awareness of its origin. The United States fought a brutal war against rebels in the Philippines, in the course of which American forces pressured captured guerrillas to supply information with an interrogation tactic now known as "waterboarding." For its part, Germany suppressed a tribal rebellion in Southwest Africa with massacres so severe they are now considered genocidal.[9]

All the great powers also sent troops to China in 1900 to suppress the Boxer Rebellion, which had threatened Western embassies in Peking. Greatly outnumbered by native rebels, all the western troops seem to have relied on intimidating displays of violence on their way to Peking. The German Kaiser expressly admonished his troops to disregard any notion of restraint, urging them to show themselves "Huns of the Twentieth Century." That remark provoked some clucking comment in foreign newspapers. It was from this episode that the term *Huns* came to be attached to German troops in two world wars.

Western governments did not claim that *all* tactics were acceptable when Hague rules did not apply. The Victorian world still assumed that civilized states had certain moral obligations to prove that they were civilized and at least somewhat humane. The Preamble to the Hague Convention itself said so:

> . . . [I]n cases not included in the Regulations [that is, outside the limitation to wars between "contracting parties"] . . . the inhabitants and the belligerents remain under the protection and the rule of *the principles* of the law of nations [emphasis added], as they result from the usages established among civilized peoples, from the laws of humanity, and the dictates of public conscience.

The force of such avowals, however, may be judged from the actual reaction of the leading nations of that day to the brutal methods deployed in ensuing colonial conflicts. In 1907, delegates from all the same countries assembled for a second Peace Conference at The Hague. The official host—that is, the national leader who sent out invitations for a second round of deliberations—was the same Kaiser Wilhelm who had urged German troops to abandon all restraint in China. No one seems to have regarded his "Hun" rhetoric (nor the brutal methods of his troops in China) as disqualifying.

The 1899 Hague rules simply did not apply to a conflict with rebels in China, and the 1899 embrace of principles of restraint did not, it seems, exclude admonitions to abandon restraint. The 1907 conference did actually agree on a revised convention on "The Laws and Customs of War on Land." The changes were extremely minor, however. None changed the inapplicability of Hague rules to colonial wars outside Europe.

A third Hague conference was scheduled for 1915. By then, however, Europe was too preoccupied with war to organize a Peace Conference. The Hague rules turned out not even to restrain armies of signatory states battling each other across the trenches in Western Europe. By the time the war ended, there was much less confidence in general treaties on the conduct of war. There were no new Hague peace conferences in the era between the wars.

A small conference of jurists and technical advisers was convened at The Hague in 1923 to propose limits on air warfare. Yet the major states, particularly Britain, decided that they did not want to commit to restraints on military uses of this technology. Britain, in fact, was already employing air power to suppress rebellions in its new mandates in the Mideast—where the Royal Air Force proved it was quite ready to enforce submission by bombing Arab villages.[10]

There was more success at a conference convened by the League of Nations in 1925, which produced a "Protocol" reaffirming (despite wartime experience) the prewar ban on poison gas in warfare. But despite its professed aim of securing a "universally accepted" prohibition, "binding alike the conscience and the practice of nations," this 1925 Geneva Protocol took care to stipulate that signatory powers would only "be bound as regards other Powers which have already deposited their ratifications" (that is, pledged to comply).[11]

What if a signatory power did not honor its pledge even with regard to other signatories? General Dwight Eisenhower seemed to have a clear view: he took the precaution of stockpiling poison gas in the Italian theater in 1943.[12] The 1936 London Protocol, though it did not specify that its limitations on attacks without warning applied only between signatories, did not survive the first weeks of war. But the Second World War unleashed military tactics so ferocious that submarine warfare hardly registered among the new horrors.

The conference assembled in Geneva in 1949 was quite sober, therefore, in its expectations. It produced four new conventions: on the treatment of wounded combatants "in the field," on protection for wounded or shipwrecked combatants "at sea," on protection of "prisoners of war," and on protection of "civilian persons in time of war." None dealt with actual conduct of military operations. Even the fourth convention (on protection for civilians) focused only on "occupied territory"—that is, places where fighting was presumed to have ended.

Even the first Hague Convention on Land Warfare, adopted in the optimistic climate of the late Victorian era, had acknowledged, in its preamble, that it was "inspired by the desire to diminish the evils of war, *as far as military requirements permit*" (emphasis added). Nobody was sure, in the aftermath of the world wars, which "evils" could be diminished without unduly interfering with "military requirements." The United Nations Charter itself authorized the Security Council to enforce compliance with its resolutions by unleashing an international bomber force. (Article 45 refers to "air-force contingents for combined international enforcement action.") That provision contained no caution against bombing civilians, though it was approved by delegates to the San Francisco conference in the late spring of 1945, only four months after the firebombing of Dresden.

The Nuremberg trials implicitly endorsed the prevailing understanding. Though rules set down in The Hague conventions were frequently invoked against Nazi commanders, the rules protecting civilian centers from "bombardment" were not invoked against those who ordered the bombing of Warsaw, Rotterdam, and London in the first year of the war. The far greater Allied bombardments of German cities in ensuing years seemed to prove restrictions on aerial bombardment had ceased to be part of international law. So, too, the judges at Nuremberg declined to endorse charges against Grand Admiral Karl Dönitz, commander of the German U-boat fleet, for directing attacks on merchant shipping in violation of prewar rules, after Dönitz's lawyers submitted documents showing that the U.S. Navy had followed the same policies in the Pacific.[13] Whatever their other results, the Nuremberg trials did not try to uphold the doctrine that rules of restraint remain binding rules, even in wars where they were generally disregarded.

II. HOW THE RULES WERE REWRITTEN

Some three decades after the Geneva conference of 1949, a new international conference attempted a new codification of the rules of war. The conference that met periodically in Geneva, between 1974 and 1977, ultimately produced two new "additional protocols" to the 1949 Conventions. Additional Protocol I was designated for "Protection of Victims of International Armed Conflicts" and Additional Protocol II for "Protection of Victims of Non-International Conflicts." Despite the term *Additional Protocol*, these conventions actually covered a considerable range of new issues (or at least Protocol I on *international conflicts* did). The changed political context explains a great deal of the change in content.

The 1949 Geneva conference had included representatives from 64 nations, already a large increase from the cozy gathering of 26 nations at the first Hague Peace conference, and a few more than attended the conference that drafted the U.N. Charter in San Francisco in 1945. As in San Francisco, the Geneva gathering in 1949 was a gathering of the victorious allies: Germany and Japan were not invited to participate.

The Geneva conferences of the mid-1970s, however, included representatives of 126 nations—virtually the whole U.N. General Assembly of that era. U.N. membership had nearly tripled since 1945. The new states were mostly former colonies in Africa and Asia, now forming a block in world politics frequently called the *Third World*. At the insistence of this block, even "national liberation movements" were invited to the new Geneva conferences as observers. Both the Palestine Liberation Organization (the PLO, then pledged to the destruction of Israel) and the African National Congress (the ANC, waging a violent guerrilla struggle against the white government of South Africa) attended.

A strong anti-Western wind then seemed to be blowing in international affairs. As the conferees were meeting in Geneva, the 1973 peace settlement in Vietnam was brushed aside by North Vietnam with no American response. The communist government of the North simply annexed the territory of South Vietnam, which the United States had been trying to defend for over a decade. Apart from war exhaustion, Washington was preoccupied with political scandals at home and an economy struggling simultaneously with high inflation and high unemployment. There was still no American response when, in 1975, Soviet-equipped troops from Cuba landed in Angola and Mozambique to assist guerrilla forces battling Portuguese colonial control.

Simultaneously, at the U.N. General Assembly, the Third World majority (with the support of the communist states) passed, over Western objections, a series of resolutions calling for a "New International Economic Order." The idea was to promote international cartels to raise the price of minerals and other basic commodities, on the model of the Organization of Petroleum Exporting Countries (OPEC), which had forced a tripling of oil prices in 1973 as a weapon against Western support of Israel in its struggles against Arab adversaries. In 1974, the General Assembly also passed a resolution—again over Western objections—calling for a New International Information Order. This resolution urged regulation of journalistic access to developing countries in order to prevent "biased" (or unflattering) accounts of conditions there reaching outside media.

Yet another resolution adopted by the General Assembly over strong Western objections in 1975 underscored the new balance of power in international fora. This one condemned "Zionism" as a form of "racism"—effectively calling for the elimination of Israel as a sovereign state. The resolution ignored the fact that the U.N. had itself helped call the Jewish state into existence in the late 1940s, when it resolved that Britain's Palestine Mandate should be divided into separate Jewish and Arab states. And the U.N. had promptly agreed to Israel's membership in the organization, soon after it achieved its independence in 1949. The U.N. of the late 1940s clearly had quite a different political balance than the UN of the mid-1970s.

By the 1970s, with the U.N.'s Third World majority flexing its diplomatic muscles on so many fronts, rewriting the law of war did not seem out of reach. As the General Assembly called for redressing Western advantages in trade and information flows, Third World representatives demanded that the Geneva conference should develop new rules of war to assist Third World nations and their clients and causes. At an early planning meeting for the conference, delegates from African and Arab countries argued that

> lack of balance between Powers with substantial technological means at their disposal, on the one hand, and newly independent states and national liberation movements on the other, has led to an escalation of guerrilla warfare and . . . these conflict situations have eroded reciprocity as a *de facto* element of compliance with international humanitarian law. . . .[14]

The ensuing conference pushed for redressing this "lack of balance" by changing earlier understandings of the law of armed conflict.

So, where the 1949 Geneva Conventions had stipulated that their provisions would apply to conflicts "between the contracting parties"—to conflicts where both sides acknowledged their obligations to the same rules—Additional Protocol I [hereinafter AP I] insisted that its provisions must also apply to "armed conflicts in which peoples are fighting against colonial domination and alien occupation and against racist regimes in the exercise of their right of self-determination." (Article 2)

This provision did not mean that all combatants in all conflicts would be covered by the same rules. AP I took the trouble to specify that *mercenaries*—defined as those fighting for "financial gain"—should not be given prisoner-of-war protections. (Article 47) It was aimed at soldiers (mostly British army veterans) recruited by the government of South Africa to resist Cuban forces in neighboring states.

An entire separate convention, Additional Protocol II, was supposed to cover "non-international conflicts" and it was very much shorter, less detailed, and less constraining. Third World states at the Geneva conference wanted to ensure protection for "anti-colonial" struggles like that of the PLO against Israel or of rebels against Portuguese rule in Angola. What they did not want to do was impose constraints on Third World governments facing their *own* rebellions, as with the civil war in Nigeria in the late 1960s.

But how was one to distinguish *alien occupation* by Israelis in "Palestine" from the "occupation" of a Hausa-dominated government in the heartland of the Ibo tribe in Nigeria? Throughout the newly independent states of the Third World, there were restive tribes and competing loyalties. If armed rebels resisted the "national" government, how could one tell whether they were fighting a "non-international conflict" or "fighting against colonial domination and alien occupation"? Such distinctions—along with that between "mercenaries" and Cuban "volunteers"—were apparently to be left to the Third World majority to determine on the basis of its own political calculus.

In the following decades, internal wars in Central Africa (and a few other places) were fought with no regard for humanitarian constraints. Both rebels and opposing governments slaughtered civilians as a deliberate tactic of war. For the most part, international authorities simply shrugged.[15]

Delegates to the Geneva conferences in the 1970s focused most of their attention on international conflicts—increasingly now said to include conflicts between a "people" and some outside oppressor—where providing new protection for guerrilla fighters was still a priority. The traditional view, enshrined in The Hague Conventions and the 1949 Geneva Convention did not provide protection for guerrilla fighters. By their standards, soldiers could only qualify for prisoner-of-war (POW) protections under certain conditions: they would have to operate under clearly defined insignia (to distinguish themselves from civilians); they would have to be subject to command discipline (so they would stop fighting when their superiors agreed to a truce or a surrender); and they would have to fight in conformity with accepted rules of war (so they would not put others at a disadvantage by continuing to honor these rules).[16]

Defenders of guerrilla forces, such as the PLO and the ANC, urged that such traditional restrictions would make it impossible for guerrillas to operate lawfully. Given the much greater resources of their opponents, they had to rely on dispersal and concealment. The traditional view was that fighters who concealed themselves by blending in with the civilian population were spreading the risks of war to civilians and therefore undermining efforts to spare civilians from the effects of conflict.

The "compromise" written into Additional Protocol I endorses "the generally accepted practice of states with respect to the wearing of the uniform by combatants" and stipulates that even fighters who cannot so distinguish themselves should at least display their weapons "openly" when "engaged in a military deployment preceding the launching of an attack." (Article 44, Paragraphs 7 and 3) But the same provision then asserts that any fighter "failing to meet [these] . . . requirements" "shall, nevertheless, be given protections equivalent in all respects to those accorded to prisoners of war." (Article 44, Paragraph 4)

While loosening traditional restrictions on guerrilla warfare, the Additional Protocol imposed new constraints on the use of air power—the sort of force that advanced states might use against guerrillas but guerrillas could not usually deploy themselves. Air attacks must be confined to "military" objects. Attacks on "civilian objects" were to be prohibited, even if they merely destroy valuable property without loss of life. (Article 51, Paragraph 1) What if guerrillas use civilian settings to shield their munitions or their staging areas from attack? The Protocol insists that where there is uncertainty whether an apparently civilian building or institution "is being used to make an effective contribution to military action, it shall be presumed not to be so used." (Article 52, Paragraph 3). Another provision insists that civilian "objects" (that is, buildings, equipment, and property) may not be "the object of attack" even as "reprisals"—including, it seems, for reprisals against terror attacks on civilian lives. (Article 52, Paragraph 1) Meanwhile, even attacks on military objects are prohibited if they "may be expected" (by whom is not specified) "to cause incidental loss of civilian life . . . [or] damage to civilian objects [that is, buildings or equipment] . . . which would be excessive in relation to the concrete and direct military advantage anticipated." (Article 51, Paragraph 5)

The Protocol does gesture toward traditional standards, but only in a way that simply reinforces the underlying change. The provisions on prisoner-of-war status do endorse efforts to distinguish active combatants from civilians, but still provide POW protections to those who fail to distinguish themselves. In a similar way, AP I admonishes that "parties to the conflict shall, to the maximum extent feasible . . . avoid locating military objectives within or near densely populated areas" and "take the other necessary precautions to protect the civilian population . . . under their control against the dangers resulting from military operations." (Article 58) But the failure of defenders to take such "precautions"—even their evident determination to use civilians as human shields for military supplies or fighters—does not (so far as AP I recognizes) affect the obligations of the attackers.

One of the final sections of Protocol I underscores the new priorities. It sets out obligations to punish "grave breaches" of the standards in the Protocol. Denying protection to POWs is classified as a grave breach, but disguising guerrillas as civilians, even in the midst of an attack, is not. Launching attacks on civilians is classified as a grave breach, even when the attacks aim at military targets and cause harm to civilians or civilian property is unintended but still "excessive." Using civilians as human shields for military assets is not, however, listed as a grave breach. (Article 85, Paragraph 3)[17] Again, the rules seem designed to protect guerrilla fighters, while restraining regular armies fighting against them. Guerrilla forces get the same protections as disciplined soldiers, regardless of what terror tactics the guerrillas may deploy.[18]

These deals did not look very attractive to Western nations. Among other things, Western delegations repeatedly urged some acknowledgment that when one side in a conflict violates the rules, the opposing side should be authorized to retaliate in kind in belligerent reprisals.[19] Such appeals, however, were consistently rejected, and in its final form, AP I seems to prohibit almost all reprisals.[20] So Western nations did not rush to commit their forces to the new rules codified in Additional Protocol I. Ten years after the completion of AP I, it had been ratified by 65 states, but only three members of NATO: Belgium, Denmark, and Norway, states by then among the least likely to be engaged in actual combat operations.

But in the following decade, the Cold War waned, the Berlin Wall fell, the Soviet bloc in Eastern Europe crumbled, and, finally, the Soviet Union itself fell to pieces. In the course of the 1990s, almost all other members of NATO subscribed to the Additional Protocols. By then, it seemed unlikely that rules of war would again be put to the test. Even so, France, Britain, and the United States—the most serious military powers in the Alliance—held back. But by the beginning of the new century, the idea that there was a transcendent humanitarian law already seemed well established.

III. HUMANITARIAN ADVOCACY—THE IMPARTIAL VOICE THAT ISN'T

What gave new credibility to the idea of a transcendent humanitarian law in the 1990s was the new prominence of humanitarian advocacy groups. Most of these non-governmental organizations had only recently come to be involved in commenting on the conduct of warfare. Most non-governmental organizations (NGOs) in this field, in fact, had sprung up in the 1980s (and a few a bit earlier) to advocate for human rights in more general terms. Only one humanitarian organization, the International Committee of the Red Cross (ICRC), had already been in the field before the world wars. Yet even the ICRC now operates much differently than it did in earlier times. The conditions that allowed the ICRC to change its operating style have encouraged many others to follow its new, more activist stance.

The change is reflected in one remarkable contrast: The International Red Cross has criticized the American detention facility at Guantánamo Bay far more than it criticized Nazi concentration camps during the Second World War. The Red Cross was, in fact, completely silent about the murder of millions in Nazi death camps.

After 1945, the Red Cross insisted that it had engaged in "a long series of protests" to German authorities, resulting in "countless improvements in the [concentration] camps."[21] Meanwhile, it conferred an award on the head of the German Red Cross—an SS doctor responsible for gruesome experiments on concentration camp inmates.[22] Some scholars claim that the Red Cross of the 1940s was influenced by anti-Semitism; others emphasize the concern of the Geneva-based organization to accommodate the priorities of the neutral (and vulnerable) Swiss government, which was itself anxious to avoid offending Germany.[23] Certainly, the Red Cross did not play a heroic role in the greatest humanitarian catastrophe of modern times.

But the ICRC's traditional role required that it remain on good terms with both sides in the conflict. Under the 1929 Geneva Convention, the Red Cross could inspect prisoner-of-war camps to assure signatory states that their prisoners were being accorded proper treatment while in the hands of the enemy. To provide this service, the Red Cross depended on the cooperation of detaining powers. But actual enforcement of prisoner treatment rules was left to reciprocity, and in the hands of governments—which might withdraw protections from enemy prisoners in their own hands, if they found that their troops in enemy hands were denied the full range of protections.

On the Eastern front in Europe, neither Soviet nor German authorities were prepared to offer better treatment of enemy prisoners to secure better treatment of their own troops in enemy hands. Until the last months of the war, Nazi officials were unwilling to make any concessions in their war of extermination against Jews and Gypsies. But almost from the outset, German authorities did seek to protect their pilots and later on, their soldiers and seamen, captured by British and American forces. So the ICRC focused on doing what it could do, as it explained in a lawyerly postwar defense: "For the Committee to protest publicly would have been not only to outstep its functions, but also to lose thereby all chance of pursuing them, by creating an immediate breach with the government concerned."[24]

A similar dynamic obtained in the air war. During the Battle of Britain, the Red Cross offered to monitor bomb damage in British and German cities, so the two sides could cooperate in limiting harm to civilians. British Prime Minister Winston Churchill, however, dismissed the offer out of hand. As he explained to his cabinet, it was not in Britain's interest to submit to a neutral arbiter of bombing tactics, when it was trying to win a war: "Bombing of military objectives, *increasingly widely interpreted,* seems at present our main road home."[25]

For similar reasons, Allied leaders dismissed repeated calls from the Vatican (the last as late as Christmas 1944) to negotiate peace with Germany. The continuation of the war certainly caused terrible suffering. But it was equally clear that a continuation of Nazi rule would also have caused terrible suffering—and a Nazi victory even more. It is quite unlikely that a Vatican appeal to reduce the violence of war, such as by limiting Allied bombing of German cities, would have been heeded either. And indeed such debates involved troubling dilemmas. Would such measures have saved lives or simply prolonged the suffering by deferring the Allied victory? Were Vatican officials in a better position to weigh such terrible dilemmas than the military chiefs of the Allied powers? And if the Vatican had little to contribute, why expect more from the officials of the Red Cross?

Yet by the late 1980s, humanitarian advocacy came to seem a more promising venture. One reason was that international human rights treaties and associated monitoring efforts had developed enough status to be noticed by a wider public. It was only in 1976 that the first and most general U.N. human-rights treaties—the Covenants on Civil and Political Rights and on Economic and Social Rights—secured enough ratifications to be given legal effect for the signatories. It was not until the early 1980s that the U.N. Human Rights Commission agreed to issue criticism of human rights records of specific countries. Amnesty International and Human Rights Watch, which first emerged as monitoring organizations in the 1970s, began to gain wider notice for their own reports. This helped pave the way for a greater role for such NGOs, not as neutral observers but as advocates.

The biggest change was not legal or institutional, but political. By the mid-1980s, as Cold War tensions subsided, it came to seem—at least to many people—more plausible to think about "humanity" in abstract, nonpolitical terms. At the height of the Cold War, defending freedom meant taking sides with the Western states against the communist powers. To talk about human rights in abstraction from the Cold War seemed no more promising than pronouncements from Pope Pius XII about peace and justice in 1943, as the Vatican continued to disclaim support for either side in the Second World War.

Trans-political human rights advocacy came to seem more plausible in the 1980s, as a more relaxed international environment allowed advocates to find fault on both sides. Organizations like Human Rights Watch criticized Soviet repression in Eastern Europe along with violence and repression in countries like El Salvador, then battling a Soviet- and Cuban-backed communist insurgency. Then, it seemed a natural extension of human rights advocacy to invoke the Geneva Conventions as further grounds for criticism of embattled states such as El Salvador.

The collapse of communist rule in Eastern Europe, and finally in Russia by the end of 1991, seemed, for a time, to give even more prestige to human rights claims. Why not accord the same authority to humanitarian standards in times of conflict? When the United Nations published a collection of all its human rights documents in the mid-1990s, it included the Geneva Conventions and the Additional Protocols, as if they were all parts of the same overarching international project.[26]

But there remains a fundamental difference. One nation's human rights failures do not, in most circumstances, affect the capacity of others to protect human rights. If Saudi Arabia fails to abide by all the provisions of the Convention on the Elimination of Discrimination Against Women, that will not make it harder for Canada to honor such rules. But if one army disregards humanitarian constraints in warfare, the nation it is fighting may, in fact, find that it is placed at a great disadvantage by continuing to adhere to those constraints. What if the force that ignores humanitarian constraints is, not just in this respect but overall, more brutal in its aims and methods? Is it clearly more "humane" or "humanitarian" to let totalitarian forces prevail, by hobbling those who fight against them?

That question is no easier to answer today than in the past. Even if one believed that humanitarian advocates had no distracting interests of their own, there might be reason to doubt that such advocates are uniquely well positioned to provide the right answers in all such painful debates. And there are, in fact, several good reasons to believe that the priorities of these organizations are indeed distorted by other interests.

In the first place, as non-governmental organizations, they must raise funds from contributors who can decline to pay—and who will not open their wallets unless sufficiently motivated—so they must win attention from news media, which are themselves similarly free to ignore the NGOs if they like. In earlier times, the ICRC did not need to seek publicity to woo activist funding and support. Its role as an intermediary made it useful to governments, who could prod national Red Cross chapters to keep funds flowing to Geneva. Modern NGOs operate in a different world, however, where quiet, unobtrusive memoranda to governments are not the main game. Today, eye-catching publicity is necessary for survival. If the NGOs simply echoed the priorities or perspectives of Western governments, they would be redundant. To prosper, they must, instead, provide arguments and information which play to potential donors' demands for alternative perspectives and to media interest in novelty and reader- or viewer-attracting controversy.

In practice, therefore, such NGOs have incentives to provide critical perspectives, since there are large and affluent constituencies—even within Western countries, and even within the United States—quite interested in hearing about supposed abuses caused by American policy or the actions of American allies. Human Rights Watch, the largest human rights advocacy organization, has become so eager to emphasize the failings of Western democracies (especially the United States and Israel) that its own founder has denounced it for loss of balance.[27] The organization has become so hungry for donations, in fact, that it ended up trolling for contributions in Saudi Arabia—a place, of course, where many donors were less interested in "human rights" than in denunciations of Israel. Human Rights Watch has proved all too eager to provide such donors with value for their money.

One might think these NGOs would have competing incentives to highlight abuses of anti-Western forces in the world. Such abuses might certainly also stir genuine humanitarian concern. But in practice, it is much harder to gather information about the most repressive regimes, since investigators cannot operate freely in North Korea, Burma, or Saudi Arabia—let alone in terrorist enclaves in embattled war zones such as Afghanistan or south Lebanon. Where they can operate at all, NGOs are at the mercy of local authorities in repressive regimes or in war zones. That fact is bound to induce caution in reporting there, and to increase reliance upon safer Western sources about Western problems, or official government sources elsewhere.

In the summer of 2003, for instance, as violence erupted in Iraq against the Western coalition that had ousted Saddam Hussein's regime, the ICRC announced that it was withdrawing all its personnel from Iraq, rather than leave its field agents there dependent on American protection. But as the President of the ICRC conceded, half of its field agents were then in Muslim-majority countries. Whether dependence on local authorities in these countries might have some impact on their activities was not discussed.[28] But it is likely to make a difference. Two decades earlier, when Red Cross officials were trying to operate in Lebanon, in the midst of an Israeli invasion, the ICRC issued a stream of denunciations of Israeli tactics, endorsing all claims advanced by the Palestinian Red Crescent Society (PRCS) about civilian casualties from Israeli attacks—at a time when the PRCS was headed by the brother of PLO chief Yasser Arafat. If Palestinian fighters might possibly have violated humanitarian law themselves, the ICRC did not find such incidents worthy of comment.[29]

NGOs also have a more enduring incentive to skew their reports against the perspective of Western governments. The more attention humanitarian advocates focus on regimes already opposed by Western governments, the more they risk sounding like cheerleaders for Western government policies. (As noted above, this might constitute financial suicide.) So, for example, to have harped on the abuses of communist regimes in the 1970s might have made NGOs sound like North Atlantic Treaty Organization (NATO) auxiliaries. Humanitarian advocacy groups, however, were extremely concerned to maintain their posture as "impartial" bystanders. Accordingly, Amnesty International refused to say anything about repression of Soviet dissidents in the 1970s. It even failed to denounce mass murder by the Khmer Rouge government that took power in Cambodia after the American withdrawal.[30]

Finally, and perhaps most fundamentally, the premise of humanitarian advocacy is that the rules must be observed. Once it is acknowledged that the rules are somewhat contingent and their application to particular cases both complicated and contestable, there is no particular reason why humanitarian advocates should have more moral or legal authority than officials of actual elected governments, who are responsible to voters for actual outcomes in the ambiguous business of war making. Perhaps, for example, lives would be saved, overall, by pursuing a speedy victory, even if doing so risks more casualties in the short run. Strict adherence to rules, if it prolonged the conflict and substantially increased the casualty count—let alone if it inhibited a democracy's war effort enough to give victory to a brutal tyrant—might then be judged *less* humane.

It is easier to leap over painful trade-offs or moral dilemmas and simply insist that "the rules are the rules." It is certainly much easier for advocacy groups to pretend that the right answer is always clear. Indeed, they have a stake in exaggerating the precision of international standards and their relevance to each conflict. Advocacy organizations may boast of their detachment from national loyalties and their potential bias, such as by saying that they give their loyalty to the "international community." Even then, however, it is not the actual, existing "community" of today's divided world that claims their allegiance, but at best an abstractly imagined, fully law-bound international community in a better world of some future day—a world that they feel it their job to interpret and prescribe to present-day actors.

The consequences of these incentives and loyalties are on ready display. The International Red Cross now competes with other human rights organizations for attention. Instead of merely serving as a mediator, it tries to serve as a moral proctor for nations at war. After years of *ad hoc* admonitions, it published in 2005 a multivolume work, *Customary International Humanitarian Law*.[31] The premise was that the standards set out in the Additional Protocols have now become "customary law," binding as such even on nations which have not ratified the protocols.

The ICRC has thus set itself up, quite literally, as a kind of public voice for humanity, explaining to the nations what it was they have agreed to accept. The United States had explicitly refused to accept this sort of open-ended arbitral authority for the U.N.'s International Court of Justice in 1945.[32] But the ICRC, in effect, took it upon itself to fill this gap by offering its own guidance to the nations of the world on their international obligations under customary humanitarian law. And the Red Cross did so, of course, without even bothering to seek any actual government's consent to this role. As it turned out, in fact, securing the consent of states was quite peripheral to the Red Cross understanding of international law.

In the view of the ICRC, when it comes to humanitarian law, international custom need not rest on the actual practice of nations, as in the traditional view of customary law, but can be established by what governments merely say about humanitarian standards—and then not even what they say uniformly but what they might happen to have said in special circumstances. Having shifted the emphasis from actions to words, the ICRC saw no need to focus on actual nations at war, or even to focus on actual governments. As a result, the ICRC commentaries frequently cite, as a circular sort of "precedent" for evolving international custom, pronouncements of fellow advocacy groups like Human Rights Watch and Amnesty International.[33]

Even references to government pronouncements are often quite . . . imaginative. The commentaries cite as precedents, for example—without any acknowledgement of incongruity—the pronouncements of Saddam Hussein's government decrying attacks on civilians. That is balanced by a citation to a policy statement of British Prime Minister Neville Chamberlain, in February 1940, avowing that air attacks on German cities would be improper.[34] That Chamberlain's successor pursued rather different policies—with much more acclaim through most of the world—doesn't seem to matter. (Anyway this latter inconvenient fact is not mentioned.)

Elsewhere the ICRC study cites, as a sign of international custom, not even what a government minister said in Australia but what an opposition member of Parliament said in criticism of that country's military targeting policies during the first Gulf War.[35] Actual Australian practice was precisely contrary to what the opposition member criticized—hence the occasion for the criticism—but at least someone said what the ICRC wanted to hear, and hence this became the relevant citation. When words are the crucial thing, it doesn't seem to matter much who actually pronounces them.

The ICRC must have thought that such whimsical manipulations of evidence could be justified by the good intentions of the project. Indeed, such advocacy organizations seem to presume quite a lot on behalf of good intentions. Human Rights Watch was not only comfortable raising money from Saudi Arabia (one of only two states to vote against the U.N.'s Universal Declaration of Human Rights in 1948). The organization even assigned its assessments of Israeli military tactics to an analyst who turned out to be an avid collector of Nazi memorabilia and had expressed gushing enthusiasm for the pleasures to be derived from owning authentic SS regalia. No one at Human Rights Watch seems to have taken any pains to protect the organization's own reputation, given the high moral prestige of its underlying intentions.[36]

Meanwhile, Amnesty International (AI) expanded its concerns from the protection of political prisoners (those imprisoned for their ideas or expressed views) to a range of new issues—on many of which (such as Amnesty's total opposition to capital punishment, even for aggravated murder) it could show purported evenhandedness by denouncing the United States as being uniquely out of step with evolving international standards. It also offered guidance to the world on the lawful requirements for peace between Israel and the Palestinians, embracing positions on the rights of Palestinian refugees more extreme than those adopted by any European Union government, but in close parallel to positions advanced in peace proposals from Saudi Arabia.[37]

Inevitably, after the United States began its counterterrorist campaign in Afghanistan after the attacks of September 11, 2001, AI also embraced the claims of detainees held at Guantánamo Bay. When the head of the organization's "gender unit" protested against top AI officials appearing on platforms with an advocate for the notoriously rights-abusing Taliban, in fact, she was promptly removed from her position.[38]

All these organizations purport to be better interpreters of international humanitarian law—even on questions of military necessity that might or might not justify particular tactics or bombing targets—than the actual military officers, lawyers, and statesmen of states actually responsible for actual or potential warfare. Perhaps they are not.

IV. SOMETIME ALLIES AND NEUTRALIST TEMPTATIONS

The predilections of such advocacy organizations would not greatly matter if they were not influential. And they would not be "influential" if governments did not let themselves be influenced. Governments that have little at stake, however, are more easily swayed than those with real responsibilities in the area of law at issue. In this sense, the most interesting question may be why so many governments have come to think they have little at stake when humanitarian advocates rewrite the rules of war—especially in ways deliberately designed to disadvantage states.

The United States has continually declined to ratify Additional Protocol I, though it embraces many of its standards. Israel has not ratified, though it also has indicated acceptance of many humanitarian constraints. The United Kingdom did not ratify until 1999, and then did so with a long list of qualifications, emphasizing that it would not be bound by constraints that were not observed by forces it might be fighting. Others, including Germany, offered qualifications in somewhat similar spirit.[39] But by no means all.

That there is some division within the Western Alliance should not be altogether surprising, if one takes a long view of the relevant history. NATO was founded in 1949, when there was much concern about a Soviet invasion of Western Europe. A decade earlier, when there was much reason to fear German invasions, all the smaller countries in Western Europe had left Britain and France to cope with the danger on their own—with nearly catastrophic results. Norway, Denmark, the Netherlands, and Belgium, originally professing neutrality, were only drawn into the war when actually invaded in 1940. These experiences seem to have swayed them to join NATO in 1949. Countries not invaded in 1940—

notably Sweden, Ireland, Switzerland—clung to neutrality even in the Cold War. They chose, in effect, to be free riders on the western defense effort.

As the Cold War waned and finally ended with the Soviet collapse, more countries in Western Europe began to disengage, functionally at least, from the Western Alliance. (On paper, of course, NATO expanded.) Most NATO states decided not to participate in the 1991 Gulf war or the conflicts in the Balkans in the late 1990s. Defense spending plummeted, and war preparations seemed both unnecessary and distasteful. And, in turn, countries that no longer envisioned themselves as potential participants in war found it much easier to embrace moralistic and state-disadvantaging claims about international humanitarian law—as it might be applied to others.

The underlying principle of contemporary humanitarian advocates—that international law imposes duties on combatants, regardless of what their enemies do—may also have special appeal for nations of the European Union. The European Union (EU) started as a trade pact among six nations in 1957 (the "Common Market") then gradually expanded in membership and authority. By the early 21st Century, it included 26 nations under a treaty pledging not only a common currency and wide-ranging regulatory powers but also a "common foreign and security policy."

But the EU has no army, no police force, nor even a criminal court of its own. It relies on member states to implement common policies, so it can only work on the assumption that international law already functions—at least in general, or in the abstract—as reliably and compellingly as national law appears to in an already well-ordered domestic community.

And the very abstractness of international law also has special appeal for EU member states. Now stretching from Portugal to Estonia, from Ireland to Bulgaria, and from Sweden to Malta, the EU embraces states facing quite different security challenges from quite different directions. It is much easier to agree on a common policy at a high level of abstraction. On the concrete question of whether to go to war against Saddam Hussein's Iraq in 2003, EU states were sharply divided. But on the abstract question of whether the conduct of war should respect humanitarian constraints—who could say no to that?

So EU members were among the leading proponents of the idea of a permanent international court to prosecute offenders against international humanitarian standards. The treaty for the International Criminal Court (ICC), negotiated at a conference in Rome in 1998, largely defined "war crimes" and "crimes against humanity" by cutting and pasting provisions from the Additional Protocols and the 1949 Conventions. At the drafting conference, humanitarian advocacy organizations, such as Amnesty International and Human Rights Watch, played a prominent role as interested observers—much as the PLO and the ANC had done at the Geneva conferences of the mid-1970s.

The United States refused to ratify the so-called Rome Statute that established the ICC. Among other holdouts were Russia and China, India and Pakistan, South Korea and Japan, Egypt and Israel—in short, almost every country that could still see itself potentially engaged in serious military conflict and did not welcome the idea of an international prosecutor looking over its shoulder as it considered what tactics to pursue. Britain and France, however, though they still maintained some military capacity, were dragged into ratifying the ICC Statute because most other EU members insisted on collective support for this new institution.

V. RESTORING REASONABLE BALANCE

One view of contemporary humanitarian law was voiced by a Red Cross legal commentator during the Geneva conferences of the mid-1970s: "If we cannot outlaw war, we will make it too complex for the commander to fight!"[40] Such a program, however, was not likely to be embraced by Third World guerrillas, who naturally preferred that only their *opponents* face such challenging complexities.

In fact, another commentator on humanitarian law therefore warned against trying to insist on traditional rules, when such approaches would necessarily be rejected by guerrilla forces. Instead, the demands of such fighters for special help vis-à-vis their state adversaries should be accepted:

> . . . [T]he visible carrying of arms and distinguishing signs may . . . be incompatible with the practicalities of the action (for example, if the guerrilla fighters use the population for support or are intermingled with it). Because of this, refusing to allow specific procedures would be to refuse guerrilla warfare. In order to remain objective and credible, humanitarian law must allow every party an equal chance in combat.[41]

In other words, if guerrilla fighters feel they need to adopt tactics endangering civilians, they must be allowed to do so in the name of equality—but Western armies must still be constrained in the name of humanity. The Additional Protocols sought to level the playing field by giving new protections to irregular forces while imposing new restraints on modern armies. This seemed to be the necessary price to pay for securing "international consensus." And even with such deliberate nonreciprocity, it was apparently ultimately felt to be too much to ask guerrillas to follow any legal rules. As a Third World delegate to the Geneva conferences acknowledged, the "Third World attitude" was that "in dealing especially with the Western countries, anything which could be formulated in the very precise terms of an operational rule was considered as nonsense."[42]

The implications were predictable. States which profess fidelity to the new humanitarian standards have to fear that their forces will be placed at impossible disadvantage, or their commanders subject to international denunciations, or both. By the 1990s, in fact, commanders had come to fear that, if they skirted the new rules, they might face prosecution by an international tribunal. Such concerns may have reinforced European disinclination to supply troops to the NATO-endorsed and U.N.-sanctioned operations against *al-Qaeda* terrorists and Taliban fighters in Afghanistan. As more and more members of the alliance retreat into passivity, the rift—in moral and political terms as in military operations—widens between fighting members of the alliance and high-minded and responsibility-free onlookers.

The trend is indeed dismaying, but neither cynicism nor despair is a reasonable response. Despair would imply that Western governments can never succeed in resisting lawless guerrilla forces. If that were true, it would imply that Western states cannot really (or lawfully) defend themselves at all, not even close to home—and *that* is a message which not many Western electorates are likely to (or should) embrace when their own countries are threatened. Nor is it likely that people will long embrace the notion that ceding authority to murderous terror networks is inherently more moral than resisting them. That is not a morally serious position; it is an unstable compound of cynicism and escapism. As an alternative, I offer some suggestions.

At the very least, the success of Israeli efforts in suppressing the violence of the 2000–03 intifada and American efforts at suppressing the Iraqi insurgency in 2007–08 show that difficult measures can have quite dramatic effects on the ground where there is the will to pursue them with adequate patience and resolve. The same lesson might be drawn from American success in penetrating the *al-Qaeda* courier network, allowing Navy SEALs to stage their successful raid on Osama bin Laden's safe house near Islamabad in May 2011. Nor is it true, on the other hand, that successful military efforts require steely indifference to humanitarian considerations. Indeed, Western armies take humanitarian restraint quite seriously, and domestic support for ongoing conflicts seems to require at least some serious effort to restrain unnecessary violence and continue to emphasize the moral difference between Western forces and those they fight.

But it remains crucial not to let the rules be defined by nonparticipants who claim to be neutral but are, in fact, lacking in any responsibility for consequences and often have crosscutting (and sometimes quite mischievous) agendas of their own. To be sure, there is now an established place for nongovernmental advocacy organizations; that is part of the modern landscape. Western countries cannot silence these organizations, and can no longer take for granted that participants in their own domestic political debates will feel stronger loyalty to the policies of their own elected governments than to the criticisms leveled by such groups. Western states are open to self-criticism and debate, while their opponents feel free to use terror to silence open debate. That is one of the things Western states are fighting to preserve, and simply muzzling NGOs is today on no democracy's agenda.

One thing Western governments can do, however, is to continually emphasize that the relevant humanitarian standards remain matters of dispute. Complex real-world patterns can be very hard to squeeze into tidy legal or moral pigeonholes. In some contexts, this is already widely understood. To offer but one example, states that sympathize with terror tactics (at least in some settings, against some opponents) have blocked international institutions from embracing any clear definition of terrorism. And there is probably, after all this time, no hope of getting the United Nations to agree on a common definition of terrorism. But Western states can hope to remind people—at least in Western countries, where press freedom allows others to listen—that just as the definition of terrorism is disputed, so the definition of precisely what is required in humanitarian restraint is also disputed—and that democratic governments are not obliged to accept the definitions asserted by their adversaries or even by purported neutrals who claim to stand outside struggles against the evils of terror networks.

A second and more focused defense of responsible thinking about the law is to resist the attribution of authority to freestanding international bodies. The laws of war are what participants agree to, not simply what the ICRC or ICJ or ICC say they are absent such agreement. To allow outside authorities to determine which tactics are acceptable—such as how to balance the demands of military necessity and humanity—is to lose the capacity for self-defense, especially when these outside moral arbiters cannot enforce their supposed standards on one's adversaries.

Finally, it can be helpful to insist that allies share in the risks and in the moral responsibilities of actual combat operations. If they want to help define standards, they have to share some responsibility for living and working with them. We may hope, for example, that the experience gained in the 2011 intervention against Libya leaves some lasting impact on British and French military planners. At the outset of the conflict, Britain's defense minister insisted that air strikes were being carefully assessed for consistency with humanitarian law, and that British policy sought to assure "civilian casualties as close to zero as possible."[43] As the stalemate dragged on—and casualties mounted—British commanders were quoted in press accounts calling for more "aggressive" policies in order to force a result.[44] It is not obviously more humane to allow a war to drag on when means are available to achieve decisive results, and one might hope that Libya will be a salutary reminder of the ways that military good sense and humanity do not always point in opposite directions.

VI. A CONCLUDING THOUGHT

War is, at some level, always a political contest as well as a military struggle. For a military conflict to continue, both sides must have the political will to continue, as well as the military resources. Accordingly, in almost every war, both sides claim that their opponents are both morally and legally in the wrong. In such rhetorical contests between contending sides, appeals have often been made to legal standards that should have been followed—with each side pressing its own view of the relevant "law." These claims readily extend from the underlying *causus belli* to claims that the enemy has employed particularly dishonorable tactics.

Such accusatory discourses, which we might call propaganda, are probably as old as warfare. Today, however, there has developed a word for legal maneuvering to gain strategic advantage in war: *lawfare*. While appeals to the law of war go back many centuries, this term was coined only at the beginning of the present century.[45] It would not have made sense previously, because in earlier times, few imagined that rules of war could be maintained—if indeed they could be kept from falling silent amidst the clash of arms at all—without reciprocity and good faith. A force that sought to hobble its enemy by invoking legal restraints, while simultaneously disregarding all restraints in its own tactics, would not have found such arguments taken terribly seriously. Yet that, apparently, is no longer true today.

Coping with the advent of such lawfare—and countering its employment—should be a priority for the Western governments at which it is aimed. There is much to commend humanitarian restraint in wartime, and conflicts sometimes permit their belligerents great flexibility to moderate military tactics with this in mind. There have certainly been wars fought for limited objectives, and ones that have been settled before much damage was done on either side. To the degree that the contending belligerents think the stakes warrant a more intense effort, however, restraints can come under strain. Fundamentally, it is a state's own responsibility to balance the values of effectiveness and humanity, and if one is truly at war it is almost an obligation to resist the gamesmanship of modern "lawfare." A nation that allows its forces to be defeated merely by legal maneuvers is not one that was very committed to fighting in the first place.

We should, of course, try to preserve restraint in the conduct of war to the extent that this is feasible. But we should not allow ourselves to forget that such restraint—like war itself—requires commitments on both sides, and can only be coherently assessed in the context of what is at stake. Western states need to preserve flexibility in the law of war if they want to preserve the capacity to fight wars.

NOTES

1. "Declaration Concerning Asphyxiating Gases" (July 29, 1899), *reprinted in American Journal of International Law,* vol. 1 (1907), Supp., at 157–59.

2. "Process-Verbal Relating to the Rules of Submarine Warfare" (Nov. 6, 1936), reprinted in *American Journal of International Law,* vol. 31 (1937), Supp., at 137–39.

3. "War is the contention between two or more States through their armed forces. . . ." Because "there are no longer the forces of two States in the field . . . guerrilla war is not real war, [and therefore] it is obvious that in strict law the victor need no longer treat the guerilla bands as a belligerent Power and the captured members of those bands as soldiers." L. Oppenheim, *International Law* (New York: Longmans, Green, 1912), 2d. ed., Vol. II, at 60 (§ 54) & 71 (§ 60). Oppenheim's text was the leading English-language treatise on international law in the early 20th Century, and is still in print (in revised editions) seven decades after it first appeared.

4. For example, Francisco Vitoria, "On the Law of War" in E. Nys, ed., *De Indis et Iure Belle Reflectiones* (Washington, D.C.: Carnegie Institution, 1917), Part 52, at 184–85, noting that "horrors and cruelties . . . such as slaughter and torture of the innocent, rape of virgins and dishonor of matrons" might be justified in a just war "as a deterrent to the enemy or as a spur to the courage of the troops" (that is, a reward for enduring the hardships of a siege).

5. Timothy Byrnes, *Catholic Bishops in American Politics* (Princeton, New Jersey: Princeton University Press, 1991), at 101.

6. International Court of Justice, Advisory Opinion on the Legality of Nuclear Weapons (July 8, 1996). The central ruling, on which the Court was split 7–7, was as follows: "the threat or use of nuclear weapons would generally be contrary to the rules of international law applicable in armed conflict, and in particular the principles and rules of humanitarian law; however, in view of the current state of international law, and of the elements of fact at its disposal, the Court cannot conclude definitively whether the threat or use of nuclear weapons would be lawful or unlawful in an extreme circumstance of self-defence, in which the very survival of a State would be at stake." (Paragraph 105)

7. "Order of Retaliation" (July 30, 1863), in Abraham Lincoln, *Speeches and Writings, 1859–1865* (New York: Library of America, 1989), at 484. The rules on lawful military measures issued to the Union army in 1863 (the so-called Lieber Code, named after the German émigré scholar who prepared them for the U.S. government) formulated the general principle in these terms: "All troops of the enemy known or discovered to give no quarter in general, or to any portion of the army, receive none." (Article 62)

8. Here is a contemporaneous account from a participant in British actions on the Indian frontier—a writer who would become better known for his role in European wars: "I invite the reader to examine the question of the legitimacy of village burning for himself. A camp of a British brigade . . . is attacked at night [by Pathan tribesman in the Northwest Frontier Province]. Several valuable and expensive officers,

soldiers and transport animals are killed and wounded. The assailants retire to the hills. Thither it is impossible to follow them. They cannot be caught. They cannot be punished. Only one remedy remains—their property must be destroyed. Their villages are made hostages for their good behavior." Winston S. Churchill, *The Story of the Malakand Field Force* (originally published in London by Longmans, Green & Co, 1898; reprinted by W.W Norton in New York in 1990), at 165.

9. For scholarly surveys of the extreme tactics deployed in these wars, *see Anticipating Total War* (Manfred F. Boemeke et al., eds.) (New York: Cambridge University Press, 1999) with separate essays discussing American measures against the Philippine insurgency, American efforts against Indian tribes on the Great Plains, British war measures in South Africa, the German army's efforts in China and Southwest Africa.

10. Amidst general demobilization, Britain's war minister declared in 1919 that the "first duty of the Royal Air Force is to garrison the British Empire." The entire British military presence in Iraq, in fact, was placed under the control of an Air Force officer. Winston Churchill (the minister who made these arrangements) was not shy about using threats against "civilian property" to impose order. The RAF commander he sent to Iraq subsequently explained his policy in these terms: ". . . the real weight of air action lies in the daily interruption of normal life which it can effect, if necessary for an indefinite period . . . It can knock the roofs of huts about and prevent their repair, a considerable inconvenience in winter time. It can seriously interfere with ploughing or harvesting—a vital matter—or burn up the stores laboriously piled up and garnered for the winter. By attacks on livestock, which is the main form of capital and source of wealth to the less settled tribes, it can impose in effect a considerable fine or seriously interfere with the actual [food] source of the tribe—and in the end the tribesman finds it is much the best to obey the [British directed] Government." H. Montgomery Hyde, *British Air Policy Between the Wars, 1918–39* (London: Heinemann, 1976), p. 168 (*quoting* a September 29, 1923, report from John Salmond [the air commander in Iraq] to Hugh Trenchard [chief of the air staff in London]).

11. "Protocol for the Prohibition of the Use in War of Asphyxiating, Poisonous or Other Gases" (June 17, 1925), reprinted *American Journal of International Law*, vol. 25 (1931), Supp., at 94–96. The restriction on who is "bound" appears in the last substantive paragraph.

12. This mustard gas ended up accidentally causing fatalities to hundreds of civilians, when German bombing happened to hit the storehouse in Bari where the gas was stored. Even then, the existence of the stockpile was kept secret for decades. The episode is described in Rick Atkinson, *The Day of Battle* (New York: Henry Holt &Co, 2007), at 275–78.

13. Telford Taylor, *The Anatomy of the Nuremberg Trials* (New York: Knopf, 1992), at 325–27 (on bombing) & 399–409 (submarine warfare).

14. *See* Proposal submitted by experts of Algeria, Jordan, Mali, Nigeria, Norway, the Sudan, Tanzania, Yemen, and Yugoslavia, Conference of Government Experts on the Reaffirmation and Development of International Humanitarian Law Applicable in Armed Conflicts, 2d Sess, Geneva, 3 May—3 June 1972, *Report on the Work of the*

Conference, Vol. II (Annexes) (Geneva: International Committee of the Red Cross, 1972), at 116.

15. Benjamin Valentino, Pual Huth, Dylan Balch-Lindsay, "Draining the Sea: Mass Killing and Guerrilla Warfare," *International Organization,* vol. 58 (2004), at 375–407, describing deliberate targeting of civilians by government forces in conflicts between Ethiopia and Eritrea, and between the government of Guatemala and internal rebels in the 1980s. Kristine Eck and Lisa Hultman, "One-Sided Violence Against Civilians in War," *Journal of Peace Research,* vol. 44 (2007), at 233, 237, estimate that of some 75,000 civilian casualties from episodes of mass killing of civilians between 1989 and 2004 (excluding the genocide in Rwanda), some 40 percent were perpetrated by governments against their own people. In the last phase of the Sri Lankan government's campaign to suppress Tamil rebels, the army bombed and shelled a previously proclaimed safe haven for civilians (after it had been infiltrated by Tamil guerrillas): the civilian death toll was estimated to exceed 20,000. The U.N.'s Human Rights Council rejected a proposal to organize an investigation. *See* Catherine Philip and Michael Evans, "Photographs Expose Sri Lanka's Lie on Civilian Deaths at Beach," *The Times* (UK) (May 29, 2009).

16. These limitations are spelled out in Article 4 of the 1949 Geneva Convention on Prisoners of War and in the 1899 and 1907 Hague Regulations Respecting the Laws and Customs of War on Land, Art 1. The traditional rule was acknowledged even in trials of Nazi war criminals, where American judges ruled that German commanders had not violated the law of war by executing partisans in Yugoslavia when they were operating without insignia and without reliable command structures. "Trial of Wilhelm List and Others" (Case No. 47), *Law Reports of Trials of War Criminals* (U.N. War Crimes Commission, 1948), vol. 8, at 57.

17. But the same provision (Article 85, Paragraph 4) does stipulate that "grave breaches" include "the transfer by the Occupying Power of parts of its own civilian population into the territory it occupies"—a provision aimed at criminalizing Israeli government policies allowing voluntary settlement of Israelis in territory captured in the 1967 war (including East Jerusalem, Hebron, and other places where Jews had lived for centuries until forcibly expelled by the Jordanian army in 1948). It says much about the priorities of the Geneva conference that building houses in disputed locations was classified as a war crime but deliberately using civilians as human shields was not.

18. Individual acts of terrorism can certainly be punished under AP I—but, in the Red Cross view, doing so requires evidence of personal involvement in such actions, rather than mere membership in an organization or military force involved in terror attacks. Article 96 stipulates that when there are "people engaged . . . in an armed conflict" [people claiming to be battling "colonial domination, alien occupation or racist domination"], the authority representing such people can invoke the protections of AP I by "unilateral declaration of adherence," even though not a recognized state. (Article 96, Paragraph 3) (Article 96, of course, provided only the simulacrum of traditional reciprocity, by permitting "both sides" to be bound by rules that in fact specified asymmetrical compliance obligations.)

According to the ICRC *Commentary on the Additional Protocols of 8 June 1977* (Yves Sandoz et al., eds, Geneva, 1987), at 1089, where there are several different groups involved in a conflict (that is, splinter groups on the same side), the protections may apply to those claiming to adhere to Geneva rules, even if allied groups repudiate all obligation to Geneva rules. (The commentary does not bother to explain how a counter-insurgency force could be expected to sort out such identity problems.) Subsequent ICRC pronouncements have simplified the challenge by insisting that there are really only two categories of captured fighters: either they are accorded the protections of POW status or they must be considered civilians, subject to criminal prosecution but only with full protections of due process before established tribunals. *See* Hans-Peter Gasser, "Acts of Terror, "Terrorism" and International Humanitarian Law," *International Review of the Red Cross*, vol. 84 (2002), at 547, 568.

19. *Official Records of the Diplomatic Conference on the Reaffirmation and Development of International Humanitarian Law Applicable to Armed Conflicts* (Bern: ICRC, 1978), vol. XIV, at 55 (Canada), 65 (France), 139 (Great Britain), & 162 (Australia).

20. That is certainly the ICRC view. Its *Commentary on the Additional Protocols* insists that AP I prohibits any form of reprisal whatever against prisoners of war, civilians (defined as anyone not embraced by the category of *military personnel*) and civilian objects, regardless of "military necessity" and these prohibitions "now bear the stamp of customary law" (meaning that they are binding even on non-signatories to AP I). Sandoz et al., *supra*, at 626–28.

21. Michael Barnett, *Empire of Humanity, A History of Humanitarianism* (Ithaca: Cornell University Press, 2011), at 136, quoting a "1948 booklet" published by the ICRC.

22. Caroline Moorhead, *Dunant's Dream: War, Switzerland and the History of the Red Cross* (New York: Harper-Collins, 1998), at 444.

23. David Rieff, *A Bed for the Night: Humanitarianism in Crisis* (New York: Simon and Schuster, 2002) at 76–77.

24. Barnett, *supra*, at 136 (quoting from the same 1948 booklet).

25. *Quoted by* Martin Gilbert, *Winston S. Churchill*, Vol. VI, *Finest Hour, 1939–1941* (New York: Houghton Mifflin, 1983), at 832, n. 1 (emphasis added). Four months later, Britain's minister to the Vatican proposed to issue a statement explaining that Britain had "deferred to the Pope's request to spare Rome on account of its Christian tradition." Churchill vetoed this suggestion, as well: "It would be unwise to try to make this point because we shall soon be bombing Rome." *Id.*, at 885, n. 2.

26. *Human Rights, A Compilation of International Instruments* (New York and Geneva: United Nations, 1994).

27. Robert Bernstein, "Rights Watchdog, Lost in the Middle East," *The New York Times* (October 19, 2009).

28. ICRC President Kellenberg explained the organization's reason for declining to accept "an escort of coalition forces" in Iraq—"The ICRC will not allow itself to be swallowed up by any power. . . . We bring help on the basis of neutrality"—in an interview with the journalist Marlene Schneiper, which originally appeared in the

Swiss newspaper *Tages-Anzeiger* on November 8, 2003, and was subsequently posted (in translation) on the ICRC website.

29. W. Hays Parks, "Air War and the Law of War," *Air Force Law Review,* vol. 32 (1990), at 166. Colonel Parks was part of the American team sent by the Reagan administration to make independent findings of what was happening in Lebanon. He concluded that the precautions employed at the time by Israeli forces were "among the highest imposed by any nation in any armed conflict" while "actions of the PLO were a direct cause of civilian losses. . . . The ICRC's singling out of one party to the conflict in its call for restraint and its reliance upon disinformation provided it by one party to the conflict are but two examples of its . . . abandonment of the principles of neutrality." *Id.* at 166, n. 94.

30. On Amnesty's reluctance (as late as 1977) to associate itself with "conservative opinions" warning of genocide in Cambodia, *see* Samantha Power, *"A Problem from Hell: America and the Age of Genocide* (New York: Basic Books, 2002), at 113–14. On Amnesty's "striking" record of "non-involvement" in human rights advocacy for Soviet political prisoners during the 1970s and 80s, *see* William Korey, *NGOs and the Universal Declaration of Human Rights* (New York: St. Martin's Press, 1984), at 169.

31. Jean-Marie Henckaerts and Louise Doswald-Beck, *Customary International Humanitarian Law* (Cambridge and New York: Cambridge University Press, 2005).

32. The so-called Vandenberg amendment to U.S. ratification of the International Court of Justice (ICJ) Statute reserved U.S. consent to the court's jurisdiction in "disputes arising under a multilateral treaty, unless all parties to the treaty affected by the decision are also parties to the case before the Court." The United States sought to invoke this reservation when Nicaragua tried to bring claims against the United States at the ICJ arising out of U.S. support for the *Contra* rebels there in the mid-1980s. The Court ruled in *Nicaragua v. U.S.* (1984) that it could proceed to judgment by basing its decisions on customary international law rather than multilateral treaties (Paragraph 67)—a distinction which (among other aspects of the Court's ruling) provoked indignant response from the U.S. government and a decision to withdraw all U.S. consent to compulsory jurisdiction under the ICJ. The ICRC volumes are in a different category because they do not claim to be binding interpretations. As the Nicaragua case demonstrated, however, the United States is sometimes prepared to say the same about rulings of the International Court of Justice.

33. *See* Henckaerts and Doswold-Beck, *Customary IHL,* Vol II, at 236 ¶ 685 (HRW), 331 ¶ 191 (ICRC), & 190, ¶ 369 (AI).

34. *Id.,* Vol. II, at 146, ¶ 85 (Saddam Hussein).

35. *Id.,* Vol. II, at 310, ¶ 82.

36. David Bernstein, "Human Rights Watch Goes to Saudi Arabia," *Wall Street Journal* (July 15, 2009).

37. "The Right of Return: The Case of the Palestinians" (March 30, 2001) (MDE 15/013/2001) insists that all descendants of Palestinians who fled from Israel in 1949 continue to have an unlimited right to return.

38. Richard Kerbaj, "Amnesty International 'damaged' by terror link," *Sunday Times* (UK) (February 7, 2010).

39. A convenient survey of reservations appears in Adams Roberts and Richard Guelff, *Documents on the Law of War* (3d edition) (Oxford University Press, 2000), at 499–512.

40. Jean Pictet, author of ICRC's commentaries on the 1949 Conventions and co-editor of its commentaries on the Additional Protocols, *quoted in* Parks, *supra*, at 75.

41. *Quoted in* ICRC Commentary on AP I, Art. 44, at 529, Paragraph 1698: Charles Chaumont, "La recherche d'un critere pour l'integration de law guerilla au droit international humanitaire contemporain" in "Melanges Offerts a Charles Rousseau" (Paris, 1974, trans. by ICRC).

42. Abi-Saab, "Proceedings of the 1976 and 1977 Conferences" *in The New International Humanitarian Law of Armed Conflict* (Antonio Cassese, ed.) (Napoli: Editoriale Scientifica, 1979) at 250. Abi-Saab was the Egyptian Delegate to the Geneva Conferences.

43. "Operations in Libya," Wed. 27 April 2011, House of Commons, Defence Committee (transcript available at www.parliament.uk).

44. For example, Joseph Logan, "NATO Must Step Up Pace in Libya: British General," May 15, 2011.

45. The term has entered general use only in the past decade. While the original coinage is disputed, Major General Charles Dunlap certainly fixed the current usage in a published lecture at Harvard University's Carr Center for Human Rights ("Law and Military Interventions") on November 29, 2001, when he was Deputy Judge Advocate General in the U.S. Air Force.

Chapter 3

Targeted Killing

The Israeli Experience

Steven R. David

As the United States increases its drone attacks on suspected terrorists in Afghanistan, Pakistan, and elsewhere, it is useful to examine the Israeli experience with targeted killing, for it may offer important information that will help us assess the pros and cons of this controversial policy. Israel has pursued a policy of targeted killing since before the creation of the state. It has only been since the onset of the Second *Intifada* in 2000, however, that the policy has become so central to Israeli security. Since that point, Israel has killed hundreds of Palestinian terrorists—as well as innocent bystanders—in wide-ranging operations utilizing helicopter gunships, F-16 aircraft, and hit squads. Notable successes have been achieved, including the near elimination of suicide attacks against Israel, attacks that had killed over 1,000 Israelis during the Second *Intifada*. Reasons for this success include the impact of targeted killing in eliminating key personnel (bomb makers, planners, commanders), keeping on the run those who would otherwise be mounting attacks, and responding to the demands of a restive public. Targeted killing also has its drawbacks in that innocents are sometimes killed, it erodes the norm against assassination, and sullies Israel's reputation in the international community.

In this chapter, I will argue that targeted killing is fully consistent with Israeli law, as evidenced by a 2006 Israeli Supreme Court decision that set clear guidelines as to when it can be used. Israel's use of targeted killing also fits with traditional Just War doctrine, in that it is both discriminate and proportionate. By meting out punishment to the guilty, targeted killing also meets the retributive demands of the Israeli population.

While the policy of targeted killing makes sense for Israel, however, I argue that it can be improved upon. Israel should be forthright and unapologetic about its policy of targeted killing, for it is a moral and legal imperative in light of the situation Israel faces, and dissembling about such things is almost never justified. Israel should take extra care to avoid civilian casualties, and it must try harder to avoid killing political leaders unless there is compelling evidence that they are actively involved in terrorist operations. (These suggestions also hold true for the United States and other democracies that face threats far removed from the clear distinctions of war and peace that earlier generations confronted.) Targeted killing remains an unsavory choice, but is often the most effective and moral response to modern conditions of nontraditional conflict. The following pages will explain these points in more detail.

I. WHY IT MATTERS

Israel has openly and officially pursued a policy of targeted killing since the inception of the Palestinian uprising known as the Second *Intifada,* in September 2000. The Israelis have identified, located, and then killed alleged Palestinian terrorists with helicopter gunships, fighter aircraft, tanks, car bombs, booby traps, and bullets. All in all, 411 Palestinians have reportedly been killed during targeted killing operations, of which 239 were apparently the intended targets. (The 172 who were killed without being targeted were either companions of the victim or simply innocent bystanders.)[1] These killings have prompted international condemnation—at times even from the United States—domestic soul searching, and bloody retaliation. Given its controversial nature and obvious costs, it is worth considering whether this policy is really worth pursuing. Why has Israel embarked on this policy of targeted killings? Has the policy been effective in reducing Palestinian attacks on Israeli civilians? Are targeted killings permitted by Israeli and international law? Are they moral? Is the policy of targeted killing in the Israeli national interest?

The answers to these questions are of critical importance. For Israel, it is necessary to know whether its policy of targeted killings is pragmatically and ethically justified. If it is, it makes sense for Israel to continue or even expand upon this approach. If there are serious shortcomings, they need to be highlighted so that the policy can be modified—or discarded. For countries other than Israel, and especially the United States, assessing the worth of targeted killings is hardly less significant. Ever since the New York and Washington terrorist attacks of September 11, 2001, much of the world, with the United States in the lead, has sought ways to counter terrorism. In fact, the United States, its sometime criticism of Israel notwithstanding, has embarked on a policy of targeted killing on its own, using drones to kill hundreds of alleged terrorists in Pakistan, Afghanistan, and Yemen—a policy that has been dramatically accelerated under the Obama administration. If the Israelis have embarked upon a successful approach, it may make sense for Americans to emulate them. If Israeli policy is fundamentally flawed, it would be better to understand this as soon as possible, especially when voices demanding that terrorists be hunted down and killed have grown so loud. Either way, learning from the Israeli experience is central to those seeking to combat the threat from terrorism.

As indicated, I argue that the policy of targeted killing is in Israel's interests and, subject to certain guidelines, should be retained. Especially after the Second *Intifada,* targeted killing, in coordination with other policies, has protected Israeli civilians from terrorist attack, and done so in accordance with the principles of humanity, discrimination, and proportionality that are central to the laws of armed conflict in the 21st century. As Israel has moved to employ helicopter-fired missiles and bombs from F-16 jets, instead of exploding packages and poisons, it has also helped define the modern targeted killing as having a "military" nature that will increasingly be a necessary response for countries facing non-traditional threats in the 21st century. Targeted killing, as practiced by the Israelis, has become an evolved response to contemporary conditions of conflict in which terrorists hide among civilian populations in order to launch their murderous assaults against innocents. So long as this threat persists, Jerusalem will have little choice but to respond with its policy of targeted killing.

The remainder of this chapter will have five parts. After defining *targeted killing*, I discuss the Israeli use of this practice from before the establishment of the state of Israel to the present. I then consider the effectiveness of this policy in reducing Palestinian terrorism. Next, the legal and normative considerations of targeted killing are examined. My own case in support of targeted killing then follows, after which I conclude with some general recommendations for improving the implementation of this policy.

II. DEFINITION AND HISTORICAL BACKGROUND

Targeted killing is the intentional slaying of a specific individual or group of individuals undertaken with explicit governmental approval, and in the context of a broader armed struggle against such persons. It is not "assassination" for three reasons:

- First, assassination typically has a pejorative connotation of "murder by treacherous means." Whether the Israeli killing of alleged Palestinian terrorists is "treacherous" or not is a debatable proposition that should not be assumed *a priori* by employing loaded terms such as *assassination*. (In fact, as will be discussed herein, Israeli targeted killings are frequently done relatively openly, and with "military"-style tools such as bombs and missiles.)

- Second, assassination usually refers to the killing of a politically prominent person to bring about political change. Israel has focused on killing Palestinians engaged in armed attacks against Israeli civilians, not heads of state, and with military objectives in mind (e.g., stopping terrorist attacks).
- Finally, Israel itself does not use the term *assassination* and, instead, prefers *targeted thwarting* or *interceptions*.[2] While it is not necessary, uncritically, to accept Israeli terminology for these actions, neither does it make sense, reflexively, to accept the terminology of their critics—who prefer to label these activities *assassination*. As an alternative, *targeted killing* is a dryly descriptive term that accurately refers to what the Israelis actually do, with a minimum of semantic baggage implying approval or disapproval of their actions.

The practice of targeted killing by Israel is not new. Underground Jewish groups, such as the Hagana, Irgun, and Lehi, in the period before Israeli independence often cited Biblical and ancient historical examples to justify their own practices of targeted killing. These groups had little compunction about eliminating individuals who supported the British occupation of Palestine. A few of the victims were prominent political figures, such as the international mediator, Count Folke Bernadotte. Most, however, were fellow Jews suspected of being informers.[3] Some of the leaders of these groups, such as Menachem Begin and Yitzhak Shamir, went on to assume leadership positions in modern Israel. They did so having sanctioned targeted killings in the past, and perhaps with the belief that this policy helped them achieve their aims.

A. History

From its independence in 1948 to the present, Israel has used the policy of targeted killings to advance its interests. When the intensity of the Arab-Israeli conflict is high, especially if the main antagonist is the Palestinians, the number of targeted killings rises. At times of relative peace, such as just after the signing of the Oslo Peace Accords in 1993 and the collapse of the Second *Intifada* in 2005, targeted killings drop.

While the numbers may fluctuate, this practice has never totally disappeared. Exact figures are difficult to come by, because the Israelis often do not publicly acknowledge responsibility for a specific killing. Nevertheless, in most cases it is clear who is responsible. Israeli attacks are characterized by their professionalism, efforts to minimize innocent casualties, and (occasionally) the sophistication of the weapons used (e.g., helicopter gunships and F-16 fighters). The identity of the target also provides a strong indication of Israeli responsibility. The Israeli government will usually refuse comment regarding attacks it mounts, except where Israeli involvement is obvious, but will often deny responsibility for operations undertaken by others. In many cases, Israeli sources will unofficially admit to being behind specific attacks.

The persistence of the Israeli policy of targeted killing can be seen by a brief historical overview. (Examples of targeted killings provided are meant to be illustrative, not exhaustive.) In the 1950s, Israel focused its targeted killings on efforts to halt *fedayeen* attacks from Egypt. Two senior Egyptian military intelligence officials in charge of *fedayeen* operations were killed by mail bombs sent by Israeli intelligence.[4] In the 1960s, Israel again used mail bombs in a program of targeted killing, this time sent to German scientists developing ballistic missiles in Egypt for the government of Gamal Abdul Nasser—missiles that would have been capable of reaching Israel. The bombs, mailed to the scientists and their families, convinced these scientists to return to Germany, bringing about an end to that missile program.[5]

The occupation of the West Bank and Gaza following Israel's victory in the 1967 war, and an increase in Palestinian terror operations, dramatically increased the use of targeted killings by Israel. General Ariel Sharon commanded an anti-terror detachment in 1971 that attempted to eliminate Palestinian militants from Gaza. Often posing as Arab civilians or guerrillas, Sharon's unit killed 104 Palestinians and arrested 742 others.[6]

The slaughter of 11 Israeli athletes at the 1972 Munich Olympics by Palestinian terrorists, however, galvanized Israel's policy of targeted killing as no previous event had done. Israel established a "Committee X" chaired by Prime Minister Golda Meir and Defense Minister Moshe Dayan. The Committee oversaw a mission in which agents of the Israeli foreign intelligence service, the Mossad, systematically hunted down and killed the members of the Black September organization responsible for the Olympic massacre. Beginning in October 1972, the killings continued over the next year, resulting in thirteen deaths. (An innocent Moroccan busboy, Ahmed Bouchiki was killed by mistake in Norway, but this slowed rather than stopped the Israeli effort.[7]) Israel's war with the Palestine Liberation Organization (PLO) escalated in April 1973, when three PLO leaders were killed in separate apartments in Beirut by Israeli commando teams. Ehud Barak, the future prime minister, led the daring operation—reportedly actually disguised as a woman.

The 1980s saw Israel attempt to kill two Palestinian leaders, in one case successfully. The failed effort occurred following the Israeli intervention into Lebanon in the spring of 1982, when Israel tried several times to kill Palestine Liberation Organization leader Yasser Arafat. Despite the Israelis' use of booby-trapped cars and air attacks, Arafat was able to escape unscathed. An Israeli sniper reportedly also had Arafat in his sights during the PLO's withdrawal from Beirut, but he was not given the order to shoot on account of the presence of American and other diplomats at the farewell ceremony.[8] (In February 2002, Prime Minister Ariel Sharon lamented that Israel had not killed Arafat in Lebanon when it had the chance to do so.) Israeli efforts proved more successful in killing Arafat's second in command, Abu Jihad (Khalil el-Wazir), who died at the hands of an Israeli hit squad in Tunisia in the spring of 1988. The decision to kill Jihad stemmed from his role in planning several terrorist activities against Israel, including the bloody hijacking of an Israeli bus in March 1988. More importantly, the Israelis saw Abu Jihad as an irreplaceable leader who held the PLO together, and was key to the success of the first Arab *intifada*. Ehud Barak reportedly planned the Jihad raid—jointly conducted by the Israeli Defense Forces (IDF) and Israel's foreign intelligence service (Mossad)—drawing upon his 1973 Beirut experience.[9]

At least three major Israeli efforts at targeted killing took place in the 1990s, one successful, one a failure, and one achieving mixed results. The successful operation killed the head of the group Palestinian Islamic Jihad, Fathi Shikaki, in Malta in October 1995. To Israeli's delight, no competent successor emerged to replace Shikaki, producing disarray in Islamic Jihad. The organization limped along for several years, unable to mount any serious attacks against Israeli interests.[10]

The mixed outcome stemmed from the January 1996 killing of Yahya Ayyash, known as *the engineer*, in Gaza. Ayyash was killed while speaking on a mobile telephone that had been booby-trapped by the Israeli domestic intelligence agency, Shin Bet. Ayyash had been one of Hamas' most skilled and prolific bomb makers whose handiwork proved critical to many terror attacks against Israel. Although Jerusalem succeeded in removing a key figure from Hamas, Ayyash's death also led Hamas to mount four retaliatory suicide bus bombings in the next two months, killing more than fifty Israelis.

Finally, in an embarrassing, almost comic episode, the Israelis failed to kill Khaled Meshal, the chief of Hamas's political bureau, in Amman, Jordan, in September 1997. Two Mossad agents posing as Canadian tourists succeeded in poisoning Meshal with an exotic neurotoxin, but they were captured by Jordanian authorities before they could leave the country. In order to secure the return of the two operatives, Israeli Prime Minister Benjamin Netanyahu agreed to provide the antidote for the poison—thus permitting Meshal's recovery—and to release Hamas' founder, Sheik Ahmed Yassin, from an Israeli prison. As a result of this embarrassing and counterproductive episode, Israel damaged its relations with Jordan, a friendly Arab country. The affair also infuriated Canada after it was revealed that the Mossad agents had used Canadian passports. Most important perhaps, the aura of invincibility and shrewdness that had long surrounded Mossad, had been badly compromised.[11]

B. Targeted Killings During the Second *Intifada*

A wave of Israeli targeted killings began in November 2000, as an outgrowth of the second Palestinian *intifada.* Following the failure of the Camp David peace negotiations in the summer of 2000 and Ariel Sharon's provocative visit to the Temple Mount in late September, the Palestinians unleashed a violent revolt against Israel. Unlike the First *Intifada,* in which the ratio of Palestinians to Jews killed was roughly 25 to 1, in the Second *Intifada,* a well-armed Palestinian force making free use of suicide bombers reduced that proportion to three to one.[12] Israel responded to these increasingly lethal attacks—over 1,000 Israeli civilians were killed during the Second *Intifada*—with military incursions into Palestinian-controlled areas, increased use of checkpoints to control Palestinian movements, the erection of a security barrier, and a dramatic rise in the slayings of Palestinian militants.

In one sense, there was nothing new about Israel's policy of targeted killing during the Second *Intifada.* As indicated above, Israel has pursued targeted killings throughout its history. What was new now, however, was the scale of the effort: never before had so many militants been killed in such a short span of time. Also new were some of the tactics, particularly the use of helicopter gunships, F-16 fighter/bomber aircraft, and unmanned drones to execute individuals. Because of the extent of the campaign and the obvious use of Israeli military assets, the Israeli government has been forced to acknowledge its role in targeted killings to a much greater extent than previously, although it still refuses to routinely claim responsibility for its operations.[13]

Several high ranking Palestinians have been killed during the Second *Intifada.* They include the head of the Palestinian Front for the Liberation of Palestine (PFLP), Abu Ali Mustafa; the Secretary-General of the PFLP, Mustafa Zibri; one of the leaders of the Tanzim movement, Raed al-Karmi; and a senior official of Hamas, Sheik Salah Shehadeh. Shehadeh was killed by a one-ton bomb dropped by an F-16, an operation that proved especially controversial since 14 civilians, including 9 children, also perished in the strike. While attacks on leaders grabbed the headlines, most of those killed during this period were in fact mid-level fighters, important enough that it was hoped that their deaths would disrupt a terrorist cell but not so important as to provoke murderous retaliation.

The targets of these attacks were identified through Israel's intelligence apparatus and through collaborators, and usually knew they were being sought. The Israelis claim they only target those who are on their way to a terrorist attack or are actively planning one. During the early months of the Second *Intifada,* when the Israelis had ongoing talks with the Palestinian Authority (PA), they would hand over to the PA a list of suspected terrorists. If the PA did not arrest the individuals, Israel killed them.[14] Once talks broke down with the PA in the spring of 2002, however, such efforts to cooperate dwindled, resuming only after the death of Yasser Arafat and the 2005 election of Mahmoud Abbas as leader of the Palestinian Authority.

Although the great bulk of its targeted killing has been against Palestinian militants, Israel is also suspected of employing this strategy against Iranian scientists who are actively working on producing a nuclear bomb. On November 29, 2010, Iranian scientist Majid Sharriari was killed by a magnetic bomb attached to his car, while another scientist, Fereydoun Abbasi Davani, barely escaped death from a similar bomb attack. Other Iranian scientists have been killed or died under mysterious circumstances. While Israel has not claimed responsibility, it is widely believed that the Jewish state is behind these operations. The goal appears to be similar to the attacks against the German scientists in Egypt in the 1960s, namely to kill key personnel while frightening away others who may be considering taking their place.[15]

III. HOW EFFECTIVE IS ISRAEL'S POLICY OF TARGETED KILLING?

A. Successes

There is no question that Israel's policy of targeted killing has hurt the capability of its Arab adversaries to prosecute attacks against Israel. Terrorism is essentially an offensive action, making counteroffensive actions such as targeted killing an especially effective response. It is exceedingly difficult for Israel directly to defend against or deter terror attacks from Palestinians. In terms of defense, there are tens of thousands of potential targets in Israel for Palestinian terrorists. (The list is endless: power stations, government bureaus, bus depots, airports, skyscrapers, open-air markets, sports stadiums, or indeed anywhere people congregate.) It is impossible to defend all such targets, especially against a determined adversary that can choose the time and place of attack. While some level of deterrence of terrorism is achievable, and Israel's security barrier seems to have had a significant effect in reducing Palestinians' ability to bring weapons and explosives into Israel, dissuading potential terrorists is not easy when they are eager to die for their cause. In such situations, the best response to terrorism may be to go on a counteroffensive—that is, to eliminate the terrorist threat *before* it can be launched. One of the most successful means of eliminating terrorists before they can strike is the policy of targeted killing.[16]

As alluded to above, Israel has achieved some notable triumphs in its policy of targeted killing. In the 1950s, terrorist infiltration from Egypt lessened as a result of the killing of Egyptian intelligence officers in charge of the operation. In the 1960s, Nasser's plan to build ballistic missiles capable of reaching Israel collapsed when his German scientists fled in the wake of Israeli mail bomb attacks. Black September was all but destroyed as a functioning terrorist organization in the 1970s, following the Israeli campaign to avenge the Munich massacre. The 1995 Israeli assassination of Palestinian Islamic Jihad leader Fathi Shikaki in Malta undermined the effectiveness of this group for several years, as successors struggled over policy and power. The elimination of Yahya Ayyash also hurt the effectiveness of Hamas, though only at the cost of many Israeli lives due to Hamas retaliation.[17]

Several other benefits of Israel's policy of targeted killing became apparent from its heightened practice during the Second *Intifada*. First, targeted killings have impeded the effectiveness of Palestinian terrorist organizations where leadership, planning, and tactical skills are confined to a few key individuals. There are a limited number of people who have the technical ability to make bombs and plan attacks. If they are eliminated, the ability to mount attacks is degraded.

There is indeed some evidence that targeted killings have reduced the effectiveness of Palestinian terror operations. The large number of intercepted suicide bombers (Israelis estimate that they stop over 80 percent of attempts) and poorly planned attacks (e.g., suicide bombers with faulty munitions or bombs easily visible to security service officials, or detonations that occur with little loss of life) indicates that there are problems either with the organization of the operations or the quality of those available to carry them out.[18] Daniel Byman points out that the lethality of Hamas attacks declined dramatically from 3.9 deaths per attack in 2001 to a mere 0.11 deaths in 2005. The number of Israeli deaths dropped as the policy of targeted killing continued, with Hamas killing 185 Israeli civilians in 2002 as compared with 21 in 2005.[19] This record illustrates that there are individual leaders whose charisma and organizational skills keep a group together. If such figures are eliminated, they are not easily replaced.[20] Shikaki of the Islamic Jihad falls into this category. Israel appears to have had some success in disrupting and degrading Hamas' operational capabilities.

Another, and related, benefit of targeting killing is keeping would-be bombers and bomb makers on the run. When the Israelis informed the Palestinian Authority who they were after, this information was often passed to the targeted individuals so that they knew they were being hunted. Some voluntarily chose to place themselves in Palestinian custody to avoid being slain, and the threat they posed to Israel was consequently diminished. There are numerous accounts of others on the "hit" list taking precautions against being killed—precautions such as sleeping in a different location every night and not letting others know of their whereabouts.[21] Even for those Palestinians who have not been told they are being hunted, the very possibility they might be targeted is likely to cause a change in behavior. Whether or not Israeli forces actually kill them, their fugitive status can redound to the benefit of Israel: time and effort undertaken to avoid Israeli dragnets are time and effort *not* undertaken carrying out operations.

Targeted killing also acts as a deterrent. In one sense, it might appear virtually impossible to deter people willing and even eager to lose their lives. But for every eager suicide bomber there are others who might not be as ready for martyrdom. The large numbers of Palestinian commanders who surrendered meekly to Israeli forces during the large-scale military incursions in the spring of 2002 lend support to the notion that many senior officials do not actually wish to die for their cause. It is also reasonable to assume that there are skilled, capable Palestinians who do not engage in terrorist operations for fear of Israeli reprisals.

Most important, there is strong evidence that the policy of targeted killing hurts Palestinian organizations, a dynamic visible in the extent to which they are willing to alter their behavior in order to escape it. When Israeli Prime Minister Ariel Sharon, for example, met with three Palestinian leaders (though not Yasir Arafat) on January 30, 2002, he asked the Palestinians what they wanted from him. The first thing on their list was an end to targeted killings.[22] In December 2001, moreover, Palestinian Islamic Jihad and Hamas agreed to refrain from launching attacks within the pre-1967 boundaries of Israel, so long as Israel refrained from killing their leaders. Although these cease-fires eventually broke down, these organizations' willingness to undertake such obligations, even temporarily, indicates the deterrent power of targeted killing.

Targeted killing is popular with the Israeli public. A poll conducted by *Ma'ariv* and the Mutagim Institute in July 2001—one year into the Second *Intifada*—found that 90 percent of the Israeli public supported the policy. Although subsequent polls showed a small drop in support, robust majorities of the Israeli public continue to believe that targeted killing represents an appropriate response to the terror attacks that afflict the population. No other

Israeli counterterrorism policy, in fact—including incursions into Palestinian territory, arrests of militants, the erection of a security barrier, or forced transfer of Palestinians from the territories to neighboring Arab countries—enjoys the support received by targeted killing. Since the approval spans the Israeli body politic, it is well-received by coalition governments representing diverse Israeli views. Democracies follow public opinion, and targeted killing is a policy that has never lost favor with the Israeli electorate.

Targeted killing has also proven effective in the battle for public relations throughout the world. Although Israel has been criticized in the media for slaying Palestinian militants, the criticism has been far less than afforded to other policies. When, for example, Israel attacks Palestinian cities, there is no lack of coverage of the innocent deaths that result or the widespread suffering imposed on Palestinian civilians. Targeted killings, at least, focus on specific adversaries who mean Israel harm. (That there is rarely television coverage of the actual operation is another benefit.)[23]

In sum, the policy of targeted killing has prevented many attacks against Israel, weakened the effectiveness of terrorist organizations, kept potential bomb makers on the run, deterred terrorist operations, gained the support of the overwhelming percentage of the Israeli population, and done so while largely avoiding the sharp glare of publicity. It has not prevented *all* acts of terrorism, nor can it. But as part of a larger array of policies, including blockades, checkpoints, barriers, and incursions, it is seen to be a successful response to an intolerable threat.

B. The Limited Effectiveness of Targeted Killing

Strong arguments have been made that targeted killings have done little to reduce the overall terrorist threat against Israel. During the Second *Intifada,* the Israelis embarked on more targeted killings than at any time in its history. At the same time, however, record numbers of Israeli civilians became victims of Palestinian attacks. After reviewing several studies examining the effectiveness of targeted killing, political scientist Avery Plaw concluded that there was no definitive evidence that this policy suppressed Palestinian violence, at least in the short term.[24] If targeted killing really did not save innocent Israeli lives, its value is called into question.

It is not difficult to understand why targeted killing may not have been particularly effective in stopping terrorism. Organizations such as Hamas, Palestinian Islamic Jihad, and (to some extent) the Palestinian Authority, promoting terror against Israel, are often very decentralized. Terrorist groups are frequently made up of many cells, the destruction of some having little or no impact on others. Moreover, the number of young men (and women) who are willing and eager to be suicide bombers appears to be virtually limitless. Outfitting these martyr wannabes with primitive bombs capable of wreaking murderous assaults appears to be relatively easy.

There is also no doubt that targeted killing, at least in some instances, *increases* the terrorist threat against Israel by producing murderous retaliation. The killings of "the engineer" (Yahya Ayyash), PFLP leader Rehavam Ze'evi, Tanzim chief Raded al-Karmi, and Hamas head Sheik Salah Shehadeh all resulted in dramatic escalations in attacks against Israelis, with revenge explicitly cited as the motivation for the actions. Targeted killing may also hurt Israeli interests by removing current adversaries who may prove to be useful negotiating partners in the future. One of the vexing problems confronting Israeli decision makers for many years was the absence of any credible alternatives to the failed leadership of Yasir Arafat. (Ironically, this was sometimes said to be a reason why Israel had not, or should not, kill Arafat.) Israel itself, however, contributed to this sorry situation. When Israel killed Arafat's second-in-command, Abu Jihad, in 1988 it eliminated not only an individual behind several bloody operations, but also someone who many saw as a pragmatist capable of making peaceful compromises.

By diverting scarce resources away from the collection and analysis of intelligence on the threat posed by adversarial states to individual terrorist subjects suitable for targeted killing, moreover, Israel runs the risk of paying less attention to existential threats in order to combat critical but less vital challenges to its security. Following the Munich Olympics massacre, for instance, Israel focused much of the attention of its intelligence services on tracking down and killing the perpetrators. This effort may have led, in part, to diverting Israel's attention away from the growing threat posed by Egypt and Syria, which led to Israel being caught by surprise at the outbreak of the October 1973 War.[25]

Even where the effect is not so dramatic, targeted killing can hurt Israel's ability to gather critical intelligence on other subjects. Locating and killing key Palestinian terrorists requires timely information, much of which can only be supplied by informers. Given that only a limited number of people will know the whereabouts of the targets, it is often not too difficult, in the wake of a targeted killing, to isolate those who have collaborated with Israel. Increasing reports of informers being killed during the Second *Intifada*, with their bodies publicly displayed, may be a result of their identities becoming known as a result of the targeting killing policy.[26] Those informants, clearly, could provide no additional intelligence to their Israeli contacts.

When Israel kills militants abroad, it also opens itself up to withering criticism from a host of aggrieved parties. The 2010 slaying of Hamas commander Mahmoud al-Mabhouh in Dubai, by what is believed to have been an Israeli hit squad that smothered him in his hotel room, subjected Israel to protests not only from Dubai but from Britain, France, Germany, and Ireland—all of whom objected to Israel allegedly using passports from their countries in mounting the attack. Finally, Israel's overall policy of targeted killing has been condemned by the Arab world, Europe, the United Nations, and even the United States. Clearly, targeted killing is a policy that can have high costs.

IV. NORMATIVE AND LEGAL ISSUES

Norms are broad guidelines of behavior that are largely followed by states and other actors. There is no established norm against targeted killing, but there is one against assassination. Although I have argued there is a substantial difference between the two concepts from a lawyer's perspective, they are related in public perceptions. Part of the difficulty Israel has had in justifying the practice of targeted killing stems, in part, from the norm against assassination. More important, continued Israeli employment of targeted killing could work to erode the norm against assassination, with negative consequences for Israel and the world community.

The norm against assassination is relatively recent. Before the 17th century, assassination was a normal means of states doing business, similar to diplomacy and war. Statesmen, philosophers, and even the Catholic Church approved of the practice as a means for states to pursue their interests while limiting harm done to innocents.[27] The support of assassination dropped precipitously, however, in the 1600s. The norm against assassination became so strong, that even as odious a character as Hitler was not seen as a legitimate target by the British who deemed any effort to kill him as "unsportsmanlike."[28]

What changed? According to the political scientist Ward Thomas, who has done some of the best work in this area, norms stem not only from moral considerations, but also from the interests of the great powers. Moral concerns regarding assassination existed before the 17th century, but so long as assassination served the interests of the major states, they were not enough to support a norm against its practice. The rise of the sovereign state and the mass army in the mid-1600s, however, changed thinking about the acceptability of assassination. By limiting "legitimate" conflict to clashes of large military forces, the leaders of the great powers established rules of the game that maximized their advantages while sidelining the weaker states that did not have mass armies with which to compete. Similarly, the norm against assassination protected the leaders of great powers by depriving weaker players of an instrument that otherwise might have allowed them to level the playing field by threatening those leaders directly. So long as there was general agreement that the way to resolve violent conflicts was through conventional war and that assassination was unacceptable, the hierarchy of the international system and the interests of the leaders of the major powers would be preserved.[29]

The reasons for the emergence of the norm against assassination illustrate some of the costs Israel (and other countries) could be expected to bear if the norm were eroded. Assassination is a weapon of the weak. It benefits those with limited resources, but with fanatical devotion to a cause. In other words, it plays to Palestinian strengths. So long as conventional military operations hold sway, Israel is in an unassailable position. Its ability to call upon sophisticated, multimillion-dollar aircraft, modern tanks manned by well-trained crews, and world-class electronic warfare and surveillance makes it the strongest military power in the Middle East. But when the arena switches to the world of assassination, young men and women armed with a couple of hundred dollars' worth of explosives eager to achieve martyrdom are able to inflict grievous harm on Israel that Arab armies cannot match. Insofar as Israel erodes the norm of assassination, it transforms the rules of conflict in a manner that benefits its most fervent adversaries.

It is, of course, true that norms do not determine behavior. Terrorists, almost by definition, are not constrained by established norms. The long history of plane hijackings and other murderous attacks against innocent civilians by terrorists throughout the world gives brutal testimony to their willingness to violate established codes of conduct. In confronting this challenge, states have also sometimes had to depart from usual norms. Terrorists typically do not appear in identifiable uniforms or hold clear swaths of territory, making conventional military responses to their threats all but impossible. Insofar as Israel (and other states) need or choose to make war on terrorists, traditional norms of combat may have to be eroded no matter what the long-term implications may be.

Nevertheless, when a major regional power and democracy such as Israel openly proclaims its right to pursue a policy of targeted killing, it helps to create a new standard of behavior that may work to its and other states' detriment. Norms may not be determinative, but neither are they irrelevant. Rather than simply disregarding norms because they interfere with its war on terror, Israel needs to act in a way that preserves its right of self-defense without bringing about future harm to itself and to the international community. Doing that requires that Israel preserve a clear distinction between targeted killing and assassination, a goal that Israel does not always achieve.

The policy of targeted killing is fully consistent with Jewish and Israeli law, and is in accordance with most interpretations of international law as well. Regarding Jewish law, the *Rodef* injunction that appears in the Hebrew Bible (Shemot 22:1) makes it abundantly clear that if someone is coming to kill you, you are obligated to kill them first. The Torah (the first five books of the Hebrew Bible) teaches that if a thief is tunneling through into one's house, the members of the household need to kill the would-be intruder before he can enter. The rule that emerges states, "If someone comes to kill you, act first and kill him." This obligation applies not only for one's own protection, but for the defense of the community as well. As such, killing a terrorist before he can act is not only permitted by Jewish law, it is *required*.[30]

Israeli law is a bit more problematic, but here, too, the legality of targeted killing is not in much doubt. It is true that Israel does not allow capital punishment for its citizens. It is also true that Israel's Basic Law (the closest Israel comes to a constitution) guarantees that "[t]here shall be no violation of the life, body or dignity of any person as such." However, the Basic Law does allow these rights to be suspended, "by a law befitting the values of the State of Israel, enacted for a proper purpose, and to an extent no greater than is required, by a regulation enacted by virtue of express authorization in such law."[31]

And indeed, Israeli law has allowed for just such a suspension. In February 2002, the Judge Advocate General of the IDF, Menachem Finkelstein, issued four conditions under which targeted killing can take place. Before suspected terrorists are killed, he declared, there must be solid information showing that the terrorist will plan or carry out an attack in the future, the Palestinian Authority must first ignore appeals for their arrest, the Israelis must conclude that they would be unable to arrest the individuals themselves, and the attack must not be carried out to avenge past events. The Israeli High Court supported these conditions in a strongly worded opinion that rejected petitions calling for an end to targeted killing.[32]

Of even greater importance, in December 2006, the Israeli Supreme Court, building on the Finkelstein conditions, issued a ruling that presented five guidelines to determine when targeted killing was legal. There must be "convincing and well-formed information" that the individual is indeed a terrorist; attacking the terrorist can only be done if other less harmful means (e.g., arrest) cannot work; the terrorist must present an ongoing threat and not be attacked for actions committed in the past; the attack must be followed by an independent investigation to determine its appropriateness; and every effort must be made to minimize innocent civilian casualties.[33] If these guidelines from the Israeli Supreme Court are followed, targeted killing is clearly within the scope of Israeli domestic law.

As for international law, the situation is more complicated. Both international treaty and customary law outlaw assassination. The 1937 Convention for the Prevention and Repression of Terrorism and the 1973 New York

Convention are prominent examples of efforts undertaken to formally codify the illegality of assassination. Customary prohibitions against assassination have been even more influential than written law. The notion that assassination is not an accepted practice of statecraft became prominent with the writings of Hugo Grotius and Emmerich de Vattel in the 17th and 18th centuries. The prohibition against assassination was strengthened in the mid-1970s in the United States, following congressional investigations into activities by American intelligence agencies. The Church and Pike Committee investigations were especially outraged by Central Intelligence Agency efforts to assassinate several world leaders including Patrice Lumumba of the Congo and Cuba's Fidel Castro. Their committee hearings led to the establishment of an Executive Order stating that "[n]o person employed by or acting on behalf of the United States Government shall engage in, or conspire to engage in, assassination." This Executive Order has been reaffirmed by each succeeding American president. Although pertaining only to the United States, given America's leading role in the world, the Executive Order has contributed to the general agreement that assassination is unacceptable.[34]

There is, therefore, a clear consensus that assassination violates international law. Nevertheless, the key issue is what precisely constitutes *assassination*—and, as already discussed, there are strong reasons to believe that the Israeli policy of targeted killing is *not* the same as assassination. As the Director of the Center for National Security Law and the University of Virginia Law School, John Norton Moore, explains, "[i]f one is lawfully engaged in armed hostility, it is not 'assassination' to target individuals who are combatants." An American military lawyer, Charles J. Duncan, has agreed: "Contrary to popular belief, neither international law nor U.S. domestic law prohibits the killing of those directing armed forces in war. Nations have the right under international law to use force against terrorists."[35]

There are two points of ambiguity in the Israeli case regarding its adherence to international law, however. The first is whether Israel is actually at war with the Palestinians. As the head of the international law branch of the Israeli army's legal division remarked,

> International law actually only recognizes two situations: peace or war. But life isn't as simple. Israel is not at war since war is between two armies or two states and the Palestinians have neither. But since Israel is in armed conflict with Palestinians, you are allowed to target combatants.[36]

The Israeli Supreme Court has weighed in on this issue and in a series of decisions left no doubt that Israel considers itself to be in "armed conflict" with the Palestinians since the First *Intifada* (which began in the late 1980s).[37]

If Israel is in "armed conflict" with the Palestinians (at least during the *intifadas*) that is tantamount to war—and, in war, Israel has every right to target those combatants it believes are its enemy. Just as a soldier in wartime will feel no compunction about firing on an opposing army before they attack, so Israel is legally justified in preemptively killing terrorists regardless of whether they have attacked Israel. War—or armed conflict—is a legal license to kill opponents whether via targeted killing or in more traditional combat.

The second area of ambiguity rests in whether Israel is using "treacherous" means when it kills suspected terrorists. For many, *assassination* is murder by treacherous means, and so *how* one is killed is as important as (or even more important than) *who* is killed when it comes to determining whether the ban on assassination applies. As former American Secretary of Defense Casper Weinberger noted,

> it is considered lawful in warfare for a skilled and daring soldier (perhaps a Delta Force commando) to steal into the enemy's camp and enter the general's tent and kill him. But it would be a forbidden assassination if someone disguised as the general's doctor was admitted to his tent, and then killed him.[38]

The issue of what constitutes "treacherous" killing is not just semantics. The United States had little trouble justifying its efforts to kill Libyan leader Muammar Qaddafi in 1986, Osama bin Laden in 1998, or Saddam Hussein in 2003 using bombs and cruise missiles. U.S. President Barack Obama also received scant criticism after he sent a commando team to Pakistan in 2011 to kill terrorist leader Osama bin Laden. Precisely because they were military operations against leaders in an adversary's military hierarchy and not carried out under false pretenses, the ban against assassination did not apply.

It is true that the Israelis have used deception in some of their killings, and this is potentially problematic. There are reports that Israelis have disguised themselves as women or Arabs to facilitate getting their targets. The hit team that killed the Hamas official, Mahmoud al-Mabhouh in Dubai in 2010 posed as foreign tourists, clearly crossing the line from targeted killing to assassination. Nevertheless, what distinguishes most of the killings in the Second *Intifada* from the past is precisely the comparatively open and *military* nature of the attacks. The use of helicopter gunships or F-16s to kill suspected terrorists, for example, fits much more the conventional modes of warfare than it does the shadowy, deceitful world that characterizes assassinations. International lawyers may disapprove of Israeli actions, but most would agree that Israeli targeted killings usually do not violate the ban on assassination.

V. IN SUPPORT OF ISRAEL'S POLICY

Thus far, the case for targeted killing may appear weak. While it may disrupt and deter some attacks, there is no proof that targeted killing has saved Israeli lives. As one of the few Western democracies that openly proclaim the right to commit such extrajudicial killings, however, Israel has been fiercely criticized by the United States, its Arab neighbors, the international community, and the United Nations. While it may be technically legal, the policy has helped erode the norm against assassination, thus endangering the lives of world leaders while empowering the weak and fanatic. Based on its past record and likely future impact, there is seemingly little basis to continue this failed approach.

And yet, the policy of targeted killing makes sense for Israel for several reasons. First is the question of morality. Yes, there is widespread agreement that targeted killing raises disturbing moral issues. After all, Israel is killing individuals without any trial or due process. Innocent people are sometimes killed in these operations. It offends our sense of moral sensibility when government officials are reduced to the role of hit squads, as if they were part of some Mafia-like organization. The bedrock of Western democracy established by philosophers such as Thomas Hobbes and John Locke is limited government. How can that principle reconcile itself with a government that deprives people of their lives without proper judicial proceedings? The moral squeamishness that the policy evokes is demonstrated by the reluctance that Israel itself manifests when it refuses to comment on various killings for which it is clearly responsible. Israel may defend its right in the abstract to pursue a policy of targeted killing, but clearly the specifics of doing so are not something with which it is particularly comfortable.

Its qualms notwithstanding, however, the Israeli policy of targeted killing rests on an unassailable moral foundation. Just War tradition, from the time of Saint Augustine to the present, has emphasized the need for armed conflict to be discriminate and proportionate in the pursuit of legitimate ends; this is necessary for the use of force to be moral.[39] There is no question that the policy of targeted killing meets these criteria. Targeted killing is discriminatory—in the good sense of not being *indiscriminate,* which the law forbids killing to be—in that it aims to focus exclusively on one's adversaries. Civilian casualties and collateral damage are minimized. It is also proportionate, in that it seeks to use only enough force to accomplish the task. Targeted killings does not employ large numbers of troops, aerial bombardment, artillery attacks, or other means that can leave in their wake far more destruction than they prevent.

Finally, Israeli targeted killing serves a legitimate end by striking at those who threaten the lives of innocents. Since the policy is applied against those on their way to terrorist attacks or those who make such attacks possible, targeted killing enables Israel to protect its civilians by eliminating those who would murder them. Targeted killing might still be unobjectionable if it only focused upon protecting Israeli military targets, but the moral and legal argument is even more powerful inasmuch as it targets not lawful combatants who restrict their assaults to an adversary's military but terrorists who would otherwise slaughter innocents. Far from being morally questionable, therefore, it would be difficult to come up with an approach in warfare that rests on stronger moral ground.

Targeted killing also serves Israel's interests because it meets the demands of the Israeli public to *do something* in the face of murderous attacks. Failing to respond to Palestinian terrorism leads to despair, frustration, and anger. Politically, this can bring about the downfall of governments unwilling or unable to answer attacks on its people. Withstanding repeated attacks without responding can also lead to a sense of impotence and malaise that ultimately weakens a society's ability to protect itself. One could not, of course, defend the position that killing someone is appropriate *only* because the public cries out for action in response to terrorist atrocities, but neither is this irrelevant: a democratic society has both a right and a duty to defend itself.

To be sure, retaliation becomes problematic when there are no guidelines for how to act, or against whom. If there is too much space for arbitrary retaliation, attacks can indeed get out of hand and become disruptive, immoral, and unlawful. That is why states regulate and oversee the exercise of retaliatory strikes, and why the law articulates the ideals of proportionality and distinction to govern their exercise. For domestic infractions, society protects itself through the rule of law. In the international realm, security is pursued through foreign policy, ranging from diplomatic rebukes to war.

Yet in addition to its arguable utility as a prophylactic aimed at preventing future attacks against Israel, Israel's use of targeted killing is also a form of state-sanctioned retaliation. Since the government decides on who is to be killed according to established criteria, the issue of arbitrary retaliation is resolved. Because the killers of Israeli civilians are themselves killed, the desire for justice from both families of the victims and the society at large is met. Anger at the government is dissipated as the perpetrators of terror receive the same punishment as their victims.

Retribution is thus also a powerful justification for the Israeli policy of targeted killing, albeit with concerns that it must not get out of control or violate the law of armed conflict. Retribution, in its purest sense, has no utilitarian component. It is not motivated by vengeance. In such a view, even if the victims do not care about the offense committed or are opposed to punishing the aggressors, punishment nevertheless must be carried out. Nor is retribution motivated by deterrence or a need to satisfy the demands of an aggrieved population. If it can be shown that deterrence will not be enhanced by retaliation or that the community has no wish to strike back, retribution *still* demands the punishment of the guilty. Retribution is driven by the belief that offenders need to be punished *purely and simply* because such punishment is warranted. This concept of *just deserts* is compellingly put forward by the theorist Michael Moore who writes, that "[r]etributivism is the view that punishment is justified by the moral culpability of those who receive it. A retributivist punishes because, and only because, the offender *deserves* it."[40]

Israel's policy of targeted killing is driven, in part, by the desire for retribution. Palestinian suicide bombers seek out the most innocent of Israeli civilians—old men, women, children, and infants—and attempt to kill as many of them as they can. Stopping these operations before they can inflict their horrific harm is of obvious importance and provides some of the justification for targeted killings. But what of those who plan the attacks, arm the bombers and send them on their way? How are they to be not simply stopped but punished? During the Second *Intifada,* the Palestinian Authority was unwilling or unable to arrest many perpetrators, many of whom were PA officials. Hamas, which now rules in Gaza, far from seeking to punish suicide bombers, is a principal sponsor. Who, then, aside from us—Israelis ask—will provide the just deserts to these terrorists? Even if the policy of targeted killing does not reduce Israeli causalities, even if it increases them, such a policy is felt to be justified because it is only through this approach that the terrorists get what they inflict on others—a violent death.

While retribution may be emotionally satisfying, however, it alone cannot serve as the basis of Israel's policy of targeted killing. Retribution and state interest do not necessarily go hand in hand. For example, in order to protect its security, Israeli leaders may decide to kill someone who seeks to attack Israel in the future, even if he has not actually done anything yet for which retribution could be invoked. Conversely, Israeli officials may decide to *refrain* from attacking someone who, despite richly deserving retributive justice because of responsibility for atrocities, is seen, nonetheless, as someone who should be usefully spared in the name of some greater state interest. (The abovementioned decision not to kill Yasser Arafat falls into this category.) Retribution can be in conflict with Israeli law, moreover, as the Supreme Court explicitly prohibits revenge as a basis for targeted killing. The reasonable fear that a policy determined by retribution will lapse into rogue lawlessness also limits its role in guiding targeted killing.

In order to meet these concerns, several limits on retribution as a driver for targeted killing need to be followed. First, the punishment must fit the crime. Retributivists emphasize that the response to an action must be proportionate to that action. Since Palestinian terrorists are bent on killing Israeli civilians, killing them in return (or those who send them on their missions) is an appropriate reaction. Only those bent on killing Israelis, however, should be subject to targeted killing. Second, the punishment must be focused on those who are actually committing the offense, with innocents spared. As the moral philosopher Judith Lichtenberg writes,

> while the principle of retribution says that the guilty must be punished, equally important is its demand that *only* the guilty may be punished. Punishment must be tailored to reach those who have done wrong and leave untouched those who have not.[41]

Thus are the key legal principles of distinction and proportionality reflected in retributivist thinking.

Targeted killing, when done properly, achieves this goal by focusing retaliation on the actual perpetrators of terrorism. To be sure, targeted killing that also produces innocent casualties weakens the retributive rationale. But given the greater risks of innocent Palestinians being killed by other forms of retaliation such as military strikes against urban areas, targeted killing best fits the retributive model of appropriate punishment for the guilty. Moreover, the Israeli Supreme Court has explicitly demanded independent reviews of targeting operations to make certain that appropriate steps are undertaken to protect the lives of the innocent. Finally, although this principle departs from pure retribution, targeting must be directed only against those who present an ongoing and *future* threat of terrorism, not those who may have committed terrorist actions in the past. Retribution then, becomes subordinate to the larger goal of combating terrorism.[42] Israeli guidelines are clear that targeting can only take place when an individual poses an active threat of launching a terrorist attack, not for punishment for past crimes. Israel can help avoid political and legal problems, in other words, by limiting retributive action to those retribution-deserving targets that *also* pose a threat cognizable under more prophylactic norms of military necessity well-established in international law.

Israeli security concerns should trump the desire for retribution in formulating a policy of targeted killing, and indeed operations such as the one that avenged the killing of the Israeli Olympic team have become increasingly rare. In place of such principally retributive policies are efforts employing targeted killing driven by the desire to protect Israelis from terrorist attacks, whether by those who have already launched assaults or those who are planning to do so. Nevertheless, the retributive impulse will never fully go away. Jewish history is too filled with unavenged wrongs to completely dismiss the desire for retribution among Israeli decision makers. Retribution may be subordinate to other, larger purposes when developing guidelines for targeted killing, but it is foolish to believe that it will play no role in making these life-and-death decisions.

Public opinion polls support the retributive goals of targeted killing. In the United States, for example, 65 percent of Americans polled supported assassinations—legally speaking, a far more extreme policy than targeted killing—in the Mideast, even though 40 percent said such actions would *increase* the likelihood that more attacks would be carried out against the United States. (Only 28 percent said assassinations would decrease attacks against Americans.) Similarly, only 19 percent of Israelis polled said targeted killings have decreased terrorism while 32 percent said it has done the opposite (37 percent believe it has had no effect on terrorism). And yet, more than 70 percent of Israelis surveyed in that same poll *supported* the policy of targeted killing. In both the United States and Israel, therefore, there seems to be a shared belief that targeted killing (or assassinations) will not enhance security, may in fact hurt security, and yet should *still* be carried out. Although the polls do not ask the question directly, the desire for retribution appears to be stronger than the quest for security.

Notwithstanding such complications, however, targeted killing supports Israel's interests because, among the possible responses Israel can mount against terrorism, it is the least bad option. As discussed, Israel has responded to Palestinian terror in several ways, all of which have major drawbacks. Checkpoints humiliate and inconvenience large numbers of the Palestinian population, producing resentment and seething hatred. The Israeli security barrier has swallowed up Palestinian territory and separated villagers from their land. Even Israeli raids merely to arrest militants result in civilian casualties. Responses such as these hurt innocent Palestinians in an effort to get at the guilty. Such alternative policies thus also have costs—both morally and in their potential to plant the seeds for future terrorism.

Major incursions into Palestinian territory to root out the terrorist infrastructure—that is, a more conventional type of military response—have been especially controversial, and costly. In the spring of 2002, for instance, the Israelis carried out two massive interventions producing thunderous international condemnation. Following the Israeli incursion of early March 2002, United Nations Secretary General Kofi Annan sent a letter to Israeli Prime Minister Ariel Sharon that was sharply critical of Israel's actions. The message of the letter, however, seems to suggest that more discrete, focused actions—such as targeted killing, though the Secretary General does not *quite* say this—would be preferable to the policy of mass intervention that Israel had undertaken. As the letter says,

> In the process [of undertaking the military incursions] hundreds of innocent non-combatant civilians—men, women, and children—have been injured or killed and many building and homes have been damaged and destroyed. . . . Israel is fully entitled to defend itself against terror. . . . It is incumbent on all parties to take urgent steps to de-escalate the level of violence. Israel should contribute to this effort by ensuring that the IDF uses only weapons and methods that minimize the danger to the lives and property of Palestinian civilians, in conformity with its humanitarian obligations. . . .[43]

Targeted killing is clearly a policy that "uses weapons and methods that minimize the danger to the lives and property of Palestinian civilians." Similarly, the *New York Times,* which had editorialized *against* targeted killings, seemed to endorse the policy when confronted with the bloodier alternative of full-scale Israeli military incursions. As a March 14, 2002, editorial stated,

> Israel must cut way back in its use of military force as Washington urges, and direct its actions against suspected terrorists rather than against the broader Palestinian civilian population. Its current methods are causing great civilian suffering and unnecessary humiliation. With Palestinian police failing to make arrests, Israel is justified in sending its own forces after specific terrorist suspects.[44]

A stronger defense of targeted killing would be difficult to find.

The far greater Israeli intervention into the West Bank following the March 28, 2002, Passover massacre—in which 30 Israeli civilians were killed by a suicide bomber—produced even more international opposition. This intervention saw a massive call-up of Israeli reserves as key Palestinian cities, including Jenin, Nablus, Ramallah, and Bethlehem, were attacked in an effort to destroy terrorism at its roots. However legitimate the intentions may have been, the operation produced casualties in the hundreds, including the deaths of 23 Israeli soldiers, and widespread destruction of civilian areas. Both sides acknowledged that innocents were killed, though they differed greatly on the numbers.

Inevitably, the Israeli action provoked harsh international criticism, to the point where only the United States stood by Israel—and even American support was called into question. The European Union, for the first time, threatened sanctions against Israel. Public opinion polls revealed greater support for Palestinians than Israelis in such countries as France, Italy, and England. The U.N. envoy to the Middle East, Terje Roed-Larsen, an architect of the Oslo accords, called the destruction wrought by the Israeli army "morally repugnant," and declared that "combating terrorism does not give a blank check to kill civilians." The Israelis found themselves defying President Bush's order to withdraw their troops "without delay," while American officials from the United States Assistant Secretary of State for Near Eastern Affairs William J. Burns to Secretary of State Colin Powell criticized Israeli actions.

Even *greater* destruction occurred during Israel's incursion into Gaza in December 2008. In response to repeated rocket attacks, Israel invaded Gaza with ground forces and air strikes, killing over 1,000 Palestinians, many of them women and children. Worldwide condemnation predictably followed, reinforcing Israel's status as a pariah among nations.

The Israeli incursions harmed noncombatant Palestinians to a far greater degree than the policy of targeted killing. According to the Israeli human rights group, B'Tselem, less than ten percent of Palestinians killed by Israeli security forces died as a result of targeted killing operations.[45] These Israeli incursions also produced much more intense condemnation of Israel throughout the world than targeted killing operations have produced. It is not the purpose of this essay to assess whether such operations were nonetheless justified. What is clear, however, is that Israel—to say nothing of the Arab people—must pay a large price when they occur. If Israel can achieve the security it needs through policies such as targeted killing that obviate the need for large scale incursions, Israel and the Palestinians both benefit.

As this review of Israeli policies suggests, it is not enough simply to oppose Jerusalem's policy of targeted killing. Critics of this approach need to provide an alternative. Aside from anti-Israeli extremists and pacifists, few counsel Israel to simply *endure* suicide bombing attacks and do nothing. The question then becomes what for Israel is the correct response to terrorism. For hawks, Israeli incursions into Palestinian areas are attractive options, though not so much to replace targeted killings as to supplement them. For Israel's legion of international critics, there are precious few suggestions for how Israel should combat terrorism, only condemnation of whatever armed response Israel undertakes—and complaints about nonlethal steps (e.g., the security barrier or the Gaza blockade) as well. In the end, targeted killing may deserve international approval in retrospect not so much for what the policy has inarguably achieved, but rather because it is less objectionable than the alternatives. Although this is clearly not a ringing endorsement, targeted killing may survive because it is indeed the last bad choice for a state confronted with the threat of terrorism.

Finally, it is worth briefly revisiting the question of the effectiveness of targeted killing. Some have argued that there has been no clear benefit from this approach, for record numbers of Israeli civilians were killed in terror attacks during the Second *Intifada* at the same time that targeted killings reached unprecedented levels. Logically, however, this mere coincidence does not answer the question, for it is open to argument what the cost of terrorism would have been *without* such killings. (Perhaps it would have been worse.) Moreover, even the absence of a short- or medium-term benefit does not necessarily mean that targeted killings have not, over the long haul, eventually undermined the infrastructure of terror constructed by the Palestinians. Indeed, in the last several years, the number of Israeli civilians killed by Palestinian terrorists has plummeted, and life has returned to something akin to normal in Israeli cities. Other actions such as the erection of the barrier and better relations with the Palestinian Authority have surely contributed to this decline of terrorism against Israelis. Nevertheless, it would also seem that, over time, the relentless elimination of the foot soldiers and planners of terrorism has played a major role in defeating or preventing Palestinian suicide attacks.

VI. CONCLUSION

It is my contention that, all in all, the policy of targeted killing is in Israel's interest. Terrorists on their way to operations against Israeli civilians are intercepted before they unleash their assault. Bomb makers and commanders are eliminated, with skilled replacements not always being thereafter available. Enemies spend time trying to survive rather than planning attacks, and potential recruits are discouraged from offering their support. Targeted killing signals the Israeli people, adversaries of Israel, and the world at large that those who seek to kill the innocent in an effort to spread fear for political purposes will pay the ultimate penalty. Retaliation helps mollify a restive Israeli population, enabling the government to remain in power and preventing social upheaval. Given the Palestinian inability or unwillingness to punish terrorists (at least during the *intifada*), the task of rendering justice to those who attack innocent civilians falls, if anywhere, into the hands of the Israelis. It is true that targeted killing can provoke murderous retaliation and expose informers, sometimes kills innocents, and preoccupies scarce intelligence resources. But, given the range of options open to the Israeli government to respond to terror, targeted killing remains the most effective way to save Israeli lives and the least morally problematic policy for Israel to follow.

NOTES

1. *See* B'Tselem, *Human Rights in the Occupied Territories*, <http://www.btselem.org/english/statistics/Casualties.asp>.

2. Samantha M. Shapiro, "Announced Assassinations," *New York Times Magazine* (December 9, 2001), at 54.

3. Nachman Ben-Yehuda, *Political Assassinations by Jews: A Rhetorical Device for Justice* (Albany: SUNY Press, 1993), at 99–104.

4. Ben-Yehuda, *supra*, at 304; Dan Raviv & Yossi Melman, *Every Spy a Prince: The Complete History of Israel's Intelligence Community* (Boston: Houghton Mifflin, 1990), at 122.

5. Raviv & Melman, *supra*, at 122.

6. *Id.*, at 247.

7. Ian Black & Benny Morris, *Israel's Secret Wars: A History of Israel's Intelligence Services* (New York: Grove Weidenfeld, 1991), at 272–277; Raviv & Melman, *supra*, at 189. Ali Hassan Salameh, the Black September operations officer who planned the Munich massacre and was the target of the Lillhammer attack, was eventually killed by a car bomb in Beirut in 1979.

8. Raviv & Melman, *supra*, at 276.

9. *Id.*, at 392.

10. Michael Eisenstadt, "Pre-Emptive Targeted Killings As a Counter-Terror Tool : An Assessment of Israel's Approach," *Peacewatch*, no. 342 (Washington Institute for Near East Policy, August 28, 2001), at 1.

11. Barton Gellman, "For Many Israelis, Assassination is Only as Bad as Its Execution," *Washington Post*, (October 12, 1997), at A01.

12. James Bennet, "Mideast Turmoil, News Analysis," *New York Times* (March 12, 2002).

13. Samantha M. Shapiro, "Announced Assassinations," *New York Times Magazine* (December 9, 2001), at 54.

14. Aaron Harel & Gideon Alon, "IDF Lawyers Set 'Conditions' for Assassination Policy," *Ha'aretz* (English Edition) (February 4, 2002); Shapiro, *supra*, at 54.

15. Christopher Dickey, R.M. Schneiderman, & Babak Dehghanpisheh, "The Shadow War," *Newsweek* (December 20, 2010), at 28–33.

16. For a similar view regarding dealing with terrorism in general, see Richard K. Betts, "The Soft Underbelly of American Primacy: Tactical Advantages of Terror," *Political Science Quarterly* (Spring 2002) at 33.

17. Ben-Yehuda, *supra*, at 304, 307, 318; Eisenstadt, *supra*, at 1; Avery Plaw, *Targeting Terrorists: A License to Kill?* (Ashgate: Burlington, 2008), at 59.

18. Eistenstadt, *supra*, at 2.

19. Daniel Byman, "Do Targeted Killings Work?" *Foreign Affairs*, vol. 85, no. 2 (2006), at 103. Only three Israelis were killed as a result of suicide attacks in 2007.

20. Brian Michael Jenkins, *Should Our Arsenal Against Terrorism Include Assassination?* (Santa Monica: Rand Corporation, 1987), at 4.

21. *See,* e.g., the account of a victim in "Israel's Assassination Policy: Extra-Judicial Executions," by Yael Stein, translated by Maya Johnston, available at <www.btselem.org>, at 6.

22. William Safire, "Sharon Enters Armistice Talks," *New York Times* (February 4, 2002), at A27.

23. Jonathan Snow, "Countering Global Terrorism: Lessons from the Israeli Experience," unpublished manuscript (undated), at 21.

24. Avery Plaw, *Targeting Terrorists, supra*, at 173–75. Plaw also made the point, however, that the studies did not support the view that targeted killing *increased* violence either.

25. Raviv & Melman, *supra*, at 194.

26. On the killing of informers, *see*, e.g., Joel Brinkley, "Israel Promises a Pullback as Death Toll Keeps Rising," *New York Times* (March 15, 2002), at A9.

27. Ward Thomas, *The Ethics of Destruction: Norms and Force in International Relations* (Ithaca: Cornell University Press, 2001), at 56.

28. *Id*, at 60.

29. Thomas, *supra*, at 60–62.

30. The *Rodef* injunction achieved notoriety when Yitzhak Rabin's assassin, Yigal Amir, claimed that Rabin was a *Rodef* (a pursuer) because his pursuit of peace through the Oslo process constituted a danger to the Jewish community. The overwhelming consensus of Jewish scholars was that this justification had no foundation. *See,* e.g., Rabbi Howard Jachter, "The Halacha of Rodef and the Rabin Shooting," *available at* <http//www.koltorah.org/ravj.rodef-rabin>.

31. Sefer Ha-Chukkim, "Basic Law: Human Dignity and Liberty," (1992) at 150; *Id*, at n. 13, Art. 8 (*cited in* Stein, *supra*, at 8).

32. Harel & Alon, *supra*.

33. Plaw, *supra*, at 84.

34. Thomas, *supra*, at 49; Tim Weiner, "Rethinking the Ban on Political Assassinations," *The New York Times* (August 30, 1998), at 3.

35. Harry Levins, "Military Experts Debate Moral Ramifications of Killing Leaders," *Post Dispatch* (August 3, 2001).

36. Tim Weiner, "Making Rules in the World Between War and Peace," *New York Times* (August 19, 2001), at A1 & A4.

37. Plaw, *supra*, at 139.

38. Henry Levins, "Military Experts Debate Moral Ramifications of Killing Leaders," *Nation and World* (August 3, 2001), at A10.

39. For one of the best accounts of Just War theory, *see* Michael Walzer, *Just and Unjust Wars* (New York: Basic Books, 1992).

40. Michael S. Moore, "The Moral Worth of Retribution," in *Punishment and Rehabilitation* (3rd ed.) (Jeffrie G. Murphy, ed.) (Belmont, California: Wadsworth, 1995), at 94, 97 (emphasis added).

41. Judith Lichtenberg, "The Ethics of Retaliation," *Philosophy and Public Policy Quarterly*, vol. 21, no. 4 (Fall 2001), at 5 (emphasis in original).

42. I am grateful to Avery Plaw for making this point. *See* Plaw, *supra*, at 205.

43. "Kofi Annan's Blunt Words Criticizing Israeli Tactics," *New York Times* (March 19, 2002), at A12.

44. "Israel's Unwise Offensive," *New York Times*, (editorial) (March 14, 2002), at A30.

45. *See,* e.g., the data provided by B'Tselem *available at* <htttp://www.btselem.org/english/statistics/Casualties.asp>.

Chapter 4

Guarding the Guards in the War on Terrorism

Yuval Shany

There is little doubt that the "war on terror" could bring about dramatic changes in the configuration of governmental power, and indeed much such power has been claimed in recent years. The novelty and magnitude of the threats presented by terrorist organizations such as *al Qaeda* and Hezbollah—and the need for swift and decisive response to this threat—have served as a justification for the executive branch of various governments to seek more power at the expense of the other branches, and to strike a new balance between security interests and individual rights.[1] Hence, members of the executive branches in the United States, United Kingdom, Israel, and other countries have asserted the necessity of subjecting terrorist suspects to some form of detention without trial[2] or extended pretrial detention;[3] enhanced interrogation techniques;[4] trials before special courts and commissions;[5] control orders and other restrictions on liberty, privacy, and property rights;[6] and, in the most extreme cases, extrajudicial killings.[7]

Since the application of all, or almost all, of these counterterrorism measures hinges on decisions by the executive branch or involves actions by the executive, their introduction following terror attacks or in response to terror threats typically entails the dramatic empowerment of that same executive—inevitably at the expense of other branches of government. For example, the introduction of administrative detention schemes can also be understood as a transfer of the power to detain from the civilian legal system, where courts occupy a central role, to a decision-making process largely controlled by the executive branch (often, by the military), and monitored only to a limited degree by the judiciary.[8] In the same vein, the resort to emergency powers may lead to the suspension of ordinary safeguards established by the legislature, such as *habeas corpus* or statutory limits on clandestine intelligence gathering.[9] Of course, such measures—separately and jointly—also have dramatic implications for the human rights of many individuals directly or indirectly affected by counterterrorism measures.

From a strict act-consequentialist perspective, it is difficult to contest that some or all of the aforementioned measures could be morally justified in extreme circumstances.[10] Since counterterrorism measures are designed to save human lives and to protect a number of additional human rights of potential terror victims, it may be difficult to reject under all circumstances governmental acts and policies that prioritize the rights and interests of victims over those of suspected terrorists. Even if we neutralize any notion of blameworthiness assigned to suspected terrorists[11]—a sensible proposition given that at the time in which right-infringements occur the persons in question are typically only terror suspects, not proven social deviants—the sheer numbers involved (i.e., the ratio between suspects and potential victims), may sometimes justify resorting to extreme right-limiting measures affecting the few, as a response to extreme threats directed against the many.

But this right-balancing analysis may be far too crude or simplistic in nature. In order to better understand the full costs of counterterrorism measures, we must also take into consideration the risk of chronic *misapplication* of such measures. We must, in other words, undertake a rule-consequentialist analysis of the costs associated with striking an inappropriate balance between security needs and human rights—or, put differently, between the human rights of suspected terrorists and those of their potential victims.[12] Significantly, the misapplication of counterterrorism measures appears to be a common occurrence; hence, its effects are far from negligible.[13]

Furthermore, since the executive—the branch most responsible for running the war on terror—is also, as I argue below, the branch most prone to abuse its discretion or apply it in a tendentious manner, executive branch empowerment under counterterrorism laws and practices may lead to more abuse and bias. Concomitantly, eroding the oversight powers of courts and parliaments over the executive is likely to result in the availability of fewer correcting mechanisms that could remedy instances of norm misapplication.[14] Thus, even if *act*-consequentialist arguments would support flexible rules that may authorize governments to curb, when necessary, the rights of terror suspects, *rule*-consequentialist arguments may point in the other direction, suggesting the need for more rigid rules and stronger corrective mechanisms.

Another "second-order cost" one needs to include in a cost-benefit analysis of counterterrorism laws and policies is the long-term impact of deviations from preexisting power-allocating configurations and decision-making procedures—departures which the war on terror facilitates. Such deviations may have a long-lasting impact on the prevailing constitutional equilibrium, could tarnish the reputation of some institutions of government, and might lead to erosion of public trust in their operation.[15] Thus, for example, requiring courts to conduct *ex parte* proceedings in terror-related cases may project an image of the judiciary serving as a mere "rubber stamp" for executive power.[16] This may, in turn, undermine the judiciary's reputation as a bulwark against infringement of individual liberties in other areas of its operation as well.[17] In the same vein, authorizing intelligence services to participate in terror-related criminal investigations in a manner deviating from past insistence on the erection of a "wall" between intelligence gathering and criminal prosecution may have long-term effects on the power of the executive, and could raise concerns about its ability to manipulate the legal system.[18]

In other words, a debate on the propriety of any counterterrorism strategy should arguably address not only the substantive merits of specific acts pursued under the existing policy—that is, whether the targeted killing of dangerous terrorists, or the torture of terrorists under "ticking bomb scenarios" can ever be justified—but also the policy's institutional or second-order implications. Following these introductory comments, Part I will identify three principal institutional settings in which key decisions in the war on terror are reviewed and discussed; I claim that in all of these settings the executive branch is subject to insufficient oversight and that, as a result, given the executive's structural incentives, an improper application of counterterrorism norms can be expected to occur.

Thereafter, Part II describes some of the political dynamics that cause the executive to perform inadequate right balancing, and which limit the ability of other branches of government to correct such decisions and actions. Part III then discusses the possibility of remedying the inadequate oversight procedures which are currently in place by way of strengthening international supervision over counterterrorism policies, clarifying the law governing counterterrorism policies—in particular, norms governing the invocation of the "armed conflict paradigm," where some of the most critical measures and decisions are adopted—and, most importantly, introducing absolute procedural and substantive norms, which limit the potential for norm-abuse by all involved branches of government.

I. THREE INSTITUTIONAL SETTINGS FOR REVIEWING COUNTERTERRORISM MEASURES

A. No Interbranch Review

In the aftermath of the terrorist attacks on New York and Washington of September 11, 2001 (a.k.a. "9/11"), President George W. Bush declared that the United States was in a "war on terror" of a global dimension.[19] One of the consequences of this particular framing of the administration's policy and the ensuing invocation of the president's war-making powers[20] has been the pursuit of significant parts of America's counterterrorism efforts by military and intelligence agencies subjected only to limited oversight by the other branches of government—and especially, to very limited judicial control.[21] The propensity to channel counterterrorism into less-than-fully accountable operative frameworks has been exacerbated as a result of the introduction of extraterritorial counterterrorism measures, such as the special *renditions* program (for sending detainees to other countries for interrogation and imprisonment) and the establishment of detention facilities outside U.S. territory, specifically designed to insulate such measures from judicial review.[22]

It goes without saying that many substantive aspects of these new counterterrorism policies have been criticized for unduly favoring security interests at the expense of individual liberties.[23] Indeed, key counterterrorism policies have been reversed over time as the result of public pressure inside and outside the United States, and rejection by the U.S. judiciary of the some of the executive branch's key positions on the geographical and other limits of judicial review.[24] Thus, it appears that the U.S. response to the 9/11 attacks supports the claim that empowering the executive and eroding individual rights tend to go hand in hand.

A similar attempt to insulate key aspects of the war on terror from judicial oversight can also be identified in Israel, where the executive has tried to allege that certain counterterrorism strategies, such as targeted killings or the utilization of Palestinian civilians to assist arrest operations executed by the military, are nonjusticiable.[25] One may also regard the adamant refusal of the Israeli Defense Forces (IDF) to expose its investigations of troop conduct in counterterrorism operations—such as "Operation Cast Lead" (a large-scale military operation which took place in Gaza between December 27, 2008, and January 18, 2009)—to meaningful external monitoring either in the form of an independent commissions of inquiry, or by way of cooperation with international bodies, such as the Goldstone Commission,[26] as indicative of the same impulse to press simultaneously for a new substantive equilibrium between security needs and individual rights, and to insist on the executive's exclusive power to strike such a balance without meaningful external review.

B. Limited Interbranch Review

When the first "line of defense" has been breached—i.e., if courts or political institutions insist on exercising their powers of jurisdiction over executive decisions and actions in a way that frustrates attempts to create an unreviewable institutional setting, then a second "line of defense" may be erected in the form of new institutional settings offering only limited review processes.

Note, however, that such an institutional configuration may also be created in a more proactive fashion at the executive's initiative, or with its acquiescence. The executive branch, for instance, may support the introduction of some review over its actions in order to attain the legitimacy benefits that accrue to institutional oversight and deflect pressures for full interbranch review, while minimizing, through insistence on the limited nature of the review process, the policy-constraining effects of such oversight.[27]

An example of the establishment of such a limited oversight scheme at the executive's own initiative can be found in the U.S. government's move to create a system of military commissions in the aftermath of 9/11.[28] Not only did the military commissions represent an *intrabranch* system of oversight—as opposed to the *interbranch* review process associated with channeling terrorism trials to the ordinary court system—but as originally constituted, the commissions were authorized to receive evidence inadmissible in ordinary courts' proceedings (e.g., hearsay evidence or evidence procured by coercive interrogations), to deny defendants access to secret evidence, and to restrict their right to legal representation.[29] In other words, the commissions' rules of procedure and evidence made it easier for the government to secure convictions, and thus limited the commissions' potential for constraining governmental policy options with regard to the incarceration of suspected terrorists.

The introduction, through an Executive Order, of Combatant Status Review Tribunals (CSRTs) to monitor executive decisions to indefinitely detain enemy combatants[30]—in response to Justice Sandra Day O'Connor's opinion in the *Hamdi* case[31]—and the enactment of the Military Commissions Act in reaction to the Supreme Court's judgment in *Hamdan,*[32] exemplifies *reactive* institutional reforms. After Justice O'Connor expressed discomfort with the executive's reliance on unreviewable "enemy combatant" designations, and following the holding of the majority in *Hamdan* that the president had exceeded his authority in creating military commissions that deviate in their procedures from statutory and international standards, the executive branch established CSRTs. At that point, Congress moved on to pass legislation authorizing the operation of military commissions—initially, with only few modifications to the original procedures set out in the president's Order—introducing only limited powers of congressional and judicial review over the CSRT procedures. Ultimately, the Military Commission and Detainee Treatment Acts facilitated the prolonged detention of suspected terrorists deemed by the executive to belong to or be associated with *al Qaeda* or the Taliban, with only limited interbranch review. In particular, both Acts explicitly sought to curb the power of civilian courts to exercise *habeas corpus* powers of review over the relevant executive branch decisions and procedures.[33]

Special court procedures have been devised for some terrorism-related liberty-restricting measures in other jurisdictions as well. For example, in the United Kingdom, the issuance of control orders restricting the freedom-of-movement and privacy rights of terror suspects has been subject to an *ex parte* judicial review process, in which the interests of the suspected individual are represented by "special advocates."[34] Such a system has been regarded by some House of Lords judges as leading to an unacceptable dilution of judicial oversight over executive decisions in this field.[35] An *ex parte* hearing system was also introduced in the Canadian Immigration and Refugee Protection Act.[36] (Only in 2007 were special advocates allowed to examine secret evidence on the part of the detained individual.[37]) In Israel, secret evidence has been relied upon routinely in administrative detention cases.[38] In addition, a 2006 amendment to Israel's Criminal Procedure Law permitted the conduct of criminal pretrial detention hearing in the absence of the accused.[39] In the same vein, political supervision over sensitive security measures is sometimes granted in both the United States and Israel to special legislative subcommittees that hold discussions in closed sessions.[40]

Of course, there can be perfectly good substantive reasons supporting the introduction of special trial and detention procedures in terror-related cases. International terror offences are notoriously hard to prove, especially given their cross-border dimensions, and the compartmentalized nature of many terror groups.[41] Hence, it may be impossible, or extremely difficult, to effectively curb some terrorism networks through the conduct of ordinary criminal trials.[42] Furthermore, the magnitude of the threat represented by terrorism could justify some right-balancing outcomes designed to protect society from terrorists on the loose, leading to a certain degree of procedural and evidentiary flexibility in criminal trials, or the utilization of noncriminal law detention frameworks.[43]

Still, bending existing procedures to accommodate terrorist prosecutions and other counterterrorism measures exacts certain prices from society. First, the new procedures introduced may curtail the ability of oversight bodies to effectively monitor counterterrorism policies. In particular, the loosening of admissibility-of-evidence rules in court cases and the dilution of some adversarial features of the process (e.g., permitting *ex parte* proceedings) reduce the reliability of the factual basis of the judicial decision in question. In addition, the new court procedures often represent a withdrawal from the "equality of arms" principle in court cases, and tend to under-protect the rights and interests of suspected terrorists in ways which throw into doubt the fairness and legitimacy of the process. Finally, the less-than-transparent nature of the new oversight procedures—trials with limited evidence disclosure, and detention proceedings subject to limited judicial review or *in camera* subcommittee hearings—limits public scrutiny of the monitoring bodies' decisions[44] and may even complicate these bodies' ability to publicly justify bad outcomes (e.g., ordering the government to release suspected terrorists, which the government claims to be dangerous). In other words, such counterterrorism policies' lack of transparency, which some of the post-9/11 procedural reforms exacerbate, raises the problem of *Quis custōdiet ipsōs custōdōs?*—that is, who will watch the watchmen themselves?—and increases the risk of abuse of discretion by the executive and/or the bodies reviewing their conduct.

What's more, the same problem of right and interest balancing described below—that is, the tendency of courts and parliaments to align themselves *substantively* with the executive in terror cases, and to ascribe excessive weight to security interests over individual rights—also afflicts their *procedural* balancing decisions, such as deciding on the admissibility of controversial evidence, or on whether or not to conduct *ex parte* proceedings.[45] As a result, if we perceive due process rights as relative rights that can be waived in the face of overwhelming security interests, there is considerable likelihood that they too will be chronically misapplied by organs of the state addressing terror threats and suspects.

C. The Limits of Interbranch Review

Even if counterterrorism measures undertaken by the executive are reviewed by courts and other oversight bodies that apply their ordinary oversight power vis-à-vis the policies in question, such a review is often characterized by deference extended towards the executive's positions. Such deference may be grounded in legal doctrines restricting the ability of courts to "second guess" executive discretion,[46] or it may reflect approval by the judiciary or the legislature of the executive's policy choices.[47] Either way, the result may be that the executive enjoys a "home court" advantage when defending its counterterrorism acts and policies before the country's own courts and parliament.[48]

A pro-executive bias is, however, not surprising. In fact, it would be extraordinary if national courts would habitually side with terrorist suspects *against* the national government that is fighting terrorists on the nation's behalf. So, while judicial review (and other forms of review) can work to mitigate *some* excesses on the part of the executive, it tends to support the executive's core positions on the war on terror.[49] Hence, at the end of the day, courts and parliaments may operate more to legitimize than to inhibit executive policies in the war on terror—thus ensuring a shift in the balance between human rights and security interests.[50]

For example, the U.S. Supreme Court in *Hamdi* required *habeas corpus* rights be afforded to suspected terrorists, but actually *reaffirmed* the power of the executive to detain enemy combatants—including U.S. citizens—without trial for extended periods of time (and perhaps indefinitely).[51] In the same vein, the Israeli Supreme Court in *Beit Sourik* ordered the removal of parts of the West Bank separation barrier constructed by the Israeli military, but confirmed the IDF's right to construct a barrier in occupied territories even in order to defend controversial settlements.[52]

The aggregate effect of these three typical institutional configurations governing counterterrorism measures—the removal of certain measures from all forms of review, the introduction of limits on review procedures, and the tendency of review bodies to defer to the executive and to support key aspects of its counterterrorism policies—is a cause for serious concern.[53] Simply put, the empowerment of the executive during the war on terror may invite abuse, and the existing review mechanisms do not appear to be capable of effectively curbing the power of the executive and ensuring that a proper balance between individual rights and security interests is maintained. To the contrary, limits on the power of review and excessive deference to the executive leaves terror suspects bereft of many important procedural and substantive protections. As noted above, the tendency of courts and legislatures to side with the government with relation to counterterrorism also adversely affects their reputation in the eyes of important local and international constituencies.

II. WHY IS STRIKING THE BALANCE IN TERROR CASES DIFFERENT?

The very reluctance on the part of the executive branch to subject counterterrorism measures to meaningful interbranch oversight, and the willingness of other branches of government to accept a more limited monitoring role, is already suggestive of the perceived exceptionality of the threat of terrorism—a perception stemming from the scope of violence that can be generated by terror groups, their robust organizational structures, and fanatic ideological bent—and of the view that the threat of terrorism justifies the striking of a new balance between individual rights and security interests.[54] Still, such perceptions are enhanced by some unique features of the politics surrounding terrorism and counterterrorism policies.

First, given the seriousness of the threat of terrorist attacks, the executive is under considerable public pressure to do "whatever it takes" to curb future attacks (and to punish the perpetrators of past attacks).[55] Hence, the executive is likely to adopt a task-oriented approach vis-à-vis the war on terrorism, and strong pressures are likely to be applied throughout the government bureaucracy to get the job done, even at the price of significantly eroding human rights protections.[56] To illustrate, the performance of a security service interrogator might be expected to be primarily measured on the basis of the number of attacks he or she has foiled, and not by the number of the interrogated detainee's human rights he or she observed or violated.

Second, what may be important in understanding the decreased public appetite for assuming security risks in the face of international terrorism is the perception of international terrorists as the ultimate *others*[57] and as *outlaws*.[58] The international terrorist is a foreigner, who not only speaks a foreign language but also holds a radically different set of values, which are anathematic to the societies he struggles against. (The latter feature, at least, characterizes "homegrown" fundamental terrorists as well.) In addition, the terrorist not only violates the governing law, but his campaign is also aimed at the destruction of the social and political order that this law sustains.[59] In this respect, terrorists can be distinguished from other criminals, including dangerous and reprehensible criminals, who do not challenge the very foundations of the legal, social, and political system of the polity in question.

The twice-removed position of the international terrorist—as a foreigner *and* an antisocial deviant—minimizes any empathy decision makers and the public at large may feel towards his or her human rights.[60] Hence, the executive branch may enjoy considerable popular support in its effort to curb the threat posed by terrorism through measures that radically restrict his human rights, and in taking the position that ordinary rules that apply to ordinary criminals both should not and do not apply to terrorists.[61] Furthermore, the general antipathy towards terrorists underscores the difficulty of protecting their rights in social institutions, such as parliaments and governments, whose policy decisions are inevitably shaped by the preferences of the majority within the given society.[62]

In addition, the characterization of terrorists as aliens and/or outlaws underlies the belief that counterterrorism laws and policies that derogate from ordinary practices employed by the executive branch—and which are not overseen by ordinary review mechanisms—can nonetheless be safely contained, being managed in a way that produces little if any "spill-over effect" to taint *other* areas of law enforcement.[63] But the ability to contain precedents generated in the field of counterterrorism may be merely illusory. In particular, once review bodies, especially judicial bodies following legal precedents, start adopting rulings that reflect a new equilibrium between individual rights and collective interests, such norms could easily lend themselves to application in many other contexts as well, thus also damaging rights protections in other areas.[64]

One may finally note another strong undercurrent of the opposition to strong judicial review and political oversight over executive counterterrorism measures: appeals, or excessive deference, to *professionalism*. Governments tend to argue that only the military and the other security services fully understand the nature of the threat of terrorism and know what counterterrorism measures would actually work.[65] The subtext underlying the claim for superior professional capabilities is that civilian judges or politicians are either two naïve, softhearted, or detached from the actual difficult realities to second-guess decisions of the executive in the field of counterterrorism, and that such nonexecutive officials should thus defer to the judgment of the more competent executive branch. (A related claim has to do with executive officials' special access to or experience with the classified information upon which some important counterterrorist decisions are taken.) In Waltzerian terms,[66] it may be posited that only the executive is capable of getting his hands "dirty" and confront the real dilemmas (or "tragic choices")[67] that the war on terror presents.

The perceived professionalism of the executive branch often accounts for the reluctance of judges, and officials involved in other review mechanisms, to assume responsibility for high-stakes and highly unpopular decisions *against* executive counterterrorism initiatives. A 2009 decision of the Israeli Supreme Court on the resumption of the punitive house demolition policy[68] perhaps exemplifies this problematic dynamic. Israeli secret service experts have claimed for years that demolition is an effective counterterrorism policy, although little if any empirical data has been presented in support of this hypothesis. (In fact, some indications point in the other direction.[69]) The Israeli Supreme Court, however—which had no independent tools for ascertaining the veracity of the causality claim—has been reluctant to prevent such demolitions, apparently as a result of the danger that if it did so, it would be blamed for undercutting the government's counterterrorism strategy.[70] The government's own lawyers, who may have also played a certain mediating role between the two action-inaction poles, also find it difficult to stand up to the full-time security officials in such matters. Since the Court is likely to side with the executive—indeed, the Israeli Supreme Court has approved throughout the years hundreds of punitive house demolition decisions[71]—the government lawyers cannot easily object to what the courts will most certainly approve, and risk being perceived as "holier than the pope." The result of this dynamic may be that demolition, a controversial counterterrorism measure of limited proven effectiveness, is routinely approved and applied.

III. REESTABLISHING MEANINGFUL SUPERVISION OVER THE EXECUTIVE

In the previous sections of this chapter, I have claimed that the war on terror tends to take place in institutional settings that are unlikely to ensure a proper balance between individual rights and security interests, and that the human rights of the terror suspects might therefore be chronically underprotected by the responding state's legal system. To summarize, certain counterterrorism measures taken by the executive occur wholly outside the scope of any form of review; other measures are only reviewed by (deliberately) weak review mechanisms; and domestic review mechanisms tend to defer to the executive and operate in ways that under protect the rights of foreign terrorists. How might one prevent such suboptimal decision-making and monitoring processes?

A. International Supervision

One way to break the vicious cycle of weak interbranch supervision—which, as we have seen, may lead to new unchecked excesses on the part of the executive—is to delegate greater monitoring authority to international actors, such as international courts, committees, international public opinion, international nongovernmental organizations (NGOs), and the like.[72] Unlike domestic branches of government, external actors do not always share the perception of the terrorists as the ultimate *other* and as existential threats to society.[73] Instead, they may sometimes view terrorists with some degree of *sympathy,* as fighting for a just cause, albeit through unlawful means. International actors also tend, at times, to be skeptical or suspicious of the real motives behind the domestic executive's draconian counterterrorism measures.[74] In short, external monitoring bodies may be more inclined than their domestic counterparts to assert jurisdiction over counterterrorism measures in some cases, and to second-guess executive discretion in the field of counterterrorism.

The invocation of international review mechanisms, in parallel to domestic review, is important because it may partly compensate for the accountability deficit associated with the operation of purely domestic oversight procedures. Moreover, the involvement of international actors may also embolden national review mechanisms—such as domestic courts—to assert more robust powers of review, on the grounds that their local review would be more palatable to local constituencies than international review, and may operate to limit the scope of the latter.[75] Indeed, one possible explanation for the fact that the record of UK courts in monitoring counterterrorism measures appears more impressive than that of their U.S. counterparts, is the "shadow" cast by the European Court of Human Rights (ECtHR) in its exercise of broad supervision over the UK legal system. The *potential* for ECtHR intervention, in other words, legitimizes intrusive exercise of "preemptive" jurisdiction by the local courts—which might not otherwise have occurred.[76] (The same dynamics may also explain the degree of UK parliamentary opposition to some of the government's more expansive counterterrorism initiatives).[77] In Israel too, one may explain the Supreme Court's increasingly robust exercise of supervisory powers over IDF and secret service counterterrorism measures—especially when comparing judicial responses to allegations of human rights violations during the Second *Intifada* (2000–05) to those during the First *Intifada* (1987–91)—at least in part as a result of the growing prominence since the late 1990s of foreign and international courts (especially in the criminal sphere) claiming jurisdiction over Israel and Israelis.[78]

Still, international supervision has its own array of deficiencies. International governmental and nongovernmental organizations, and international courts, suffer from their own kind of democratic and accountability deficits,[79] and may irresponsibly encourage societies afflicted by terrorism to assume unnecessary risks. Moreover, international actors are often hampered by lack of expertise and information about the specific challenges confronting targeted societies, and may produce under-informed and insensitive decisions.[80] Finally, the application of international review tends to be haphazard and uncertain, and has been perceived, in many cases, to be biased, if not extremely politicized, and thus illegitimate.[81] As a result, international supervision can only supplement and support—not substitute for—domestic review mechanisms. It is, in other words, only the *combination* of these two levels of supervision that can offer significant prospects of effective and legitimate curbs to executive excess in the war on terror.

B. Normative Limits on Executive Power Outside Judicial Review

Another possible direction that can be explored for restricting the ability of the executive to resort to excessive counterterrorism measures could involve the normative elaboration of criteria for derogating from ordinary monitoring procedures. This approach would not *deny* executive claims that special threats justify more permissive rules, but it would seek to ensure that the invocation of such circumstances—and the more flexible rules this entails—only occurs when this is truly warranted.

As noted above, the first institutional challenge that the war on terror presents is the inclination of governments to try to remove counterterrorism measures from *any* form of review by courts and other oversight bodies. Such attempts are facilitated by international and constitutional law norms, which reflect the basic notion that situations of armed conflict and emergency are qualitatively different than "peaceful" and/or "ordinary" situations, and thus merit special regulation. In particular, it has been suggested that the invocation of the laws of war to counterterrorism operations implies the "*dis*-application" of human rights law norms, including some of the procedural guarantees they would otherwise offer terror suspects.[82] Similarly, it has been argued that the invocation of exceptional powers available in states of emergency (under international human rights law and/or domestic constitutional law) enables the executive to suspend certain rights, including important procedural guarantees.[83] Indeed, Article 4 of the International Covenant on Civil and Political Rights (ICCPR) permits derogation in times of emergency from most human rights at times of war, including the right to liberty (Article 9) and due process (Article 14). Thus, the legality of controversial counterterrorism measures—things such as targeted killing (i.e., extrajudicial executions), prolonged detention without trial of suspected terrorists, and the referral of terror trials to special courts—may depend on the question of whether the situation at hand qualifies as an armed conflict, or meets the conditions for declaring a state of emergency.[84]

The paradigmatic shift from "peace" to "war," and from ordinary legal rules to the exceptional states of emergency, allegedly justifies a dramatic shift in the balancing formula between individual rights and security interests.[85] The normative approach to guarding against the unjustified assertion of such a shift would require executive officials seeking such additional powers first to demonstrate that the situation they are facing really *should* be properly categorized as an armed conflict (normally defined as a high intensity conflict between organized groups)[86] or a state of emergency (which, in the words of Article 4 of the ICCPR, "threatens the life of the nation"). If they can make such a showing, they would be authorized to invoke the extraordinary powers that such states convey. Otherwise, they would not. Although some terrorist campaigns would indeed meet these requirements—at least at certain points in time—other campaigns would probably fall short of them.[87]

The laws of war and human rights law—and actors applying them at the national and international level, directly or indirectly, through the mediation of parallel constitutional law norms—have an important role to play in elucidating the conditions for such paradigm shifting in the course of the war on terror, and in monitoring compliance with such conditions. In this regard, it is interesting to note the particular significance that Article 4 of the ICCPR assigns to monitoring the invocation of emergency powers. The article does not merely provide that a situation inviting derogation should meet a high threshold of gravity,[88] in addition to any other applicable constitutional criteria. It is also clear that the claimed derogation must also be *publically stated,* and notified to the other state parties to the Covenant—and the *reasons* leading to the adoption of specific derogating measures need thus to be communicated.[89]

Thus, in exchange for permission to shift into a paradigm in which there are fewer substantive and procedural protections for individual rights, states are expected to invite closer international scrutiny of their conduct and, in particular, of their decision to invoke the emergency paradigm. Still, the new equilibrium set by the ICCPR's Article 4 appears to have had little impact on state practice: state notifications have been scarce and sparse,[90] and have attracted limited reactions from international actors. In addition, the precise criteria governing the invocation of emergency powers remain unclear, and states have declared, in practice, emergency situations in a wide array of circumstances.[91]

This does not, however, undercut the importance of the ICCPR's basic insight: there is value in forcing states seeking emergency powers to more clearly justify their claims of necessity. Constituencies concerned about the erosion of individual rights protection in the war on terrorism should therefore focus efforts and attention on creating new norms, and on clarifying and monitoring existing norms governing the invocation of extraordinary executive powers, with a view to ensuring that paradigm shifting occurs only under well-justified circumstances. A better understanding by local and international review bodies of what constitutes an armed conflict or an emergency situation, for instance—either of which would justify right-restricting measures—could facilitate more effective review of executive determinations and subsequent measures.

Significantly, moreover, even if one were to accept that certain situations do justify an extraordinary response, some degree of ongoing monitoring may still be required as a doctrinal legal matter, under the theory that at least some procedural elements attendant to non-revocable rights are in themselves non-revocable, and would continue to apply under all circumstances.[92] For example, counterterrorism measures interfering with the right to life, such as targeted killings, should arguably be subject to special procedural requirements—such as the duty to collect and retain specific information *ex ante*, as well as to investigate *ex post* alleged cases of misapplication—in order to reduce the danger of abuse and facilitate after-the-fact accountability for decisions that are taken. Indeed, in both the *Targeted Killings*[93] and *Intifada Compensation* cases,[94] the Israeli Supreme Court has suggested that the substantive obligation to respect the principle of proportionality when restricting the human rights of suspected terrorists and uninvolved civilians (harmed as "collateral damage") entails procedural obligations, such as the duty to conduct investigations and to allow tort cases to be filed in local courts. There is also rich case law from the European Court of Human Rights, which ties substantive rights to procedural obligations even in times of armed conflict.[95]

As a result, a new international norm appears to be developing, if it has not emerged already, that requiring states engaging in counterterrorism measures that potentially violate human rights to always undertake some form of investigation, which should itself meet certain international standards (e.g., independence, credibility, and effectiveness).[96] Still, the specific contours of such an investigation and its remedial implications have not been fully worked out in the legal doctrine. Nor is there consistent state practice on the matter.[97] Consequently, this is an area of future development, which can serve to correct some of the accountability problems associated with current counterterrorism measures and campaigns.

C. Treating Certain Individual Rights as Absolute

(1) The Need for Absolute Rights

As described above, executive branch counterterrorism measures are sometimes afforded exceptional deference by the other branches of government. Such deference may attach to substantive outcomes (reflecting assumptions of a new equilibrium between individual rights and security interests), or to balancing decisions taken with relation to procedural matters, such as the creation of less demanding review mechanisms (marking, again, a new equilibrium between rights and interests). As we have seen, one possible explanation for the significant deference afforded by courts and other review mechanisms to the executive is the pressure of public opinion supporting the executive's war on terror and opposing attempts to uphold the individual rights of unpopular terror suspects in ways that may be regarded as hindering the counterterrorism effort. Another possible explanation I alluded to above is the expertise gap between the executive and other branches of government, rendering it difficult for lawyers and politicians to challenge the discretion exercised by professional counterterrorism experts in the executive branch.

If I am right that existing oversight mechanisms are inadequate, in the sense that they tend to lead to improper balancing decisions that are overly restrictive of individual rights, then one corrective strategy that can be considered is explicitly to move away, in some legal areas, from balancing formulas to absolute norms. By disallowing balancing in favor of absolute norms, one could reduce the problems of misapplication and abuse.

Admittedly, discretionary norms are normally superior to absolute norms, since they enable decision makers to precisely tailor legal norms to new and complex factual scenarios.[98] (For example, the proportionality principle authorizes decision makers to measure the specific gains and specific harms associated with any particular measure they consider taking, and to develop accordingly the most suitable policy.)[99] Nevertheless, discretionary norms may raise significant second-order problems, as they are open to chronic misapplication and abuse. Specifically, I have claimed above that the application of discretionary norms in the war on terror is afflicted by structural problems that lead to norm application in a manner tilted against the rights and interests of terror suspects.

Both at the procedural and substantive levels, absolute norms provide a partial remedy to the second-order problem identified above. By restricting the discretion of the executive and the review bodies overseeing its policies, the potential for abuse of the substantive norms in question and the review process attended to their application is reduced.[100] Moreover, absolute norms send a strong rights-protecting message and help insulate courts and other oversight bodies and functionaries (including government lawyers) from the rights-disadvantaging external pressures associated with the exercise of balancing discretion. Absolute norms also minimize any risk of spillover to other areas of law, and reduce the problems that relative norms present of "slippery slopes" within counterterrorism law.[101]

A key question raised in this regard involves the identification and delineation of the norms ought to be construed as absolute in nature. Which norms should be made absolute? Note that I do not make any deontological claim concerning moral imperatives that support the absolute nature of certain norms. (I accept that from an act-consequentialist point of view, rights are always relative in nature.) Instead, I make a *rule*-consequentialist claim informed by second-order concerns about the potential misapplication of counterterrorism norms under the existing institutional setting in place in many states. Still, the relative importance of the values protected by the right in question *is* an important consideration in designating certain norms as absolute in nature.[102] Other important considerations for designating a norm as absolute in nature may include available empirical data suggesting the chronic abuse of balancing formulas in certain fields of counterterrorism law and practice,[103] the feasibility and quality of supervision available to oversee the balance struck by the executive, and the probability that limiting the right in question presents an *exclusive* method leading to attainment of the desired security outcome. (Put differently, this last factor looks to whether the means/goal relationship is rational and that the goal cannot be attained through other, less offensive means.)[104]

When viewed from this perspective, one may criticize some Israeli court decisions pertaining to counterterrorism laws, which have failed to designate key norms as being *absolute* in nature, and commend other precedents which have indeed gone down that path. For example, the Israeli Supreme Court may deserve criticism for allowing the admission of evidence *ex parte* in administrative detention cases, without introducing a corrective mechanism that could adequately represent the interests of the implicated individual—e.g., by appointing a special advocate.[105] Tolerating prolonged deprivation of liberty on the basis of uncontested evidence appears to critically harm individual interests, to seriously dilute the quality of the monitoring process, and to damage the reputation of courts as being fair and evenhanded. An absolute procedural norm, however, always requiring some form of adversarial vetting of incriminating evidence in legal procedures, would have arguably helped courts in addressing these problems, without excessively curbing the government's counterterrorism policy options. Indeed, some of the aforementioned due process and fairness concerns have led UK courts to insist that even some due process elements relating to the special advocate procedure cannot be removed,[106] and other courts should consider following this example.

The review of executive decisions in Israel involving punitive house demolitions provides another example of an area of counterterrorism law in which the application of an *absolute* norm should have been considered. In particular, the importance of the values at stake—specifically, the abhorrent technique of collective punishment and the value of one's place of residence as a locus of attachment—and the lack of empirical evidence suggesting that the measure in question is particularly effective,[107] should have encouraged the Israeli Supreme Court to consider reading the prohibition on collective punishment under Israeli and international law as an absolute, rather than merely a relative norm, subject to right balancing in circumstances involving a highly charged public opinion.

At the same time, other decisions reached by the Israeli courts seem to be consistent with the general criteria I suggest for imposing *absolute* rules upon executive branch counterterrorism policies. For example, the Israeli Supreme Court's decision to totally bar the use of the "early warning procedure"—a detention protocol, applied in the West Bank, which permitted using Palestinian volunteers in arrest operations—cites as a principle concern the risk of abuse and misapplication of the procedure.[108] It is also encouraging that the Israeli Supreme Court has recently struck down as unconstitutional a piece of legislation authorizing the conduct of *ex parte* detention hearings for suspected terrorists, citing concerns about the negation of judicial review that *ex parte* proceedings entail—especially, when combined with other restrictions on the rights of the detainees.[109] Although the judgment in that case refrained from identifying the right to *habeas corpus* review as being absolute in nature, the position taken by the majority comes close to postulating that restrictions on the right to court appearance can never be justified.

To be clear, one should not construe norms as being absolute or relative in nature on a case-by-case basis, because such a norm-making strategy would defeat the purpose of insulating the resolution of certain questions from discretionary application. Instead, a systematic study of national and international norms governing the war on terror should be undertaken by constituencies interested in improving the protection of individual rights and executive branch accountability. Such analysis would powerfully advance efforts to advance claims about the absolute nature of certain rights (or right components) given the contemporary threats and the institutional settings in place in the relevant society. Such a systematic study—which should be based on both normative and empirical data—exceeds the scope of ambitions of the present chapter, but is important nonetheless.

As a rule of thumb, one may argue that given the dual role of due process rights—serving, as they do, both as independent individual rights and as instrumental rights supporting the proper application of substantive rights—there should be a particularly strong inclination to identify, within procedural norms, *absolute* elements that cannot be deviated from under any circumstances.[110] The introduction of absolute procedural norms is also important for protecting the integrity of courts and maintaining public trust in their fair and independent operation. Analogous arguments may be developed, as well, with regard to other review procedures—such as parliamentary oversight—which may also seek to maintain integrity and attract public trust.

(2) How Absolute Is Absolute?

Since my concern with the nature of norms is not deontological in origin, it is important to acknowledge that the absolute norms to which I refer above are absolute, one might say, in a relative sense only. First, they are not fixed in time and space. When the threat of abuse decreases—either because the effectiveness of a counterterrorism measure or strategy is proven over time, or because adequate institutional safeguards have been developed—the *raison d'être* of the move to absolute norms may disappear. (Because it is necessary to impose absolute norms in order to prevent abuse or misapplications of counterterrorist rules, if a particular application is shown to be effective and/or it becomes clear that there is little risk of abuse of this particular rule, the need for absolute checks diminishes.) In the same vein, the dangers of abuse and ineffective oversight may be stronger in some national constellations than in others.

Moreover, the absolute nature of the norm in question merely implies that courts and other decision makers are not entitled to maintain the legality of right-restricting measures. But some degree of flexibility could, and probably should, be retained withal, at the stage of norm *enforcement*. Hence, for example, in extraordinary circumstances—such as interrogations taking place in "ticking bomb" scenarios—officials charged with violating absolute rights might be excused from criminal liability, or at least lightly punished for expedient violations.[111]

(3) The Risk of Backlash

One serious risk associated with entrenching court procedures through the introduction of absolute norms—and, more generally, with making courts and parliaments into fora less deferential to executive branch counterterrorist expertise—is that of eliciting a substantive backlash. The rising costs of interbranch review for the executive, in other words, may create strong incentives for the latter to resist *all* review of counterterrorism acts and policies, or, as a secondary strategy, to divert review from interbranch to intrabranch mechanisms such as military commissions.

Although such concerns are valid, I believe that they do not present an overwhelming case against the introduction of absolute norms—at least, not against absolute norms governing the operation of the domestic judiciary. Simply put, the cost of corner cutting *by the judiciary* in terrorism cases would seem to be particularly high.

First, it is questionable whether special intrabranch procedures are inferior to interbranch procedures conducted under less-than-fully-acceptable due process standards. At least in terms of legitimizing executive conduct, circumscribed court proceedings leading to the *affirmation* of controversial policies may generate more harmful long-term consequences than the damage inflicted by less credible social institutions, such as military commissions or internal review boards. Moreover, the channeling of review powers to special procedures is more conspicuous, and thus more transparent, than small deviations from normal procedures performed by ordinary courts in the course of the war on terror. Hence, the avoidance of judicial review in some counterterrorism contexts flags such procedures as problematic in nature and helps in focusing the attention of rights-sensitive constituencies, inside and outside the country, upon the measures and procedures in question. Finally, by protecting courts from engaging in improper review practices, one may prevent harm to the courts' reputation and integrity. As a result, the risk of a backlash may be lower than the risk of long-term damage to the judiciary and the legal systems it serves.

IV. CONCLUSION

The war on terror does not only mean redrawing the balance between individual rights and security interests (which are, of course, also reflective of the individual rights of terror victims). It also implies a shift in the institutional balance of power, and the removal of executive branch acts and policies from meaningful oversight by courts and other social institutions, such as parliaments. These two developments are interrelated: the more the executive is likely to adopt counterterrorism policies which are underprotective of the rights and interests of terror suspects, the more it is likely to try to render courts and other oversight bodies incapable of serving as effective corrective mechanisms. In the same vein, the less effective interbranch supervision is, the more the executive will be emboldened to adopt individual right-restricting measures.

The rights-deprivileging nature of the dynamic between the branches of government involved in establishing, implementing, and reviewing counterterrorism policies is such that it may be necessary to resort to *external* correcting devices in order to guarantee a more appropriate substantive balancing formula. In the foregoing pages, I have offered a number of relevant suggestions, operating at both the institutional and normative levels, that would offer a corrective to executive branch excess: international institutions can be brought into the picture in order to offer some supplementary monitoring services; clearer norms can be developed to govern the exigencies under which supervision may be curtailed (e.g., to regulate the *invocation* of more executive-privileging crisis norms); and one could develop and articulate absolute norms—either procedural or substantive, or both—to prevent the exercise of discretion by state actors relating to important rights that tend to be chronically under protected.

These suggestions should be only the beginning of a discussion. Absolute norms, for instance, cannot resolve all of the institutional problems identified here. Nor did I clearly identify the norms that need to be absolutized, or address in a fully satisfactory manner the risk of overkill—that is, of a redrawing of the balance in a way that would under-protect *the state's* security interest. One should therefore regard this chapter as a call for more study and research designed to articulate, with much greater specificity and authority, which corrective measures could be introduced, under what circumstances they are needed, and what degree of rigidity they should have. Without more such work, one may expect executive branch overreaching to continue.

The author would like to thank Mr. Ohad Abrahami for his excellent research assistance.

NOTES

1. *See*, e.g., Seth Weinberger, *Restoring the Balance: War Powers in an Age of Terror* (Westport, Connecticut: Praeger, 2009), at 16 ("the executive branch is the arm of government best suited to commanding military operations . . . the war on

terrorism, in particular, demands both the flexibility and speed of decision making enjoyed by the president"); Philip Bobbitt, *Terror and Consent: The Wars of the Twenty-First Century* (New York: Anchor, 2008), at 242 ("Governments do claim more authority for law enforcement and for executive action generally in times of crisis and our liberties are correspondingly curtailed"); Eric A. Posner and Adrian Vermeule, *Terror in the Balance: Security, Liberty and the Courts* (Oxford: Oxford University Press, 2007), at 15–16 (discussing the view that "[d]uring an emergency, it is important that power be concentrated . . . Constitutional rights should be relaxed so that the executive can move forcefully against the threat"); Richard A. Posner, *Not a Suicide Pact: The Constitution in a Time of National Emergency* (Oxford: Oxford University Press, 2006), at 5 ("the more numerous or dangerous the nation's enemies are believed to be, the greater the pressure to curtail civil liberties in favor of executive discretion and unity of command, in order to enable the government to wield its great power more effectively"); *see generally*, John E. Owens & Riccardo Pelizzo (eds.), *The "War on Terror" and the Growth of Executive Power?: A Comparative Analysis* (London: Routledge, 2010).

2. *See*, e.g., Uniting and Strengthening America by Providing Appropriate Tools Required to Intercept and Obstruct Terrorism Act of 2001 [hereinafter USA PATRIOT Act], at § 412, 115 Stat. 272; Immigration and Refugee Protection Act, sec. 81 (2001, c. 27)(Canada) Incarceration of Unlawful Combatants Law, 2002 (Israel), at § 3, S.H. 5762 at 192.

3. *See*, e.g., Terrorism Act, 2006 (c. 11, UK), §§ 23 & 25; Anti-Terrorism Act 2004, § 7 (No. 104, Australia); Spanish Penal Code, § 509 (as amended in 2003) (permitting 13 days of detention *incommunicado* for terror suspects); Act No. 2003–239 of 18 March 2003 (France) (extending pretrial detention in terror offence up to six days).

4. *See*, e.g., U.S. Department of Defense General Counsel William J. Haynes, Action Memo to Secretary of Defense (November 27, 2002), <http://www.au.af.mil/au/awc/awcgate/dod/d20040622doc5.pdf>.

5. *See*, e.g., Military Commissions Act of 2006, 120 Stat. 2600 (U.S.); Incarceration of Unlawful Combatants (Amendment and Temporary Provision) (2008), 2178 S.H. 828 (Israel) (establishing a system of administrative detention before military courts at times of wide-scale hostilities).

6. *See* e.g., USA PATRIOT Act, *supra*, §§201–202, 209–210, & 215; The Prevention of Terrorism Act 2005 (c.2, UK), §1; "EU backs biometrics visa database" (June 8, 2007), *available at* <http://www.euractiv.com/en/security/eu-backs-biometrics-visa-database/article-164422>; *see also* Security Council Resolution 1267 (1999), UN Doc. S/RES/1267 (1999).

7. *See*, e.g., U.S. State Department Legal Advisor Harold H Koh, *The Obama Administration and International Law* (March 25, 2010), <http://www.state.gov/s/l/releases/remarks/139119.htm> ("a state that is engaged in an armed conflict or in legitimate self-defense is not required to provide targets with legal process before the state may use lethal force"); David Kretzmer, "Targeted Killing of Suspected Terrorists: Extra-Judicial Executions or Legitimate Means of Defence?" *European Journal*

of International Law, vol. 16 (2005), at 171, 173 (noting that Israel and the United States argue "that the killings were legitimate acts of war carried out as part of the state's inherent right to self-defence").

8. Many such limits have been introduced through rules of procedure and evidence that limit the power of the judiciary to second-guess executive acts and decisions, and/or reduce the burden of proof which the government incurs in the relevant legal procedures. *See,* e.g., Detainee Treatment Act 2005, §1005(e) (28 U.S.C. § 2241(e)) (barring the right of all courts, except the D.C. Circuit Court of Appeals, to review cases relating to the detention of aliens at Guantánamo Bay, and limiting the grounds for review by the D.C. Circuit); Incarceration of Unlawful Combatants Law 2002, at Art. 7 (reversing the burden of proving individual risk from the state to the incarcerated person).

9. *See,* e.g., the *habeas corpus* suspension clause of the U.S. Constitution (Art. 1, § 9); James Risenand and Eric Lichtblau, "Bush Lets U.S. Spy on Callers without Courts," *New York Times* (December 16, 2005) (describing the Bush Administration's extraordinary communication monitoring program conducted outside the scope of the Foreign Intelligence Surveillance Act); Basic Law: The Government, § 39 (Israel) ("In a state of emergency the government may adopt emergency regulations. . . . Emergency regulation may change, suspend or stipulate upon any law. . . .").

10. Eyal Zamir & Barak Medina, *Law, Economics and Morality* (Oxford: Oxford University Press, 2010), at 24–27.

11. For a discussion of the argument that terror suspects and terrorist groups should incur moral responsibility for their harsh treatment, *see,* e.g., Yuval Ginbar, *Why Not Torture Terrorists* (Oxford: Oxford University Press, 2008) at 139; Matthew Waxman, "Detention as Targeting: Standards of Certainty and Detention of Suspected Terrorists," *Columbia Law Review,* vol. 108 (2008), at 1365, 1439 ("erroneous bombardment and detention of civilians thought to be terrorists are both due in part to *al Qaida*'s refusal (for obvious reasons) to designate clearly its personnel"); Darrell Cole, "09.11.01: Death before Dishonor or Dishonor before Death? Christian Just War, Terrorism, and Supreme Emergency," *North Dakota Journal of Legal Ethics & Public Policy,* vol. 16 (2002), at 81, 98 ("it is the terrorists who are to blame for the deaths of innocent people they hide among").

12. *See,* e.g., Yuval Shany, "The Prohibition Against Torture and Cruel, Inhuman, and Degrading Treatment and Punishment: Can the Absolute Be Relativized under Existing International Law?" *Catholic University Law Review,* vol. 56 (2007) [hereinafter Shany I], at 837, 844; Oren Gross, "Are Torture Warrants Warranted? Pragmatic Absolutism and Official Disobedience," *Minnesota Law Review,* vol. 88 (2004), at 1481, 1496 ("distortion would result from biased focus on isolated cases that ignores long-term and systemic implications of particular courses of action"). For a criticism, see J.J.C. Smart & Bernard Williams, *Utilitarianism: For and Against* (Cambridge: Cambridge University Press, 1973), at 10 (referring to rule-utilitarianism as "rule worship"); Posner & Vermeule, *supra,* at 682 ("arguments for prohibiting all coercive interrogation because of concerns about the decisional capacities of officials in the legal system are unduly pessimistic").

13. *See*, e.g., *Al-Rawi & Ors v the Security Service and Secret Intelligence Service* [2010] EWCA Civ 482, at Paragraph 69 ("it is a melancholy truth that a procedure or approach which is sanctioned by a court expressly on the basis that it 'is applicable only in exceptional circumstances nonetheless often becomes common practice'").

14. *Cf.* Alpheus Thomas Mason, "The American Supreme Court Under Fire," *Jahrbuch des öffentlichen Rechts der Gegenwart: Neue Folge*, vol. 17 (1968), at 395, 403 ("Judicial self-restraint . . . is defensible only if one assumes the reliability, rationality and availability of the political process as a corrective against abuse of power. In the eyes of those who framed the constitution this was not a reasonable expectation"); Matthew Groves & H.P. Lee, *Australian Administrative Law: Fundamentals, Principles and Doctrines* (Port Melbourne: Cambridge University Press, 2007), at 48 ("Pursuant to the monopoly power conception of public power then, judicial review can perhaps be regarded as a kind of corrective mechanism that serves, in certain respects, to simulate the effects of competition upon the exercise of monopoly power").

15. *See*, e.g., James P Pfiffner, *Power Play: The Bush Presidency and the Constitution* (Washington: Brookings Institution, 2008), at 245 ("Insofar as President Bush . . . refused to acknowledge the constitutional limits on his executive authority, he undermined two of the fundamental principles upon which the United States was established: the rule of law and the Constitution"); Nadine Strossen, "Terrorism's Toll on Civil Liberties," in *The Trauma of Terrorism: Sharing Knowledge and Shared Care—an International Handbook* (Yael Danieli *et al.*, eds.) (London: Routledge, 2005), at 365, 373; *but see* John E. Owens, "Presidential Aggrandizement and Congressional Acquiescence in the 'War on Terrorism': A New Constitutional Equilibrium?," in *America's "War on Terrorism": New Dimensions in U.S. Government and National Security* (John E. Owens and John W Dumbrell, eds.) (Lanham, Maryland: Lexington Books, 2008) 25, 29 ("[B]y late 2007, the balance of congressional-presidential relations looked remarkably similar to that during the previous period of single-party government").

16. *See*, e.g., James Hugessen, "Watching the Watchers: Democratic Oversight," in *Terrorism, Law and Democracy* (David Daubney et al., eds.) (Montréal: Éditions Thémis, 2002), at 386 (describing the role of the Canadian judiciary in *ex parte* proceedings under the Immigration and Refugee Protection Act as a "fig leaf").

17. *See*, e.g., *AF (No 3) & Ors v Secretary of State for the Home Department* [2009] UKHL 28, at 63 (per Lord Phillips) ("Resentment will understandably be felt, not merely by the controlee but by his family and friends, if sanctions are imposed on him on grounds that lead to his being suspected of involvement in terrorism without any proper explanation of what those grounds are. Indeed, if the wider public are to have confidence in the justice system, they need to be able to see that justice is done rather than being asked to take it on trust"); MCR [Misc. Criminal Request] 8823/07 *v. State of Israel* , judgment (February 11, 2010) [hereinafter *Anonymous* Case], at Paragraph 17 (opining that *ex parte* detention extension proceedings undermine public trust in the judicial system).

18. *See*, e.g., Norman C Bay, "Paradigm Shifts, Executive Power, and the War on Terror," *Enemy Combatants, Terrorism and Armed Conflict Law: A Guide to the Issues*

(David K. Linnan, ed.) (Westport, Connecticut: Praeger, 2008), at 67, 77 ("lowering the wall between foreign and domestic intelligence creates the risk that foreign intelligence and methods used to acquire foreign intelligence will be used for domestic law enforcement purposes in an effort to circumvent legal safeguards that would otherwise apply, even in cases unrelated to international terrorism"); Mikhail Rykhtik, "Asymmetric Threats and Counter-Terrorism Strategies in Russia," in *National Counter-Terrorism Strategies: Legal, Institutional and Public Policy Dimensions in the US, UK, France, Turkey and Russia* (Andrei S Makarychev and Robert W Orttung, eds.) (Washington, D.C.: IOS Press, 2006), at 165, 174 ("critics say that anti-terror rhetoric provides an excuse for the significant expansion of federal investigative authority").

19. *See,* e.g., Office of the White House Press Secretary, "President Bush Releases National Strategy for Combating Terrorism," February 14, 2003) *available at* <http://georgewbush-whitehouse.archives.gov/news/releases/2003/02/20030214–7.html> ("The war against global terror will be hard and long").

20. Authorization for Use of Military Force (September 18, 2001), Public Law 107–40.

21. *See,* e.g., Report of the Special Rapporteur on Extrajudicial, Summary or Arbitrary Executions, Philip Alston: Study on Targeted Killings, UN Doc. A/HRC/14/24/Add.6 (2010), at Paragraph 87 (criticizing lack of transparency and oversight over U.S. and other states' targeted killing policies); Richard H. Kohn, "Using the Military at Home: Yesterday, Today, and Tomorrow," *Chicago Journal of International Law,* vol. 4 (2003), at 165, 181–82 (discussing the post-9/11 expansion of government authority in the United States without judicial oversight).

22. *See,* e.g., Joseph Margulies, *Guantánamo and the Abuse of Presidential Power* (New York: Simon & Schuster, 2007), at 224 ("[The Administration] deliberately created a network of prisons beyond the law in order to evade existing legal constraints."); Heinz Duthel, *Who Watch the Watchman?* (Lulu: 2008), at 187 ("The central effect of the post 9/11 rendition programme has been to place captured terrorist suspects outside the reach of any judicial system and keep them there.").

23. *See,* e.g., Seth Weinberger, "Presidential War Powers in a Never-Ending 'War,'" *ILSA Journal of International and Comparative Law,* vol. 13 (2006), at 221, 239; Erwin Chemerinsky, "Civil Liberties and the War on Terrorism," *Washburn Law Journal,* vol. 45 (2005), at 1, 19.

24. *See,* e.g., John O. McGinnis, "Losing the Law War: The Bush Administration's Strategic Errors," *Georgia State University Law Review,* vol. 25 (2008), at 377, 395–396; Jenny S. Martinez, "Process and Substance in the 'War on Terror,'" *Columbia Law,* vol. 108 (2008), at 1013, 1028.

25. Initially, the Supreme Court of Israel accepted the position that the targeted killing policy is nonjusticiable. H.C.J. 5872/01, *Barrake v. Prime Minister,* 56(3) P.D. 1 (in Hebrew). This ruling was reversed in the 2006 *Targeted Killings* judgment of the Supreme Court. *See* H.C.J. 769/02 *Public Committee against Torture in Israel v. Government of Israel,* 46 ILM (2007) [hereinafter PCATI Case], at 375.

26. *See,* e.g., Israeli Ambassador Aharon Leshno-Yaar, letter to Justice Richard J.Goldstone(July2,2009),*availableat*<http://www.mfa.gov.il/MFA/Foreign+Relations/

Israel+and+the+UN/Issues/Letter_from_Israel_Ambassador_Leshno-Yaar_to_Goldstone_2-Jul-2009.htm>.

27. Ariel L Bendor, "Investigating the Executive Branch in Israel and in the United States: Politics as Law, The Politics of Law," *Miami Law Review,* vol. 54 (1999–2000), at 193, 229–230.

28. U.S. Department of Defense, Military Commissions Order No. 1, Procedures for Trials by Military Commissions of Certain Non-United States Citizens in the War Against Terrorism (March 21, 2002), *available at* <http://www.defenselink.mil/news/Mar2002/d20020321ord.pdf>.

29. *But see* Harold H. Koh, "The Obama Administration and International Law," remarks at the Annual Meeting of the American Society of International Law (March 25, 2010) *available at* <http://www.state.gov/s/l/releases/remarks/139119.htm> (discussing changes in the 2009 Military Commissions Act).

30. U.S. Deputy Secretary of Defense, Order Establishing Combatant Status Review Tribunals (July 7, 2004), <http://www.defense.gov/news/Jul2004/d20040707review.pdf>. (This order, however, has been implicitly endorsed by the Detainee Treatment Act of 2005.)

31. *Hamdi v. Rumsfeld, 542 U.S. 507, 538 (2004)* ("There remains the possibility that the standards we have articulated could be met by an appropriately authorized and properly constituted military tribunal").

32. *Hamdan v. Rumsfeld,* 548 U.S. 557 (2006).

33. Military Commission Act of 2006, § 9 (10 U.S.C. § 950g); Detainee Treatment Act, 2005, § 1005(e)(2)(C); *see also* Benjamin Wittes, *Law and the Long War: The Future of Justice in the Age of Terror* (New York: Penguin Books, 2008) 123 ("judicial review has so far amounted to so little in practical terms"). One should note that the Supreme Court struck down in *Boumediene* as unconstitutional the *habeas corpus* sections of the MCA and DTA. *See Boumediene v. Bush,* 553 U.S. 723 (2008).

34. United Kingdom, Prevention of Terrorism Act 2005 (c.2), Section 11—Schedule, Part 7(1).

35. *See,* e.g., *AF (No 3),* at 84 (per Lord Hope) ("for a judge to hold that a hearing in which the party affected has had no opportunity to answer is a fair hearing negates the judicial function which is crucial to the controlled order system").

36. Immigration and Refugee Protection Act, § 78(e). This provision was repealed in 2008.

37. Canada, Immigration and Refugee Protection Act, S.C. 2001, c.27, s. 85.4(1) (2008, c.3, s.4).

38. Emanuel Gross, "Human Rights in Administrative Proceedings: A Quest for Appropriate Evidentiary Standards," *California Western International Law Journal,* vol. 31 (2001), at 215, 224; *see also* <http://www.law.idf.il/603–3160-en/Patzar.aspx> ("administrative detention measure can be used only on an exceptional basis when the evidence in existence is clear, concrete and trustworthy, but for reasons of confidentiality and protection of intelligence sources, cannot be presented as evidence in ordinary criminal proceedings").

39. Criminal Procedure Law (Detainee Suspected of a Security Offence) (Temporary Order), 5766–2006, 2059 S.H. 364, 365, s.5. The amendment was nullified by the Supreme Court of Israel in the *Anonymous* Case.

40. For example, the U.S. administration confidentially notified only the Congress leadership about its extrajudicial eavesdropping program. Lionel Beehner & Greg Bruno, "Council on Foreign Relations Backgrounder: NSA Eavesdropping" (January 28, 2008), <http://www.cfr.org/publication/9763/>. In Israel, a recent law governing detention of suspects in security offences (Criminal Procedure (Enforcement Powers—Detention) (Detainee Suspected of Security Offense) (Temporary Order) 2006) was passed after closed hearings in the Knesset subcommittee on secret matters.

41. *See*, e.g., Kelly Moore, "The Role of Federal Criminal Prosecutions in the War on Terrorism," *Lewis & Clark Law Review*, vol. 11 (2007), at 837.

42. *See*, e.g., M. Cherif Bassiouni, "Effective National and International Action against Organized Crime and Terrorist Criminal Activities," *Emory International Law Review*, vol. 4 (1990), at 9, 42.

43. *See*, e.g., Posner, *supra*, at 147.

44. *See*, e.g., Rita Galsionov, "In Furtherance of Transparency and Litigants' Rights: Reforming the State Secret Privilege," *George Washington Law Review*, vol. 77 (2008–2009), at 458, 474 *et. seq*.

45. *See* Cass R. Sunstein, "Judging National Security Post-9/11: An Empirical Investigation," *2009 Supreme Court Review* (2008), at 269, 271 ("The overall rate of invalidation is low. The government loses only 15% of the litigated cases—a lower figure than in almost all other domains of federal law.").

46. *See*, e.g., *A. v. Secretary of State for the Home Dep't [2004] QB 335* (C.A.), Paragraph 40 of Lord Woolf's opinion ("decisions as to what is required in the interest of national security are self-evidently within the category of decisions in relation to which the court is required to show considerable deference to the Secretary of State because he is better qualified to make an assessment as to what action is called for"); H.C.J. 2056/04 *Beit Sourik Village Council v. Gov't of Israel, International Legal Materials*, vol. 43 (2004), at 1099, 1116 ("We, Justices of the Supreme Court, are not experts in military affairs. We shall not examine whether the military commander's military opinion corresponds to ours—to the extent that we have an opinion regarding the military character of the route. So we act in all questions which are matters of professional expertise, and so we act in military affairs as well. All we can determine is whether a reasonable military commander would have set out the route as this military commander did."); *Chae Chan Ping v. United States* (The Chinese Exclusion Case), 130 U.S. 581, 606 (1989) ("The government, possessing the powers which are to be exercised for protection and security, is clothed with authority to determine the occasion on which the powers shall be called forth; and its determination . . . is conclusive upon the judiciary."); *but see A. v Secretary of State for the Home Department, [2005] 2 AC 68 (H.L.)*, Paragraph 44 of Lord Bingham of Cornhill opinion (" . . . [T]he duty of the courts to protect convention rights, would in my view be emasculated if a judgment at first instance on such a question were conclusively to preclude any further review. So would excessive deference, in a field involving indefinite detention without charge or trial, to ministerial decision.").

47. *See,* e.g., *Al-Bihani v. Obama, 590 F.3d 866,* 873 (2010) ("Viewed in full, the facts show Al-Bihani was part of and supported a group—prior to and after September 11—that was affiliated with *al Qaeda* and Taliban forces and engaged in hostilities against a U.S. Coalition partner. Al-Bihani, therefore, falls squarely within the scope of the President's statutory detention powers."); HCJ 9132/07 *Al Bassiouni* 9132/07 *Al Bassiouni Ahmad v. Prime Minister of Israel,* ILDC 883 (IL 2008), at Paragraph 11 (per Beinisch) (" . . . [T]he State of Israel has no obligation to allow passage of an unlimited amount of electricity and fuel into Gaza strip in circumstances in which some of it is in fact being used by the terrorist organizations for the objective of striking at the civilian population of Israel.").

48. Sunstein, *supra,* at 271.

49. David Cole, "Judging the Next Emergency: Judicial Review and Individual Rights in Times of Crisis," *Michigan Law Review,* vol. 101 (2003), at 2565, 2566.

50. *Cf.*, Ronen Shamir, "'Landmark Cases' and the Reproduction of Legitimacy: The Case of Israel's High Court of Justice," *Law & Society Review,* vol. 24 (1990), at 781.

51. *Hamdi, v. Rumsfeld,* 542 U.S. 507 (2004).

52. *Beit Sourik, supra.*

53. *See,* e.g., Michael Welch, "Trampling Human Rights in the War on Terror: Implications to the Sociology of Denial," *Critical Criminology,* vol. 12 (2004), at 1, 5–11.

54. *See,* e.g., Victor V. Ramraj, "Terrorism, Risk-Perception and Judicial Review," in *Global Anti-Terrorism Law and Policy* (Victor V. Ramraj *et al.*, eds.) (Cambridge: Cambridge University Press, 2005), at 107, 114–115.

55. *See,* e.g., H. L. Pohlman, *Terrorism and the Constitution: The Post 9/11 Cases* (Plymouth: Rowman & Littlefield, 2008), at 13 ("One major concern with leaving the issue of balancing civil liberties and national security during wartime to one of the two political branches of the federal government, or to both of them together, is that they are subject to shifts of public opinion, including the hysteria that all too often accompanies wartime crises and emergencies. For that reason, both the president and Congress are arguably less well suited for performing this responsibility than the unelected federal judiciary.").

56. *See,* e.g., Darius Rejali, *Torture and Democracy* (Princeton, New Jersey: Princeton University Press, 2007), at 455 ("The State endorses torture for either intimidation or information. Once it does so, the incentives are that torture 'is carried out with positive probability.'").

57. *See,* e.g., Adrian Theodoor Peperzak, *To the Other: An Introduction to the Philosophy of Emmanuel Levinas* (West Lafayette, Indiana: Purdue University Press, 1993), at 19–20 ("Another comes to the fore as *other* . . . when the other's invasion of my world destroys my empire.").

58. *See,* e.g., Slavoj Žižek, *For They Know Not What They Do: Enjoyment as a Political Factor* (2nd ed.) (Brooklyn, New York: Verso Books, 2002), at 204.

59. *See,* e.g., Kenneth Anderson, "What to Do with Bin-Laden and *Al-Qaeda* Terrorists? A Qualified Defense of Military Commissions and U.S. Policy on Detainees at Guantánamo Bay Naval Base," *Harvard Journal of Law & Public Policy,* vol. 25

(2001–2002), at 591, 610; Richard Jackson, "Security, Democracy and the Rhetoric of Counter-Terrorism," *Democracy and Security,* vol. 1 (2005), at 147 (appearing on page 2 of the online version, *available at:* <http://cadair.aber.ac.uk/dspace/bitstream/2160/1962/1/Security,%20Democracy.pdf>).

60. *See,* e.g., Lynn M. Kuzma, "Security versus Liberty: 9/11 and the American Public," *in The Politics of Terror: The U.S. Response to 9/11* (William Crotty, ed.) (Boston: Northeastern University Press, 2004), at 160, 163.

61. *See,* e.g., Victor M. Hansen & Lawrence Friedman, *The Case for Congress: Separation of Powers and the War on Terror* (Farnham, Surrey: Ashgate, 2009), at 84 (discussing the argument that "representatives of *al-Qaeda* in custody, simply did not deserve the protections we afford criminal defendants").

62. *See,* e.g., Fiona de Londras & Fergal F. Davis, "Controlling the Executive in Times of Terrorism: Competing Perspectives on Effective Oversight Mechanisms," *Oxford Journal of Legal Studies,* vol. 30 (2010), at 19, 36–37.

63. *See,* e.g., David Jenkins, "In Support of Canada's Anti-Terrorism Act: A Comparison of Canadian, British and American Anti-Terrorism Law," *Sask Law Review,* vol. 66 (2003), at 419, 453.

64. *See,* e.g., John Ferejohn & Pasquale Pasquino, "The Law of the Exception: A Typology of Emergency Powers," *International Journal of Constitutional Law,* vol. 2 (2004), at 210, 235.

65. *See,* e.g., Ramraj, *supra,* at 115–16 ("It can be argued that when it comes to threats to national security, the executive, with the advice of the security intelligence community and other security experts within the bureaucracy, is in a much better position to assess and respond to the risk of terrorism than the public, the legislature or the judiciary.").

66. *See* Michael Walzer, "Political Action: The Problem of Dirty Hands," *Philosophy & Public Affairs,* vol. 2 (1973), at 160, 161–162.

67. *See* Posner & Vermeule, *supra,* at 187.

68. H.C.J. 9353/08, *Abu Dahim v. IDF Home front Commander,* judgment of January 5, 2009.

69. In fact, some anecdotal evidence suggests that house demolitions are counterproductive. *See,* e.g., Aryeh Shalev, *The Intifada: Causes and Effects* (Jerusalem: Jerusalem Post Press, 1990), at 127–131 (in Hebrew). One may speculate that the position of the security service reveals an "action bias" because its officials are pressed to respond to terrorist acts, and because no response is perceived by the general public as worse than an under-effective response. For a possibly interesting analogy, *see* Michael Bar-Eli et al., "Action Bias Among Elite Goal Keepers: The Case of Penalty Kicks," *Journal of Economic Psychology,* vol. 28 (2007), at 606 (arguing that an "action bias" leads goalkeepers to jump to one side or another of the soccer goal in order to save a penalty kick, even though the most rational response may actually be to remain in the center of the goal).

70. Thus, whereas the security services may be afflicted by an action bias, the Court may suffer from an "omission bias." For a general discussion of omission bias, *see* Jonathan Baron & Ilana Ritov, "Omission Bias, Individual Differences

and Normality," *Organizational Behavior and Human Decision Processes,* vol. 94 (2004), at 74.

71. *See* David Kretzmer, *The Occupation of Justice: The Supreme Court of Israel and the Occupied Territories* (Albany, NY: SUNY Press, 2002), at 145 *et seq.*

72. *See,* e.g., Philip Alston et al., "The Competence of the UN Human Rights Council and its Special Procedures in Relation to Armed Conflicts: Extrajudicial Executions in the 'War on Terror,'" *European Journal of International Law,* vol. 19 (2008), at 183, 207–209.

73. *See,* e.g., Geoffrey Robertson, "Fair Trials for Terrorists?" in *Human Rights in the "War on Terror"* (Richard Ashby Wilson, ed.) (Cambridge: Cambridge University Press, 2005), at 169, 173 *et seq.*

74. *See,* e.g., *Legal Consequences of the Construction of a Wall in the Occupied Palestinian Territory,* 2004 ICJ 136, 184 ("Whilst the Court notes the assurance given by Israel that the construction of the wall does not amount to annexation and that the wall is of a temporary nature (see paragraph 116 above), it nevertheless cannot remain indifferent to certain fears expressed to it that the route of the wall will prejudge the future frontier.").

75. For example, the rule of complementarity under the Rome Statute provides that the International Criminal Court will be barred from assuming jurisdiction over cases pursued effectively and in good faith by local judiciaries. *See* Rome Statute of the International Criminal Court (July 17, 1998), at Art. 17, 2187 U.N.T.S. 90.

76. *See,* e.g., *A. v. Secretary of State for Home Affairs,* [2005] 2 AC 68; *Secretary of State for Home Affairs v. MB,* [2008] AC 440; *Secretary of State for Home Affairs v. JJ,* [2008] AC 385.

77. *See,* e.g., Joint Committee on Human Rights, *Twenty-First Report* (2008) at Paragraph 43–44 (citing ECtHR case law to support opposition to a 42-day detention without charges of terror suspects).

78. *See,* e.g., PCATI Case, *supra,* at Paragraph 53 (". . . [T]he types of questions examined by this Court have also been decided by international courts. International law dealing with the army's duties toward civilians during an armed conflict has been discussed, for example, by the international criminal tribunals for the former Yugoslavia and Rwanda. . . . These courts have examined the legal aspects of the conduct of armies. Why can't an Israeli court perform that same examination? Why do those questions, which are justiciable in international courts, cease to be justiciable in national tribunals?"); *see also* Orna Ben Naftali, "A Judgment in the Shadow of International Criminal Law: the Decision of the Israeli High Court of Justice on the Legality of Targeted Killings," *Journal of International Criminal Justice,* vol. 5(2) (2007), at 322.

79. *See generally,* Thomas D. Zweifel, *International Organizations and Democracy: Accountability, Politics and Power* (Boulder, Colorado: Lynne Rienner, 2006).

80. Indeed, some of the criticism leveled against the United Nations fact-finding mission led by Justice Richard Goldstone investigating human rights violations committed during Israel's counterterrorism operation in Gaza (December 27,

2008–January 18, 2008) has focused on the limited understanding of the mission members of military operations and the historical context of the conflict. *See*, e.g., Alan Dershowitz, "The Case against the Goldstone Report: A Study in Evidentiary Bias," Harvard Public Law Working Paper No. 10–26, at 49 *available at* <http://ssrn.com/abstract=1542897> (suggesting that mission members lacked the expertise to "assess credibility, determine intentions, and arrive at both legal and political conclusions").

81. *See*, e.g., *id.*, at 49 (accusing the Goldstone fact-finding mission of one-sidedness and bias); *see also* U.S. House of Representatives Resolution 867 (November 3, 2009), available at <http://frwebgate.access.gpo.gov/cgi-bin/getdoc.cgi?dbname=111_cong_bills&docid=f:hr867eh.txt.pdf>.

82. *See*, e.g., The second and third periodic reports of the United States of America to the Human Rights Committee, U.N. Doc. CCPR/C/USA/3 (2005) at Paragraph 130 ("The United States also notes that the legal status and treatment of such persons is governed by the law of war."); Replies of the Government of Israel to the List of Issues (CCPR/C/ISR/Q/3/) to be taken up in connection with the consideration of the third periodic report of Israel, UN Doc. CCPR/C/ISR/Q/3/Add.1 (2010), at 3 (" . . . [I]n the current state of international law and state-practice worldwide, it is Israel's view that these two systems-of-law, which are codified in separate instruments, nevertheless remain distinct and apply in different circumstances.").

83. *See*, e.g., Derogation by the State of Israel from the International Covenant on Civil and Political Rights (October 3, 1991) ("Since its establishment, the State of Israel has been the victim of continuous threats and attacks on its very existence as well as on the life and property of its citizens. These have taken the form of threats of war, of actual armed attacks, and campaigns of terrorism resulting in the murder of, and injury to human beings. In view of the above, the State of Emergency which was proclaimed in May 1948 has remained in force ever since. This situation constitutes a public emergency within the meaning of article 4 (1) of the [International] Covenant [on Civil and Political Rights]. The Government of Israel has therefore found it necessary, in accordance with the said article 4, to take measures to the extent strictly required by the exigencies of the situation, for the defence of the State and for the protection of life and property, including the exercise of powers of arrest and detention. In so far as any of these measures are inconsistent with article 9 of the Covenant, Israel thereby derogates from its obligations under that provision."); Derogation by the United Kingdom from the International Covenant on Civil and Political Rights (December 18, 2001) ("There exists a terrorist threat to the United Kingdom from persons suspected of involvement in international terrorism. In particular, there are foreign nationals present in the United Kingdom who are suspected of being concerned in the commission, preparation or instigation of acts of international terrorism, of being members of organisations or groups which are so concerned or of having links with members of such organisations or/and who are a threat to the national security of the United Kingdom. As a result, a public emergency, within the meaning of Article 4(1) of the Covenant, exists in the United Kingdom. As a result of the public emergency, provision is made in the

Anti-terrorism, Crime and Security Act 2001, *inter alia,* for an extended power to arrest and detain a foreign national which will apply where it is intended to remove or deport the person from the United Kingdom but where removal or deportation is not for the time being possible, with the consequence that the detention would be unlawful under existing domestic law powers.").

84. *See,* e.g., International Covenant on Civil and Political Rights (December 16, 1996), at Art. 4, 993 UNTS 3; Human Rights Committee, General Comment 29, UN Doc. CCPR/C/21/Rev.1/Add.11 (2001); *see also* PCATI Case, *supra,* at 382–83 (describing the role of the laws of armed conflict in addressing question regarding the legality of targeted killings).

85. For a general discussion of the subject, *see* Yuval Shany, "Human Rights and Humanitarian Law as Competing Legal Paradigms for Fighting Terror," *in* XIX/1 *Collected Courses of the Academy of European Law: Human Rights and International H¶umanitarian Law* (Orna Ben Naftali, ed., forthcoming in 2010).

86. *See,* e.g., *Tadic v. Prosecutor,* ICTY AC Decision (July 17, 1995), at ¶ 70 (Case No. IT-94–1-T).

87. For a recent discussion of the possibilities of regarding terror and counterterror campaigns as armed conflicts, *see Prosecutor v. Boškoski,* ICTY TC Judgment (July 10, 2008) (Case No. IT-04–82).

88. *See* HRC General Comment 29, *supra,* at ¶ 3 ("Not every disturbance or catastrophe qualifies as a public emergency which threatens the life of the nation.").

89. *Id.,* at Paragraph 17 (". . . [N]otification by States parties should include full information about the measures taken and a clear explanation of the reasons for them.").

90. *Id.* ("States parties have failed to notify other States parties, through the Secretary-General, of a proclamation of a state of emergency and of the resulting measures of derogation from one or more provisions of the Covenant.").

91. *See* Oren Gross & Fionnuala Ní Aoláin, *Law in Times of Crisis: Emergency Powers in Theory and Practice* (Cambridge: Cambridge University Press, 2006), at Ch. 4.

92. HRC General Comment 29, *supra,* at ¶ 15 (". . . [T]he provisions of the Covenant relating to procedural safeguards may never be made subject to measures that would circumvent the protection of non-revocable rights.").

93. PCATI Case, *supra,* at 396.

94. H.C.J. 8276/05, *Adalah v. Minister of Defense,* judgment of December 12, 2006.

95. *See,* e.g., *Isayeva et al v. Russia,* ECtHR judgment February 24, 2005, at ¶ 208 ("The obligation to protect the right to life under Article 2 of the Convention, read in conjunction with the State's general duty under Article 1 of the Convention to secure to everyone within [its] jurisdiction the rights and freedoms defined in [the] Convention,' requires by implication that there should be some form of effective official investigation when individuals have been killed as a result of the use of force."); *Kaya v. Turkey,* ECtHR judgment of February 19, 1998, at ¶ 86 ("The Court recalls at the outset that the general legal prohibition on arbitrary killing by agents of the State contained in Article

2 of the Convention would be ineffective, in practice, if there existed no procedure for reviewing the lawfulness of the use of lethal force by State authorities.").

96. *See generally,* Joseph Isanga, "Counter-Terrorism and Human Rights: The Emergence of a Rule of Customary Int'l law from UN Resolutions," *Denver Journal of International Law and Public Policy,* vol. 37 (2009), at 233 (describing the emergence of customary law on the application of some human rights standards during the "war on terror").

97. *See,* e.g., Israel Ministry of Foreign Affairs, Gaza Operation Investigations: An Update (January 2010), at 25 (comparing the military investigation procedures of Israel with those of the US, UK, Canada, and Australia).

98. *See,* e.g., Kathleen M Sullivan, "The Supreme Court 1991 Term, Forward: The Justices of Rules and Standards," *Harvard Law Review,* vol. 106 (1992–93), at 22, 66–69.

99. *See,* e.g., Dale Stephens, "Human Rights and Armed Conflict—The Advisory Opinion of the ICJ in the Nuclear Weapons Case," *Yale Human Rights & Development Law Journal,* vol. 4 (2001), at 1, 19–20.

100. Shany I, *supra,* at 844.

101. Oren Gross, "Chaos and Rules: Should Responses to Violent Crises Always Be Constitutional?" *Yale Law Journal,* vol. 112 (2003), at 1011, 1052.

102. Shany I, *supra,* at 843–844.

103. *See,* e.g., Michael Ignatieff, "The Torture Wars," *The New Republic* (April 22, 2002) ("As reports by the Israeli human rights group B'Tselem show, in Israel it has proved difficult to keep the use of physical force in interrogation under effective judicial and executive control.").

104. *See,* e.g., Michel Rosenfeld, "Judicial Balancing in Times of Stress: Comparing the American, British, and Israeli Approaches to the War on Terror," *Cardozo Law Review,* vol. 27 (2006), at 2079, 2121.

105. *See,* e.g., B'Tselem—The Israeli Information Center for Human Rights in the Occupied Territories, "Administrative Detention" (undated), *available at:* <http://www.btselem.org/English/Administrative_Detention/>.

106. *See,* e.g., *MB & AF v. Secretary of State for the Home Department* [2008] 1 AC 440, at ¶ 91 (per Lord Brown) ("I cannot accept that a suspect's entitlement to an essentially fair hearing is merely a qualified right capable of being outweighed by the public interest in protecting the state against terrorism (vital though, of course, I recognize that public interest to be). On the contrary, it seems to me not merely an absolute right but one of altogether too great importance to be sacrificed on the altar of terrorism control.").

107. In fact, as noted earlier, some anecdotal evidence suggests that house demolitions are counter-effective. *See,* e.g., Shalev, *supra,* at 127–31.

108. *See* HCJ 3799/02, *Adalah et al. v. Commander of the Israeli Army in the West Bank et al.*, ILDC 155 (IL 2005), Separate Opinion of Judge Mishael Cheshin, at ¶ 7, * Separate Opinion of Judge Dorit Beinisch, at Paragraph 5.

109. The *Anonymous* Case, *supra.*

110. *See*, e.g., Larry Alexander, "Are Procedural Rights Derivative Substantive Rights?" *Law & Philosophy*, vol. 17 (1998), at 19, 23–26.

111. *See* H.C.J. 5100/94, *Public Committee against Torture in Israel v. State of Israel*, 38 I.L.M. 1471 (1999); *Gäfgen v. Germany*, ECtHR Judgments 30 June 2008 (Chamber) & 1 June 2010 (Grand Chamber).

Chapter 5

The Foreign Intelligence Surveillance Puzzle

We Know How We Got Here—Now, What Do We Do?

John H. Shenefield

The Foreign Intelligence Surveillance Act[1] (FISA) is the statutory framework for enabling the U.S. government to engage in electronic surveillance in the United States as well as, since 2008, outside the United States (including of U.S. persons) in certain defined circumstances—all for the purpose of gathering foreign intelligence. This statute, enacted in 1978, gave rise to a system notable today both for its durability notwithstanding digitization and other technological developments, on the one hand, and a long process of legislative tweaks, on the other. What has become increasingly obvious in recent years is that FISA stands in need of reform. The statute's history and development help to suggest the ways in which a "modern" FISA might pass both the national security and the political tests.

I. WHAT IS FISA, AND HOW DOES IT WORK?

As FISA has been amended over the years, it also regulates physical searches, pen registers, and trap-and-trace devices[2]—as well as demands for business records and other tangible things—when undertaken for foreign intelligence purposes.

The statute is based on the idea that electronic surveillance of certain persons who have foreign intelligence significance should not require a full-fledged warrant, as is the case when using such techniques in a criminal investigation. Nevertheless, the policy judgment was made in 1978 that *some* form of warrant-like regulation was appropriate for foreign intelligence surveillance—albeit a form that involves lower thresholds, simplified procedures, and approval from a specially designated court. Until the enactment of FISA, the executive branch had undertaken domestic surveillance for foreign intelligence purposes essentially at its discretion. FISA was intended to provide a degree of oversight and accountability, yet without subjecting intelligence collection to all of the strict U.S. rules governing the acquisition of criminal intelligence.

FISA treats U.S. citizens and foreigners differently. For pure aliens—that is, nonpermanent residents of the U.S.—a finding of probable cause to believe that they are members of a terrorist group or agents of a foreign power is enough to justify approval of an intercept under FISA. For *U.S. persons,* which means citizens or permanent resident aliens, there must be probable cause to believe that a person is "knowingly" engaged in activities that "involve or may involve" a violation of the criminal statutes of the United States.[3]

Applications for FISA warrants go to the Foreign Intelligence Surveillance Court (FISC), made up of federal judges picked by the Chief Justice. Only government lawyers are present when the court, almost always a single judge, is conducting business. There is appeal to the court of review—the Foreign Intelligence Surveillance Court of Review (FISCR)—but that process has been used only rarely in the life of the statute.

FISA is a complex statute with many moving parts. A variety of factors may affect the way the rules apply:

(1) Whether the target is a U.S. person or a foreign national;
(2) Whether the target is located in the U.S. or overseas;
(3) Whether the collection actually takes place in the U.S. or abroad;
(4) Whether the means of communication at issue is wire (or fiber-optic cable) or wireless; and
(5) Whether the surveillance is targeted at a particular person or is, instead, incidental to targeting a different person.

FISA is not meant to cover communications that occur overseas (except in certain limited cases, and between two foreign nationals). To what extent FISA covers international communications between a foreign national overseas and a U.S. person within the United States, however, is more complicated—and has been controversial.

If you were to conclude that some of these distinctions are arbitrary and bear little, if any, relationship to expectations of privacy or the imperatives of collection, you would be correct. Indeed, the evolution of communications technology and changes in the nature of the threats facing the United States—shifting, to a major extent, from the hostile foreign powers originally envisioned by the statute to nebulous terrorist groups seeking to employ terrifying lethality in open societies—have made the careful definitions and fine nuances of FISA less and less efficient. For instance, the original focus on the location of the target persists despite the fact that it is no longer possible, in today's boundary-obscuring world of Internet-based communications links and packet-switched data routing, to ascertain with a high degree of reliability where exactly the target is.

Thus, the time surely has arrived to examine the FISA regime fundamentally, and to attempt to replace it with an up-to-date statute that is effective against current threats while still protecting the civil liberties of U.S. citizens.

II. THE PAST

A. Some History and Some Constitutional Law

In the early part of the 20th century, the executive branch routinely engaged in warrantless wiretapping. The issue finally reached the Supreme Court in 1928, in *Olmstead v. United States*.[4] In that case involving the admissibility of intercepted information in a conventional criminal trial, Chief Justice William Howard Taft, speaking for a narrow 5–4 majority, wrote that because a telephone conversation involved people intending to project their words outside their homes, if there had been no any physical intrusion into their homes, the Fourth Amendment to the U.S. Constitution—prohibiting unreasonable searches and seizures—simply did not apply. Tapping their telephone wires, therefore, was unproblematic.

But there was a strong dissent. Justice Louis Brandeis, sensing, as he so often did, where the law *should* be heading, thought the Court ought to be interpreting the Constitution in such a way as to protect the citizen from the government's increasingly sophisticated means of invading privacy in order to use in court "what is whispered in the closet." In other words, Brandeis felt the Fourth Amendment should be less about protecting the *premises,* and more about protecting the *person* and reasonable expectations of privacy.

After *Olmstead,* and for the next decade, the executive branch was legally free to engage in wiretapping in criminal and national security cases alike, without having to seek any kind of warrant. But the executive branch faced increasingly insistent demands from Congress that there be some regulation of surveillances, particularly in the area of criminal law enforcement, and gradually the controversy spilled over into the national security area. Nevertheless, with the onset of World War II, President Franklin Roosevelt unilaterally approved the use of national security surveillances, and successive presidents thereafter came to the same conclusion.

But the courts were narrowing the executive branch options. From the 1940s through to the 1960s, the notion of requiring a warrant based only upon some actual entry to physical premises increasingly gave way to a concern about individual privacy and the need to protect it even in the absence of physical intrusion. Even President Lyndon Johnson felt some pressure to limit national security surveillances in 1965, although the record still shows some 1,350 warrantless wiretaps and 250 secret microphone installations ("black bag jobs") over the next 10 years.

Then, in 1967, in *Katz v. United States,*[5] the Supreme Court specifically discarded the *Olmstead* doctrine for criminal cases, holding that—with a few exceptions such as searches incident to arrest, stop-and-frisk searches, border searches, and the like—warrantless searches are "*per se* unreasonable," and hence a Fourth Amendment problem. But in a footnote that set up further debates over the next 10 years, the Court expressly carved out national security surveillance from the sweep of its decision. Justice Byron White—the former Deputy Attorney General—emphasized this point in his concurring opinion, concluding that if the president or the attorney general found a national security surveillance reasonable, no prior judicial review should be necessary.

A year later, Congress enacted a statute regulating the use of electronic surveillance in criminal cases, Title III of the Omnibus Crime Control and Safe Streets Act.[6] Significantly, however, that statute disclaimed any intention to affect the powers of the president to obtain foreign intelligence to protect national security: domestic surveillance for foreign intelligence purposes was not affected. Once again, the executive branch believed the inherent power of the president included the power to collect foreign intelligence using warrantless electronic surveillance.

The same issue was touched lightly in another Supreme Court case five years later. In the so-called *Keith* case,[7] there was a challenge to the use of warrantless surveillance in a case involving domestic security—or, as the court described it at places in the opinion, "internal security." There had been an attempted bombing of a Central Intelligence Agency (CIA) office in Ann Arbor, Michigan, by a domestic organization, and the defendants charged in the case challenged the proposed introduction of evidence as having been tainted because it had been obtained by electronic surveillance undertaken without a Title III warrant. Justice Lewis Powell, writing for the Court, concluded that the government had not made the case for a departure from normal Fourth Amendment warrant requirements.

The *Keith* Court first looked at language in Title III itself that spelled out that nothing contained in the criminal warrant statute "shall limit the constitutional power of the President" to protect the national security or obtain foreign intelligence. Dealing with the government's argument that the language of the statute thus created a national security exception that came into play in domestic security cases, however, the Court decided that both the language of the statute and the legislative history demonstrated no such legislative intention. Instead, they reasoned, Congress by that language had only made clear that it did not intend to legislate with respect to national security surveillances. "Congress simply left presidential powers where it found them," and had not *created* any new national security exception.

That, however, raised the question of what exactly the constitutional powers of the President actually were. In confronting that issue, the Court explained that the facts of the case required "no judgment on the scope of the President's surveillance power with respect to the activities of a foreign power, within or without this country." There was in fact no evidence in the case of any involvement, direct or indirect, of a "foreign power." (The bombing had apparently been undertaken by Americans acting at home, and on their own.) In a footnote, Justice Powell distinguished between national security threats involving foreign intelligence and foreign powers—which were not at issue in the case—and national security threats emanating from *domestic* organizations, which triggered the Fourth Amendment analysis of reasonableness. A key to the constitutional analysis, therefore, was not the existence of a security threat *per se,* but rather whether it could be traced in some way to a "foreign power."

Of course, the president has the constitutional duty under Article II to protect the Constitution and the government from those who would overthrow or subvert it. Nor, however, was there any question that national security cases involve Fourth Amendment (search and seizure) and First Amendment (free speech) values, albeit in ways somewhat different from ordinary criminal cases. ("Though the investigative duty of the executive may be stronger in such cases, so also is there greater jeopardy to constitutionally protected speech.") Assessing the government's arguments for special treatment in this domestic security case, the Court found none of them persuasive: the facts are not too subtle for courts, federal judges are capable of handling the difficult issues involved, and secrecy can be well protected by federal courts. Therefore, it was held in *Keith,* the normal warrant requirements must apply, and the government was required to divulge the contents of its surveillance evidence to the defendants.

Notably, however, as if by way of exclamation point, the majority opinion concluded by once again calling attention to the fact that the decision did *not* address issues involving activities of foreign powers or their agents. And it was this repeated allusion in the *Keith* opinion to national security involving *foreign* powers and *foreign* intelligence—though the Court actually reached no formal decision on the subject, which, as the opinion stated, had *not* been raised by the facts of *Keith*—that paved the way for, first, an extensive debate and, finally, six years later, for the enactment of the Foreign Intelligence Surveillance Act (FISA). Coming as it did in an era of antigovernment protest and concern about executive overreaching at home and abroad, such explicit talk of a foreign intelligence exception to the now-normal warrant requirements for electronic surveillance set a slow legislative process in motion.

The lower federal appellate courts, meanwhile, were being forced to confront the "foreign power" national security issue. Most of them in fact did end up recognizing a foreign intelligence exception to the warrant requirement.[8]

B. President Ford and the Levi "Compromise"

In the wake of Watergate and the associated popular suspicion of the propriety of various executive-branch activities, there developed an intense battle within the administration of President Gerald Ford over whether to continue to engage in national security wiretaps unilaterally (without the participation of Congress in any way) or to endorse legislation that was acceptable to the members of the Judiciary Committee and most of the other members of Congress, thus sharing responsibility between the two branches of government. The debate culminated in a meeting in the "Situation Room" at the White House on March 12, 1976, in which the then counsel to the president, Philip Buchen, discussed possible legislation with Secretary of State Henry Kissinger, Secretary of Defense Donald Rumsfeld, CIA Director George H.W. Bush, Attorney General Edward Levi, and National Security Advisor Brent Scowcroft.

Following the meeting, Buchen wrote a decision memo for the president in which he reported that any objection to the so-called Levi "share-the-responsibility" approach had been stilled, and that there was "no adamant opposition" to moving forward with some legislation. His decision memo recommended that the president endorse the legislative approach and that he meet with congressional leaders, and reported both that Senator Edward Kennedy (D-MA) had offered to be a co-sponsor and that the attorney general was confident that the measure would not be opposed by any member of the Judiciary Committee in either chamber of the legislature.

Legislation was duly sent to the Senate soon thereafter, and there followed two years of hearings and debate, focusing mostly on the issues of targeting Americans for foreign intelligence surveillance and whether the president had inherent authority to proceed without involving Congress in any way. With the advent of the administration of President Jimmy Carter, which likewise favored a compromise with Congress, more consideration of the legislative options ensued, and finally in October 1978, Congress passed the Foreign Intelligence Surveillance Act.

And for over 20 years, the FISA regulatory regime did its job adequately, supported by able staffs sprinkled throughout the relevant executive branch agencies. The rate of applications for surveillances gradually increased, and the professional staffs in the Justice Department and at the FBI gained valuable practical experience, but the years were mostly uncontroversial. Then came 9/11.

III. 9/11 CHANGES EVERYTHING

Modern FISA history began the day that two hijacked airplanes slammed into the World Trade Center towers in New York City, a third into the Pentagon, and a fourth into a field near Shanksville, Pennsylvania. Immediately, the traditional FISA regime was perceived as being inadequate and in need of overhaul. A major focus in such debates was on the bureaucratic complexity that seemed to characterize the statute's everyday life and to limit its flexibility and usefulness.

A. The FISA "Wall"

The infamous FISA "Wall"—a perceived absolute legal and institutional barrier between any comingling of "intelligence" and "law enforcement" investigative activity which many believe helped to keep the U.S. government from being able to "connect" some of the 9/11 "dots" in advance of the attacks—probably got its start in the language of the original 1978 statute itself. The statute required that each FISA surveillance operation have "the purpose" of obtaining "foreign intelligence information." That language raised two questions:

- First, how much of the "purpose" of the surveillance must be to obtain foreign intelligence information? Must it be the government's *sole* purpose, its *primary* purpose, a *substantial* purpose, a *significant* purpose, or merely a *nontrivial* purpose?
- Second, what exactly is "foreign intelligence information" anyway?

Based on the "purpose" language, federal courts during the 1980s began construing the statute to preclude a FISA surveillance unless its "primary purpose" was to gather foreign intelligence. This tended to rule out the use of FISA where criminal prosecution became—or was perceived to have become—the primary purpose.[9] Once that happened, so the reasoning went, what was being sought was no longer "foreign intelligence information" but instead conventional "law enforcement" information. At that point, therefore, the FISA surveillance would have to stop, and a conventional Title III warrant for law enforcement purposes would have to be obtained. Were the FISA surveillance then to be maintained, and were it to pick up incriminating information, all of this evidence would be subject to a motion to suppress at any subsequent trial. (Technically, therefore, FISA could still be used to collect information, but none of it could be used in court.)

The somewhat confusing fact that both kinds of surveillances sought precisely the same information from the same person using the same communications devices was less important to the courts. Of greater importance—through this legal-analytical prism—were the government's *intentions,* and the moment at which it began to focus in specifically on potential prosecution. As in the *Truong* case, one key to understanding this was found in the nature of internal executive branch consultations. The more consultations involving the Criminal Division's prosecutors occurred, the more likely the court was to find that the purpose of the surveillance was *really* law enforcement.

And thus there developed a powerful but perverse incentive to have *no* consultations, to maintain duplicative and uncoordinated investigations in parallel institutional "stove pipes," and—when in doubt—not to share any leads, tips, or insights across the resulting bureaucratic "wall." The "backdoor" channel between the Federal Bureau of Investigation (FBI) and the Justice Department's Criminal Division, for instance, was shut down. At the FBI the word went out from the Deputy Director's office that to violate the new rule of separation was "a career-ending move."

To be sure, there was no *official* rule or decree erecting such a bureaucratic wall. But the situation was at least confusing to line agents and prosecutors, despite several efforts to clarify things, and officials clearly perceived that no contacts across the "wall" should take place. To try to clear things up a bit, the Department issued a memorandum in 1995 in connection with the twin investigations of Omar Abdel Rahman and the first World Trade Center bombing. That memorandum was followed almost immediately by a set of procedures designed to encourage coordination. But instead of clarifying the situation, this memorandum and these procedures regulated and constrained information sharing in a variety of ways, and were apparently—according to the 9/11 Commission's subsequent report—"almost immediately misunderstood and misapplied." A bureaucratic culture of constraint had gotten out in front of applicable laws and regulations.

In an effort to help, the Office of Intelligence Policy Review (OIPR) in the Justice Department appointed itself as the gatekeeper for cross-wall information sharing, and demanded to be present at all meetings between the Criminal Division and the FBI. The result was delay, and some of the participants described such meetings as "intimidating," "surreal," and even "weird." Rather than facilitating communication and coordination, this OIPR role turned into a new procedural bottleneck.

At about this same time, the FBI and the Department were working through issues related to an investigation and possible prosecution of Wen-Ho Lee, a nuclear weapons scientist at the Los Alamos National Laboratory who was suspected of espionage in connection with the unauthorized release of nuclear weapons information to the People's Republic of China. The Lee affair was complicated and involved many issues, but according to subsequent investigations, one of the many problems the government faced in its own ill-handled work on the case was a crippling lack of coordination between intelligence and criminal investigators—in a word, the FISA "Wall."[10] Again there was misunderstanding of the rules, and failures to follow procedures. Again, the result was confusion and miscommunication, demonstrating that the FISA infrastructure and procedures were simply not working satisfactorily.

Further attempts to improve coordination took place throughout the spring and summer of 2001, but in July 2001, the General Accounting Office (GAO)[11] issued a report calling attention to these continuing difficulties. In August 2001, another memorandum purporting to clarify and modify the 1995 procedures was issued, making yet another attempt to clear the channels of communication. By then, however, it was too late.

In the months leading up to 9/11, the lack of coordination between intelligence and law enforcement officials resulted in several missed opportunities. First was the effort to locate Khalid al-Mihdhar and Nawaf al-Hamzi, both 9/11 bombers. CIA analysts did not pass on what they knew to FBI investigators; procedures for sharing leads and tips were misused. One FBI agent in New York, wanting to open a criminal case on Mihdhar, asked another FBI agent who was working on the intelligence investigation to consent. After consulting FBI lawyers and misunderstanding the advice that was received, the second agent refused to consent. Whereupon the first agent wrote the memorable lines quoted in the 9/11 Commission's report:

> . . . [S]omeday someone will die—and wall or not—the public will not understand why we were not more effective and throwing every resource at certain 'problems.' [9/11 Commission Report p. 271]

The second agent then replied that the rules were the rules, that these restrictions had been (she said) ordered by the FISA Court, and that they applied to the entire FBI, even the FBI field office in New York. On this evidence alone, it is clear—and the 9/11 Commission so concluded—that pretty much everyone involved was confused about the rules governing the use and sharing of information gathered in intelligence investigations.

This brings us to Zacharias Moussaoui. By almost any standard, he seemed sure to raise suspicions of aircraft-related terrorism. He wanted flight training as "an ego-boosting thing" and attracted attention because, with little knowledge of flying, he wanted to learn to take off and land a Boeing 747, wanted to fly a simulated flight from London Heathrow into John F. Kennedy airport in New York, was very interested in the operation of the plane's doors, and had paid for his training with $9000 in cash but had no explanation for how he came by such a large amount.

The FBI in Minneapolis became convinced that Moussaoui was a *jihadist* and indeed suspected he might be planning to hijack a plane. Wanting to take him out of play as soon as possible, the FBI worked with the Immigration and Naturalization Service to arrest Moussaoui for visa violations. Understandably, however, they also wanted to search his laptop computer. It was here that confusion set in. The FBI agents were concerned that they might not have enough evidence to get a criminal search warrant—though they probably did—so they elected not to try, because they feared that the FISA warrant option might be foreclosed if they first applied for a criminal warrant. (A subsequent FISA application, they feared, would be rejected if a criminal warrant attempt had previously been made: the court would conclude that the FISA procedure was merely a subterfuge with criminal prosecution really in mind, in violation of the "purpose" standard.) But because the mere *discussion* of a criminal warrant was already taking place, FBI lawyers also did not initially want to try the FISA route either. (There was also concern that, on the basis of the information then available, Moussaoui could not be connected to a "foreign" power and thus the FISA statute's requirements could not be met.[12]) In effect, therefore, the allegedly mutually exclusive criminal and FISA surveillance routes interfered with, and for a time precluded, each other.

All in all, the run-up to 9/11 was—from a FISA perspective—a tale of substantial confusion, inadequate understanding of the relevant procedures, and unnecessary bureaucratic complexity. All this got in the way of understanding what was really about to happen.

B. The PATRIOT Act and the Wall

Has the "wall" now been torn down? Certainly, today it has—as a matter of law, at least. But reaching even that point, and in the wake of a terrible terrorist atrocity, proved surprisingly difficult.

The USA PATRIOT Act was enacted in October 2001.[13] It sought to break down the FISA "Wall" in several ways. First, FISA was amended so that it was no longer required in applying for a FISA surveillance that obtaining foreign intelligence information be "*the* purpose" of the surveillance. Henceforth, as long as gaining foreign intelligence information was at least "*a significant* purpose," a FISA surveillance could be obtained. (Law enforcement, in fact, could actually be its "primary purpose.") Second, Section 504 of the Act amended FISA to make it clear that intelligence officers who conduct surveillances or physical searches in pursuit of foreign intelligence information *may* consult with law enforcement officers to investigate international terrorism.

But that was not enough. In November 2001, the Foreign Intelligence Surveillance Court (FISC), in dealing with the first FISA applications prepared after the enactment of the USA PATRIOT Act, effectively blocked implementation of the FISA provisions of the Act. Remarkably, it did so by reaching back to *earlier* Department of Justice (DOJ) guidelines and imposing them generically in the post-Act world.

In response, DOJ came up with new guidelines. These March 2002 guidelines effectively permitted total exchange of information and advice between intelligence and law enforcement officials. In May, however, the FISC accepted some aspects of the new procedures but rejected others. The court was especially sensitive about any direction of foreign intelligence collection activity by prosecutors, so it put in place some constraints: law enforcement officers were prohibited from making any recommendations or directions in connection with foreign intelligence surveillances that might assist criminal prosecution. The court also imposed a "chaperone" procedure, pursuant to which prosecutors could not consult with intelligence personnel unless the DOJ's Office of Intelligence Policy Review (OIPR) were present. The "wall"—with its OIPR gatekeeper—was back, this time by actual judicial decree.

Unsurprisingly, the Department appealed to the Foreign Intelligence Surveillance Court of Review (FISCR), which had never before been asked to convene at all. The Department submitted briefs, and the American Civil Liberties Union and the National Association of Criminal Defense Lawyers were also invited to submit briefs, which supported the decision in the FISC.

In November of 2002, the Court of Review reversed the FISC and upheld DOJ's March 2002 procedures in their entirety. The court concluded that there was nothing in the text or legislative history of FISA that precluded the government from using foreign intelligence information in the criminal process. Indeed, the FISCR found it "puzzling" that the Department began sometime in the 1980s to read FISA as if it constrained DOJ's ability to seek FISA applications if the intended objective was prosecution of agents of a foreign power for foreign intelligence crimes, such as espionage, sabotage, or terrorism. That meant, of course, that the entire debate about "purpose" had been beside the point: FISA surveillance was permitted in order to assemble evidence for the prosecution of the agent of a foreign power for foreign intelligence-related offenses. Ordinary criminals were beyond the reach of FISA surveillances.

But then, in a surprising twist, the appellate court also looked at the USA PATRIOT Act's Section 218, with its "significant purpose" language, and concluded that although the original Foreign Intelligence Surveillance Act had never contemplated a "wall," the Act had actually *erected* one. After that statute, in other words, a FISA surveillance could *not* be used exclusively to gather evidence for a prosecution—even one for a foreign intelligence-related crime. Thus, a statute designed to expand the government's use of foreign intelligence information actually turned out to have contracted it, at least theoretically and at least in this one instance. In the language of the court, "even though we agree that the original FISA did not contemplate the 'false dichotomy' [of intelligence investigation versus criminal investigation], the Patriot Act actually did—which makes it no longer false."

But the Court of Review took two further steps to clarify the FISA process. First, it made it crystal clear that, while the government could use FISA surveillances to gather evidence for a crime related to a foreign intelligence threat—as long as, after the USA PATRIOT Act, a "significant purpose" of the surveillance is to gather foreign intelligence information—it could not use them to gather evidence of what it called "ordinary crime," even when committed by an agent of a foreign power. Thus, evidence of a bank robbery by such a suspect to finance terrorist attacks, or identification fraud to conceal an identity was fair game. Jaywalking, being drunk and disorderly, or domestic violence likely was not. There had to be some nexus to foreign threat activity.

Second, in assessing the purpose of the surveillance, the court turned away from the balancing of law enforcement and intelligence purposes, required under the earlier jurisprudence, and held that the foreign intelligence purpose was to be judged on its own terms. And, finally, the consultations of lower-level line prosecutors and intelligence officers were made beside the point: it was the purpose certification required of a senior national security official that would be examined and would be determinative.

And so the "wall" was indeed beginning to come down. But clearly still not without some resistance, even after the FISCR's important ruling. The USA PATRIOT Act reauthorizations confirm the point. In 2005, for instance, there was some—but not too much—controversy over Section 203 of the Act, which authorized the sharing of grand jury information between law enforcement officials and intelligence personnel. Allegations were made that the legislation permitted too much information to be shared, did not tightly control what uses were made of it, and therefore made the efficient exchange of highly relevant information more difficult. In response, defenders of the provision argued there were controls enough and that more arcane restrictions would rebuild the walls of distrust and the reluctance to share information that the provision had sought to deal with in the first place.

Bureaucratically and culturally, there is work probably still to be done in draining the swamp of decades of accumulated resistance to law enforcement and intelligence coordination in foreign intelligence-related matters. Indeed, changing the culture at the Justice Department and at the FBI, as well as at the intelligence agencies, is at least as important as any changes in the law. Part of what will help is the existence of the National Security Division at the Justice Department, established in the wake of the USA PATRIOT Act. This organization is still relatively new and is meant, among other things, to be the point of liaison between the Department and the FBI. But at last, one might say, *most* of the Wall has been torn down.

C. Other FISA-related Provisions in the USA PATRIOT Act

In addition to its "Wall" provisions, the USA PATRIOT Act modified and supplemented FISA in a number of ways. "Roving wiretap" authority—that is, surveillance authority keyed to a particular target, rather than simply to a particular telephone—was finally allowed in national security investigations, as it had been for some time in organized crime investigations. The availability of physical searches, pen registers, and trap-and-trace devices was also expanded, as was the amount of time an emergency surveillance could be kept in place before obtaining a FISA warrant.

D. The Renewal Problem

Because of the intense controversy that surrounds the topic of domestic surveillance, Congress has required various provisions to be reauthorized periodically: the roving wiretap provision; the provisions in Section 215 providing for orders to produce "any tangible things" (including books, records, papers, documents, and other items); and the provision authorizing "lone wolf" surveillances (e.g., of individuals like Moussaoui, who cannot, at least initially, be linked to a "foreign power," but are suspected of engaging in international terrorism or other relevant activity).

The "roving wiretap" provision, Section 206 of the USA PATRIOT Act, provided for roving surveillance of a target who takes measures to thwart FISA surveillance. We live in an age of cheap, "throw-away" cell phones and multiple call cards. To make life difficult for counterterrorist investigators with FISA approval to tap a specific phone, the terrorist could simply thwart the surveillance by continually changing phones. This they had learned to do.

Under the pre-9/11 law, the telecommunications carrier for the target's first phone number (e.g., Verizon) would be ordered to assist the government, but the order would cover only that carrier. If the target switched phones (and carriers), the second carrier (e.g., T-Mobile) would not be covered by the order and might not voluntarily cooperate, thereby requiring a whole new FISA petition to be prepared in order to add coverage of the second phone. And so on.

The Act's "roving wiretap" authority avoids that duplication and delay by permitting the FISA court to issue a generic order covering *any* carrier whose phone is used by the target. This kind of authority had been available for some years to the federal *criminal* prosecutors under Title III for organized crime and narcotics cases, for it had long been known in criminal circles that phone switching could defeat traditional surveillance. The USA PATRIOT Act provided this authority to foreign intelligence investigators under "sunset" provisions that require periodic renewal. There is simply no good reason not to keep it as a part of the arsenal of the counterterrorist investigator as well.

The "business records" provision, Section 215 of the USA PATRIOT Act, allows the FISA court to compel production of business records or any other tangible things, and is roughly analogous to a grand jury subpoena in more conventional criminal investigations (except that its existence must be kept secret by the entity on which the request is served, unlike a grand jury subpoena).

Before 9/11, FISA had contained a basic records-request provision, but nothing with which to obtain tangible objects, such as books. Moreover, production could only be ordered from common carriers, public accommodation facilities, storage facilities, and vehicle rental facilities. The Act changed the situation in several ways. Orders seeking the production of any tangible things were now permitted, and the limitations on the kinds of entities that receive such orders were removed.

This was the provision to which many U.S. librarians took such sharp exception. In fact the public reaction was so politically charged that the reauthorization of this section in 2005 made a variety of changes which, according to government investigators, made the entire process slower and more cumbersome, and led to the greater use of an alternate route, the National Security Letter (NSL), which is more like an administrative subpoena and is issued by the FBI rather than by the FISC.

The "lone wolf" surveillance provision, Section 6001 of the Intelligence Reform and Terrorism Prevention Act of 2004 ("IRTPA"),[14] covers situations in which the link to an international terrorist organization is absent or insufficiently established. Under the original FISA, the government had to show that the target of the surveillance was a foreign power or the agent of a foreign power—that is, that the target was working for or on behalf of a foreign power.

This whole issue arose in part because of the confusion and uncertainty during the FBI's effort to search Zacharias Moussaoui's laptop computer following his arrest for immigration violations in August 2001. As noted earlier, when the Minneapolis FBI agents attempted to get clearance for a FISA warrant to search the computer, FBI headquarters was uncertain of a link to an international terrorist organization. Frantic efforts through intelligence liaison channels discovered a link between Moussaoui and a Chechen rebel leader named Ibn al-Khattab, but there was uncertainty as to whether the Chechen rebels qualified as international terrorists. Ultimately, FBI headquarters decided that the Chechen connection was not good enough, and the FBI lawyers declined to submit the FISA application.

During the back-and-forth between the Minneapolis field office and FBI Headquarters, the communications became quite heated; the case agent and the supervisory agent, both of whom were trained pilots—and therefore perhaps more sensitive to the odd nature of Moussaoui's training requests—thought they had a potential hijacker on their hands. Headquarters admonished them that they were trying to get people "spun up." The response from Minneapolis has a fateful quality to it: the supervisor said that getting officials worried was precisely his intent: he was "trying to keep someone from taking a plane and crashing it into the World Trade Center." The reply from Washington, however, was that such a thing was not going to happen and the Bureau did not know whether Moussaoui was in fact a terrorist. And there the matter stood, in an investigation-impeding stalemate, on September 11, 2001.

But relying on Moussaoui may be too convenient a hindsight. There are other possible scenarios. The government might detect some vague links to a group, but the facts may not rise to the level of probable cause. Or perhaps there would be a link to a previously unknown group, for which the government lacks enough detail to meet every element of the "foreign power" requirement. Or perhaps, in fact, there might be *no* group involved at all—just a terrorist with the psychotic zeal to carry out universal *jihad* in solitude. Alternatively, someone might once have been an agent of an international terrorist organization but broke away from it—perhaps because of an internal dispute or because the group was insufficiently aggressive—without in any way ceasing to plot terrorist attacks. Or someone might "self-radicalize" by means of information and training available on the Internet. Absent the "lone wolf" provision, surveillance could not be authorized by the FISA Court for any of these scenarios.

So there would seem to be a gap here, small but potentially important. It has long been suspected that international terrorist movements, such as *al Qaeda*, which have learned over time that more hierarchical organizations present an easier counterterror target (e.g., by being vulnerable to "decapitation" by the arrest or killing of key leaders), may gradually be morphing into more "leaderless," semi-independent cell-based organizations or "franchises" linked merely by common reference to websites on "best terrorist practices" and promoting a "culture of jihad." The "lone wolf" provisions represented Congress' attempt to provide government investigators with tools better suited to such challenges than FISA's traditional "agent of a foreign power" approach.

The "lone wolf" provision amends FISA's definition of "agent of a foreign power" to include any person, *other than a U.S. person,* who "engages in international terrorism or activities in preparation therefore [sic]." The definition of "international terrorism" in the statute emphasizes violent acts of a criminal kind designed to intimidate civilian populations or governments that take place outside the United States or "transcend international boundaries."

Thus, as a practical matter, the "lone wolf" provision creates a presumption that any person engaged in international terrorism is an agent of a foreign power. (It is worth reemphasizing that, even here, "U.S. persons"—i.e., United States citizens and lawful resident aliens, are not subject to the "lone wolf" provision. Monitoring their communications still requires a more traditional "foreign power" nexus.) Thus, after the "lone wolf" provision became law, showing an actual link between many potential surveillance targets and a foreign power was no longer necessary.

Drafters of this provision were concerned to avoid the impact of the *Keith* case, which had held that in conventional domestic security cases the usual Title III warrant requirement was reasonable. FISA was an effort to reach beyond the *Keith* focus on domestic security to deal with the activities of international terrorist organizations, even those that took place in the U.S. Thus, what the new 2004 "lone wolf" provision required was probable cause to believe that the target was engaging in or preparing to engage in international terrorism (as defined above).[15]

Not all agree that any "lone wolf" provision is necessary or important, however. First, critics say that the Moussaoui case is not a good reason for such a provision because in that case FBI Headquarters simply did not understand the applicable law in the first place. In any event, after the USA PATRIOT Act changes in the "primary purpose" test of FISA, the government could seek a criminal warrant without any preclusive effects on a future use of FISA. In addition, it is said that given the post-9/11 enactment of broad criminal statutes relating to terrorism, in any case in which investigators could meet the FISA "probable cause" standard for a "lone wolf"—someone who "engages in international terrorism activities or activities in preparation therefor[e]"—it would also be possible to meet the "probable cause" standard for a criminal warrant. Further, they argue that the need to use sensitive information relating to intelligence sources and methods in the application for a criminal warrant would not be a barrier, because classified information is already occasionally shared with federal judges in contexts such as under the Classified Information Procedures Act (CIPA).[16]

But such critics' major point is that the benefits of the "lone wolf" provision, if any, come at a very high cost because it undermines the policy and constitutional justifications for FISA. In enacting FISA, after all, Congress made it clear that its limited exception to normal criminal warrant procedures was justified only when dealing with foreign powers or their agents. Individuals acting alone, the argument goes, do not raise the same level of foreign or military policy concern. And, it is said, in statutorily defining an individual acting alone—with no connection to any other individual, group or government—as an "agent of a foreign power," Congress may well have built into FISA a fatal vulnerability if the "lone wolf" provision is ever challenged in court.

This criticism should be taken seriously. I would argue, however, that, given that the purpose of FISA is to collect foreign intelligence information, and that the "lone wolf" provision requires the government to certify that the information sought is in fact foreign intelligence, the "lone wolf" provision is sensible policy, constitutionally sound, and a vastly superior alternative to the criminal warrant process. CIPA, for instance, does not even apply at the warrant stage—it deals only with the use of classified information once criminal proceedings are underway—and what "source" of foreign intelligence, especially a foreign government, for instance, is going to be willing to trust their most sensitive information to the somewhat unpredictable criminal justice system? The shortfalls of the ordinary criminal system for addressing foreign intelligence issues are precisely why FISA was created in the first place.

The "lone wolf" provision has in fact now been renewed until mid-2015, pursuant to administration recommendations. Although admitting that the provision had never in fact been used, frequently because the target was not a "non-U.S. person," the Justice Department maintains that traditional FISA rules left a worrisome gap and that the scenarios that might trigger "lone wolf" treatment are not remote hypotheticals but instead based upon trends observed in current intelligence reporting.

IV. THE TERRORIST SURVEILLANCE PROGRAM AND PRESIDENTIAL POWER

A. The Framework

The abiding constitutional debate that continues to pervade much of the discussion of this entire subject concerns which branch of government has the bedrock constitutional power to do what. Setting aside the area of domestic security addressed in the *Keith* case, can the president—on the basis of the inherent power of the presidency—authorize surveillance across the board? Does the existence of FISA limit his otherwise unfettered authority, or does his authority trump FISA? And what difference, if any, does the existence of the post-9/11 Authorization for the Use of Military Force[17] make? Nor, significantly, is this a debate about the executive and legislative functions alone. The judiciary has also played a major role in this field, and its constitutional power must likewise be assessed.

I start with the proposition that the federal bench—insulated by lifetime appointment from political responsibility, removed by virtue of their experience from the harsh realities of international terrorism and collection of foreign intelligence, and protected even from public criticism by the secrecy that attends their decisions in this field—is unsuited to making or implementing national security policy. The role of the judge, if any, should be to confirm that the prescribed procedures have been followed, that the required findings have been made, and that the process is not flawed on its face. Beyond that, we should not ask the courts to go.

The absolutist position on the inherent powers of the presidency is that the Constitution, its framers, every relevant Supreme Court case, and the consistent practice of presidents demonstrate that the president's authority in the area of foreign affairs, and especially foreign intelligence gathering, is supreme and plenary, and cannot be checked. When, for example, John Jay wrote in Federalist 64 that he thought the president's ability to keep secrets could be relied upon, but that he had doubts about the Senate and still more about the House of Representatives, he concluded that the president "will be able to manage the business of intelligence in such a manner as prudence may suggest."

Such thinking would seem to mean that the president's authority is unbounded. By this view, he can do whatever it takes to safeguard the national security, because without that foundation it is not possible to have a coherent discussion about legitimate government powers at all. As President Abraham Lincoln famously asked when challenged about his wartime suspension of the writ of *habeas corpus,* for instance, "are all the laws but one to go unexecuted and the Government itself go to pieces lest that one be violated?" By such logic, the president's discretionary power in foreign affairs is not subject to control by statute, with this immunized area covering most clearly the collection of foreign intelligence information—even when the collection is performed against U.S. citizens inside the United States. The result of this position is that FISA is unconstitutional, because it is an illegitimate congressional grab for power, an effort to constrain some of the inherent authority of the president in the area of foreign affairs.

The other side of this debate holds that the framers of the Constitution wanted above all to avoid having the kind of absolute monarch they perceived King George III to be—and thus that the concept of an uncheckable power in the presidency is entirely out of the question. Were it possible to show that untrammeled authority in certain areas of protecting the national security is in fact necessary—that is, that without the ability to act on the basis of inherent authority alone, the national security would be endangered—the case might perhaps be different. But no such showing has been, or likely can be, made. No one, it is said, has shown that FISA interferes with national security. And in that event, unchecked presidential power would seem to be inconsistent with the text of the Constitution (the drafters of which did not see fit themselves to compose any Fourth Amendment exception for national security); with the structure of our constitutional government (which is based on checks and balances); with the framers' intent (as evidenced by their clear distrust of executive power); and with the need to prevent the inevitable abuses that are inherent in unchecked authority.

But we are here talking about opposite poles in constitutional theory. Theory, here as in so many other cases, gets mugged by harsh reality. And that reality counsels that competing and mutually exclusive interests must adjust to each other so that both can function as a shared responsibility.

The best articulation of that concept remains Justice Robert Jackson's concurring opinion in *Youngstown,*[18] the so-called "Steel Seizure" case decided in 1952 at the height of the Korean War. Faced with labor unrest, the leading steel companies were in danger of shutting down just when their production was most crucial to the war effort. President Truman issued an executive order to his Secretary of Commerce, to seize and continue to operate the mills. Litigation ensued, and in the Supreme Court the question was whether the President had acted within his constitutional power.

It is said that President Truman was stunned when the Court, by a vote of 6–3, upheld a lower court's injunction against the seizure. Although there were six separate opinions for the majority, and although Justice Hugo Black technically wrote the opinion for the Court, it is Justice Jackson's opinion that is cited by lawyers and scholars today to analyze presidential authority.

Jackson began by observing that partisan debate and scholarly speculation about constitutional distribution of power produce quotations from respected sources on each side of the debate—opinions that effectively cancel each other out. The actual business of governing, however, will force the branches to work together productively:

> While the Constitution diffuses power the better to secure liberty, it also contemplates that practice will integrate the dispersed powers into a workable government. It enjoins upon its branches separateness but interdependence, autonomy but reciprocity. Presidential powers arc not fixed but fluctuate, depending upon their disjunction or conjunction with those of Congress.

Jackson then grouped presidential power into three categories:

(1) "When the president acts pursuant to an express or implied authorization of Congress, his authority is at its maximum, for it includes all that he possesses in his own right plus all that Congress can delegate."

(2) "When the President acts in absence of either a congressional grant or denial of authority, he can rely only upon his own independent powers, but there is a zone of twilight in which he and Congress may have concurrent authority, or in which its distribution is uncertain."

(3) "When the President takes measures incompatible with the expressed or implied will of Congress, his power is at its lowest ebb, for then he can rely only upon his own constitutional powers minus any constitutional powers of Congress over the matter. Courts can sustain exclusive presidential control in such a case only by disabling the Congress from acting on the subject. Presidential claim to a power at once so conclusive and preclusive must be scrutinized with caution, for what is at stake is the equilibrium established by our constitutional system."

This persuades me that whatever constitutional purists might prefer, on the most sensitive and controversial issues the president should always seek to be in the first category: where both legislative and executive powers are *merged,* and reinforce each other, to produce the maximum presidential authority. The more important the national security threat that is faced, the more important it should be to seek such reinforcement—for there lies the secret not simply to maximizing the changes of a successful initial response but also to ensuring that the government can continue to meet such challenges over time.

B. The TSP Controversy

This was surely the lesson of the George W. Bush Administration's difficult experience with its warrantless wiretap program, known as the Terrorist Surveillance Program (TSP)—which was ordered by the administration in the wake of 9/11 and revealed publicly by the *New York Times* in 2005. It has been reported that the *Times* story was fueled by a leak from a government lawyer, then employed at OIPR, working with a Top Secret/Secure Compartmented Information clearance. He is said to have admitted that, one day in 2004, he slipped into a Metro station and telephoned the newspaper, leading to its report that the National Security Agency (NSA)—America's electronic espionage organization—had begun one or more programs involving the interception of telephone calls and e-mails into and out of the United States as long as one of the parties to the communication was suspected of being a member of the *al Qaeda* terrorist organization.[19] (Subsequent reports suggested NSA had also been engaged in large-scale electronic data mining, searching for terrorist suspects by analyzing records potentially relating to millions of Americans[20]—though to the extent that this involved commercially available data provided to the government by commercial entities, it did not seem to raise FISA issues.) All of this, it was said, was being done without a FISA-type warrant.

The public reaction was immediate—and much of it was negative, indeed vitriolic. "Fire rained down not only from the left, but also from the right," wrote John Yoo, the DOJ lawyer who had apparently been involved in thinking through the legal basis for the NSA program [Yoo, *War by Any Other Means,* (2006) p. 101] The administration's response seemed awkward and unsure. Many observers, some informed and some ignorant, raised questions of illegality. A few voices on Capitol Hill spoke of impeachment, and one senator even introduced a motion of censure.

But what was actually behind all the sound and fury? And why had the administration chosen to operate outside FISA, even after that act had been supplemented at the administration's request by the USA PATRIOT Act? There seem to have been several reasons.

First, the NSA program apparently involved electronic surveillance. Attorney General Alberto Gonzales described the activity on several occasions as involving "intercepts of contents of communication where . . . one party is outside the United States." That activity certainly comes within the statutory definition of "electronic surveillance." If that is true, then TSP activity was covered by FISA. Indeed, Congress wrote into FISA a provision that its procedures were the *exclusive* means by which electronic surveillance may be conducted. By inserting that exclusivity provision, Congress clearly intended to curb the exercise of inherent powers of the president to conduct electronic surveillance. Quite explicitly, one might say, it sought to put electronic surveillance in *Youngstown's* third category, where the president's inherent power is "at its lowest ebb."

After the TSP became public, the administration published a 42-page white paper entitled "Legal Authorities Supporting the Activities of the National Security Agency Described by the President."[21] The principal authority cited in the white paper was the Authorization for Use of Military Force (AUMF),[22] passed by Congress after 9/11. That congressional joint resolution authorized the President to "use all necessary and appropriate force against those nations, organizations or persons" that were involved in the 9/11 attacks in order to prevent "any future acts of international terrorism against the United States." The government's argument, relying in part on the Supreme Court's *Hamdi* case[23]—in which the Court had used the AUMF to find sufficient authorization for military detention of captured combatant adversaries—was that Congress had implicitly authorized the use of signals intelligence to aid troops committed to battle, and that the authorization covered international communications between, say, Afghanistan and the United States.

But then what are we to make of the USA PATRIOT Act, which in its early forms was being considered at the same time as the passage of the AUMF? In light of the exclusivity provision of FISA, which would seem to have a preclusive effect on any reliance on other statutes unless they implicitly repeal the provision, it would appear that the AUMF cannot carry the weight the government's argument places on it. That seems particularly clear given FISA's provision for a temporary exception from its normal rules, limited to 15 days, for a surveillance initiated in the wake of a formal declaration of war by Congress.

So a separation-of-powers constitutional question is presented: does the President's constitutional power under Article II of the Constitution support the TSP *notwithstanding* FISA's exclusivity provision? The government's white paper argued that it did. But does not that argument necessarily lead to the conclusion that FISA is unconstitutional as an effort to restrict inherent presidential power? And if there is some core presidential power that FISA cannot restrict, is the NSA program within that core?

Most experts would agree that in certain circumstances there *is* a core of plenary presidential power. Defining its boundaries, however, is much harder than coming up with safe examples of power on one side or another of the boundary, wherever that is. No one would argue that Congress could pass a law ordering American soldiers to avoid using roads in Afghanistan in order to reduce injuries from IEDs; that would interfere with the military authority of the president as commander-in-chief. Likewise no one doubts that Congress can prescribe the standards and procedures for courts martial, which it has for generations.

But where is the boundary between such legal zones of authority, and how close to that boundary is electronic surveillance in a time of armed conflict? These questions recall Professor Edward Corwin's famous description of an "invitation to struggle" for primacy in the area of foreign affairs. The relevant issues here are likely to be the importance of the information sought in comparison with the invasion of privacy involved, and the substantive reasons for not using the FISA process. Those questions of course can only be answered authoritatively when more facts are known. (With regard to TSP's still extraordinarily secret operations, almost no information is today publicly available.)

There is also the Fourth Amendment question. This comes down to the nature of the predicate: is there "probable cause" to believe that one party to a communication is associated with *al Qaeda,* or just "reasonable suspicion"? That issue could become pivotal were the government to prevail on its separation-of-powers argument, but tellingly, courts that considered foreign intelligence surveillance *before* FISA all required "probable cause." Whether those courts would come out the same way in wartime is uncertain. The "reasonableness" inquiry demanded by the Fourth Amendment also cannot authoritatively be resolved in the absence of more detailed facts about the program, its accomplishments, and its intrusiveness.

Then, in January 2007, the FISC issued orders the practical effect of which seemed to be that any surveillances occurring under the TSP would thereafter have to be conducted pursuant to approval by the FISC, and the Attorney General so notified Congress. Rather quickly, however, the administration contacted Congress with the message that a subsequent ruling by another judge of the FISC—one that has never been made public—was jeopardizing essential collection efforts, and that, as a result, legislation was needed to rectify the situation.

Congress responded by passing the Protect America Act (PAA),[24] which the Bush Administration regarded as a major victory, except for the fact that Congress proposed to "sunset" this statute after only six months. The PAA allowed warrantless surveillance of foreign-to-foreign communications that were routed through the United States. But it also allowed warrantless surveillance of U.S. citizens having communications with foreigners as long as the target was "reasonably believed" to be located outside the U.S. In fact, the PAA *did* expire, and for several months the legal basis for the collection programs was gone.

Then in mid-summer of 2008, Congress passed the FISA Amendments Act (FAA) of 2008,[25] which put back in place most of the necessary legal infrastructure, albeit with increased reviews and *post hoc* reporting requirements. Even as the Bush Administration wound down and its political influence waned, it was still able to gain a very significant victory. Even presidential candidate Barack Obama, who had earlier criticized the proposal, voted in favor of the final bill. Indeed, as president, Obama appears to have left the NSA's surveillance program intact and in place.

The record thus shows that in two short years, the Bush Administration was able on at least two occasions to get out of Congress important legislative support for the TSP, or at least for a *de facto* statutory equivalent. Yet this begs the question: why had the administration decided to do unilaterally—with all of the consequent political damage when the TSP was revealed (as might have been foreseen), including a deterioration in the trust relationship between coequal branches—what it later seems to have had little trouble accomplishing, *with* the support, albeit grudging, of Congress?

In his excellent book *The Terror Presidency,* Jack Goldsmith—who headed the Justice Department's Office of Legal Counsel in 2003 and 2004—explains the answer to this puzzle, contending that "the administration's conception of presidential power had a kind of theological significance that often trumped political consequences."[26] They were, in other words, just the sort of constitutional purists discussed earlier, strongly convinced of the president's inherent authority in this area.

But at what a cost! And what rich lessons this story offers for subsequent officials keen to move ahead on a number of different fronts in the national security field. Doctrinal purity, one might conclude, may itself be a luxury that wise policymakers must be willing to forego.

Given that telecommunications providers will be involved, given that American citizens will be affected, and given, finally, the supercharged political controversy that seems inevitably to be generated by this subject—with all of its consequent costs to the body politic—it is surely far wiser to preserve one's purist constitutional views for Federalist Society or ACLU meetings, but in the meantime to get on with making the policy choices and political compromises that will get the national security job done successfully.

V. WHERE NEXT?

A. Current Law

So what is the current state of U.S. foreign intelligence surveillance law, and what does all of this teach us about where it should go in the future? Although as we have seen, much has changed, much of the 1978 FISA still applies, notwithstanding evolving technology, more complicated national security challenges, changes in Fourth Amendment jurisprudence, and evolving cultural norms relating to privacy.

In addition, the FAA of 2008 allows government investigators to engage in the electronic targeting of non-U.S. persons reasonably believed to be outside the United States, provided that they have the concurrent approval of the Attorney General and the Director of National Intelligence (a position created by IRTPA in 2004). This targeting is not limited to any specific facility or place, nor need the communication's "location" be overseas. The communication can have one end in the United States, and indeed can involve a U.S. person, as long as the *target* is a non-U.S. person reasonably believed to be abroad. ("Reverse-targeting," however, is not permitted: one cannot monitor a foreign target as a subterfuge for gathering information on a U.S. person who is really the subject of one's suspicions.)

When the target is a U.S. person abroad, however, the government must seek authorization from the FISC, based on conventional FISA probable cause that the target is an agent of a foreign power. The FAA also changed FISA so that foreign-to-foreign e-mail exchanges no longer require a FISA warrant, even if this information is acquired by accessing databases—for example, belonging to major Internet Service Providers (ISPs) such as Gmail or Hotmail—in the United States.

Accordingly, after the FAA: (1) U.S. domestic communications are still fully covered by FISA; (2) U.S.-foreign communications that target *non*-U.S. persons do not require a FISA warrant at all, regardless of where the interception takes place, but those that target U.S. persons anywhere *do* require a "probable cause" FISA warrant; and (3) foreign-to-foreign communications, if the target is a non-U.S. person, do not require a traditional FISA warrant, but if a U.S. person is targeted, a FISA warrant is obligatory.

B. The Experience of Other Countries

One potentially useful tool with which to judge the reasonableness of our own system is to look briefly at the experience of other countries. Here I rely to a major extent on facts assembled in an excellent chapter by Mark Gitenstein in a first-class new book edited by Benjamin Wittes.[27]

Gitenstein reports that, in contrast to that in place in the United States, the intelligence surveillance regimes of many other countries are more permissive—with most not requiring any advance judicial approval. In fact, only one, South Africa, has warrant requirements whose strictness, on paper, approximates our own. Spain also has a requirement for prior judicial authorization, but the requirement apparently does not apply in terrorism cases.

Other countries seem to have a more relaxed version of FISA's warrant requirement. Australia's intelligence surveillance authorizations are not approved by a court of serving judges, but instead by a group of retired judges appointed by the attorney general—a rather different dynamic from ours. In addition, surveillances may be approved to intercept the communications of people not suspected of any wrongdoing at all, when doing so *might* assist intelligence services in obtaining information relating to security.

For its part, France does not involve its judges in electronic intelligence gathering. Instead, approvals come from the prime minister, acting at the request of three other ministers. French law provides that the legislative branch has oversight responsibility, not the judiciary. Magistrates are brought into the picture if the intelligence investigation produces evidence of violations of law.

Likewise, the German system also involves the legislature, rather than courts, as the oversight authority. The intelligence service must obtain authorization from a commission created by a special parliamentary committee. Interestingly, however, according to Gitenstein, German law prohibits planting of electronic "bugs" in the home.

India uses a court-ordered warrant model. The United Kingdom, on the other hand, declines to use a judicial model, preferring instead that warrants be issued by the executive—and in the most sensitive cases by the Secretary of State or the Prime Minister—notwithstanding some unease on the basis that the European Convention on Human Rights seems to prefer a system of more broadly shared responsibility. Oversight of the warrant process for the interception of communications *after* the fact is the remit of the independent Interception of Communications Commissioner and also the Intelligence Services Commissioner.

Gitenstein also reports that in Israel, intelligence agencies may, without receiving advance judicial permission, wiretap persons suspected of endangering national security. This rule is in contrast to the rules of Israeli criminal procedure, which require permission from the president of the district court, with general *post hoc* oversight exercised by the attorney general and, annually, by a designated committee of the Knesset.

What lessons can we in the United States take away from this comparative analysis? For me, the model that gives the legislative a strong case-by-case role, as in France or Germany, is unattractive. Oversight after the fact has been difficult enough; operational involvement in each surveillance operation, and in real time, even by some select subcommittee of the intelligence committees of both houses, would be challenging indeed. (That, after all, is the reason for the wariness of the U.S. intelligence community in living up to the requirement of the Intelligence Oversight Act of 1980[28] that relevant parts of the Congress be kept "fully and currently informed" of sensitive intelligence matters. If taken literally, such a commandment would paralyze both the executive and the legislature.)

On the other hand, the legislative branch still has a vital role to play in helping to build the system under which the executive branch needs to work. The United States is a country perhaps unique among the democracies in having a strong executive branch that is nevertheless constrained in its foreign intelligence surveillance work by a highly regulatory web of very detailed laws. Among democracies subjecting national security surveillance to regulation at all, most countries have regimes involving far less regulation of executive activity than in our own, but these frameworks have been constructed entirely by the legislature, and not within a system contemplating the existence of inherent executive branch power. The result is that countries with executive authorities that are weaker vis-à-vis the legislature than our own presidency in fact endow their executives with more operational discretion in this area than we do—though such power, as in parliamentary regimes, could in theory be taken entirely away. We proclaim we have a strong executive, possessing intrinsic authorities, but it ends up exercising that authority constrained by more regulation emanating from both the legislative and the judicial branches.

The lesson for me is that the best combination is the result of a joint effort and shared responsibility between the executive branch and the legislative branch. The time is coming when the entire U.S. foreign intelligence electronic surveillance system will be overhauled. As we will see, it already needs to be. The executive and the legislative branches need to devise a compromise in which the president asks Congress to share responsibility for simplifying and clarifying this legal regime. Ideally, such a collaborative process could replace the FISA system by a modernized, streamlined statutory regime fashioned jointly by both branches in the exercise of their interdependent constitutional authority.

C. The Future: Thoroughgoing Reform

At the very least, the traditional 1978 FISA process is cumbersome, slow, and laborious. Although admittedly it was at the creation of the FISA process just after the Act was passed, my own personal experience with the FISA regime—as Associate Attorney General in 1979–81—was that each application was meticulously staffed out, with multiple reviews by staff lawyers, before it was forwarded to me or the Deputy Attorney General, and then to the Attorney General for final approval. After this, each application had to be presented to a judge of the FISC. When no local judge was available, a designated judge would have to fly into Washington and review the application in a secure room at a local airport—asking questions, as needed, of the DOJ attorney who was present—before turning around and flying back home.

The good news for me was that the process worked. I was able to be confident when I told a FISA court judge that the "minimization procedures" we put in place would prevent any undue encroachment on privacy. I was similarly confident when the FBI told me that a particular surveillance placement was necessary, and not unduly intrusive on the privacy interests of third parties. In short, the regime seemed to work—and work pretty well.

And yet it was very time-consuming. Presumably things have been considerably streamlined but still, an application-by-application process is exceedingly resource-intensive. Moreover, the statute has grown hideously complex, partially out of design, partially because the subject can be allowed to get complicated and partially because—like Topsy—it has just grown that way. This is not the way such business should be done in the 21st century. Even if nothing else were done, simplification and clarification would be a big step forward. But that would not be enough.

There are much larger questions we must also confront. We are at the point where a broad revision of FISA needs to take place, one designed to bring it up-to-date—technologically, legally, and as a matter of counterterrorist policy. Much as Congress and the executive branch would like to postpone the issue, it makes sense now to rethink the basic issues: (1) What is the nature of modern signals intelligence? (2) How, if at all, can the demands for more information from different kinds of sources be reconciled with our current view of the importance of the protection of civil liberties and expectation of privacy? (3) Is it sufficient to continue to patch the existing statute, or is a whole new regime required that embodies a new approach? (4) Or is some combination of traditional FISA and a wholly new approach possibly the best solution of all?

There are two basic problems that need to be solved. First, traditional FISA is built on a conventional law enforcement/Fourth Amendment model that is inadequate on its own for the realities of surveillance in today's electronically networked world. Even on its own terms, it is dependent on legal definitions, predicates, and thresholds, many of which are out-of-date and inefficient. Focusing upon the location of the target, for instance, is no longer adequate when it is no longer possible to ascertain where the target is. A "probable cause" standard may also be less preferable for certain communications than an "electronic frisk" procedure, in which a very brief data-sampling process is permitted in order to ascertain the merits of doing more. The use in the statute of geographic location as a proxy for U.S. person status may also risk over collection against Americans and under collection against non-Americans. In these and other threshold and jurisdictional instances, the conventional FISA approach seems out-of-date.

Second, certain important kinds of foreign signals intelligence gathering may not presently be provided for at all, or may be provided for inadequately. Programmatic surveillance—the vacuuming of whole swathes of electronic communication and the subsequent application of various filters and analytical techniques to mine the data—should either be brought within FISA more completely and comfortably, or a separate legal regime needs to be created.

In short, despite periodic legislative tweaks, FISA in its current form is already obsolete. In the words of Judge Richard Posner, FISA "retains value as a framework for monitoring the communications of known terrorists, but it is hopeless as a framework for *detecting* terrorists."[29] We can, and should, do better.

Any effort to reform FISA should address at least the following problems:

(1) The very complexity of the statute and of the individualized, warrant-based, and person-focused process is getting in the way of agile, real-time collection and timely use of valuable information. Various officials have estimated that each FISA application requires 200 person-hours, and demands the close personal involvement of the intelligence officers actually working the investigations. The government is said to file well over 2,000 applications a year, with each application itself approximately 50 to 60 pages long. Moreover, sheer complexity leads either to more mistakes, or to intelligence officials declining to approach the limits of lawfulness—resulting, respectively, either in over collection or under collection.

(2) FISA focuses on the individual target (e.g., whether he is the agent of a foreign power or engaged in terrorist activity, or whether or not he is a U.S. person) and on the target's location (e.g., in the United States or abroad). A requirement of "probable cause" or "reasonable grounds to believe" at various stages thus requires knowing something significant about the target, whereas often the point of an intelligence investigation today needs to be to find out whether someone should become a target

in the first place. As has been said, a large part of defeating the enemy consists of finding him.

(3) Because of the evolution of technology and the ways in which electronic communications are today distributed, FISA covers a greater proportion of international communications today than the original sponsors ever anticipated—and, by definition, a higher percentage of international communications intercepts thus require FISA approval.

(4) Perhaps more importantly, FISA as originally enacted left the government free to monitor foreign-to-foreign communications without seeking FISA warrants, even if the intercepts took place in the United States. But under the FISA Amendments Act of 2008, surveillance targeting a U.S. person abroad is now covered by FISA, requiring a judicial finding that there is probable cause to believe that the targeted person is the agent of a foreign power, as defined. So, in that respect, the new law has expanded traditional FISA.

(5) As technology has evolved, and fiber-optic and other cable networks have played a greater and greater role in communication, the government desired to conduct surveillance on cables inside the United States. Presumably the reason had to do with the location and accessibility of such cables, and the need to work with telecommunications providers to gain timely access to the cable traffic. The FAA now permits the targeting of persons (other than U.S. persons) reasonably believed to be abroad, regardless of where the collection takes place. But this collection must be pursuant to targeting procedures that are approved in advance by the FISA Court. Assessing whether this recent adjustment is working properly makes a persuasive case for a FISA rethink.

(6) Geographic location remains key to authorizing and conditioning surveillance under FISA, but in many situations it is not possible to tell reliably where a target is when any particular communication is made. (Just think of e-mails, for instance, which can be made by someone logging in from almost any point on earth.) Presumptions about location based on nationality—or presumptions about nationality that were based upon location—that were common under traditional FISA no longer make sense in the light of international travel. Many means of communication (e.g., mobile phones, Voice-over-Internet-Protocol [VoIP] technologies such as Skype, or e-mail) neither depend upon nor reveal the location of the sender or caller.

(7) Indeed in the case of foreign-to-foreign e-mail, many ISPs store e-mail messages on servers in the United States. In short, U.S. cyberspace is frequently visited by non-U.S. persons who are actually communicating abroad. That technological happenstance should not endow complete foreigners with constitutional rights to which they are not otherwise

entitled. Fortunately, the FAA of 2008 rectified that situation, thus contracting FISA's coverage. So perhaps that job has been done—but it is worth being sure.

(8) In addition, there is the question of follow-on monitoring after a suspicious communication. Suppose, for instance, that a known terrorist in Frankfurt, Germany, calls ten American telephone numbers, and the contents of those phone calls are intercepted. The next logical step in the investigation would be to put each of those ten numbers under at least temporary, preliminary coverage, to see whether the callers from those numbers are themselves possible terrorists. (Some may not be, but some may.) But to do that now, full FISA applications are required for each one, with all the delays that this entails. There perhaps ought to be the equivalent of a "stop-and-frisk" surveillance, designed to test quickly whether these ten callers are innocent parties or whether they are themselves suspicious. If the former, coverage should stop immediately. But if the latter, then emergency coverage should continue without a full FISA application until the paperwork can be completed and presented to the FISA Court. This kind of prudential coverage ought to be provided for in a FISA reform package.

(9) There is, finally, the immensely important issue of what is to be done with voluminous data that may be acquired under FISA, and particularly as the result of the programmatic acquisition authorized by the FAA. The retention, use, and dissemination of such data should be governed by robust minimization procedures that would reassure many Americans that there could not be misuse, including unregulated collection against Americans.

VI. CONCLUSION

FISA is a 1978 statute, studded with 1978 terms, embodying assumptions based upon 1970s-era technology, and dealing with 1970s-era threats. Much changed on 9/11, but this process of change had already been underway—and continues today.

First, the policy context is now very different. When FISA was written, in the post-Watergate era, Americans were more concerned about an all-powerful government engaging in widespread abuses of its citizens' civil liberties than they were about the national security threat the government was purportedly confronting. Although the civil liberties concern is still strong, perhaps a greater concern today is the catastrophic potential of terrorist attacks on the scale of 9/11, or even more horrendous. So the political equation has likely changed, and with it the policy options.

Second, the technology has changed. Today, the central role of the Internet and the technology of packet-switched networks make the traditional FISA approach awkward at best—and dysfunctional at worst—because it does not comport with how intelligence investigations need to be conducted today.

Third, modern signals intelligence needs to involve much more than the interception of traditional wire communications. There are oceans of data available for "vacuuming" and analysis. Filters that can be inserted into a flow of packet traffic can monitor millions of packets for certain traffic characteristics, which then permit inferences about sources of information and, in due course, about individuals who have it. Powerful analytic techniques that marry link and pattern recognition with statistical and predictive modeling can produce actionable intelligence where none was available—or perhaps even imaginable—before. Especially given the alacrity with which modern Americans routinely surrender enormous quantities of personal data to social networking sites, mobile telephony providers, ISPs, credit card companies, and all manner of other commercial entities, queasiness that the government might be engaged in massive counterterrorist data mining, the first step in a process that might reveal the identities of potential mass murderers, seems to me a luxury that we will be hard-pressed to afford.

In fact, one of the incidental costs of placing impediments in government's path in this area is not that the government cannot eventually get the information. Instead, the most likely problem is that the government cannot get it when it is most likely to *need* it: quickly. Private companies ubiquitously and uncontroversially engage in data mining—so, clearly, Americans have no illusions that such transactional and other information is really "private"—and the government already has the tools to acquire those results through some form of demand or subpoena. But this takes time, and time may be the one commodity, in an emergency, that we cannot afford.

In addition, as a people we seem to feel very differently about our relationship to our own personal data than we did 30 years ago, particularly when the data are scanned by computers rather than listened to by human beings. Spam filters, Google ads, and Amazon.com are part of many Americans' everyday life, and most people don't seem to mind. (Much of this information goes beyond the merely transactional as well. Google servers, for instance, routinely scan for keywords in the *content* of customers' e-mail message traffic, and target advertising feeds based upon what they find. Amazon also uses the subject matter of the books we browse, or purchase, in order to make recommendations to us, and to other customers.) Each of our computers contains personal data that we know nothing about and can't control, which can be harvested by any competent investigator, and yet, knowing this, we don't shy away from using e-mail or going online.

So the modern threat is different, the technology far more powerful, and our attitude toward information collection and data mining has undergone a major change. Some regime to accommodate these technological and cultural developments to constitutional requirements, in the light of intelligence needs, should be debated and approved by the Congress. Assuming they are still relevant, the questions about whether a "search" or "seizure" has in fact occurred, whether it was in the circumstances "unreasonable," and whether the entire process needs to be subjected to warrant-type regulation, need to be answered anew. And if the answer is that a *new* regulatory paradigm is more appropriate—for example, that less emphasis on prospective approval and more emphasis on regulating the *use* of information obtained makes sense—that new regime must be constructed in a way that satisfies constitutional imperatives but also meets the national security demands of our time.

The important objective ought to be to put the most efficient intelligence gathering system possible on the soundest foundation of governmental support possible, which will rely in turn on the broad public approval that follows from some degree of public debate and shared undertakings by the executive and legislative branches. Given the lessons learned from recent experience, and given the intelligent wariness our world requires of us in our own defense, no other approach is acceptable.

NOTES

1. 50 U.S.C. §§ 1801 *et seq.*

2. A *pen register* is a device that monitors the numbers called from a particular telephone, while *trap-and-trace technology* aims to identify all communications signals from a telecommunications system.

3. 50 U.S.C. at §1802(b)(2).

4. 277 U.S. 468 (1928).

5. 389 U.S. 347 (1967).

6. 18 U.S.C. §§ 2510 *et seq.*

7. *United States v. United States District Court (Keith),* 407 U.S. 297 (1972).

8. *United States v. Brown*, 484 F. 2d 418 (5th Cir. 1973); *United States v. Butenko*, 494 F. 2d 593 (3rd Cir. 1974); *United States v. Buck*, 548 F. 2d 871 (9th Cir. 1977); *but see Zweibon v. Mitchell*, 516 F. 2d 594 (D.C. Cir. 1975) (warrant required even in foreign intelligence investigations).

9. *See*, e.g., *United States v. Truong Dinh Hung*, 629 F. 2d 908 (4th Cir. 1980).

10. *See*, e.g., Senators Fred Thompson (R-TN) and Joseph Lieberman (D-CT), *Department of Energy, FBI, and Department of Justice Handling of the Espionage*

Investigation into the Compromise of Design Information on the W-88 Warhead (August 5, 1999), *available at* <http://hsgac.senate.gov/080599_china_espionage_statement.htm>.

11. As of 2004, this office began styling itself the "Government Accountability Office."

12. As it happened, on September 13, 2001, the British government gave U.S. officials sensitive intelligence information indicating that in fact Moussaoui had attended an *al Qaeda* training camp in Afghanistan.

13. Uniting and Strengthening America by Providing Appropriate Tools Required to Intercept and Obstruct Terrorism Act of 2001, Public Law 107–56 (October 26, 2001), 111 Stat. 272 (2001).

14. Public Law 108–458 (December 17, 2004), 118 Stat. 3638 (2004).

15. "Probable cause" is a standard greater than "reasonable suspicion," but of course less than "beyond reasonable doubt." It varies from one legal area to another but means generally "a suspicion, supported by facts, that something 'probably' occurred."

16. Public Law 96–456 (October 15, 1980), 94 Stat. 2025 (1980).

17. Public Law 107–40 (September 18, 2001).

18. *Youngstown Sheet & Tube Co. v. Sawyer*, 343 U.S. 579 (1952).

19. *See*, e.g., James Risen & Eric Lichtblau, "Bush Lets U.S. Spy on Callers Without Courts," *New York Times* (December 16, 2005).

20. *See*, e.g., Scott Shane & David Johnston, "Mining of Data Prompted Fight Over U.S. Spying," *New York Times* (July 29, 2007).

21. U.S. Department of Justice, "Legal Authorities Supporting the Activities of the National Security Agency Described by the President" (January 19, 2006), *available at* <http://www.justice.gov/opa/whitepaperonnsalegalauthorities.pdf>.

22. Public Law 107–40, *supra*.

23. *Hamdi v. Rumsfeld*, 542 U.S. 507 (2004).

24. Public Law 110–55 (August 5, 2007), 121 Stat. 552 (2007).

25. Public Law 110–261 (July 10, 2008), 122 Stat. 2436 (2008).

26. Jack Goldsmith, *The Terror Presidency: Law and Judgement Inside the Bush Administration* (2007), p. 272. New York: W.W. Norton & Company.

27. Mark H. Gitenstein, "Nine Democracies and the Problems of Detention, Surveillance, and Interrogation," in *Legislating the War on Terror: An Agenda for Reform* (Benjamin Wittes, ed.) (Washington, D.C.: Georgetown University Law Center & The Brookings Institution, 2009), at 7.

28. Public Law 96–450 (October 14, 1980).

29. Richard Posner, testimony to the U.S. House of Representatives, Permanent Select Committee on Intelligence (July 19, 2006) (emphasis added).

Chapter 6

Terrorism-Related Adjudication

Amichai Cohen

From a historical perspective, recent judgments of the U.S. Supreme Court, coupled with the change in policy brought about by the new administration, have created an anomalous situation. The history of colonial control, terrorism-related trials, and adjudication of asymmetrical conflicts is replete with cases in which the accused *rejected* the authority and impartiality of regular courts. States, on the other hand, used regular courts to try insurgents as criminals—thereby attempting to delegitimize their conduct, and brand it as merely criminal, and not an expression of freedom fighting.

In recent years, there has been a dramatic change in this perception. Governments have tried to avoid the use of regular courts and attempted to create mechanisms which bypass them—so much so that the recent decisions of the U.S. Supreme Court requiring the application of due process and *habeas corpus* to combatants[1] have been viewed as a revolutionary turn toward a more liberal and human rights-based approach.[2] The recent indictments against terrorists handed down in New York, which in the past would have been considered an attempt on the part of government to legitimize its conduct, have now become a sign of a potential new era of human rights *protection*.

Why has this change in perspective occurred, and why is this recent turn in events, where cases are brought to civil courts, considered so momentous a development in international and domestic jurisdiction—so much so that some commentators refer to it as a "revolution" in the ways courts deal with terrorism-related adjudications?

My main claim is that for several years, governments and lawyers have promoted a legal analysis which is based on two complimentary claims, both of which I submit are inaccurate, to say the least. The first is that there exist two separate ways of countering terrorism—the "war paradigm" and the "criminal/law-enforcement paradigm"—that legal limitations on states in the "criminal/law-enforcement paradigm" are much greater than they are in the "war paradigm," and that citizens are not and have never been protected under the "war paradigm" as they are protected under the "law-enforcement paradigm." The second claim is that courts are useful in the "criminal/law-enforcement paradigm" but are unsuited to deal with the "war paradigm." Invocation of the war paradigm, so this claim goes, means that there is or should be no threat of judicial intervention in the operations of the executive.

The first of these two claims is imprecise because there has never been, and cannot be, a complete distinction between the "war paradigm" and the "law-enforcement paradigm." Rather, there is a continuum of uses of law and its protection, between times of complete peace and times of total war. There are also specific areas where the use of law in times of emergency is even more specific and designed to grant more protection. It is true, of course, that in the event of war, states are allowed (or allow their agents) to take actions against other states (and their respective citizens) in ways that would not seem appropriate in times of peace. However, since states have no business with the territories and general citizenry of other states in times of peace, this observation actually has very little merit. The correct distinction is not between "war" and "law enforcement," but rather between territories that are controlled by states, and those which are not, and this distinction holds true in situations of both war and peace.

The second observation is imprecise because the real question is not under which paradigm the courts are working, but rather in what specific areas they are willing and able to intervene and review the actions of governments.

This chapter will uncouple both of the claims, and attempt to propose a clearer understanding of the areas in which courts intervene regarding counterterrorism measures taken by states. My claim will be that courts intervene in counterterrorism measures in specific cases: when the delicate balance between different branches of government is radically changed, or when the integrity of the political system is threatened, or when the integrity of the judicial process itself seems to be imperiled.

The first part of the chapter will provide a brief description of the development of legal thinking regarding the law-enforcement/war divide. The second part of the chapter will explain the contribution of courts to current thinking about these issues. In the third part of the chapter, I will survey decisions of various courts which have reviewed counterterrorism measures, and try to categorize these interventions. In the conclusion, I shall try to provide a comprehensive explanation of the trends identified in the behavior of the courts.

I. THE WAR PARADIGM AND THE LAW-ENFORCEMENT PARADIGM

One major question that seems to be dominant in contemporary legal discourse regarding counterterrorism is whether counterterrorism activities should be considered law-enforcement operations or war.[3] With regard to the applicability of international law, the importance of this distinction cannot be overstated: If counterterrorism operations are "law-enforcement" operations, then the body of law controlling these operations is "human rights" law, which generally regulates the behavior of states in times of peace. On the other hand, if indeed the counterterrorism operations are to be considered as "war," then the body of legal norms controlling counterterrorism should be International Humanitarian Law (IHL), a.k.a. the Law of Armed Conflict (LOAC).[4]

Human rights law and IHL are different in both their aims and their contents. The goal of human rights law is to limit the actions of governments toward their own citizens, or people under their effective control in times of peace or normalcy. IHL, on the other hand, regulates policies of governments against their enemies—combatants or civilians—in times of war.[5] This major difference in goals naturally affects the difference in content. International Human Rights Law (IHRL), as represented in various international treaties such as the International Convention on Civil and Political Rights, includes a much more limiting framework. In law-enforcement operations, for example, only a very limited amount of force can be used.[6] On the other hand, IHL includes a much more flexible framework which allows the state to use force in ways which are much less prohibitive. This distinction is treated at length elsewhere in this volume.[7]

This difference in legal regimes is based on the assumption that there are basically two possible situations where governments need to balance their interests against humanitarian and human rights considerations. One situation is where the government faces an internal problem which is of relatively small scale. Such problems should be dealt with as "law-enforcement issues," and are regulated by IHRL. On the other hand, there are external wars, where soldiers mainly fight other soldiers, and the use of force is generally required. Such situations are controlled by IHL.

This traditional dichotomy has been challenged, however, by what in recent years has become the most dominant form of armed conflict: the *non-international armed conflict*. Non-international armed conflicts have posed challenges to the existing dichotomy from several perspectives:

- First, there are today almost no armed conflicts between two states of equal powers. In almost all of the armed conflicts of the past 20 years, at least one of the belligerents has been a Non-State Actor (NSA).[8] NSAs can be an organization fighting the government from within the state (in which case the conflict is sometimes called "a civil war"), an organization fighting the state from a specific location in another state, or an organization waging a global war against the state, from wherever it can and against whichever part or agent of the state it can attack. (In this last case this conflict is called part of war involving "global" or "transnational" terrorism.)[9]

- Second, the nature of the conflict has changed. There are now almost no great battles in which thousands of tanks and other armored vehicles are positioned one against the other, and hundreds of pilots fight to death to achieve control of the skies. Contemporary armed conflicts consist of small-scale operations, directed toward specific targets. There is almost never a clear victory from a specific incident, although the warring parties always hope that the accumulation of successful operations would cause the enemy to capitulate.
- Third, the changes above have been accompanied by a significant change in the nature of persons involved in warfare. While in the past it was possible to differentiate between soldiers and civilians, and between the battlefield and civilian areas, in current conflicts this differentiation is almost never possible. In current conflicts, combatants—i.e., persons participating in the conflict—form part of a civilian population. Indeed, often they are civilians during most of their daily routine. Furthermore, NSAs use civilian populations as a basis for their operations; combatants constantly hide themselves within the civilian population, and use civilian homes as arsenals and launching sites. Non-State Actors also use the civilian population as a support group, providing the organization with whatever logistical support it needs. Civilians provide these NSAs with food and shelter, medical treatment, and all other required supplies.

Naturally, under these circumstances it is quite hard to differentiate between law enforcement and war.

As a result of these changes in the operational setting, states increasingly resorted to measures which did not squarely fall within either the law-enforcement model or the war model. On the one hand, in order to fight NSAs, states used their armed forces and applied force to a degree greater than in regular law-enforcement operations. On the other hand, this use of force did not usually amount to a full-fledged war.

It should not be surprising that until the mid-1990s, international law had relatively little to offer states regarding this specific kind of use of force. To be sure, civil wars and internal strife are not a new phenomenon. Yet, in the past, it was legally possible to bypass the need to deal with the legal questions and issues detailed above which these situations pose. Until 1976, when the major International Human Rights Covenants came into force, most states were not under any international obligation to protect human rights at all. Issues related to internal security measures and internal armed conflict almost never became a matter of international law concern. IHL was also almost never invoked, mostly because these conflicts were usually internal. Hence, as already noted, IHL was considered to regulate *external* conflicts. Indeed, as Allison Danner has shown, states were quite adamant in their attempts to oppose any international law interventions in what they considered to be their internal matters with regard to insurgencies.[10]

There were only two minor exceptions to this general rule. During the 1970s, the European Court of Human Rights (ECtHR), which is an international tribunal responsible for the application of the European Conventions Human Rights, began to take some interest in the United Kingdom's activities in Northern Ireland. In a series of decisions, it criticized some of the most severe methods used by the UK, such as certain methods of investigations.[11]

The other exception was Common Article 3 of the Geneva Conventions (1949), and the second additional protocol to the Geneva Convention of 1977, both of which sought to place some limits on the use of force in internal armed conflicts. Yet these international instruments were very limited in their substance.[12] Indeed, until the end of the 1990s there was only one conflict in which the state recognized the applicability of these international limitations.

Hence, when, during the 1990s, it became apparent that non-international armed conflicts were becoming the dominant sort of armed conflict, there seemed to be very few legal norms that could be applied to these conflicts. Since these conflicts mostly occurred in countries that were not really expected to follow the rule of law, lawyers and politicians were usually able to turn a blind eye and avoid the question of applicable law in these cases. States applied force in non-international armed conflicts, and international law generally had very little to say about these situations.

Change came, however, with the legal response to two specific conflicts: the wars in Yugoslavia and the genocide in Rwanda in 1994.[13] In these two cases, the United Nations Security Council decided to form international criminal tribunals for the prosecution of persons who committed violations of international law in these conflicts. To be sure, at first it seemed that the creation of these tribunals required no new legal norm, but rather the mere application of existing legal norms. As Danner has shown,[14] regarding Yugoslavia, the dominant opinion in the U.N. was that this was an international armed conflict between Bosnia and Serbia, and not an internal one. Hence the relevant law was considered to be the four Geneva Conventions and Customary

IHL. Regarding Rwanda, the major accusation was that of genocide, which since the Second World War has been an exception to the rule of sovereign independence. However, once these tribunals began to operate, they developed a completely new jurisprudence regarding non-international armed conflicts.

Before we describe the contribution of these courts, note must be taken of another operational development: the emergence of the "war on terrorism" after September 2001.

A. Terrorism

Until September 2001, the above-described non-international armed conflicts were considered completely different from classical "international terrorism," which involves organized groups acting in various locations against civilian targets that are distant from their own bases of support, and whose actions are usually motivated by ideology (as opposed to ethnic or territorial claims).[15] Terrorism in this sense was basically considered a law-enforcement concern, which should be dealt with under criminal law. Indeed, all the major international treaties which were drafted with this model of terrorism in mind prior to 2001 treated it as a criminal law issue, to which the solution should basically be found within the contours of criminal law.[16]

This all changed in September 2001, with the attacks on the World Trade Center in New York and the Pentagon in Washington, D.C., and the responses to these attacks led by the United States. Within a short time, several international organizations and states changed their view regarding terrorism, now considering it to be a matter which is no longer fit for treatment simply within the sphere of traditional law-enforcement activity. There began a push to consider more radical solutions and methods to fight transnational terrorism.[17] Led by the United States, the U.N. Security Council adopted Resolution 1368, which declared that the United States has a right of self-defense against *al-Qaeda,* in effect moving the center of legal discourse in this issue from law-enforcement paradigm to the war paradigm.[18]

Certainly, part of this change was due to real world change. The organization of terrorist groups has indeed become global, the effects of their actions more significant, and the dangers that they pose more serious. Moreover, terrorists identified a group of "failed states" from within which they were able to operate without hindrance from local authorities, thus making them immune to normal law-enforcement operations.

However, the conceptual change was also driven by an attempt to gain some legal flexibility, as will be discussed below. As a response to the September 11 attacks, and to ensuing global terrorism, states adopted measures of fighting terrorism that reflect a deviation from the traditional law-enforcement paradigm and, in fact, appear contrary to the obligations of states under IHRL.

B. New Claims

One example is the use of *targeted killings,* discussed elsewhere in this volume.[19] Targeted killings, for the purposes of this discussion, could be defined as the use of lethal force against people believed to be part of a terrorist organization, *even when such persons do not pose an imminent and immediate* threat, on the grounds that because of their participation in the planning or command of terrorist operations, they pose a future danger.[20] This use of force by states seems to violate IHRL as traditionally interpreted, because it allows the use of lethal force only to confront immediate and imminent danger.[21] No one would think of shooting a person in a law-enforcement operation when he is asleep, and, of course, no damage to innocent civilians would be tolerated in law-enforcement operations. In *targeted-killing* operations, as carried out by Israel and the United States, the targeted person is considered a "constant" danger, and there is no need to demonstrate his or her involvement in a specific operation or an imminent attack. Moreover, under some circumstances, some civilian casualties are allowed.[22] Hence the use of targeted killing can be legally justified only under a "war" paradigm, with the appropriate limitations emanating from IHL.

Another notable deviation from regular "law-enforcement" and human rights standards took place with regard to detentions of people suspected of participating in terrorist activities. Perhaps the best known example is the U.S. detention facility in Guantánamo Bay. The original position of the U.S. authorities was a total rejection of the law-enforcement and IHRL models with regard to detention of people suspected in terrorism.[23] Because of an especially strict interpretation of its human rights and constitutional obligations, the U.S. administration concluded that its actions at the Guantánamo base, which is outside of U.S. sovereign territory, are subject to very few limitations under human rights treaties or its constitution.[24] On the other hand, because terrorists are not "legal combatants," they are not protected by the relevant Geneva Conventions.[25] Hence, the administration concluded that no rights should be afforded to the detainees in Guantanamo by IHL. As a result, these detainees were not protected by any legal regime, domestic or international, and could have been kept in prolonged detentions, and even subjected to physical pressure, without recourse to any judicial review on their part.

This, of course, was an extreme example of how the move away from traditional law-enforcement paradigm affected the way in which states treated people suspected in terrorist activities. Other states were perhaps less extreme in their responses, but still allowed themselves to deviate from traditional human rights principles. Such was the Israeli *Incarceration of Illegal Combatants Law* (2002), which allowed the chief of general staff of the Israeli Defense Forces (IDF) to detain a member of any organization which is involved in anti-Israeli activity, or that directly or indirectly assists this organization, for the duration of the conflict.[26] While this law did involve a specific clause of judicial review, it in effect allowed the authorities to detain any persons involved with Hamas or Hezbollah, even when they had no association with activities against Israel. Some scholars claimed that a textual interpretation of this law would potentially allow the detention of 30–40 percent of the residents of the Gaza strip and Southern Lebanon, where Hamas and Hezbollah, respectively, act as the *de facto* government.

In the same vein, the United Kingdom, France, Australia, Canada, Germany, and India—among other states—passed laws which allowed governments to detain persons for longer periods[27] and to employ more liberal rules of evidence.[28] Other states created special courts (with more flexible rules) to deal with people detained for terrorism-related offenses.[29] As Yuval Shany has noted, the common denominator of all these and other measures undertaken by states with the intention of restricting persons suspected of terrorist activities was the weakening of human rights protections.[30]

The claim also caused a change in traditional territorial categorization: while in the past all activities within a state were controlled by domestic law and human rights law, the claim resulting from the move to the war paradigm was that regular laws should not now be applied even *within* the state in certain situations. One prominent example is the U.S. administration's attempt to bypass the Foreign Intelligence Surveillance Act (FISA) legislation, allowing the administration to conduct eavesdropping on a massive scale without the judicial authorization required by the statute.[31]

To sum up this part, states indeed faced changing realities challenging the traditional concept of a divide between law enforcement and war, and the resulting dichotomy between human rights obligations and obligations resulting from IHL. Yet, it seems that, at least with regard to the "war on terror," states manipulated this apparent lack of clarity in law. States defined counterterrorism measures as "a war on terror" in order to gain more flexibility in using their powers, and to evade legal limitations. Of course, if the law were indeed lacking, then states could not be said to act in an illegal manner when they manipulated it. The only institutions with the potential to clarify the norms, however, were national courts and international tribunals. The next part of this chapter will evaluate the response of the courts to the changing policy of states.

II. COURTS AND NON-INTERNATIONAL ARMED CONFLICT—PRIOR TO 2001

As was already shown, the gradual erosion of the law-enforcement/war paradigm can be traced back to the 1980s and early 1990s, when internal armed conflicts gradually became the more dominant form of armed conflicts. As already mentioned, until the mid-1990s, international law had very little to say about this development. However, two important processes in international law changed this situation; both resulted from activities taken by international tribunals—the International Criminal Tribunal for the former Yugoslavia (ICTY) and the International Court of Justice (ICJ).

A. The ICTY and Non-International Armed Conflicts

As already noted, when the ICTY was formed in 1993, it was established under the idea that the conflict in Bosnia was basically international in character. However, in its first major decision, the *Tadic* case (1995), the ICTY pointed out that the conflict was actually a *non*-international one, posing the Bosnian government against the *Republica Srepska*—a political organization of the Bosnian-Serb minority. This raised the issue of the applicable law in non-international armed conflicts.[32]

In a series of revolutionary decisions, the court offered Customary International Law as the source of prohibitions and legal norms during armed conflicts. In its famous *Tadic* opinion the ICTY declared that:

> . . . [i]t follows that in the area of armed conflict the distinction between interstate wars and civil wars is losing its value as far as human beings are concerned. Why protect civilians from belligerent violence, or ban rape, torture or the wanton destruction of hospitals, churches, museums or private property, as well as proscribe weapons causing unnecessary suffering when two sovereign States are engaged in war, and yet refrain from enacting the same bans or providing the same protection when armed violence has erupted 'only' within the territory of a sovereign State? If international law, while of course duly safeguarding the legitimate interests of States, must gradually turn to the protection of human beings, it is only natural that the aforementioned dichotomy should gradually lose its weight. [33]

It added later that

> . . . elementary considerations of humanity and common sense make it preposterous that the use by States of weapons prohibited in armed conflicts between themselves be allowed when States try to put down rebellion by their own

> nationals on their own territory. What is inhumane, and consequently proscribed, in international wars, cannot but be inhumane and inadmissible in civil strife. [34]

The declaration of the ICTY paved the way for a significant migration of IHL norms from international armed conflicts to non-international armed conflicts in Customary International Law.[35] Viewing this development in retrospect, the comprehensive study of Customary International Law, supported by the ICRC, declared most major rules of Customary IHL applicable to international and non-international armed conflicts.[36]

B. ICJ and the Parallel Application of Norms

A second major development in this area was the ICJ's *Advisory Opinion on the Legality of Threat or Use of Nuclear Weapons*.[37] In its advisory opinion, the ICJ dealt with the problem of the relationship between IHL and international human rights law when both apply. What happens when in a single situation a state is obligated by the two sets of norms, and these collide?

The solution of the ICJ was simple. IHL and IHRL are not mutually exclusive. They both apply to cases of, for example, an internal military conflict. However, human rights law is the *lex generalis* (general law applying to all cases) and IHL is the *lex specialis* (special law applying only to armed conflicts). Hence, IHL would receive precedence in cases of direct conflict between norms emanating from the two systems.[38] Whenever there is a direct conflict between IHL and IHRL, the legal norms of IHL would prevail. However, when there is no conflict between these bodies of law, IHRL should be used to determine the extent of obligations on states.[39]

What emerged from the moves of both IHL to encompass and regulate non-international armed conflicts (the path taken by the ICTY), and IHRL to regulate cases of armed conflict (that of the ICJ), is a new legal paradigm, which David Kretzmer dubbed "the mixed model."[40] In essence, the underlying premise of the mixed model is that some armed conflicts do not belong either in the sphere of law enforcement (and IHRL) or in war (and IHL), but rather in both. These situations, in which states fight NSAs, have a distinct body of law controlling them. "Pure" IHRL is inappropriate in these cases, and so is "pure" IHL.

It is perhaps impossible to overstate the importance of these two decisions. They both created a framework for applying international law in non-international armed conflicts, and sent a signal that these forms of conflicts would be controlled by international law, and not left without any legal norms to control them.

Yet, without in any way diminishing the importance of these decisions, it is vital to understand that they included a problematic intellectual move. In order to create norms that effectively control the application of force in non-international armed conflicts, these courts had to lower the barriers which previously existed between internal law enforcement (controlled by domestic law and IHRL) and war (controlled by IHL). If states were unwilling to apply the entire gamut of human rights obligations in internal and non-international conflicts, the courts, using international law, allowed them more flexibility: states could base their operation on the more permissive norms included in IHL. The result was that the previously existing barriers between the law-enforcement paradigm and war paradigm became porous.

There is a direct connection between this intellectual move and the development of states' practice regarding counterterrorism. The absence of a clear border between law enforcement and war tempted states to view counterterrorism activities as "war," in order to gain more flexibility in their responses to terrorism. Hence, even though the "war against terrorism" is a figure of speech, and most operational activities against transnational terrorism are basically law-enforcement in nature, states juxtaposed them within the framework of a "war against terrorism." From the legal point of view, this means that states allowed themselves greater flexibility in the fight against transnational terrorism, under the *mixed-model paradigm,* flexibility that would not have been allowed under the traditional law-enforcement model.

The next part of this chapter will review the response of national courts and international tribunals to this practice of the states and international organizations.

III. COURTS AND COUNTERTERRORISM MEASURES

As Yuval Shany has correctly stated, the move toward a more flexible mode of IHRL, or the adoption of the mixed model, actually signified a more profound institutional claim. The idea was that it was not courts, the traditional bearers of human rights, which should control national security. Rather, courts should be shunted aside, and the executive should be given more control over the fight against terrorism.[41]

Hence, when state lawyers raised the claim the counterterrorism activities are part of the "war" paradigm, they were in effect arguing that *courts* should not try to uphold these laws because courts are not supposed to intervene in matters of war.[42] This claim, which is an institutional and not analytical one, is based on the assumption, supported by vast historical evidence, that courts avoid getting involved in national security matters.

This claim is based on a long tradition of scholars of domestic constitutional law. In his minority opinion in the *Korematsu* case (1944), Justice Robert Jackson famously stated:

> It would be impracticable and dangerous idealism to expect or insist that each specific military command in an area of probable operations will conform to conventional tests of constitutionality. When an area is so beset that it must be put under military control at all, the paramount consideration is that its measures be successful, rather than legal. The armed services must protect a society, not merely its Constitution. The very essence of the military job is to marshal physical force, to remove every obstacle to its effectiveness, to give it every strategic advantage. Defense measures will not, and often should not, be held within the limits that bind civil authority in peace.[43]

Note that Justice Jackson was saying not that the law in times of emergencies is different, but that upholding it in times of emergencies is different. Courts have traditionally stayed out of matters involving national security, and have traditionally adopted a series of "avoidance doctrines" intended to save them the need to interfere with the ways that legislatures and executives managed their mutual relationship and human rights.

The modern presentation of this theory was introduced in the United States by scholars such Eric Posner and Adrian Vermeule,[44] and by Richard Posner.[45] According to these commentators, courts should indeed limit their interventions in national security matters because of problems of incorrect information, inability to weigh the costs correctly, and the danger that some terrorist activities might cause damage which will far exceed the courts' expectations. For all these reasons, these scholars suggest that the correct institution to deal with antiterrorist activities is the executive, which should generally not be controlled by the court.[46] Not unexpectedly, these claims generated forceful opposition. The attempt to limit the power of courts was seen as an attempt to limit civil liberties, and a mistaken submission to executive claims, which do not lead to more safety.[47]

So, the real gist of the executive position on the "war on terror" is that it was an attempt to call upon the courts to refrain from intervention where national security matters are concerned.[48] To some degree, this proved to be a forceful claim. American courts, as well as other courts, were indeed very hesitant to intervene in what the government was doing, and frequently deferred to it. It is worth looking closer, however, at how courts have responded to this claim. Have they really taken it seriously and entirely avoided intervening in these cases?

According to Eyal Benvenisti, who has written extensively about the attitude of courts both before and after 2001, once the initial shock of the September 11th attacks wore off, several courts did begin to intervene in national security matters, even in the face of the "war on terror" claims. Benvenisti claims that national courts formed a united opposition to the attempts of government to curb constitutional rights, by limiting the ability of government to adopt measures which infringed upon basic human rights.[49]

I shall evaluate the claims raised by Benvenisti later. However, I think that this claim does not fully encompass the analytical and institutional change that took place. The question is not only whether courts opposed specific government acts, an issue to which I will return hereafter. The question is also whether the courts opposed the principled positions that governments took: that of trying to gain more flexibility in counterterrorism measures by using the "war" paradigm.

In this principled area, two issues should be closely examined. The first is the attitude of courts toward the general claim of the move from the "law-enforcement" paradigm to the "war" paradigm. Did courts accept that counterterrorism measures are actually part of the "war on terror"? The second issue is territorial: did courts accept the claim that counterterrorism operations outside the territory of the state should not be controlled by courts?

A. Law-Enforcement vs. War Models

(1) National Courts

All in all, it could be said that national courts did accept the paradigm shift from law enforcement to war, and the resulting move from human rights law to IHL. Explicit statements in this regard were voiced by the Israeli Supreme Court in several decisions. In the *Ajuri case,* for example, the court explicitly declared:

> Since late September 2000, severe combat has been taking place in the areas of Judea and Samaria. It is not police activity. It is an armed conflict.[50]

The same logic was used by the U.S. Supreme Court in the *Hamdan* case (2006).[51]

As is well known, the major cases in which the U.S. Supreme Court has intervened in national security matters focus on the treatment of what the U.S. government terms "enemy combatants" of various sorts. In *Hamdi v. Rumsfeld*[52] and *Rasul v. Bush,*[53] both in 2004, the Supreme Court decided that as long as detainees are effectively under the control of the United States, whether or not they are American citizens, they are entitled to some level of *due process of law* both under U.S. law and under the Geneva Conventions.

Significantly, however, the U.S. Supreme Court in these cases accepted the basic premise of the applicability of IHL to the war on terror, especially in Afghanistan, where it seemed that the operation was indeed similar to war. Following this decision, President George W. Bush authorized the creation of military commissions to try the detainees in Guantánamo. In 2006, in *Hamdan v. Rumsfeld,* the Supreme Court held that these military commissions lacked "the power to proceed because their structures and procedures violate both the Uniform Code of Military Justice and the four Geneva Conventions signed in 1949." In its *Hamdan* opinion, the U.S. Supreme Court also accepted without debate the position of the U.S. government that IHL applied to the "war on terror." The government's difference of opinion with the court was regarding the question of whether Common Article 3 of the Geneva Conventions applies to the conflict between the United States and *al-Qaeda*. Accordingly, it could safely be said that the U.S. Supreme Court accepted the position of the government that counterterrorism is controlled by IHL.

One decision in which a national court might have opined differently is that of the German Federal Constitutional Court to strike down Article 14 (3) of the German Air Transport Security Act (2005). This important provision authorized the minister of defense to order that a passenger airplane be shot down, if it could be assumed that the aircraft would be used against the life of others and if the shooting is the only means of preventing this present danger.[54] The court declared that this law was incompatible with the German Basic Law (Constitution). Among other issues, the court declared that the minister of defense lacked the power to intervene in matters which lie within the sphere of authority of the *Lander* (the "states" of the German Federation), which are responsible for internal security.

According to the German Constitution, the armed forces are constituted "for the purpose of defense."[55] At least one commentator understood this decision as a rejection of the attempt by the German government to present counterterrorism activity as a "war on terror" which justifies self-defense, and hence the use of the federal armed forces.[56] According to this interpretation, the German Federal Court stood by the traditional view, according to which counterterrorism should be analyzed under the human rights (law-enforcement) model, and resisted recourse to any version of the "war" paradigm.

The abovementioned interpretation, however, is at least arguable. The German court did *not* focus on the question of the limits of self-defense against terrorism, but rather on the division of authority between various branches of the Federal government in cases of emergency, as will be explained below.[57]

(2) International Bodies

It seems that international tribunals, especially in Europe, were much readier to reject the paradigm shift from law enforcement to war. In a series of decisions relating to British counterterrorism measures, to the conflict in Chechnya, and to the conflicts between Turkey and the Kurdistan Workers' Party (PKK), the court applied the framework of the European Convention of Human Rights without formally recognizing *any* of these cases as allowing more flexibility, or derogation from human rights obligations, to the state involved in counterterrorism or international conflict.[58] Thus, in the *Isayeva* case, the court applied human rights norms to a battle between the Russian armed forces and more than one thousand armed insurgents. The Court explicitly described the Chechnyan forces as involved in "active resistance to . . . law-enforcement bodies,"[59] and criticized the armed forces for not showing "the degree of caution expected from a law-enforcement body in a democratic society."[60]

A somewhat similar position was advanced by the European Court of Justice in its *Kadi* decision.[61] U.N. Security Council Resolution 1267 required all states to impose aircraft and financial sanctions and an arms embargo against the Taliban in Afghanistan. In addition to laying down provisions for monitoring the implementation of the measures, the resolution also mandated the creation of the so-called Sanctions Committee. Subsequent resolutions arising out of the Resolution 1267 terrorist sanctions regime require enforcement by U.N. member states against any person or entity designated on the "Consolidated List" created by the Sanctions Committee. The 1267 regime, however, contains only minimal allowance for due process: decisions to list or delist a party are by Committee consensus; little information about the grounds for being listed is shared with the listed parties; listees are not represented before the Sanctions Committee; and no judicial review or remedy is available. Kadi was added to the list by the Sanctions Committee, and consequently the European Union, acting according to the U.N. Security Council decision, "blacklisted" him and applied the sanctions.

> In accepting Kadi's appeal against the decision to blacklist him, the ECJ declared that [i]t follows from the foregoing that the Community judicature must, in accordance with the powers conferred on it by the [European Commission] Treaty, ensure the review, in principle the full review, of the lawfulness of all Community acts in the light of the fundamental rights forming an integral part of the general principles of Community law, including review of Community measures which, like the contested regulation, are designed to give effect to the resolutions adopted by the Security Council under Chapter VII of the Charter of the United Nations. [62]

Once again, even without explicitly saying so, it seems that the European Court of Justice rejected the claim that terrorists should be dealt with by the "war" paradigm and insisted that the regular human rights regime should apply.

To sum up, it could be said that national courts were hesitant to oppose the basic contention of governments that the fight against terrorism is basically a war, and that limitations arising out of IHRL should be relaxed. International tribunals, on the other hand, were much more ready to oppose governments on this point. This is only natural since after all, national courts are a branch of government of the state, and judges in these courts feel responsible first and foremost for the welfare of the citizens of the state.

B. The Territorial Limits

Even when courts were ready to impose limitations on governments, the question was whether these limitations applied globally, or only in specific areas. There is some debate in international law as to whether IHRL applies outside the area controlled by the state, on the actions of its agents abroad.[63] Apart from this question, however, there is also the institutional issue: are courts willing to impose any limitation (be its source in IHRL or IHL) on the actions of governments outside their territories?

A short survey of cases shows that judicial review of counterterrorism measures is strongly connected to territorial concerns. Thus, the Guantánamo cases mentioned above deal exclusively with cases arising from the United States and the Guantánamo base—a territory controlled by the United States. In a parallel case to that of *Boumedienne,* dealing with the *habeas corpus* rights of suspects detained in the Bagram air base in Afghanistan, the U.S. Court of Appeals for the D.C. Circuit rejected the claim that such rights should be afforded also to persons detained there, because Bagram is clearly outside the *de facto* territory of the United States. (By contrast, the Guantánamo base is under the complete and total control of U.S. authorities, although technically not on land under American sovereignty.)[64] Similarly, in the case of *El-Masri v. Tenet,* federal courts dismissed the lawsuit brought by a person who claimed to have been mistakenly arrested by the Central Intelligence Agency (CIA) and held in various prisons around the world.[65]

The Israeli Supreme Court, dealing with Israeli obligations toward Palestinians in the Gaza strip after the Israeli disengagement, declared that the area is no longer under Israeli occupation, and therefore Israel's obligations toward Palestinians in the Gaza strip are down to the bare "minimum humanitarian level."[66] In further cases, the court rejected all of the petitions against the Israel government arising out of the Gaza strip.[67]

All these decisions lead to the same conclusions: though national courts were willing to impose some limitations, based on human rights and IHL, on counterterrorism measures employed by governments, they did so only within strict territorial limits. National courts were usually very hesitant to extend the reach of their decisions *outside* the territory in which there is "effective control" of the government. I shall deal with what I think are the reasons for these self-imposed limitations at the conclusion of this chapter.

Once again, international tribunals seem to be more flexible. The European Court of Human Rights, while still limiting the application of human rights norms based on a territorial control test, found some exceptions to this rule. The basic rule was set out in the *Bankovic* case.[68] There, the court declared that the reach of the European Convention of Human Rights, although territorial in nature, extends also to areas in which a person is under the control agents of the states.[69] Further, the court declared that the application of the convention extends to areas that are under the effective control of states.[70] In other decisions, the court further developed this test to extend the reach of its authority to areas that are temporarily under the control of the state.[71]

In the *Al-Skeini* decision, the UK House of Lords applied this test to the Basra area of Iraq, and declared that this area *was not* under the effective control of the UK, hence refusing to apply the obligations under the European Convention to this area.[72] The European Court of Human Rights, in its *Al Skeini* decision, reiterated the "effective control" principle, while rejecting the view of the UK House of Lords that the UK had no effective control over Basra in the month following the Iraq war.[73] In summary, it is possible to see that the European Court of Human Rights was much less strict on applying the territorial limitations on the obligations on states.

C. Substantive Areas of Intervention

Clearly, despite the limitations I just mentioned, courts did intervene in some cases to limit counterterrorism measures taken by states. My claim in this part is that interventions by national courts and international tribunals took place in two main areas. One consists of protection of the *constitutional order* and institutional separation of powers. The other is the protection of *due process* and *the integrity of the judicial process*. There are very few interventions of courts in counterterrorism measures outside these two areas.

(1) Institutional and Separation of Powers Issues

Under this rubric, I refer to issues which are usually considered part of the constitutional order of the state. Specifically, which branch of government is the appropriate one to make decisions in which matter?

The first case in which the Israeli Supreme Court (ISC) chose this path is the *Public Committee Against Torture* case of 1999.[74] In this case, a nongovernmental organization (NGO) petitioned the ISC against the approval given by the government (and approved by a special parliamentary committee) to General Security Service investigators, to use "moderate physical pressure" and other methods in investigations of persons suspected in terrorist activities.[75] In its decision, the court did not opine regarding the morality or constitutionality of the methods, or the degree of the approval's consonance with international law. Instead, the ISC declared that since Israeli criminal law does not include any specific authorization for the use of such methods, any approval would have to be given by the Knesset, Israel's parliament.

The same logic was used by the U.S. Supreme Court in *Hamdan v. Rumsfeld* in 2006, mentioned above, in which the Court held that military commissions set up by the Bush Administration to try detainees at Guantánamo Bay lack "the power to proceed because their structures and procedures violate both the Uniform Code of Military Justice and the four Geneva Conventions signed in 1949." In short, the Court *required the executive to receive express Congressional authorization for its actions*[76]—which is to say, the Court required more legislative input into the counterterrorism measures that were being taken.

Perhaps the most elaborate body of jurisprudence regarding the institutional division of power in the fight against terrorism is that of the German Federal Constitutional Court. In several important decisions, that court outlined the limits on the executive and on the *Bund* (the federal government) regarding the use of force in general and the fight against terrorism in particular.

First let us look at its treatment of the use of force. In several decisions dating back to the 1990s, the Federal Constitutional Court emphasized the need for parliamentary authorization for every major use of force outside Germany. If possible, this authorization should receive prior authorization. In emergencies, the *Bundestag* should be notified after the fact and approve the continuance of the mission. Any lack of parliamentary authorization—even to a support mission such as operating airborne warning and control system (AWACS) aircraft during the 2003 Iraq War—will render the operation illegal.[77]

The German *Aircraft Security Act* case has already been mentioned. As we already saw, there is an interpretation of the decision which views it as a rejection of the "war" model regarding counterterrorism measures. A different, perhaps more plausible interpretation of the decision, however, is that it was about the proper separation of powers. First, the court was clearly worried that the act gives the Federal Government more powers than the constitution intended. The Court, in its decision, focused on the analysis of Article 35 of the German Constitution, which deals with the division of powers between the *Lander* and the Federal Government in case of emergency. Its conclusion is that the Federal Government is not allowed to intervene in internal security matters of the *Lander* without the express request of the *Lander*. Furthermore, even if the Federal Government could intervene, the court mentions that intervention in the matters of the *Lander* can be done only by a decision of the full Federal Cabinet, and not the minister of defense, as the law declares.

To sum up this catalogue of institutional decisions, it appears that in several cases, national courts did indeed fear that counterterrorism measures were tilting the constitutional balance toward giving more powers to the executive and to the central government, and worked to halt this change. In the theoretical discussion among lawyers and political scientists regarding whether the executive should really receive more powers to fight terrorism, some courts clearly found themselves on the side cautioning against interference with the constitutional balance, and calling for a more traditional separation of powers.

(2) Courts as Protectors of the Integrity of the Judicial Process

Courts, of course, did not limit themselves to citing institutional reasons for limiting counterterrorism measures. They also referred to substantive claims of violations of rights. I submit that the specific area in which courts found themselves involved regarding counterterrorism measures is the protection of the integrity of the judicial process itself, and protection of *due process of law*.

In his comprehensive analysis of decisions of national courts regarding counterterrorism measures, Eyal Benvenisti depicted a "ladder" of judicial decisions, moving from the least activist, to the most activist decisions.[78] Benvenisti claims that because courts are hesitant to intervene in matters of national security in general, and counterterrorism in particular, they use various techniques to avoid having to directly strike down measures enacted by the government.

The lowest level, according to Benvenisti, are cases in which the court makes a decision, based on rules of administrative law, to order the government to reconsider its position. In cases such as the Canadian *Suresh* decision, the court ordered the government to take into account matters which were not taken into account earlier.

The second level of review consists of returning the decision back to the legislature, on the grounds of the lack of clarity of the authorization. In some senses, these decisions are close to the institutional framework I presented above, but usually they are made with regard to the specific human rights violations that should be dealt with by the legislature. In the same vein, the UK House of Lords has declared an Act permitting the indefinite detention of some foreign terror suspects pending their deportation from the UK to be incompatible with the European Convention on Human Rights.[79] The Law Lords also prohibited the use of evidence procured through torture, restricted the use of secret evidence in terror-related judicial proceedings, and criticized the extreme implications of "control orders" issued by the government (as a substitute for prolonged detention).[80] A good example of this is the UK's *Belmarsh Detainees* case, in which the British House of Lords declared an item of UK legislation to be incompatible with the European Convention of Human Rights. According to the British *Human Rights Act,* this decision means that the Parliament should reconsider the measure. However, as Parliament has never reenacted a law declared incompatible with a European convention, it seems that the court was quite sure that no further action would be required.

The highest level of review in Benvenisti's analysis is when a national court declares a counterterrorism measure to be unconstitutional, or an international tribunal declares a measure to be contrary to the international obligations of the state. In both cases, the only option available to the domestic political system is to change the constitution or the international treaty, something that is done only rarely, if at all.

Very few court decisions have struck down counterterrorism laws on the grounds that these measures violated the protections of human rights in the constitution, and hence cannot be approved even by the legislature. Moreover, most of these decisions deal with one specific issue area: the integrity of the judicial process.

This course of action was principally adopted with regard to decisions regarding detentions and their judicial review. Three examples are indicative:

- First, in the 2008 case *Boumedienne v. Bush,* Justice Anthony Kennedy wrote the opinion for the 5–4 majority of the U.S. Supreme Court holding that the prisoners had a right to *habeas corpus* review under the United States Constitution and that the MCA (Military Commissions Act) was an unconstitutional suspension of that right.
- Second, the Israeli Supreme Court declared amendments to the Torts Ordinance to constitute an unconstitutional infringement on the right to private property. At issue was the fact that the amendments immunized the state from tort litigation concerning a tort caused by soldiers in any area in which counterterrorism activity took place.[81]
- Finally, in February 2007, a decision by the Supreme Court of Canada declared incompatible with the Canadian Charter of Rights and Freedoms the procedures allowing deportation of noncitizens suspected of terrorist activities on the basis of confidential information, as well as denying prompt hearing to foreign nationals.[82]

International tribunals have also declared security measures taken by governments to be contrary to international law. In the *Kadi* decision, mentioned above, the European Court of Justice declared as illegal the regulation of the European Commission to seize assets of people suspected in terrorist activity because they were lacking in terms of *due* process. The European Court of Human Rights also issued some judgments in the same direction. In the *Belmarsh detainees* case, it declared as incompatible with the European Convention a UK law allowing the indefinite detention of aliens suspected in terrorist activities. In a series of decisions regarding the Russian operations in Chechnya and Turkish operations against the Kurdish minority, it also required independent investigations of the behavior of the armed forces, an investigation that would be effective and could lead to criminal prosecution, and hence to the involvement of courts.

In national courts, there are only very few cases in which the courts struck down a government counterterrorism policy on any other ground than the ones listed here.[83] Once again, perhaps international tribunals, especially the European Court of Human Rights, are willing to intervene more on the basis of violations of human rights other than *due-process* related rights.[84] However, these are the exceptions, and definitely not the majority of cases.

IV. CONCLUSION

This chapter is an attempt to explain, review and analyze the forms of intervention of courts in counterterrorism measures. One point seems to me to be clear: the question whether the paradigm used is that of "war" or "law enforcement" has little bearing on this question. The Israeli Supreme Court, one of the only two courts which explicitly accepted the "war-on-terror" paradigm in the first place, has also been the most active national court in its willingness to review national legislation and government policies. However, the Israeli experience is unique: other national courts, although willing to intervene, have done so only on a limited basis.

Courts intervene in two main areas when reviewing counterterrorism measures. First, they protect some form of balance of powers between the different branches of government. Second, they protect the *right of due process*. In a sense, courts are protecting the integrity of their own branch of government: the authority of courts to perform judicial review over government actions, even with regard to matters of national security.

Indeed, the attempt to protect the authority and integrity of the judicial system might also explain why courts intervened in the institutional aspects of counterterrorism measures. They did so as part of the attempt to protect their power. A stronger executive and a weaker legislature would necessarily mean that the courts would become weaker too, because in national security matters courts and legislatures are indeed the "least dangerous branches," and when the power of one is weakened vis-à-vis the executive, so, too, is the power of the other.

If this explanation is correct, it also clarifies why courts were willing to accept the position of the government in the basic question of IHRL versus IHL, and to limit the territorial reach of their jurisprudence. What the courts oppose is the attempt to curb their powers. Hence, as long as there is a valid legal mechanism according to which judicial review can be performed, such as IHL, courts are willing to accept this as a basis for their review. Similarly, national courts never asserted the power of judicial review over acts that took place outside the territory of the state, and hence they saw no need to assert this authority regarding counterterrorism measures.[85]

The second thing protected by courts in these cases is the right of due process, which is the gateway to all other rights. If the right of due process is protected, all other rights might be protected as a result of the power of the courts to order the government to respect these rights in cases that come before it.

However, due process rights in general suffer from one grave fault: they are exactly that, only due process rights. Due process protects a value which is not independent but rather is contingent upon other decisions. Such values as freedom of speech, the right to life, the right to human dignity, the right to equality, are all independent rights that would be protected by the court only if the court is willing to stand up to government and protect them. By themselves, due process and *habeas corpus* review afford very little protection. In terrorism cases, though courts have insisted upon due process protections, they have still remained generally deferential to governments on underlying substantive issues.

So, if courts are willing to protect the right of *due process* and are not really protecting other rights, are they doing something meaningful? On the one hand, it could be said that the mere fact that judicial review exists for counterterrorism measures taken by governments is, in and of itself, an important and useful contribution to the rule of law. Even without protecting any substantive right, the fact that governments are aware of a possibility of review may be enough to deter them from implementing some of the most extreme measures. The fact the judge would allow a person to appear before him means that the government would have to provide at least some credible evidence in order to detain him.

On the other hand, if judicial review and due process are the only things that are protected, this might have a negative effect. Judicial review has the effect of legitimizing government action that withstands it. If a judge reviews a specific action, the perception is that he or she performs some meaningful examination. However, if judges do not actually protect rights beyond the fact that there is some review, government can use this as a proof for the legality and legitimacy of their action, even if it is not so.

Perhaps in contrast to Benvenisti, therefore, I see no signs of a meaningful judicial review of actual rights developing beyond the contours discussed in this chapter. In the United States, it seems that the doctrine of deferring to the executive in matters pertaining to national security still holds. This, I submit, is also true in other countries. Hence it is quite unlikely that we would see any significant further intervention of U.S. courts in the "war on terror" apart from their traditional role—that of preserving the integrity of the criminal system and the rights of *due process*.

NOTES

1. *See*, e.g., *Boumediene v. Bush*, 553 U.S. 723 (2008).

2. *See*, e.g., Amanda McRae, "*Boumediene v, Bush:* Another Chapter in the Courts Jurisprudence on Civil Liberties at Guantanamo Bay," *Duke Journal of Constitutional Law*, vol. 4 (2009), at 247; Nathaniel H. Nesbitt, "Meeting Boumediene's Challenge: The Emergence of an Effective Habeas Jurisprudence and Obsolescence of New Detention Legislation," *Minnesota Law Review*, vol. 95 (2010), at 244.

3. *See generally* Ariel N. Zemach, "The Unpleasant Responsibilities of International Human Rights Law," *Denver Journal of International Law & Policy*, vol. 38 (2010), at 421 (claiming that human rights should control counterterrorism measures).

4. *See* Yuval Shany, "Human Rights and Humanitarian Law as Competing Legal Paradigms for Fighting Terror," in: Orna Ben Naftali (ed.), *Collected Courses of the Academy of European Law: Human Rights and International Humanitarian Law*, Vol. XIX/1 (2011) 13–33.

5. David Kretzmer, "Targeted Killing of Suspected Terrorists: Extra-Judicial Executions or Legitimate Means of Defense?" *European Journal of International Law*, vol. 16 (2005), at 171, 201; Orna Ben-Naftali & Keren Michaeli, " 'We Must Not Make a Scarecrow of the Law': A Legal Analysis of the Israeli Policy of Targeted Killings," *Cornell International Law Journal*, vol. 36 (2003), at 233; Rosa Ehrenreich Brooks, "War Everywhere: Rights, National Security Law, and the Law of Armed Conflict in the Age of Terror," *University of Pennsylvania Law Review*, vol. 153 (2004), at 675, 719–20.

6. Marco Sassoli, "Use and Abuse of the Laws of War in the 'War on Terrorism,'" *Law & Inequality*, vol. 22 (2004), at 195, 213.

7. *See*, e.g., Christopher A. Ford, "Living in the 'New Normal': Modern War, Nonstate Actors, and the Future of Law" elsewhere in this volume.

8. Upsala University database on Armed Conflicts. Available at: <http://www.pcr.uu.se/research/ucdp/database>.

9. There are various definitions of terrorism, in different legal instruments. For an analysis of different definitions and their use, *see* Jean-Marc Sorel, "Some Questions about the Definition of Terrorism and the Fight Against its Financing," *European Journal of International Law*, vol. 14 (2003), at 365.

10. Allison Marston Danner, "When Courts Make Law: How the International Criminal Tribunals Recast the Laws of War," *Vanderbilt Law Review*, vol. 59 (2006), at 1.

11. *Ireland v. UK*, ECtHR, application No. 5310/71 (1978).

12. Common Article 3 to the Geneva Convention places some very limited restrictions on parties to an armed conflict not of an international character. Common article 3 appears in all Geneva Conventions. *See*, e.g., Geneva Convention Relative to the Protection of Civilian Persons in Time of War (August 12, 1949), 6 U.S.T. 3516, 75 U.N.T.S. 287, 318–38, at Art. 3.

13. For a full description of the history of these courts, *see* Gary J. Bass, *Stay the Hand of Vengeance: The Politics of War Crimes Tribunals*, (Princeton: Princeton University Press, 2000), at Chapter 6.

14. Danner, *supra*.

15. Tim Krieger & Daniel Meierrieks, "What Causes Terrorism?" *Public Choice*, vol. 147 (2011), at 3.

16. Convention on Offences and Certain Other Acts Committed on Board Aircraft, Sept. 14, 1963, 704 UNTS 219; Convention for the Suppression of Unlawful Seizure of Aircraft (Hijacking) (December 16, 1970) UNTS 105; Convention for the Suppression of Unlawful Acts Against the Safety of Civil Aviation (Sabotage) (September 23, 1971), 974 UNTS 177; Protocol for the Suppression of Unlawful Acts of Violence at Airports Serving International Civil Aviation (September 23, 1971), 1589 UNTS 473; Convention on the Prevention and Punishment of Crimes Against Internationally Protected Persons (December 14, 1973), 1035 UNTS 167; Convention on the Physical Protection of Nuclear Materials (October 26, 1979), 1456 UNTS 125; International Convention Against the Taking of Hostages, (December 17, 1979), 1316 UNTS 205; Convention for the Suppression of Unlawful Acts Against the Safety of Maritime Navigation (March 10, 1988) 1679 UNTS 221; Protocol for the Suppression of Unlawful Acts Against the Safety of Fixed Platforms Located on the Continental Shelf (March 10, 1988), 1678 UNTS 303; Convention on the Marking of Plastic Explosives for the Purpose of Identification (March 1, 1991), UN Doc. S/22393 (1991); International Convention for the Suppression of Terrorist Bombings, (December 15, 1997), 37 ILM (1998) 249; International Convention for the Suppression of the Financing of Terrorism (December 9, 1999), 39 ILM (2000) 270.

17. Richard A. Posner, *Not a Suicide Pact: The Constitution in a Time of National Emergency*, (Oxford: Oxford University Press, 2006) at 72.

18. Another country which declared itself in armed conflict with terrorist organizations was Israel, which defined its conflict with Palestinians as "an armed conflict short of war." During certain parts of the Palestinian *intifada*, the conflict indeed seemed to be a real "armed conflict," yet in other phases of this conflict, Palestinian operations seemed more like classic terrorism.

19. *See*, e.g., Steven David, "Targeted Killing: The Israeli Experience," herein.

20. For a discussion of the U.S. policy of targeted killings, see Kenneth Anderson, *Targeted Killing in U.S. Counterterrorism Strategy and Law* (Brookings Institute, 2009), *available at* <http://www.brookings.edu/papers/2009/0511_counterterrorism_anderson.aspx>. For a description of the Israeli policy of targeted killings, *see* Hilly Moodrick Even-Khen, "Can We Now Tell What 'Direct Participation in Hostilities' Is?" *Israel Law Review*, vol. 40 (2007), at 213 (2007).

21. *See*, e.g., *McCann v. UK*, ECtHR (GC), application No. 18984/91 (September 27, 1995).

22. The Israeli Supreme Court allowed the use of targeted killing provided certain conditions are followed. *See* HCJ 769/02 *The Public Committee Against Torture in Israel v. The Government of Israel* (2006), available in English at: <http://elyon1.court.gov.il/files_eng/02/690/007/a34/02007690.a34.pdf> (the targeted killings case).

23. For a description of the U.S. position (supporting it) *see* John C. Yoo, *War by Other Means: An Insider's Account of the War on Terror* (New York: Atlantic Monthly Press, 2006), especially chapter 6. For a description of other detaining methods of the United States during the Bush administration *see* Margaret L. Sutterthwaite, "The Story of *El-Masri v. Tenet*: Human Rights and Humanitarian Law in the 'War on Terror,'" *in Human Rights Advocacy Stories* (Hurwitz et al., eds.) (Foundation Press, 2009), at 535–77.

24. For a full discussion see Ford *supra*.

25. The Third Geneva Convention gives the right to be considered a prisoner of war only to "soldiers" which fight for a state, and identify themselves as soldiers. See Geneva Convention Relative to the Treatment of Prisoners of War (August 12, 1949), at Art. 4(A)(2), 6 U.S.T. 3316, 75 U.N.T.S. 135.

26. Incarceration of Illegal Combatants Law (2002), at Article 3, 7 (Israel).

27. *See*, e.g., Anti-Terrorism Act 2004 (Australia), Sch 1, Sec. 5, 7; Criminal Justice Act 2003 (UK) § 306; Terrorism Act 2006 (UK) § 23; Code of Criminal Procedure (France), at Art. 78–2-2 (as amended in 2001); Criminal Procedure Law (Detainee Suspect of a Security Offence) (Temporary Measure) 2006 (Israel), § 3–5.

28. *See*, e.g., Terrorism Act 2000 (UK), § 109; Anti-Terrorism Act 2001 (Canada), Part 3.

29. *See*, e.g., Prevention of Terrorism Act 2002 (India), § 23; Military Order of 13 Nov. 2001, *supra*; *see also* Country of Origin Information Report; Turkey, State Security Courts (Devlet Güvenlik Mahkemesi), <http://www.ecoi.net/>.

30. Shany, *supra*.

31. *See*, e.g., John H. Shenefield, "The Foreign Intelligence Surveillance Puzzle: We Know How We Got Here—Now, What Do We Do?" herein.

32. *The Prosecutor v. Tadic* IT-94–1-AR72 Appeals Chamber, Decision of October 2, 1995 (Decision of the Defense Motion for Interlocutory Appeal on Jurisdiction), at ¶ 73.

33. *Id.*, at ¶ 97.

34. *Id.*, at ¶ 120.

35. Later decisions of the ICTY applied various parts of IHL to the conflict, e.g., The Prohibition on Indiscriminate attacks on Civilians (*The Prosecutor v. Strugar*

IT-01–42-AR72 (Decision on interlocutory appeal) Appeal chamber (November, 22, 2002), at ¶ 10. A similar statement was made by the International Criminal Tribunal for Rwanda in *The Prosecutor v. Jean Paul Akayesu*, Case No. ICTR-96–4-T, ¶ 618–27.

36. Jean-Marie Henckaerts & Louise Doswald-Beck, *Customary International Humanitarian Law* (Cambridge: Cambridge University Press, 2005).

37. *Advisory Opinion: Legality of the Threat or Use of Nuclear Weapons, Advisory Opinion*, 1996 I.C.J. (July 8), at Paragraph 25; *see also Advisory Opinion: Legal Consequences of the Construction of a Wall in the Occupied Territory*, 2004 I.C.J. 136 (July 9), at Paragraph 106.

38. The rule that *lex specialis* receives precedence over *lex generalis* is a general principle of law in all systems.

39. For an analysis and criticism of this decision, *see* William Schabas, "*Lex Specialis*? Belt and Suspenders? The Parallel Operation of Human Rights Law and the Law of Armed Conflict, and the Conundrum of Jus In Bello," *Israel Law Review*, vol. 40 (2007), at 592.

40. Kretzmer, *supra*.

41. Shany, *supra*.

42. The claim was raised by government lawyers in both the Israeli targeted killings case, *supra*, and the U.S. Guantánamo case, discussed *infra*.

43. *Korematsu v. United States*, 323 U.S. 214, 244 (1944).

44. Eric A. Posner & Adrian Vermeule, *Terror in the Balance: Security, Liberty, and the Courts*, (Oxford: Oxford University Press, 2007).

45. Richard Posner, *Not a Suicide Pact: The Constitution in a Time of National Emergency*, (Oxford: Oxford University Press, 2006).

46. *Id.* at 35–36.

47. *See*, e.g., David Cole & Jules Lobel, *Less Safe, Less Free: Why America Is Losing the War on Terror* (New York: The New Press, 2007).

48. It is quite probable that many government lawyers, perhaps even most, actually thought that the use of the term "war on terror" would provide legal backing for the executive to act at will. Not only would no court enforce laws, but the laws themselves would all be relaxed. This, for example, was clearly John Yoo's position, even before he was appointed to government office and long before September 11, 2011. However, the application of these theories to the "war on terror," which is in my opinion erroneous, was allowed to stand without any meaningful judicial review precisely because courts were reluctant to intervene in these matters.

49. Eyal Benvenisti, "Reclaiming Democracy: The Strategic Uses of Foreign and International Law by National Courts," *American Journal of International Law*, vol. 102 (2008), at 241.

50. HCJ 7015/02 *Ajuri v. The Military Commander of the Judea and Samaria Area*, Piskei Din vol. 56(6) (2002) at 352, 358.

51. *Hamdan v. Rumsfeld*, 548 U.S. 557 (2006).

52. 542 U.S 507 (2004).

53. 542 U.S. 466 (2004).

54. 1 BvR 357/05 (15 February 2006). An English translation of the decision is available at <http://www.bundesverfassungsgericht.de/en/decisions/rs20060215_1bvr035705en.html>.

55. German Basic Law, at Art. 87A.

56. Oliver Lepsius, "Human Dignity and the Downing of Aircraft: The German Federal Constitutional Court Strikes Down a Prominent Anti-terrorism Provision in the New Air-transport Security Act," *German Law Journal*, vol. 7 (2006), at 761.

57. Emanuel Ladiges "Comment: Oliver Lepsius Human Dignity and the Downing of Aircraft," *German Law Journal*, vol. 8 (2007), at 307.

58. For an analysis and critique of these decisions see William Abresch, "A Human Rights Law of Internal Armed Conflict: The European Court of Human Rights in Chechnya," *European Journal of International Law*, vol. 16 (2005), at 741.

59. *Isayeva v Russia*, ECtHR, application No 57950/00 (February 24, 2005), at ¶ 180.

60. *Id.*, at ¶ 191.

61. Joined Cases C-402/05 P & C-415/05 *P, Kadi & Al Barakaat v. Council of the European Union and EC Commission*, 3 C.M.L.R. 41 (2008) [hereinafter *Kadi*].

62. *Id.*, at ¶ 287.

63. For an analysis of the various opinions, *see* Orna Ben Naftali & Yuval Shany, "Living in Denial: The Application of Human Rights in the Occupied Territories," *Israel Law Review*, vol. 37 (2003–04), at 17.

64. *Maqaleh v. Gates*, (D.C. Cir.) 605 F. 3d 84 (2010).

65. *El-Masri v. US*, 479 F.3d 296 (4th Cir. 2007), cert denied 128 S. Ct. 373 (2007). Although the case was dismissed on other grounds, it seems to me that the territorial issue lay at the background of this case.

66. HCJ 9132/07 *Jaber Al Bassiouni Ahmed v. The Prime Minister* (2008), available in English at: <http://elyon1.court.gov.il/files_eng/07/320/091/n25/07091320.n25.htm>.

67. *See*, e.g., HCJ 4258/08 *Gisha—Legal Center for Freedom of Movement v. Minister of Defense* (2008).

68. *Banković v. Belgium*, ECtHR [GC], application No. 52207/99, decision as to the admissibility, (12 December 2001), at ¶ 59.

69. *Al-Saadoon and Mufdhi v. the United Kingdom* , ECtHR, application no. 61498/08, at ¶ 86–89, (30 June 2009). In this case, the Court held that two Iraqi nationals detained in British-controlled military prisons in Iraq fell within the jurisdiction of the United Kingdom, since the United Kingdom exercised total and exclusive control over the prisons and the individuals detained in them. In *Medvedyev and Others v. France* ECtHR [GC], application no. 3394/03 (2010), at Paragraph 67, the Court held that the applicants were within French jurisdiction by virtue of the exercise by French agents of full and exclusive control over a ship and its crew from the time of its interception in international waters.

70. *Ilașcu and Others v. Moldova and Russia*, ECtHR [GC], Application no. 48787/99 (2004), at ¶ 311–16; *Loizidou v. Turkey*, (preliminary objections), ECtHR (1995), at ¶ 62; *Loizidou v. Turkey*, (merits), ECtHR (1996), at ¶ 52 (noting that

the obligation to secure, in such an area, the rights and freedoms set out in the Convention, derives from the fact of such control, whether it be exercised directly, through the Contracting State's own armed forces, or through a subordinate local administration).

71. *Issa and Others v. Turkey*, ECtHR. Application No. 31821/96 (16.11.04).

72. *Al-Skeini and Others v. the Secretary of State for Defence*, [2007] UKHL 26.

73. *Al Skeini v. The United Kingdom*, ECtHR [GC] Application no. 55721/07 (July 7, 2011).

74. HCJ 5100/94 *The Public Committee Against Torture v. Government of Israel*, Piskei Din vol. 53(4) (1999), at 817.

75. The methods included: dangling the suspects, deprivation of sleep, covering the head of suspect for long periods of time, tying the suspect to low chairs for extended periods of time, and keeping the suspects in cold rooms.

76. The *Boumediene* decision, which dealt with the constitutionality of these commissions, will be mentioned later.

77. BVerfGE, 2 BvE 1/03 (May 7, 2008).

78. Eyal Benvenisti, "United We Stand: National Courts Reviewing Counterterrorism Measures," in *Counterterrorism: Democracy's Challenge* (Andrea Bianchi and Alexis Keller, eds.) (Oxford: Hart Publishing, 2008) at 251.

79. *See A v. Secretary of State for the Home Dept.* [2004] UKHL 56.

80. *Secretary of State for the Home Department v JJ* [2007] UKHL 45.

81. HCJ 8276/05 *Adalah—The Legal Center for Arab Minority Rights in Israel v. Minister of Defense* (December 12, 2006).

82. *Charkaoui v. Canada* (Citizenship and Immigration), 2007 SCC 9 (February 23, 2007).

83. One example is the Israeli Supreme Court's decision in the Neighbor Policy case (HCJ 3799/02 *Adalah—The Legal Center for Arab Minority Rights in Israel v. OC Central Command*, Piskei Din vol. 60(3) (2005), at 67 (declaring illegal a policy by which the IDF used civilians as messengers to suspected terrorists which refused to turn themselves in). Another is a set of decisions in which the court intervened in the route of the Separation barrier. *See*, e.g., HCJ 2056/04 *Beit Sourik Village Council v. The Government of Israel*, Piskei Din vol. 58(5) (2004), at 807. The Israeli Supreme Court is indeed unique in its willingness to intervene in national security matters. *See generally* Amichai Cohen & Stuart A. Cohen, *Israel's National Security Constitution* (London: Routledge, 2011), especially at Chapters 6 & 7. A second important instance, however, is the German decision in the *Aircraft Security Act*, mentioned above. Yet the Court there based its decision on an alternative ground, according to which the proposed act violates the right to life.

84. *See*, e.g., *Isayeva v. Russia, supra.*

85. As we have seen, the European Court of Human Rights was much more flexible in its willingness to impose limitations on governments acting extraterritorially. As in the matter of the law-enforcement/war dichotomy, an international tribunal is not subject to the political pressures which national courts have to take into account.

Chapter 7

Necessity, Proportionality, and Distinction in Nontraditional Conflicts

The Unfortunate Case Study of the Goldstone Report

Elizabeth Samson

This chapter highlights the challenges of applying the international humanitarian law principles of military necessity, proportionality, and distinction to nontraditional armed conflicts, exploring these issues through an examination of the *Report of the United Nations Fact-Finding Mission on the Gaza Conflict,* also known as the "Goldstone Report." In the years since the September 11, 2001, terrorist attacks upon the United States, the shift in the dominant paradigm of armed conflict from a state-vs.-state framework to one of state-vs.-violent non-state actors has required a fresh analysis of the relevance of existing international legal instruments to various combat scenarios. While international law can indeed bind non-state actors, they commonly disregard the law and enforcement is difficult. The Goldstone Report illustrates some of the problems the international community has had in struggling to make sense of modern irregular conflicts through the prism of international humanitarian law.

The Goldstone Report illustrates the confusion and errors that can result by approaching irregular and asymmetric conflicts by assuming the sort of reciprocity and regularity that is traditionally associated with state-on-state clashes, but which was nowhere apparent in the Gaza conflict of 2008–09 between Israel, a state, and its adversary Hamas, which has been internationally recognized as a terrorist group. Justice Richard Goldstone, the chief architect of the report, having now accounted for those errors through a retraction of his position, offers an important lesson for the international legal community about how to assess—or perhaps *not* to assess—the behavior of terrorist groups and their state adversaries.

I. A NEW POST-9/11 ERA

Almost a decade after the terrorist attacks of September 11, 2001, against the United States ("9/11"), the international community continues to grapple with the questions of how to apply the laws of armed conflict to nontraditional armed conflicts. The eruption of global terrorism as a prevalent model of warfare against states has required a reassessment of the sufficiency of the laws that currently exist, as well as the practicality of their application. There have been several conflicts over the past ten years that have required an examination of the actions of parties to a conflict, state and non-state actors alike, for the purpose of determining the legality of the use of force.

One relatively recent instance, in particular, is illustrative of the challenges that both states and the international community face when trying to apply international law to a situation of armed conflict. The incursion of Israel into the Palestinian territory of Gaza by air and ground forces as a countermeasure to Gazan rockets raining on Israeli territory—an operation best known by its Israeli name as Operation Cast Lead—commenced on December 27, 2008, and continued for three weeks. Operation Cast Lead resulted in over 1,000 Palestinian deaths and 13 Israeli deaths.

On January 12, 2009, the United Nations Human Rights Council passed a resolution establishing a fact-finding mission to investigate alleged human rights and humanitarian law violations committed by Israel against the Palestinian people in Gaza.[1] Justice Richard Goldstone, former judge of the Constitutional Court of South Africa and chief prosecutor for the international criminal tribunals for the former Yugoslavia and Rwanda, was appointed by the Human Rights Council on April 3, 2009, to head this mission into Gaza.[2]

His *Report of the United Nations Fact-Finding Mission on the Gaza Conflict,* also known as the "Goldstone Report," was published on September 15, 2009,[3] and has been highly controversial, with potentially important implications for the laws of armed conflict, particularly with respect to the ability of states to fight terrorist groups. While the Goldstone Report is, indeed, an important reflection of how the international community approaches the acts of states during a nontraditional armed conflict, its significance may be viewed beyond Operation Cast Lead as an example of how the international community is generally struggling—and not always successfully—with the theoretical and practical questions raised by such irregular conflicts. The report raises questions about the relevance of the international response in undertaking future analyses of nontraditional armed conflict.

Israel's Prime Minister, Benjamin Netanyahu, has stated that the Goldstone Report is one of the greatest existential threats to the State of Israel, and specifically that Goldstone has become "a codeword for an attempt to delegitimize Israel's right to self defense."[4] Despite Israel's assertions of self-defense against Hamas, and due to the contrast between the number of lives lost and damage caused on each side, the Goldstone Report comes across as more critical of Israeli measures taken against Hamas than it is of the Hamas rocket attacks against civilian towns and villages in Israel, often from civilian areas within Gaza itself, to which Israel's campaign was a response.

Hamas, recognized as a terrorist organization by the United States, the European Union, Japan, and Canada,[5] may be disinterested in protecting human life in the areas under its attack—and may even have deliberately imperiled Palestinian civilians by mounting military operations from their midst, in order either to deter Israeli counterstrikes or indeed actually to *provoke* them, so as to tar Israel for causing civilian casualties. The Goldstone Report, however, condemns Hamas only in passing, reserving its attention for the actions of Israel, the state with the misfortune of having to face an adversary committed to terrorist tactics. The report's willingness to play along with Hamas' approach has, of course, caused Israel significant political harm. It also, however, presents broader problems for international law, because it seems to suggest, wrongly, that it is not possible to confront terrorist adversaries in ways that are both lawful and militarily effective. It also risks leaving the impression that Hamas' policies were *not* particularly objectionable or problematic—or at least not by comparison to Israel's response—and by seeming to validate them it may end up making terrorism seem a more attractive tactic in the future.

In the early days after the Goldstone Report was published, Justice Goldstone responded to criticism of the report with professed disbelief as to why the "international community, Israel and the United States and others, do not give as much attention to how the report condemns Hamas as well and only focuses on the criticism of Israel."[6] He should not, perhaps, have been so surprised at the criticism.

There are three main critiques put forward by the report's detractors, including this author. The first is that the mission's criticism in the report does not single out Hamas by name as the aggressor and only generally talks about unspecified—and hence largely unaccountable—Palestinian militants or combatants in any event. (The very specific state of Israel, however, is mentioned and criticized frequently.) The second is that, besides the absence of a fully comprehensive discussion of Hamas, a much larger part of the report focuses on Israel's actions rather than on the Palestinians' actions. The third complaint is that because Palestine is not a state, it is not a signatory of the Geneva Conventions or any other relevant treaties. It is, therefore, difficult to hold Hamas—a recognized terrorist organization—to the international standards to which Hamas does not hold itself, but Israel can be held to international legal standards because it is a state and it has chosen to subject itself to the same laws and standards as other states in the international community.[7] It is a common critique of Israel that an end must be put to "impunity" for violations of international law,[8] but to such critics the most troubling "impunity" is not that of an Israel that is frequently and loudly accused of violations but rather the impunity of its terrorist adversaries such as Hamas—who few in the international legal community seem even to *try* to hold legally accountable.

On April 1, 2011, Justice Goldstone issued a public retraction of the main premise of the report of his mission—that Israel purposely targeted civilians and civilian objects, the most egregious of war crimes. After having made this allegation for nearly two years in the most public possible way, Justice Goldstone now states that

> we know a lot more today about what happened in the Gaza war of 2008–09 than we did when I chaired the fact-finding mission appointed by the U.N. Human Rights Council that produced what has come to be known as the Goldstone Report. If I had known then what I know now, the Goldstone Report would have been a different document.[9]

Favorably comparing internal Israeli investigations into alleged abuses to Hamas' apparent disinterest in such self-examination, Goldstone also conceded that "[i]n the end, asking Hamas to investigate [its actions] may have been a mistaken enterprise."

The Goldstone Report, with both Justice Goldstone's endorsement and later retraction, demonstrates the complexity and difficulty of applying the laws of armed conflict to nontraditional armed conflicts. Very often, the actions of one party may not be entirely clear after initial analysis, with later evidence demonstrating instances of law-abidingness or legal violation. Indeed, the scope of lawful action available to one side or another does not always even seem to be entirely clear in the first place. Due to the modern paradigm shift toward the dominance of nontraditional armed conflict, the questions of whether the existing law is sufficient in guiding, being binding on, and being capable of enforcement against both states and violent non-state actors is more important than ever. But it apparently still remains to be answered.

II. THE SHIFTING PARADIGM OF ARMED CONFLICT

Modern armed conflicts—particularly since the terrorist attacks of September 11, 2001—can be characterized by having shifted away from the traditional state-vs.-state paradigm of armed conflict towards a new one in which a state is pitted against violent non-state actors. Such modern-style conflicts are generally characterized by the use of unconventional tactics and dynamics of asymmetric warfare.

Under the conventional or symmetric model of warfare, belligerents have relatively similar military powers—being by no means necessarily similar in actual size and power, but at least being so in *types* of military power, organization, and tactics—and they engage in combat in a generally linear fashion (e.g., with "front lines"), targeting the opposition's strategic assets, as well as his actual combatants and weapons systems/platforms, etc. In such wars, one body of national armed forces fights against another. However, when there is a lack of such organizational and behavioral similarity between the powers, or when one side is notably weaker than the other, the challenge to find alternative means of attack arises, with the weaker party seeking to gain advantage by way of unconventional methods of combat. Due to the inability to compete with the larger force, in such asymmetric warfare combatants focus on avoiding strengths, and engage the superior enemy by using alternative means of attacking the opposition's vulnerabilities.[10]

Traditional examples of asymmetric warfare include guerrilla warfare and partisan activity, but it is terrorism, the most contemporarily pervasive form of asymmetric warfare, that poses one of the greatest emerging global threats. The reach of today's "terrorist network" has permeated the globe, with terrorists enjoying an extensive "toolkit" of methods that can be adapted to reflect the changes in the battlefield—or to bring that "battlefield" to the enemy's rear, including to its civilian population. Combat-type actions such as individual suicide bombings in Israel and highly coordinated bombing or other operations like those in London in July 2005, in Madrid in March 2004, and in the United States in September 2001, have wreaked havoc on civilians who are militarily unprepared for a terrorist attack. Additionally, other asymmetric tactics, such as the use of human shields—a commonly used tactic in other regional conflicts such as Afghanistan, where the Taliban has used women and children as shields against coalition forces[11]—have been utilized by Palestinians[12] in order to generate propaganda benefits and/or to neutralize the Israelis' overwhelmingly stronger force.

III. INTERNATIONAL HUMANITARIAN LAW AND NON-STATE ACTORS

International conventions are clear about their intent to bind any party to a conflict—states and violent non-state actors alike—to International Humanitarian Law (IHL), that is, to the laws of armed conflict. Under Article 3 common ("Common Article 3") to the four Geneva Conventions of 1949

("Geneva Conventions"),[13] all parties who engage in armed conflict "not of an international character" in the territory of a High Contracting Party are bound to follow the Geneva Conventions. The Conventions govern the actions between that Party and "dissident armed forces or other organized armed groups."[14]

Violent non-state actors are predominantly considered bound by IHL through the territorial link of the State Party to the Geneva Conventions on whose territory they are acting.[15] When Common Article 3 was drafted, its novelty was that each contracting state established binding rules for its own conduct, but also for involved non-state parties. The authority to establish those rules is derived from the contracting state's domestic legislative sovereignty, thereby creating a territorial requirement for Common Article 3.[16] However, terrorist groups often do not deem themselves bound to the rules adopted by a state against whose regime they are fighting—if indeed they acknowledge the legitimacy of legal restraint at all. For that reason, it remains difficult to enforce the Geneva Conventions against violent non-state actors when they engage in conflicts with states. Despite whatever legal justifications may be provided to argue that terrorists are bound by IHL, enforceability of the law is problematic when there is no reciprocity between the parties.[17] In some circumstances, in fact, this allows law-disregarding parties to use *against* their opponents these opponents' own desire to *comply* with IHL rules (e.g., by hiding military assets among innocent civilians). This can present worrying challenges, not just to the enforceability but, perhaps, even to the perceived legitimacy of IHL.

In the case of Israel and Gaza, Gaza's status as a no-man's land—annexed by no state and belonging to no one—allows Hamas the purported justification for ignoring international humanitarian law that it is fighting the Israeli "regime" and will not allow itself to be bound by "Israeli" rules. The Goldstone Report presumes that both parties—Israel, a state, and Hamas, a non-state actor—are bound by international law and are therefore both required to investigate their actions. It calls upon them to do so, presupposing that the parties deem themselves to be bound.

The fallacy of those presumptions can be seen in Justice Goldstone's own confession that after recommending that the parties investigate the incidents to which the Goldstone Report referred, it has been found that "Israel has done this to a significant degree; Hamas has done nothing."[18] Goldstone went further to admit that "[s]ome have suggested that it was absurd to expect Hamas, an organization that has a policy to destroy the state of Israel, to investigate what we said were serious war crimes." Goldstone confessed that he had hoped, even if unrealistically, that Hamas would undertake investigations, especially if Israel did as well. But those hopes were in vain. Not only were rocket attacks not curtailed but "hundreds more rockets and mortar rounds have been directed at civilian targets in southern Israel."[19]

And so, notwithstanding the theoretically binding character of IHL on Hamas, Goldstone's naïve expectation and ultimate disappointment underscore the challenge of holding non-state actors legally accountable.

IV. THREE PRINCIPLES: NECESSITY, PROPORTIONALITY, AND DISTINCTION

The changing landscape of modern wars, which look less and less like traditional armed conflicts, thus requires a reexamination of international legal norms, particularly with respect to the application and interpretation of the general founding principles of international humanitarian law—"military necessity," "distinction" and "proportionality"[20]—when dealing with violent non-state actors.

IHL is the branch of international law specifically intended to preserve humanitarian values during armed conflict by protecting those who do not, or no longer, directly participate in hostilities. IHL also limits the right of parties to the conflict to use armed force only to the degree necessary to achieve the aim of the conflict, which is to weaken the military capabilities of the opposing party. IHL governs the behavior of states vis-à-vis one another and consists of the two complementary components of *jus ad bellum* and *jus in bello*.[21]

Jus ad bellum—the law regulating the decision to resort to the use of force—governs actions of states before hostilities begin. Resorting to force is generally prohibited by Article 2(4) of the United Nations Charter,[22] which requires that "[a]ll Members shall refrain in their international relations from the threat or use of force against the territorial integrity or political independence of any state, or in any other manner inconsistent with the Purposes of the United Nations."[23] However, there are two exceptions to the general rule: Security Council enforcement actions to restore international peace and security,[24] and circumstances of self-defense. The self-defense exception is described in Article 51 of the UN Charter[25] which states:

> Nothing in the present Charter shall impair *the inherent right of individual or collective self-defence* if an armed attack occurs against a Member of the United Nations, until the Security Council has taken measures necessary to maintain international peace and security. Measures taken by Members in the exercise of *this right of self-defence* shall be immediately reported to the Security Council and shall not in any way affect the authority and responsibility of the Security Council under the present Charter to take at any time such action as it deems necessary in order to maintain or restore international peace and security.[26]

That self-defense is the only legitimate reason for a state to use force has been expressed as the policy of most states in the international community.

Jus ad bellum is characterized by a constant tension in IHL between the principles of military necessity and humanity[27]—recognizing the state's need to protect its interests and defend itself while at the same time treating the adversary humanely, with pity and mercy to varying degrees. The Preambles to the Hague Conventions of 1899 and 1907—what has become known collectively as the Martens Clause—discuss humanity as a guiding principle for warfare.[28]

> Until a more complete code of the laws of war is issued, the High Contracting Parties think it right to declare that in cases not included in the Regulations adopted by them, populations and belligerents remain under the protection and empire of the principles of international law, as they result from the usages established between civilized nations, from the *laws of humanity* and the requirements of the public conscience.[29]

A state's engagement in self-defense is an act of military necessity, therefore, but that engagement is also inextricably linked to the humanity principle.

Military necessity, moreover, is a concept that itself needs to be understood as having limits. Though, as we have seen, the right of a state to act in self-defense is recognized by the UN Charter, the requirement for military necessity is found reflected in historical military documentation such as the St. Petersburg Declaration of 1868,[30] which stated that "the only legitimate object which states should endeavour to accomplish in war is to weaken the military . . . of the enemy."[31] The justifiable utilization of military necessity rests on an assumption that the force being used is regulated and not otherwise prohibited, and that this force is necessary to achieve partial or complete submission of the adversary. Military necessity also requires that the use of force is no greater than what is needed to achieve that submission.

Once the determination is made to use force in self-defense, this triggers the introduction of *jus in bello*—the law regulating states as they engage in use of force, the law that applies during an armed conflict. However, military necessity remains relevant to *jus ad bellum* as well as *jus in bello,* because military necessity applies both to the initial decision to resort to use force and to demonstrating necessity subsequently throughout the ongoing conflict (e.g., in specific military operations).[32]

Before engaging in the use of force, a state must apply the principle of proportionality, a preliminary assessment the goal of which is to reduce incidental damage caused by military operations.[33] Prohibiting *all* acts that cause civilian losses is irreconcilable with the principle of military necessity, which permits military action to be taken in self-defense.[34] Therefore, proportionality only prohibits attacks that "may be expected to cause incidental loss of civilian life, injury to civilians, damage to civilian objects, or a combination thereof, *which would be excessive* in relation to the concrete and direct military advantage anticipated."[35] Proportionality accounts for the expectation that injury may occur, even when undesired, as a result of an attack on a legitimate target, so long as there is no intentional or reckless targeting of civilian objectives.[36]

To determine the proportionality of a response, military planners examine the facts on the ground, determine where the targets are located, what military significance they have, and what potential destruction and loss of life might result from attacking them. On the basis of these considerations, they make a calculated decision regarding costs to life versus advantages for self-defense or military necessity. The test for determining whether a response is proportional is applied before a party engages in an armed conflict and cannot be retroactive: one cannot look to the *results* of a military measure and determine, after the fact, that the measure was disproportionate to the circumstances of the threat. The legality of a decision relies upon its foundation in good faith and reasonable judgment based upon the anticipated civilian costs and anticipated military gains as understood in light of the information available at the time. Everything does not actually have to turn out as planned, in other words; it is enough that one acted reasonably at the time.

The principle of distinction prohibits direct attacks on civilians or civilian objects, and is employed to distinguish between civilians and combatants to determine the potential level of damage that may be caused, and ultimately to decide whether the advantages of military action outweigh the costs—that is, the proportionality of the response. Article 48 of Additional Protocol I[37] to the four Geneva Conventions describes the principle of distinction as requiring the parties to a conflict to "distinguish between the civilian population and combatants and between civilian objects and military objectives and accordingly only direct their operations against military objectives."[38] The goal of the principle of distinction is to facilitate the recognition and protection of civilians in a combat zone[39] by distinguishing them from combatants, as well as the recognition of civilian and military objects. The general rule is that military objects are lawful targets and civilian objects are not.

Article 52(2) of Additional Protocol I[40] defines military targets as "limited to those objects which by their nature, location, purpose or use make an effective contribution to military action and whose total or partial destruction, capture or neutralization, in the circumstances ruling at the time, offers a definite military advantage." [41] All objects which are not military are considered civilian, and in case of doubt there is an assumption that the object has civilian status. Though the principle of distinction appears to be fairly simple, the practical application of the principle is difficult, particularly when applied to violent non-state actors who often engage civilians or civilian objects for military objectives.[42]

The principles of military necessity, proportionality, and distinction are linked at all times during a state's decision-making process when engaging in use of force. The state must continuously ask the following questions: Does the exercise of force further the goal of subduing the adversary, or is it extraneous? Is the force used against the adversary not in excess of what is needed for the adversary's submission? In furthering the goal of self-defense, are steps being taken to identify, and therefore avoid, harm to noncombatants to the greatest degree possible?

V. THE GOLDSTONE REPORT AND THE THREE PRINCIPLES

The Goldstone Report purports to call into question Israel's proper exercise of these three principles during Operation Cast Lead. The report's conclusion with respect to targeting civilians, though now erroneous according to Goldstone, creates a basis for examining the norms of IHL as they pertain to *jus ad bellum* and *jus in bello* and the principles of military necessity, proportionality, and distinction in the context of a nontraditional armed conflict between a state and a terrorist entity.

The assumption of the report is that Israel did not exercise distinction, and either purposely or recklessly targeted civilians, and that Israel's response was not proportional to the threat that was presented. Although the report did not deny that Palestinian combatants caused serious destruction to Israeli territory, the report also makes no mention of Article 51 and Israel's right to respond to those attacks by invoking the right to self-defense under the U.N. Charter, but rather calls the invocation of that right into doubt.

In the early period after the initial publication of the Goldstone Report, Justice Goldstone had stated that his report was unreliable as a source of evidence,[43] and, indeed, many claims in the report were insufficiently substantiated and unsupported, by international legal standards, to give rise to actual *charges*—as opposed merely to public allegations—of war crimes.[44] Nonetheless the report reached several malicious and damaging conclusions regarding the behavior of Israel, particularly that Israel intentionally targeted the civilian population of Gaza for destruction—the most egregious sort of IHL violation. The Goldstone Report concluded that the actions Israel undertook in Operation Cast Lead to root out Hamas were *intended* to attack Gaza's civilian population.

Although Israel responded to the threat Hamas posed it by mounting a counterstrike in self-defense, invoking its right under Article 51 of the U.N.

Charter, the Goldstone Report attempted to criminalize Israel's strategy to weaken Hamas[45]—both in general and in particular, by depicting Operation Cast Lead as having been directed not at legitimate military targets for military reasons but instead at civilians. Goldstone's later retraction indicates that the subsequent investigations published by the Israeli military, and which were recognized in the U.N. committee's report, attest to the fact that "[Palestinian] civilians were *not* intentionally targeted as a matter of policy."[46] By then, however, much political and legal damage had been done.

The Goldstone Report, after all, had explicitly stated the following regarding military necessity/self-defense:

> While the Israeli Government has sought to portray its operations as essentially a response to rocket attacks in the exercise of its right to self-defence, the Mission considers the plan to have been directed, at least in part, at a different target: the people of Gaza as a whole.[47]

Regarding proportionality, it averred that:

> what occurred in just over three weeks at the end of 2008 and the beginning of 2009 was a deliberately disproportionate attack designed to punish, humiliate and terrorize a civilian population, radically diminish its local economic capacity both to work and to provide for itself, and to force upon it an ever increasing sense of dependency and vulnerability.[48]

Regarding distinction, the message was no less damning:

> [Israel's] repeated failure to distinguish between combatants and civilians appears to the Mission to have been the result of deliberate guidance issued to soldiers, as described by some of them, and not the result of occasional lapses.[49]
>
> . . . The Mission found numerous instances of deliberate attacks on civilians and civilian objects (individuals, whole families, houses, mosques) in violation of the fundamental international humanitarian law principle of distinction, resulting in deaths and serious injuries. [T]he Mission found that the protected status of civilians was not respected and the attacks were intentional, in clear violation of customary law reflected in article 51(2) and 75 of the First AP [Additional Protocol], article 27 of the Fourth Geneva Convention and articles 6 and 7 of ICCPR [International Covenant on Civil and Political Rights]. In some cases the Mission additionally concluded that the attack was also launched with the intention of spreading terror among the civilian population.[50]

These conclusions suggest how little the authors of the report seem themselves to have understood about the contours of the key IHL principles of military necessity, proportionality, and distinction. The report does not account for the possibility, or more likely the probability, that Hamas, a terrorist organization, foreseeably and perhaps deliberately increased risks to the Palestinian population by embedding their combatants and military assets in heavily populated civilian areas. Such a step, if it occurred, would not only suggest a possible Israeli legal defense rooted in military necessity sufficient to justify incurring *some* civilian casualties in the face of a need to attack those particular targets, but would also raise the question of whether Hamas should be considered in some measure responsible for civilian losses the report blames entirely upon Israel.

Instead, however, the Goldstone Report noted that while there was evidence of some such Hamas actions, there was no proof of criminal intent. Although the report does recognize that although "Palestinian armed groups launched rockets from urban areas[,] it was not able to obtain any direct evidence that this was done with the specific intent of shielding the rocket launchers from counterstrokes by the Israeli armed forces." Moreover, though the report also indicates that "members of Palestinian armed groups were not always dressed in a way that distinguished them from civilians," it nonetheless "found no evidence that Palestinian combatants mingled with the civilian population with the intention of shielding themselves from attack."[51]

In fact, as Goldstone himself admitted later,[52] the mission seems to have had no direct evidence of Israeli intent to target civilians either. This lack of evidence, however, did not stop the report's authors from assuming Israel's malevolent intent essentially from the bare fact that civilian casualties had occurred. With respect to Hamas, however, they seem to have felt no such inference appropriate. It does not seem to have occurred to the report's authors that the asymmetry in capabilities between Israel and the Palestinians could cause Hamas to use alternative means, outside of what is permitted under IHL, to achieve its goals—a strategy that Hamas arguably indeed had strong incentives to employ. (Ironically, of course, the political impact of the Goldstone Report in tarnishing Israel's reputation for having "intentionally" targeted Palestinian civilians is *itself* strongly suggestive of precisely why such a strategy might have been attractive to Hamas).

The principle of distinction is difficult to employ when dealing with terrorists who entrench themselves in the civilian population, which Hamas has been shown to do, thereby making it extremely difficult for the Israeli military to distinguish between combatants and noncombatants—increasing the risk of errors and ensuring that even when legitimate strikes were made against Hamas combatants or military assets, some Palestinian civilians were very likely also to suffer. Such incidents are clearly tragic, but who is legally to blame for them, if anyone, is of vital importance. Hamas appears to have used the principle of distinction itself as a weapon—thus threatening the rule of law in war entirely—and at the deliberate cost of civilian life.

VI. RESPONSES TO GOLDSTONE

As previously mentioned, there were three responses to Goldstone's initial query about why the international community does not give as much attention to how the report condemns Hamas and only focuses on the criticism of Israel.

With respect to the first response that the mission's criticism does not single out Hamas and only generally talks about Palestinian militants or combatants, the criticism seems well-founded. Though it does mention attacks against Israel, the report illustrates a lack of a comprehensive understanding of the deeper struggle that Israel has engaged in with Hamas in Gaza, thereby allowing the mission to ignore Israel's right to defend itself against the terrorist activities of a terrorist organization. While it may seem like it is simply a matter of parsing words—"terrorist" versus "militant" versus "combatant"—words create the powerful distinction between acts of terrorism which are never legally justifiable, and military acts or combat which may be permitted by the laws of war.

By not identifying the Palestinian militants as Hamas, a terrorist group, the report implies a moral equivalency between the actions of both sides in misleading ways—undermining Israel's ability to invoke the military necessity of self-defense against a terrorist threat as a justification for resorting to the use of force while yet making it appear that it is Israel's *response* to that terrorist threat that is the crime. Meanwhile, Hamas, itself, apparently escapes accountability, for it is ineffectual to criticize the actions of a party that you do not name. (If anything, by not naming Hamas, the report allows it a certain level of legitimacy by not identifying that group as an entity that engages in prohibited terrorist behavior.) In effect, the mission elected to write Hamas and its activities out of the equation, alleging that Israel was not targeting terrorists dressed as and embedding themselves among civilians, but rather intentionally taking aim at the civilians themselves, a violation of IHL.

The second criticism of Goldstone—that a much larger part of the report focuses on Israel's actions and not the Palestinians' actions—speaks to the issue of Israel's proportional response, exercise of distinction, and the report's accusation of disproportionate use of force. Goldstone argued that the number of sections devoted to each party should not matter. However, to the public's perception, the amount of space dedicated to discussion or criticism is often an indication that harsher criticism is warranted and that there is less culpability on the part of the less-criticized party.[53] It is hard to argue balanced treatment between a party whose actions are criticized extensively over many pages and one whose misdeeds are mentioned only, in effect, in passing.

Goldstone also asserted that since the number of casualties on the Palestinian side far surpassed the Israeli casualties, this is a clear indication that Israel used force that was disproportionate to the threat that was posed and consequently an inordinate number of people suffered as a result.[54] This shows great confusion about the content of IHL and its principle of proportionality, for the amount of destruction, while certainly an indication that force was used, does not necessarily indicate that this force was disproportionate. As outlined in our discussion of the aforementioned standards for assessing proportionality in international law, one cannot look at the outcome of a military incursion to judge the legality of the action.[55] The legality is assessed on the basis of what was known, intended, and planned at the outset—looking at how a party has tried to balance necessity and humanity, utilize distinction, and minimize collateral damage. Apparently knowing essentially nothing in these respects about Israeli targeting, other than the fact that the end result was that some civilians were indeed killed, Goldstone lacked a sufficient basis for his conclusion.

Since the publication of the Goldstone Report, many scholars have issued counter-reports refuting the allegations that Israel indiscriminately targeted civilians and civilian objects such as water installations, mosques, homes, and schools.[56] The refutations brought evidence in the form of testimony and satellite images, which demonstrate that the locations from which Hamas fighters launched their rockets were, in fact, in the middle of heavily populated civilian areas, indicating the possible prohibited use of human shields. Some evidence of Israeli efforts to minimize Palestinian casualties, in fact, was available to the authors of the Goldstone Report even before its publication, specifically information about Israeli attempts to warn the civilian population to evacuate to bomb shelters, or to leave locations that were about to be targeted. The report does acknowledge these warning attempts, but it describes them as insufficient—even though the fact that warnings were issued at all calls into question the report's premise that Israel intentionally targeted civilians, and speaks quite powerfully to Israel's good faith compliance with the laws of armed conflict.

The third criticism, regarding a lack of Palestinian statehood and the international community's inability to apply the same legal standards to the Palestinians as it can to Israel, highlights the ongoing challenge of applying the laws of armed conflict to violent non-state actors. Despite not being signatories to international treaties, non-state actors are in theory still obligated to apply their provisions, but enforcement remains a problem and may be impracticable in reality. Goldstone's treatment of Hamas underscores this problem.

Because it seems to penalize state efforts to strike a balance between military necessity and humanity, while yet rewarding terrorist tactics that deliberately endanger civilians, one might wonder whether the report will encourage, or *discourage,* lawful behavior in the future. To minimize the danger of moral hazard problems resulting from the report's imbalance and confusions, the international community could, at the very least, acknowledge the very real challenges that states like Israel face when confronting terrorist groups. Additionally, the best legal defense for a state that confronts violent non-state actors is to constantly monitor its progress during armed conflict to be sure that its own obligations under IHL are fulfilled, and to document all actions it undertakes to demonstrate compliance with the laws of war. To judge by Goldstone's subsequent retraction of his contentious conclusions, Israel seems in practice to have been adequately able to demonstrate its *bona fides* to him—albeit long after the fact. Faced with the possibility of future inquiries that might show the same weaknesses as did the Goldstone Report, states should prepare themselves as best they can for biased scrutiny.

VII. CONCLUSION

In theory, the laws of armed conflict apply equally to both parties to a conflict, whether they be state actors or violent non-state actors. However, the practical application of international humanitarian law is difficult when violent non-state actors, particularly terrorist groups, do not themselves play by the rules of warfare. The principle of distinction is especially difficult for states to employ when terrorists disguise themselves as civilians, which ultimately can throw off the equation when a state calculates the proportionality of a response.

It is tempting to claim that in light of the growing difficulties that states face in dealing with terrorism—with violent non-state actors that increasingly dominate the landscape of modern armed conflicts—that the laws of armed conflict should be revised. It is the contention of this chapter that even though they may have in the Goldstone case been seriously misunderstood or misrepresented, the laws themselves *are* sufficient. What is needed is understanding of and clarity about the challenges entailed in lawfully fighting such conflicts, and alteration in how we apply the rules to the parties, as well as the expectations we have of the parties.

There can no longer be the assumption that both sides are playing by the same rules although they are both legally bound. We cannot ascribe a moral equivalency to their undertakings, or presuppose that when the parties are taken to task that they will both be equally engaged in assuming responsibility for their actions. This is a lesson that Justice Goldstone learned a little too late. His rush to judgment came with a heavy price of condemning a state that was acting in self-defense—and seems to have been acting in good faith to strike a balance between military necessity and distinction—against a terrorist group that does not play by the rules.

After closer examination of the information available to him and his mission, Goldstone retracted his support from the claims of the Goldstone Report that Israel intentionally targeted civilians. By admitting that Israel investigated the legality of any civilian deaths resulting from Operation Cast Lead while Hamas conducted no investigations into its actions at all, Justice Goldstone acknowledged his own error in expecting too much from a terrorist group that cares little for international laws and principles.

The error of the Goldstone Report offers a lesson to the international community, but its confusions do not mean that international law no longer serves the purpose for which it was designed. When understood and correctly applied, the principles of necessity, proportionality, and distinction remain adequate guides to operational behavior in counter-terrorist war. The law need not necessarily be changed, but rather our understanding and expectations of the parties must evolve as international law is applied to nontraditional armed conflicts.

NOTES

1. *The Grave Violations of Human Rights in the Occupied Palestinian Territory particularly due to the recent Israeli military attacks against the occupied Gaza Strip,* U.N. Human Rights Council, 9th Special Session, U.N. Doc. A/HRC/S-9/L.1/ (2009), *revised by* U.N. Doc. A/HRC/S-9/L.1/Rev.2 (2009).

2. United Nations Fact-Finding Mission on the Gaza Conflict, U.N. Human Rights Council, *available at* <http://www2.ohchr.org/english/bodies/hrcouncil/specialsession/9/FactFindingMission.htm>.

3. *Report of the United Nations Fact-Finding Mission on the Gaza Conflict,* U.N. Human Rights Council, 12th Session, Agenda Item 7, U.N. Doc. A/HRC/12/48 (2009) [hereinafter Goldstone Report].

4. "PM: Israel faces the 'Goldstone threat,'" *Jerusalem Post* (December 23, 2009).

5. Hamas is considered a terrorist organization by Canada, the European Union, Israel, Japan, and the United States. Australia and the United Kingdom classify only the military wing of Hamas, the Izz ad-Din al-Qassam Brigades, as a terrorist organization.

6. Elizabeth Samson, interview with Justice Richard Goldstone, Fordham Law School, New York, NY, USA (November 24, 2009).

7. Response of Elizabeth Samson, interview with Justice Richard Goldstone, *supra.*

8. Richard J. Goldstone, Statement on behalf of the Members of the United Nations Fact-Finding Mission on the Gaza Conflict before the Human Rights Council, U.N. Human Rights Council, 12th Session (September 29, 2009) (decrying existence of "culture of impunity" in the region and expressing "regret" that "Israel avoids dealing with the substance of the report").

9. Richard J. Goldstone, "Reconsidering the Goldstone Report on Israel and war crimes," *Washington Post* (April 1, 2011).

10. W. Chadwick Austin & Antony Barone Kolenc, "Who's Afraid of the Big Bad Wolf?: The International Criminal Court as a Weapon of Asymmetric Warfare," *Vanderbilt Journal of Transnational Law*, vol. 39 (2006), at 291, 293.

11. *See*, e.g., "Taliban used civilians as 'human shields," *Associated Press* (May 9, 2009).

12. *See* Michael N. Schmitt, "Human Shields in International Humanitarian Law," *Columbia Journal of Transnational Law*, vol. 47 (2009), at 292.

13. Article 3, common to the four Geneva Conventions, Aug. 12, 1949, 75 U.N.T.S. 287, (entered into force Oct. 21, 1950) [hereinafter Geneva Conventions].

14. Geneva Conventions, *supra*, at Art. 3, Paragraph 2: "In the case of armed conflict *not of an international character* occurring in the territory of one of the High Contracting Parties, each Party to the conflict shall be bound to apply, as a minimum, the following provisions . . ." [emphasis added].

Article 1.1 of the Additional Protocol II to the Geneva Conventions further states that "This Protocol shall apply to all armed conflicts which are not covered by [Additional Protocol I] and which take place in the territory of a High Contracting Party between its armed forces and *dissident armed forces or other organized armed groups . . .*" [emphasis added].

15. *Empowered Groups, Tested Laws, and Policy Options*, Report of the Transnational and Non-State Armed Groups Legal and Policy Challenges, Program on Humanitarian Policy and Conflict Research, Harvard University (November 2007), at 32, *available at* <http://www.tagsproject.org>.

16. Nils Melzer, *Targeted Killing in International Law* (Oxford: Oxford University Press, 2008), at 258.

17. Lindsay Moir, *The Law of International Armed Conflict* 52–58 (Cambridge Studies in International and Comparative Law 2002).

18. Goldstone, "Reconsidering the Goldstone Report on Israel and war crimes," *supra*.

19. *Id.*

20. Michael N. Schmitt, "Asymmetrical Warfare and International Humanitarian Law," *Air Force Law Review*, no. 62 (2008), at 1.

21. Michael N. Schmitt, "The Principle of Discrimination in 21st Century Warfare," *Yale Human Rights & Development Law Journal*, vol. 2 (1999), at 143, 145. For further information, *see infra*.

22. United Nations Charter, at Art. 2(4).

23. *Id.*

24. The second exception, a Security Council enforcement action, is derived from Article 42 of the U.N. Charter:

> Should the Security Council consider that measures provided for in Article 41 would be inadequate or have proved to be inadequate, it may take such action by air, sea, or land forces as may be necessary to maintain or restore international peace and security. Such action may include demonstrations, blockade, and other operations by air, sea, or land forces of Members of the United Nations. *Id.*

25. U.N. Charter, at Art. 51.

26. *Id.* (emphasis added).

27. Robin Coupland, "Humanity: What is it and how does it influence international law?" *International Review of the Red Cross*, vol. 83, no. 844 (2001), at 969.

28. Hague Convention (II) with Respect to the Laws and Customs of War on Land and its annex: Regulation concerning the Laws and Customs of War on Land (July 29, 1899), 32 Stat. 1803, 1 Bevans 247, 26 *Martens Nouveau Recueil* (ser. 2) 949, 187 Consol. T.S. 429; and Hague Convention (IV) Respecting the Laws and Customs of War on Land and its annex: Regulations concerning the Laws and Customs of War on Land: (October 18, 1907), 36 Stat. 2277, 205 Consol. T.S. 277.

The purpose of the Hague Convention of 1899 was to ban the use of certain types of modern technology in war. The Convention also set up the Permanent Court of Arbitration. The 1907 Hague Convention expanded upon the 1899 Convention. The clause was named for Fyodor Fyodorovich Martens, the Russian delegate at the 1899 Convention, and was based upon his words. (The Preamble from the 1907 Hague Convention varies slightly from the original version.)

29. *Id.* (emphasis added).

30. Declaration Renouncing the Use, in Time of War, of Explosive Projectiles Under 400 Grammes Weight, Saint Petersburg, Russian Empire (November 29–December 11, 1868). The St. Petersburg Declaration preceded the Hague Conventions of 1899 and 1907.

31. *Id.*

32. H. McCoubrey, "The Nature of the Modern Doctrine of Military Necessity," *Revue de Droit Militaire et de Droit de la Guerre*, vol. 30 (1991), at 215.

33. Judith Gail Gardam, "Proportionality and Force in International Law," *American Journal of International Law*, no. 87 (1993), at 391, 407.

34. *Id.* at 412.

35. Protocol Additional to the Geneva Conventions of August 12, 1949 and Relating to the Protection of Victims of International Armed Conflict, June 8, 1977, 16 I.L.M. 1391, at art. 51.5(b). (1977) (emphasis added) [hereinafter Additional Protocol I].

36. Schmitt, "The Principle of Discrimination in 21st Century Warfare," *supra*, at 150.

37. Additional Protocol I, *supra*, at Art. 48.

38. *Id.*

39. Schmitt, "Asymmetrical Warfare and International Humanitarian Law," *supra*, at 15 (*citing* Jean Pictet, *Commentary: III Geneva Convention* 52 (ICRC, 1960);

Commentary on the Additional Protocols of 8 June 1977 to the Geneva Conventions of 12 August 1949 (Yves Sandoz, Christophe Swinarki, & Bruno Zimmerman, eds.) (ICRC 1987), at ¶ 1577–78).

40. *Id.*

41. *Id.*

42. *See* Schmitt, "The Principle of Discrimination in 21st Century Warfare," *supra*, at 157.

43. Gal Beckerman, "Goldstone: 'If this was a court of law, there would have been nothing proven'," *The Forward* (October 7, 2009) (*quoting* Richard Goldstone: "We had to do the best we could with the material we had. If this was a court of law, there would have been nothing proven.").

44. Laurie Blank & Gregory Gordon, "Goldstone, Gaza and (Dis)Proportionality: Three Strikes," *The Jurist* (November 11, 2009), *available at* http://jurist.law.pitt.edu.

45. *Id.*

46. Goldstone, "Reconsidering the Goldstone Report on Israel and war crimes," *supra* (emphasis added).

47. Goldstone Report, *supra*, at ¶ 1680.

48. *Id.* at ¶ 1690.

49. *Id.* at ¶ 1686.

50. *Id.* at ¶ 1718.

51. Goldstone Report, *supra* note 46, art. 482–83.

52. Goldstone, "Reconsidering the Goldstone Report on Israel and war crimes," *supra* (noting that when writing the report he had "had no evidence on which to draw any other reasonable conclusion" about Israel).

53. Interview with Justice Richard Goldstone, *supra*. *See also* David Kaye, "The Goldstone Report," *ASIL Insight*, vol. 13, no. 16 (October 1, 2009).

54. Howard LaFranchi, "Goldstone Report: UN Votes for Probe into Gaza War Crimes," *Christian Science Monitor* (November 5, 2009); *see also* Graham Usher, "Law-fare, not Warfare," *Al-Ahram Weekly*, no. 972 (November 12–18, 2009).

55. *See* Gradam *supra*, and accompanying text.

56. Moshe Halbertal, "The Goldstone Illusion: What the U.N. report gets wrong about Gaza—and war," *The New Republic* (November 6, 2009); *see also* Dore Gold & Jonathan Dahoah Halevi, *The U.N. Gaza Report: A substantive Critique*, expanded presentation by Amb. Gold, originally given at Brandeis University (November 5, 2009), *available at* <http://www.jcpa.org/text/GoldGoldstone-5nov09.pdf>.

Chapter 8

Confronting Terrorism

Human Rights Law, or the Law of War?

Juan Carlos Gómez Ramírez

In our present era of terrorism, human rights (HR)[1] law and the law of war or international humanitarian law (IHL),[2] and the relationship between the two, are fundamental in state security and defense policy. After the atrocities and the excessive number of civilians killed in the wars of the 20th century, including during the post-Cold War period,[3] the development of compelling norms securing human beings' fundamental rights is understood to be one of humanity's most important victories over barbarism. Few are willing to compromise the belief that these norms protect everyone regardless of race, religion, gender, age, political ideology, or economic situation. The development of IHL is also a signal achievement, representing as it does the principle that even in the conduct of war itself, states are bound to conform their conduct to standards of lawful behavior.

From conventional threats and the potential for "industrial" wars, however, we have emerged into an era of wars in the midst of the people,[4] which bring a concurrent increased risk of asymmetric threats, including terrorist actions. Today, most wars faced by states are with enemies who, like criminals, operate in small groups and in ways that are nebulous and covert. Such enemies engage in armed actions within the civilian population and, more frequently, against them.[5] How do states wishing to follow and preserve the rule of law cope with such adversaries?

The leaders of modern democracies face an immense responsibility in their effort to guarantee defense and security in societies that are intolerant of crime and terrorism[6] but at the same time cherish hard-won freedoms and rights. How can such governments rise to these challenges and yet safeguard a state's most valuable intangible good, its legitimacy? No action of defense or security can be taken outside of the parameters of legality and legitimacy, because the center of gravity of such a state's power, and its capacity to act against any sign or outbreak of violence, lies squarely in society's perception of the government it elected.

HR law and IHL are the legal tools society currently uses to face any criminal or otherwise hostile manifestation. By some accounts, however, terrorists and their actions do not fit within or deserve the legal guarantees established by HR treaties and conventions,[7] while yet not always meeting the minimum requirements for the application of IHL that permit and expand the possibility of use of force by states and international organizations to prevent and contain extremely hostile actions.

Legislative and doctrinal advances at an international level in the area of HR, especially in the last 20 years, have been driven by academics and scholars who, in many cases, come from countries and systems that were once authoritarian and dictatorial. These HR norms have helped justify radical changes in policy in such systems, and in respect for the basic rights of their citizens. With the appearance of certain radical and vindictive ideologies, however, some have gone beyond defending HR to trying to use it as a political tool for exercising opposition and confounding legitimate state efforts against subversion. Using HR issues to political advantage is not a new strategy in politics, nor is it always the monopoly of the Left. (Conservatives in the U.S. Congress in the late 1970s, for instance, picked up the human rights issue to reject economic aid to leftist regimens like Vietnam, Laos, Cambodia, Mozambique, and Angola.[8])

What body of law governs state actions in a contemporary irregular conflict? If the threats faced by states are limited to those coming from unorganized or partially organized criminals not rising to the level of an armed or insurgent group—and if these criminals have no territorial control or command structure that is responsible for the actions of the group, thus bringing it in line with the definitions of IHL—it is very probable that state action should be limited to the application of criminal law and HR. This would be done within a legal and judicial framework that safeguards human rights. And it would fall under the authority of the police and the justice system, whose primary function is to protect and to enforce the law, rather than of the military authorities.[9]

For its part, IHL has advanced little in terms of legislation on methods for the use of force since war was generally proscribed by the United Nations Charter of 1945.[10] Today, customary law is the main instrument for developing the law of war. In terms of jurisprudence, when states have not justified their actions in the framework of IHL—that is, as taking place within the ambit of an armed conflict—international human rights courts have given priority to the right to life in the framework of HR, a situation that doubtless works to a great disadvantage to armed forces facing a conflict.[11]

I. WHAT ABOUT TERRORISM?

Until nations reach general agreement and decide to legislate on whether or not some freedoms and rights may, in exigent circumstances of hostile threat, be sacrificed in favor of defense and security—which, by the way, is an issue transcending ethical and moral principles—countries and their leaders must adhere to the laws in effect as they face each and every one of the threats and aggressions besieging them.

In response to the dilemma of which set of standards applies to the neutralization of terrorism, the most important thing is to be able to identify the threat in each case and deal with it based on its description, determining whether confrontation under IHL is viable. This body of law is known by some as the law of war, deriving in part from the Hague Convention,[12] and as humanitarian law, and it incorporates the Geneva Convention and the Additional Protocols. But it was really born out of customs long before any convention was signed. Those who participated in armed conflicts and those who suffered their rigors set about establishing codes of honor and ethics to limit the suffering of those who did not participate in hostilities—or those who, having previously participated in the conflict, had ceased doing so—by preventing attacks upon, or at least limiting damage to, such persons.

The laws in the conventions are not as robust or prohibitive as some would desire, but this has its logic. If they had been extremely restrictive, very few countries would have signed them, which would limit their range of applicability and the protections they provide in the event of an armed confrontation. If, however, they had been too lax, their use would be innocuous, and therefore it would not be worthwhile to even sign or ratify them. Usefully protecting noncombatants, therefore, required striking a balance.

Unlike international armed conflicts, for which the laws restricting belligerent conduct are relatively broad-scoped, the laws for non-international conflicts cover merely the basics. And this is not to speak of the contemporary "war on terrorism," in which a perceived absence of relevant rules has been said to lead to an enormous vacuum. Unlike the situation with traditional warfare, the limits of IHL as applied to modern irregular conflict illustrate why it is so important to go deeper in the interpretation of IHL, treating it as a "Law of Minimums," and seek where possible to go beyond its scanty provisions in search of a more juridical response to the challenge of terrorism.

Without a doubt, humanitarian law has arisen out of lessons from the past. This can mean, however, that it is always one or two wars behind in its development. Such a lag may be seen in the Geneva protocols of 1977, the protocols limiting and prohibiting the use of certain weapons in 1980, the Ottawa Convention of 1997, and the International Criminal Court of 1998—all of which offer rules that still lack the levels of general adherence hoped for, and indeed still remain controversial in some circles.

Based on the actual conflicts of the real world, it is worth analyzing the impact customary IHL has had on the way hostilities are conducted, and on the evaluation of the concept of military objectives, in an attempt to develop the notions established by Additional Protocol I of 1977—which did attempt to articulate rules restraining state conduct in conflicts with guerrillas and other irregular adversaries. To do that, it is worth determining when the humanitarian laws apply that allow security forces to operate under "military," as opposed to "civilian" or "law-enforcement," rules. The following pages will examine these challenges through the prism of Colombian practice.

II. IHL VERSUS HR IN COLOMBIAN PRACTICE

From the point of view of the Colombian armed forces, independent from the political discussion—which has *not* recognized the existence of an armed conflict[13]—the application of IHL is a necessary reality. Colombia has signed and ratified the conventions and protocols that regulate this area,[14] and the crimes that constitute IHL infractions are part of its constitutional and legal system.[15] In addition, the aggression exercised by groups that subvert the democratic order in Colombia, despite the fact that these groups have been weakened, still meets the characteristics listed by IHL that require and permit its full application in certain parts of the country.

Moreover, and with the purpose of clearing up any remaining doubt as to whether or not IHL applies to a determined situation, the International Committee of the Red Cross—which is an authority in this area—endorses the application and development of IHL in times of conflict *and other situations of armed violence* in order to prevent violations of the laws that protect basic rights and values.[16] IHL, therefore, is useful as a default framework, so that no state action is ever entirely *lawless*.

Once one clearly understands the application of IHL, one must then determine the way military objectives are designated and established.

A. Military Objectives

Although some commentators believe that military objectives are limited to material assets, it is clear that Additional Protocol I of the Geneva Convention divides the concept into two parts. The section on Combatant Status—Article 43 of Section II—mentions the armed forces and speaks of the right of their members to participate in hostilities and therefore, to be an object of an attack.[17]

Subsequently, in Article 52, relative to objects, the second paragraph states that attacks will be limited to military objectives: "*In so far as objects are concerned,* military objectives are limited to those objects which by their nature, location, purpose, or use make an effective contribution to military action. . . ."

It is obvious that the introduction to this paragraph expands the definition of military objective beyond just *objects,* to include the *persons* who may be targeted by an attack. In the case of non-international conflicts, Additional Protocol II defines those involved in hostilities as armed forces, dissident armed forces, or other organized armed groups. Part II,[18] *Humane Treatment,* describes the basic protections enjoyed by those who are not participating directly in the hostilities, or who have ceased to participate in them. Therefore, relative to the concept of military objective, IHL does not exclude combatants or members of organized armed groups, nor those who participate directly in the hostilities. Both persons and objects, therefore, can be legitimate military targets.

Once we have clarity on the interpretation of a military objective, it is important to look at the role played by the Principle of Distinction in the selection of military objectives in Colombia.

B. Selection of Objectives

In recent years, as a result of the offensive launched by the state's security policy, hostile *organized armed groups* in Colombia have been weakened, little by little, and have changed their belligerent actions. From large, well-armed, equipped, and uniformed military units they have been forced to transition to small groups, often without uniforms and with small or non-conventional firearms, and have come to use the typical methods of *terrorist organizations*. The Colombian armed forces have responded to this reality by adopting measures to make a careful and detailed application of the *principle of distinction* in the selection of military objectives.

The military weakening of an enemy in any confrontation brings notable changes in the tools that should be used for facing it, not only on the level of military operations, but in the legal arena also. Colombia has worked to respond to these challenges.

III. FROM WARFARE TO LAW ENFORCEMENT

The selection of military objectives when armed groups dissolve and mix with the civilian population is a difficult task, yet indispensable. IHL has some minimum conditions for its application, which are not always in place in all situations, or in the case of all the threats faced by state security forces. When a security strategy is experiencing success, the enemy tries to act more as a criminal than a combatant. In conditions where there is no armed confrontation and where the threats are purely criminal, the legal framework to be applied is that of HR. In this framework, and from a legal point of view, military objectives do not exist. This is where the clarification becomes complex as to whether action must be taken in the framework of HR or IHL; the answer will vary.

This phenomenon is a true challenge that has been met by the Colombian Operational Legal Advisors (AJO in the Spanish). In their work, AJOs regard conflicts with such shifting or ambiguous conditions as representing a middle zone along a continuum between "normality" and military-style "confrontation," and in which either IHL or HR may apply depending upon the circumstances. They call this "The Gray Zone."

A. Which Body of Law Should Be Applied?

In this conception, as one can see on the upper line in *Figure 8.1*[19], the application of IHL will diminish to the degree that the level of violence goes down and the characteristics of the organizations being faced change or weaken. This movement represents the transition from confrontation to normality, and it is in this transitional area that terrorism moves—inside the gray zone.

Figure 8.1.

The legal framework for the application of IHL is absolutely clear when the level of violence is high and the adversary has defined characteristics, as reflected on the right hand side of the graph. And it is obvious that low levels of violence, and the absence of an armed threat, will oblige state agents and armed forces to be governed by HR standards.

B. The Gray Zone

It would be ideal if, instead of uncertainty as to which set of standards to apply, as represented by the gray zone in the graph, there were a clearly defined line for determining action without hesitation, depending on the particular situation. Unfortunately, that is not so.

As long as there is no positive law validating certain practices for confronting terrorism, customary IHL takes on singular value, since proper interpretation of the conventions permits in certain cases the use of armed forces, determination of military objectives, application of the minimum force necessary, and completion of missions. Likewise, IHL establishes minimum parameters of conduct for political leaders and military commanders, which will lead, if not met, to being accused of war crimes for which the penalties and sanctions are equal or even more serious than those for HR violations.[20]

C. Proportionality in IHL versus HR

Taking action under IHL's *minimum standards* that permit an attacked party (the state) to take military action in the scope of its mission and extinguish a threat requires professionalism and broad knowledge of those standards. The IHL framework requires that any damage to protected persons and objects be proportional to the military advantage anticipated as the result of attacking military objectives. By contrast, in the framework of HR—a standard of maximums—the use of lethal force is only for legitimate defense and as a last recourse.[21] In other words, an action is considered justified when the reaction is in proportion to the threat. In the face of a real or imminent attack, therefore, the use of lethal force legally could be made. Otherwise, however, the use of lethal force cannot be considered in this juridical framework.

IV. MEETING THE CHALLENGE OF THE GRAY ZONE

It is a fundamental responsibility of governments to provide defense and security for those who live and travel in their nations, thus guaranteeing stability and the survival of the state. To do that, the state must face threats and aggressions, including everything from purely criminal actions all the way to large-scale military assault—a continuum which, as noted above, includes insurgencies and terrorist actions. This reality forces government leaders and their security forces to be creative and effective in providing protection, defense, and security in a national and international environment of fundamental guarantees, where no excess is tolerated as far as restrictions or violations of basic rights is concerned. It is, therefore, of singular importance to know and correctly use, in a generalized manner, tools that can reduce the uncertainty generated by the gray zone (*Figure 1*), a zone in which the government's response to those who perpetrate terrorist actions frequently falls.

It would be helpful if legal reforms were expressly to define terrorists as legitimate military objectives, explicitly permitting the use of IHL-governed military operations as a legal tool available to states responding to this phenomenon. That would be ideal, but it has not yet occurred. While society and the legislative apparatus work on reaching an agreement as to the ethical and moral aspects of restricting, reducing, or taking away certain rights from those considered to be potential terrorists, a lot of time will go by.

In the meantime, to maintain the legitimacy and legality that sustain and validate democratic states, the best (and only) option available is to face these threats within the legal framework of International Human Rights Law and International Humanitarian Law, depending on the situation. Some simple actions have demonstrated to be effective in Colombia:

- *Integration of agencies and efforts to improve intelligence work as a basic tool for recognizing and characterizing threats.* If the specific threat at issue in a particular operation is in the orbit of criminal activity, it should be prosecuted as such (i.e., as a law enforcement or civil order problem) and it will be the judges of the appropriate court system who take action, based on the evidence, to impose the penalties determined by law. In other words, the actions will take place in the framework of HR.
- If state intelligence characterizes the threat as being within the precepts of IHL—based on the principles of military necessity,[22] distinction,[23] limitation,[24] and humanity[25]—every effort may be made to locate and neutralize the military objectives in a "military" way, within the strictures of IHL. Damage to persons and objects not part of the objective must be minimized relative to the anticipated military advantage.[26] This last principle is in strict application of the principle of Proportionality.[27]
- *The Operational Legal Advisors (AJO) established in article 82 of Additional Protocol I of the Geneva Convention.*[28] These officials are one of a commander's most important tools for determining the material and legal framework for the application of IHL. The participation of attorneys

in the process of planning, executing, and evaluating military and police operations reduces the level of uncertainty for commanders at the time of decision making.

- *Rules of Engagement (ROE).* ROE establish the basic policies and procedures governing actions taken by commanders and their forces during operations.[29] These simple instructions regulating security-force actions are a key instrument for limiting the use of force. They can reduce the complexity involved in knowing, for instance, whether a commander can opt for the principle of surprise and the use of lethal force as a first option for a military objective under the principle of military necessity—in other words, acting in the framework of IHL—or whether, on the contrary, he can only use force in reaction and in *response* to an attack, as per the framework of HR.
- *After Action Review (AAR).* Learning from the past is one of the best methods states and their security forces can use to repeat effective actions and procedures, and not repeat the errors of the past. Military and police doctrine should be built on the experience obtained and learned from new and growing threats. Humanity in the twenty-first century demands that regular state forces be much more precise and careful in fulfilling their missions.
- *Regional Scenario Training Groups. (GEPER for the Spanish).* This is a new mechanism in Colombia, developed as part of the Comprehensive Policy for Human Rights at the Ministry of National Defense in Colombia. The GEPER's mission is to direct and carry out scenario-based training and retraining exercises for members of the armed forces related to tactical missions. In order to avoid breaches of HR and IHL, the armed forces receive instruction relative to the operational reality they will face, and according to where they will be deployed. At the same time they train in techniques, tactics, and operational procedures for the correct application of the rules of engagement.[30]

V. CONCLUSION

Terrorism is, unfortunately, a reality in the 21st century, presenting extraordinary challenges to states—and to security services determined to uphold the rule of law while defending the state against such threats. Governments are required to fully guarantee basic rights, but they are also expected to be capable of providing defense and security. Asking society to give up, in the name of security, some of the guarantees obtained in modern times, is difficult. If such sacrifices occur, this could be a very lengthy process, for it will quite properly engender protracted ethical and moral debates. Until then, however, security challenges must still be faced somehow. What remains for states, therefore, is to use excellent intelligence systems and legal measures to address threats under existing law.

This often means prosecuting those who challenge the defense and security of states in the framework of HR—in other words, fully guaranteeing all the rights of victims and perpetrators. If the threat meets the requirements of IHL, however, the relevant conventions are broad-scoped and sufficient to provide guidance in both humanitarian terms (Geneva), and in the means and methods for the development of hostilities (The Hague).

In the arena of non-international armed conflicts, in those places or circumstances where the periods and levels of violence meet the characteristics that permit the use of IHL, the lack of a clearer body of law should not be an impediment to adopting—and adapting to analogous situations—the standards designed for international conflicts in terms of the principle of distinction. An example of this is the demonstrated effective, legal, and legitimate application of IHL by the armed forces in Colombia, despite the fact that an armed conflict has not officially been declared or recognized there.[31]

The existence of HR rules and their potential applicability in certain operational contexts increasingly affects and limits the autonomy of states facing different threats, therefore forcing them to be much more careful and precise in the use of force when facing illegal expressions of violence. It is vital to be able to shift between legal frameworks as operational circumstances demand. Integrated action by intelligence agencies, ROE, AJOS, lessons learned, and Regional Scenario Training Groups are some of the key tools used effectively by Colombia to face threats and to apply the right body of law (HR or IHL) depending on the circumstances of each case. Colombia's successful example can be used by countries and international organizations facing similar situations involving everything crime, hostilities, and terrorism—and complex and shifting combinations thereof.

Aggression and threats of different types will continue to appear, and the legitimate right of states to survive and protect themselves can indeed justify—or even require—the use of force in responding to such challenges. Neither, however, can we forsake the ideal of subjecting state power to the constraints of legal legitimacy. Because of this harsh but inevitable reality, conventional and customary IHL must continue to be applied and brought to maturity for the good of current generations and of those yet to come.

NOTES

1. *See*, e.g., Universal Declaration of Human Rights (December 10, 1948), from the Introduction. In December 1948, the General Assembly of the United Nations adopted and proclaimed the Universal Declaration of Human Rights, the full text

of which it urged be "disseminated, displayed, read and expounded principally in schools and other educational institutions, without distinction based on the political status of countries or territories."

2. International humanitarian law is the body of law which seeks, for humanitarian reasons, to limit the effects of armed conflict. (It is sometimes also referred to in this volume as the law of armed conflict, or "LOAC.") It protects persons who are not, or are no longer, participating in hostilities and restricts the means and methods of warfare. *See generally* Francois Bugnion, "Law of Geneva and Law of The Hague," *International Review of the Red Cross,* no.844 (December 2001), at 901–22.

3. F. A. Beer, *Peace against War* (San Francisco: W. H. Freeman & Co., 1981), at 37–38. In the First World War, the 1.3 million civilians killed represented only 14 percent of the total. In the Second World War, however, this figure climbed to 67 percent (34.3 million). *See* Uppsala University, Department of Peace and Conflict Research, *The victims of armed conflict—Report for the Global Campaign for the Protection of War Victims* (1991), at 8.

4. *See* Sir Rupert Smith, "Methods of Warfare" (interview), *International Review of the Red Cross,* vol. 88 (December 2006), at 719–27.

5. *Id.* at 719.

6. Boaz Ganor, *The Counter–Terrorism Puzzle: A Guide for Decision Makers.* (Piscataway, NJ: Transaction Publishers, 2005). According to Ganor, "[t]errorism is a form of violent struggle in which violence is deliberately used against civilians in order to achieve political goals (nationalistic, socioeconomic, ideological, religious, etc)."

7. *See,* e.g., William McGurn, "Holder's Al Qaeda Incentive Plan," *Wall Street Journal* (November 17, 2009), at 23.

8. *See* David P. Forsythe, *Human Rights and World Politics* (Lincoln, NE: University of Nebraska Press, 1983), at 125 & 153.

9. As used in this chapter, "law enforcement" refers to the prevention, investigation, apprehension, or detention of individuals suspected or convicted of offenses against criminal laws, including by an employee engaged in this activity who is transferred to a supervisory or administrative position, or serving as a probation or pretrial services officer.

10. United Nations Charter (June 10, 1945), from the Preamble:

> "We the peoples of the United Nations determined: to save succeeding generations from the scourge of war, which twice in our lifetime has brought untold sorrow to mankind, and to reaffirm faith in fundamental human rights, in the dignity and worth of the human person, in the equal rights of men and women and of nations large and small, and to establish conditions under which justice and respect for the obligations arising from treaties and other sources of international law can be maintained, and to promote social progress and better standards of life in larger freedom, And for these ends: to practice tolerance and live together in peace with one another as good neighbors, and to unite our strength to maintain international peace and security, and to ensure, by the acceptance of principles and the institution of methods, that armed force shall not be used, save in the common interest, and to employ international machinery for the promotion of the economic and social advancement of all peoples, Have resolved to combine our efforts to accomplish

these aims: Accordingly, our respective Governments, through representatives assembled in the city of San Francisco, who have exhibited their full powers found to be in good and due form, have agreed to the present Charter of the United Nations and do hereby establish an international organization to be known as the United Nations.").

11. *See* Daniel O'Donnell, "Trends in the application of international humanitarian law by the United Nations human rights mechanisms," *International Review of the Red Cross*, no.324 (September 1998).

12. As recounted by Kathleen Lawand, parties to an armed conflict are limited in their choice of weapons, means and methods of warfare by the rules of international humanitarian law (IHL) governing the conduct of hostilities. Relevant rules include the prohibition on using means and methods of warfare of a nature to cause superfluous injury or unnecessary suffering, and the prohibition on using means of warfare that are incapable of distinguishing between civilians or civilian objects and military targets. These are the ''cardinal rules'' of IHL applying to weapons. In addition, particular treaties and customary rules impose specific prohibitions or limitations on the use of certain weapons, for example anti-personnel mines and blinding laser weapons. Kathleen Lawand, "Reviewing the legality of new weapons, means and methods of warfare," *International Review of the Red Cross*, no. 864 (December 31, 2006), at 925–30.

13. *See* Colombian President Alvaro Uribe, remarks to the 64th UN General Assembly (September 23, 2009), *available at* <http://www.voltairenet.org/article162268.html>.

14. Law 5 of 1960 approved the Geneva Conventions of 1949 as part of Colombia's legislation. And Laws 11 of 1992 and 171 of 1994 approved the First and Second Additional Protocols of 1977, respectively.

15. The Colombian Constitution, in its Article 214, makes mention of IHL's applicability in the country. Crimes against IHL are also part of the Colombian criminal and disciplinary codes. *See* Law 599 of 2000, and Laws 734 of 2002 and 836 of 2003, respectively.

16. "Customary Law," *International Review of the Red Cross*, vol. 87, no. 857 (March 2005).

17. Additional Protocol I to the Geneva Conventions of 12 August 1949.

18. Additional Protocol II to the Geneva Conventions of 12 August 1949.

19. Graph made by the author for an ICRC presentation in Bogota in March 2008.

20. In the Colombian case, Law 599 of 2000 (Colombian Criminal Code) gives between 25 to 40 years in prison for aggravated homicide (an HR issue) and from 30 to 40 years of prison in the case of homicide of a protected person—that is, a crime of war (IHL).

21. According to Horst Fischer, "[t]he principle of proportionality is embedded in almost every national legal system and underlies the international legal order. Its function in domestic law is to relate means to ends. In armed conflict, the principle is used to judge first, the lawfulness in *jus ad bellum* of the strategic goals in the use of force for self-defense, and second, the lawfulness in *jus in bello* of any armed attack that causes civilian casualties." Horst Fischer, *Proportionality, Principle of* (undated), *available at* <http://cow.tommygonzalez.com/glossary/proportionality-principle-of/>.

22. Military necessity "is understood by modern civilized nations, consists in the necessity of those measures which are indispensable for securing the ends of the war, and which are lawful according to the modern law and usages of war." *Lieber Instructions* (1863), at Art. 14. *See The Law of Armed Conflicts* (Dietrich Schindler & Jiri Toman, eds.) (Leiden: Martininus Nijhoff Publishers, 2002), at 6.

23. The principle of distinction requires differentiation between combatants and civilians, and between military objectives and nonmilitary objects. According to the famous formulation in the Lieber Code in the nineteenth century, combatants should observe "the distinction between the private individual belonging to a hostile country and the hostile country itself, with its men in arms," with the result that "the unarmed citizen is to be spared in person, property, and honor as much as the exigencies of war will admit." *Lieber Instructions, supra,* at Art. 22.

24. The principle of limitation holds that "[i]n any armed conflict, the right of the parties to choose methods or means of warfare is not unlimited." Geneva Additional Protocol I of 1977, at Art. 35.

25. Under the principle of humanity, "the progress of civilization should have the effect of alleviating, as far as possible, the calamities of war," and that "the only legitimate object which States should have in view during war is to weaken the enemy without inflicting upon him unnecessary suffering." Brussels Conference of 1874, Final Protocol, at 22.

26. According to one influential compilation of rules, "an attack shall not be launched if it may be expected to cause collateral casualties or damage which would be excessive in relation to the concrete and direct military advantage anticipated from attack as a whole; an attack shall be cancelled or suspended as soon as it becomes apparent that the collateral casualties or damage would be excessive." San Remo Manual of International Law Applicable to Conflicts at Sea (June 12, 1994), § II, at 46(d), *available at* <http://www.icrc.org/ihl.nsf/385ec082b509e76c41256739003e636d/7694fe2016f347e1c125641f002d49ce>.

27. Under the principle of proportionality, combatants must "refrain from deciding to launch any attack which may be expected to cause incidental loss of civilian life, injury to civilians, damage to civilian objects, or a combination thereof, which would be excessive in relation to the concrete and direct military advantage anticipated." Protocol I Additional to the Geneva Conventions 1977, Chapter IV, at Art. 57.

28. Additional Protocol I to the Geneva Convention (August 12, 1949), at Art. 82.

29. *See*, e.g., International Law and Operational Law Department, Judge Advocate General's Center & School, U.S. Army, *Operational Law Handbook* (August 2008), at 25.

30. Republic of Colombia, Ministry of Defense, *Comprehensive Human Rights and IHL Policy* (January 2008), at 34, *available at* <http://www.mindefensa.gov.co:80/irj/go/km/docs/Mindefensa/Documentos/descargas2/anexos/9528_Comprehensive_Human_Rights_and_IHL_Policy_-_MDN.pdf>.

31. *See generally* Juan Manuel Santos, *Jaque al Terror- los años horribles de las FARC* (Barcelona: Planeta, 2009).

Chapter 9

Living in the "New Normal"

Modern War, Non-State Actors, and the Future of Law

Christopher A. Ford

It is quite common, at least in the United States, to hear it said that "everything changed" with the terrorist attacks of September 11, 2001 (a.k.a. "9/11"). Some mean by this that with those atrocities, Americans awoke to a need for robust responses to which earlier naïve legalism or political squeamishness had blinded us. Others see "everything" as having changed because *al Qaeda*'s terrorist assault led an arrogant Executive Branch to arrogate authority dangerously to itself, and to exercise this power in fundamentally lawless ways. The U.S. "war on terrorism" has sparked legal debates as intense as the political ones it likewise engendered, including controversies over the very *applicability* of law in the irregular, state-versus-non-state-actor form of warfare that seems to have become much more common today than the traditional kind.

Ten years after 9/11, what can one say about the road we have traveled—and about where we are, in these regards, going?

It is my contention that much about the "new normal" of counterterrorist war is indeed novel, in practical terms, but that both the development of these challenges *and* the principal aspects of states' responses did not appear upon a singular watershed such as 9/11. Rather, the problems presented by modern war, both tactically and legally, have been developing for some time, and one can see elements of states' characteristic post-9/11 responses well *before* that date. We are concerned here, one might say, with a much longer story arc—and thus perhaps with processes that are both less singular and more likely to persist—than the 9/11 narrative presumes.

The way in which responses to these challenges have developed, moreover, is also more complicated than a perusal of daily headlines or op-ed pages might suggest. In many regards, the advent of modern irregular conflict—especially in its specifically counterterrorist (CT) incarnation—has indeed led to some growth in the power in the Executive Branch. But this has not occurred willy-nilly, or without attendant dynamics of bargained adjustment.

Indeed, rather than being a process that could be likened to the swing of a pendulum back and forth between extremes, the intra-governmental dynamics of CT war and legality in the United States have looked more like a process of punctuated evolution. Expedient single-branch executive responses to crisis have been to some extent adjusted as the courts and Congress have stepped in—and as successive presidents have taken office—but there has been much more *ratification* than retrenchment in these respects, and more *continuity* than change in CT policy *since* the first phase of the U.S. response after 9/11. Other branches seem, in fact, to have played their most important roles not in *rejecting* "war paradigm" assertions, but rather in merely *adjusting* this paradigm as the peculiarities of today's counterterrorist "new normal" have become clearer—ultimately *legitimating* "war" rules as part of a process of buckling down, metaphorically speaking, for the long haul. Americans have ended up today with a system based upon the animating principles of the *ancien régime* of traditional conflict—and traditional approaches to its prosecution and regulation—but one in which these principles have been reconfigured and recombined in order to apply them more coherently to situations the old framework was felt ill-prepared to address (e.g., a real "war," but yet one that may not ever fully "end").

The rules of international law regulating how states may actually *fight* modern war may also be developing—or need to. Here, too, the old principles seem to remain no less valid, but they may *look* different in practice, when applied to contemporary circumstances, than what we are accustomed to seeing. Moreover, while no less *applicable* than before, the rules of war seem increasingly difficult to *apply,* as a practical matter, in the decentralized, indeterminate, and shadowy transboundary "theater" of contemporary CT conflict. As domestic systems have tried to adapt to CT challenges, so too may our understanding of how best to ensure fidelity to the ideal of law-bounded conduct need to evolve. The following pages will explore these dynamics in much more detail.

I. AMERICA AND THE NEW WAR

The initial U.S. reaction to the attacks of 9/11 was to embrace a paradigm of "warfare" based upon the domestic legal rules of traditional conflict—and to embrace it with bloody-minded vigor. The Bush administration turned to fairly executive-permissive traditional notions of "wartime" powers, and transferred them as a simple template to the "war on terrorism." Its critics frequently tried to assert, in effect, that this wasn't *really* a "war" at all, and that "peacetime" rules should still prevail. Both sides seem to have assumed that what the administration was doing was a radical departure from where things stood just before 9/11.

As observers as diverse as Benjamin Wittes[1] and Jane Mayer[2] have noted, however, many elements of the counterterrorist policy "toolkit" employed by the Bush administration existed in U.S. law and practice well before 2001. To some extent—though that is by no means the end of the story—it was merely Bush's innovation to wrap many of them together under an explicit legal theory of all-out war, and to employ these approaches on a grander scale than ever before.

A. Prehistory of a Counterterrorist Legal Revolution

Following the bombings of the U.S. embassies in Kenya and Tanzania in 1998 by *al Qaeda* terrorists, Clinton administration officials reportedly embarked upon what former national security advisor Sandy Berger called "a very intense effort to get [Osama] bin Laden," which he explained meant trying to "capture or kill" the terrorist leader.[3] The most obvious form this took was the unsuccessful cruise missile attack that year upon a site in Afghanistan where bin Laden was believed to be at the time. President Clinton, however, also authorized covert efforts by the U.S. Central Intelligence Agency (CIA) to work with local Afghan tribal forces to capture the terrorist leader—planning which actually predated the embassy bombings.[4]

These efforts were deeply controversial within the Clinton administration, with Attorney General Janet Reno reportedly fighting fiercely against the idea of undertaking a targeted killing, and even resisting the idea that bin Laden might be killed by his would-be CIA kidnappers in "self-defense." Reno is said, for instance, to have scuppered a plan to capture bin Laden and send him to Egypt to be "rudely questioned": she refused to agree to this operation unless he were first indicted.[5] The CIA was initially given authority to use lethal force against bin Laden only in "self-defense"—though this was subsequently broadened slightly to permit the CIA and its Afghan tribal allies to kill him if capture proved unfeasible.[6]

For the Clinton administration, the "preferred" option was apparently always to arrest the *al Qaeda* leader.[7] Nor, apparently, did CIA Director George Tenet during this period ever advise in favor of killing bin Laden. (Even under Bush, in fact—and only a week before 9/11—the CIA and the U.S. Air Force reportedly took positions *against* using the recently tested armed Predator drone aircraft against bin Laden in Afghanistan.)[8] Nevertheless, while U.S. leaders seem then to have had a weak stomach for covert attack, the Clinton administration's aforementioned 1998 cruise missile attack indicates that targeted killing was *in principle* available in the struggle against *al Qaeda.*

The U.S. use of the technique of *renditions*—operations in which a terrorist suspect is forcibly seized in a foreign jurisdiction, with or without the knowledge or cooperation of local authorities, and transported to another foreign jurisdiction or to the United States for interrogation, detention, or trial—also began years before 9/11. From 1993 onward, U.S. counterterrorist policy reportedly involved periodic renditions undertaken with the approval and close involvement of White House officials.[9] The Clinton administration did not do renditions frequently by post-9/11 standards, but it did them nonetheless. According to Tenet, some 70 terrorists were in fact subjected to rendition before September 2001.[10]

Both George H.W. Bush and Bill Clinton, moreover, used the U.S. Navy base at Guantánamo Bay, Cuba, for detaining foreign nationals seized outside the United States in the early and mid-1990s. These two administrations adopted this approach precisely because they believed that using Guantánamo allowed the government to hold such persons—in this case, Haitian refugees awaiting forcible return to Haiti—without them acquiring any legal rights whatsoever under U.S. law. As Wittes has observed, moreover, with regard to how detainees might lawfully be treated, the United States military had long treated irregular combatants (e.g., Viet Cong guerrillas) *as if* they were protected by the Geneva Conventions, but had insisted that this was a *policy* choice rather than something obliged by law.[11] In fact, the United States had refused to ratify the first 1977 Additional Protocol to the Geneva Conventions precisely because it aimed to make Geneva treatment of such persons obligatory.[12] (For years, moreover, standards for the interrogation of prisoners were reportedly more lax for the CIA than for the military.[13])

Remembering this "prehistory" of the war on terrorism is useful, lest we forget what *wasn't* new with George W. Bush. Indeed, even with respect to constitutional claims of inherent presidential powers in the international realm, the Justice Department's formally authoritative Office of Legal Council (OLC) under the Clinton administration took quite strong positions on behalf of the president's authority to act alone. As former OLC chief Jack Goldsmith has noted, these claims were characteristically made on behalf not of counterterrorist policy but in support of presidential unilateralism in using force for "humanitarian" purposes in Bosnia, Haiti, and Kosovo. (A counterterrorist exception was the Clinton OLC's endorsement of CIA renditions.) Regardless of their purpose, however, these were robust claims of presidential power all the same, and they notably included even arguments that the commander in chief could "disregard congressional statutes that impinged on the [constitutionally-based] Commander in Chief [power] or related presidential powers."[14]

Nevertheless, the 9/11 attacks did change how aggressively U.S. leaders approached applying and integrating such elements into an overall counterterrorist policy. It has become something of a cliché today to speak of the "existential" threat presented by modern mass-casualty terrorism in an era increasingly also defined by the proliferation of weapons of mass destruction (WMD). Especially for those who were not in Washington or New York on September 11, 2001, however, it is worth remembering just how shocking that day was—for the grave threat perceptions of the time had much to do with how things transpired.

In the space of a few hours, U.S. officials found themselves confronted with an attack bloodier than Pearl Harbor yet conducted by stealth by terrorists in our country's two most important cities. Making matters worse, 9/11 was followed within just a few weeks by mail-borne biological attacks using anthrax spores that contaminated and shut down part of the U.S. Capitol complex. (The anthrax attacks were not, as it turned out, an *al Qaeda* operation, but they were no less alarming at the time for their unknown perpetrators—and may even have been more so.) In light of all this,[15] it is hard to overstate the sense of urgency that arose in Washington, and the perceived overarching imperative of preventing further such assaults at almost any cost. One can thus perhaps begin to understand how officials—who seem to have agreed with the Scottish philosopher David Hume that "[t]he safety of the people is the supreme law," with "[a]ll other particular laws . . . subordinate to it, and dependent on it"[16]—would have concluded that a dramatic and draconian prophylactic response was required.

B. The War Paradigm

The response upon which the Bush administration settled almost immediately was to import the legal and policy paradigm of all-out warfare into this new realm of counterterrorist struggle. As the Justice Department's OLC made clear in a legal opinion provided to the White House on September 25, 2001, the terrorist attacks of 9/11 meant that the United States was officially at war. Accordingly, the president could use his full constitutional authority to fight the enemy—as well as to fight any "foreign states suspected of harboring or supporting" those involved.[17]

(1) Claims of Inherent Constitutional Power

And what was the scope of this full constitutional power? As the administration conceived it, these powers were vast. The full range of presidential authorities exercised at various points in the past against the organized armed forces of nation-state adversaries were now available—and were now felt to be available *indefinitely* and *worldwide*—against the shadowy terrorist underworld the United States now confronted. As described by one of its principal legal architects, John Yoo, the United States adopted the position that as a result of this now being a true war, it was felt that the president could now "kill enemy operatives and their leaders, detain them without trial until the end of the conflict, interrogate them without lawyers or Miranda protections, and try them without civilian juries."[18]

Furthermore, since the war with *al Qaeda* and its affiliates did not seem to have anything resembling a conventional military "front"—nor even to respect jurisdictional boundaries at all, including those of the United States itself, as the 9/11 attacks infamously demonstrated—it did not appear even to matter *where* such combat might take place. According to Mayer, White House Counsel Alberto Gonzalez at one point attempted to persuade congressional leaders to explicitly authorize the use of military force against terrorists *inside the United States.*[19] In fact, it seems to have been the Justice Department's view that the president had inherent constitutional authority to do this in any event. It was, the department is said to have believed, within the president's discretionary authority as commander in chief in time of war to decide "the method, timing, or place" of any U.S. response.[20] Moreover, the striking thing about this being an *inherent* constitutional prerogative was that the president would presumably still be able to lawfully exercise such power even if federal statutes said otherwise.

Legally speaking, this claim was by far the most significant aspect of the Bush administration's response to 9/11, and one of the few areas where its legal theories and policy approaches were *qualitatively,* as opposed to merely *quantitatively,* a departure from previous practice in the counterterrorist realm. A taste of the sweeping character of this theoretical shift can be seen in the administration's justification of the new program of widespread warrantless electronic surveillance, which was begun by the National Security Agency (NSA) after 9/11. (This "Terrorist Surveillance Program" [TSP] was apparently directed at communications between persons in the United States and those overseas believed to have some connection to terrorist activity, and it involved large-scale "data mining" of transactional and communications records.[21]) It has been reported that the administration justified the TSP as an inherent presidential power necessary to secure national security in time of war—or perhaps, more precisely, that *because* the TSP was necessary for national security in wartime, it was therefore an inherent presidential power—and that the program was explained in this vein to a handful of congressional leaders in briefings that began on October 25, 2001.[22]

As set forth in unclassified form in a letter to U.S. Senate Select Committee on Intelligence Vice Chairman Richard Shelby—in connection merely with the Foreign Intelligence Surveillance Act (FISA), and without, of course, any mention of NSA's then still highly classified TSP—the administration's constitutional argument included the contention that the U.S. Constitution permits the president to conduct "the most efficacious defense of the nation and its interests in accordance 'with the realistic purposes of the entire instrument.'" The president's inherent constitutional responsibility for protecting national security "'carries with it the inherent power to guard against the immediate renewal of the conflict'" even after an initial attack has ended.[23] As a result, it was said, he has "the primary responsibility, *and therefore the power,* to ensure the security of the United States in situations of grave and unforeseen emergencies." The Department of Justice thus declared that

> [a]s the Commander-in-chief, the President must be able to use whatever means necessary to prevent attacks upon the United States; this power, by implication, includes the authority to collect information necessary for its effective exercise.[24]

Clearly, this justification for using "whatever means [are] necessary," was not simply an argument for electronic surveillance as needed to defeat *al Qaeda*. It was a broad constitutional claim that carried within it the seeds of an argument against *any* sort of limitation upon the president's power to do what was necessary. It is thus perhaps not surprising that it has been reported that the Defense Department's general counsel advised Secretary Donald Rumsfeld in March 2003 that "the president's inherent constitutional authority to manage a military campaign" could not be constrained by mere statutory enactments such as federal anti-torture legislation.[25] It is also not surprising that the Department of Justice has been reported to have told the White House in August 2002 that international laws against torture "may be unconstitutional if applied to interrogations" undertaken where necessary in a wartime crisis.[26] In the same vein, when Congress in 2005 passed a law including a provision sponsored by Senator John McCain that prohibited "cruel, inhuman, or degrading" treatment of detainees, President Bush signed the new statute into law only upon issuing a statement declaring that this restriction might violate his inherent constitutional powers as commander in chief—and suggesting that he therefore might not comply with it.[27]

It was, in a sense, a tribute to how deeply ingrained the rule of law has become in modern American society that a presidential administration in such a crisis would feel it necessary to articulate a *legal* justification for emergency powers in the first place. After all, much of the legal work at OLC that provided the doctrinal foundation for President Bush's "wartime" power remained highly classified for several years, and some of it remains so to this day. These theories were not articulated, in other words, for outsiders:

this was a case of an administration feeling it necessary to justify action in specifically legal terms—and not to the public, in order to win support for its policies, but actually *to the rest of the government* so that the bureaucracy would be willing to act in the first place.

This says much about modern America. One suspects that most other governments today, and indeed some presidential administrations in earlier periods of U.S. history, would not have bothered—or have needed to bother—with such legal positioning. (More likely, they would have followed the path taken by Abraham Lincoln when suspending the writ of *habeas corpus* during the Civil War: to do what they felt needed doing, and if challenged, simply to insist, in effect, that no law can enjoin what necessity requires.) Be that as it may, however, the Bush administration's perhaps inadvertent homage to the rule of law cannot hide the unprecedented breadth of its explicit constitutional claims. In effect, the argument seems to have been made that the president was, in Judge Richard Posner's later characterization, lawfully able "to do *anything* if the emergency is dire enough."[28]

(2) Statutory, Case Law, and Treaty Law Analysis

Below the level of such sweeping constitutional claims and the wholesale importation of a war paradigm of presidential power, however, it bears repeating that there was much in the Bush administration's approach to counterterrorism law that merely *built upon* precedents from previous administrations and seemingly well-established legal understandings. Inherent constitutional authority was seldom, if ever, the *sole* reason the administration had for presuming itself to have the authority to conduct various aspects of its war against *al Qaeda*.

With respect to the issue of what to do with prisoners thought to be members of *al Qaeda* or its Taliban hosts in Afghanistan, for instance, an interagency task force eventually settled upon the base at Guantánamo as the best—or at least, in Rumsfeld's words, "the least worst"[29]—location to hold them. As noted previously, this was hardly unprecedented, for both the president's father and Bill Clinton had selected "Gitmo" as a detention center for Haitian refugees on the assumption that prisoners there would have no rights cognizable in U.S. courts.

This belief in the *de facto* legal invisibility of detentions at Guantánamo was not unreasonable, given existing legal precedents—including those won in this specific regard by both the George H.W. Bush and Clinton administrations. As of early 2002, it was easy for an American lawyer to conclude that the base was indeed beyond the reach of the federal judiciary. U.S. courts had previously indicated that non-U.S. nationals develop U.S. constitutional rights only to the extent that they develop "contact" with territory over which it has either *de jure* or *de facto* political control.[30] It did not appear that someone held in a *foreign* country had any such contact,[31] and the courts were still inclined to consider Guantánamo, legally speaking, to be Cuba.

With regard to what could be done with detainees, it was found to be of significance that most of the obligations imposed upon a state by the Convention Against Torture (CAT)[32] only applied in "territory under its jurisdiction."[33] In litigation over previous presidents' Haitian refugee policies, the U.S. Supreme Court had found that the term *refouler* used in Article 3 of the CAT meant only "a defensive act of resistance or exclusion at a border rather than an act of transporting someone to a particular destination."[34] Seizing Haitians on high seas and returning them forcibly to Haiti, for instance, was not *refouler* within meaning of the Convention Relating to Refugees[35] because that convention's prohibition of this practice only applied to "aliens within [a state's] territory."[36]

The U.S. Senate's reservations to the CAT, moreover—and to the International Covenant on Civil and Political Rights (ICCPR)[37]—declared that "cruel, inhuman, and degrading treatment" under these agreements, as they bound the United States, was to be regarded as being no more than coextensive with whatever the U.S. Constitution required.[38] (With respect to prisoners in the constitutional limbo of Guantánamo Bay, at least, this did not seem to be saying very much.) The Senate's reservations also expressly limited implementation of the convention to situations in which the United States "exercises legislative *and judicial* jurisdiction."[39]

At the time, there was reason to believe that Guantánamo fell outside these rules. Such courts as had addressed the issue seemed to hold that there existed no judicial jurisdiction over Guantánamo, adding further plausibility to the conclusion that neither the CAT nor the ICCPR agreement applied there as a matter of treaty law. In fact, the constitutional non-status of Guantánamo was reaffirmed as late as March 2003 by the D.C. Circuit Court of Appeals, which held that "the constitutional rights mentioned [in the earlier *Eisentrager* case] are not held by aliens outside the sovereign territory of the United States," and that "a 'foreign entity without property or presence in this country has *no* constitutional rights, under the due process clause *or otherwise*.'"[40] Read together, this mass of case precedent and treaty reservations seemed to suggest that, even though they were held there by U.S. forces, persons interned at Guantánamo were not, in fact, within U.S. legal jurisdiction and thus remained "outside" the protections not merely of U.S. law but of key parts of international conventions that might otherwise govern how such prisoners must be treated.

Nor was the Bush administration pulling legal arguments out of thin air in contending that terrorist-affiliated irregulars such as *al Qaeda* fighters—who followed none of the conventional practices set forth in the Geneva Conventions with regard to regular organization, uniforms, and the open bearing of arms—were "unlawful combatants" and not entitled to the ordinary protections afforded wartime prisoners under Geneva. Indeed, it was not much of a stretch to conclude even that "Common Article 3" of the Geneva Conventions, their baseline for the humane treatment of prisoners, did not apply to such combatants. That provision applied in armed conflicts "not of an international character occurring in the territory of one of the High Contracting Parties."[41] Additional Protocol II to the Geneva Conventions, however, indicated that *internal* armed conflicts are understood to include only

> armed conflict[s] . . . which take place in the territory of a High Contracting Party between its armed forces and dissident armed forces or other organized armed groups which, under responsible command, exercise such control over a part of its territory as to enable them to carry out sustained and concerted military operations and to implement this Protocol.[42]

A transnational fight against an entirely non-territorial terrorist network that did not engage in sustained and concerted military operations did not therefore seem to be an internal armed conflict within the meaning of these provisions. But what was it?

The drafters of Additional Protocol I clearly felt the "national liberation" wars of the decolonization period—in which irregular nationalist guerrillas, commonly based in foreign jurisdictions, conducted combat operations against European colonial forces or those of states such as *apartheid*-era South Africa—to be "international armed conflicts" within the meaning of Geneva.[43] To be sure, the United States had not ratified this protocol, and resisted the idea that a conflict pitting a government against revolutionaries drawn from its own population and seeking simply to take over that government could count as an "international" conflict. In predicting how international lawyers would characterize the globe-spanning twenty-first century U.S. struggle against the externally based, multinational, and non-territorial irregular forces of *al Qaeda* and its affiliates, however, it was reasonable to conclude that America's counterterrorism war *did* constitute a conflict of an international character. (It was not, of course, one conducted between "nations" as such. But there was equally clearly nothing "internal" about it.) As such, it would be a conflict in which terrorist prisoners would fall outside the protections offered by Common Article 3's provisions concerning conflicts "*not* of an international character."

The official commentary on the Geneva Conventions by the International Committee of the Red Cross (ICRC) lent weight to this proposition that Common Article 3 did not apply to this peculiar species of conflict. It described

Common Article 3 as having begun as an ICRC proposal in 1946 to encourage parties in *civil wars* to apply Geneva principles even though these conflicts did not fit the mold of traditional state-on-state conflicts.[44] The ICRC even suggested criteria for judging whether a conflict was "armed conflict not of an international character" within the reach of Common Article 3. These criteria seemed quite inapplicable to the *al Qaeda* war.[45] According to the ICRC,

> [t]he conflicts referred to in [Common] Article 3 are armed conflicts, with "armed forces" on either side engaged in "hostilities"—conflicts, in short, which are in many respects similar to an international war, but take place within the confines of a single country.[46]

From this perspective, the only provision of the Geneva corpus that *might* have seemed to apply to *al Qaeda* prisoners was Article 75 of the First Additional Protocol of 1977. This article covered "persons who are in the power of a Party to [a] conflict and who do not benefit from more favourable treatment under the conventions or under this Protocol."[47] As noted, however, the United States had never ratified the 1977 additions to Geneva, rejecting them precisely because they might have extended legal protections to terrorists, revolutionaries, and other irregular combatants otherwise outside the reach of the Geneva rules.[48] As one of the architects of the Bush administration's legal position has suggested, the very *existence* of the 1977 Additional Protocols indicates that there was understood to be a gap in the 1949 Geneva Conventions with regard to unlawful combatants[49]—otherwise it would never have been felt necessary to fill that hole with a new instrument. The United States' refusal to ratify those same gap-filling provisions, in turn, helped U.S. officials feel relatively confident after 9/11 that their terrorist enemies enjoyed essentially *no* protections.

The modern American counterterrorist project, in other words, could, with a degree of plausibility, be argued to be taking place against unlawful enemy combatants who—by virtue of their very irregularity, and the fact that *al Qaeda* was not a state, let alone a High Contracting Party to the Geneva Conventions—clearly did not deserve the protections of the main body of the Geneva rules, yet who *also* fell outside the rules of Common Article 3. Since there was also felt to be no relevant customary international law with regard to struggles against non-territorial, transnational terrorist groups such as *al Qaeda*,[50] the Bush administration felt the situation facing it to be entirely *sui generis:* it was writing on a blank slate. It was not, therefore, beyond reason for a lawyer to conclude in 2002 that there were essentially no restrictions on what could be done with Guantánamo detainees apart from the federal torture statue itself—which the lawyers at OLC, in response to CIA requests for guidance on what could be done in the interrogation of high-level *al Qaeda* prisoners such as Abu Zubaida and Khalid Sheik Mohammed, thus dutifully set about dissecting.[51]

Even leaving aside any constitutional claim of authority to use "whatever means [were] necessary," Bush administration officials thus believed themselves to have an enormous range of policy discretion within the bounds of what little applicable law there was. As former OLC attorney John Yoo later put it, they rejected the idea that the law was "a religion or a fully articulated ethical code that will make these decisions for us, relieving us of the difficult job of making a choice." In reality, he contended, "the law sets the rules of the playing field, but it does not set policy within that field."[52] The aim of the administration's legal analysis, therefore, was to identify the outer boundaries of what the law could be said not to prohibit, so that officials could secure for themselves as much freedom of action as possible within whatever constraints there were.

To be sure, the articulation and adoption of a stark, president-privileging war paradigm to post-9/11 circumstances did not mean that U.S. actions in the war on terrorism would *necessarily* be pursued without restraint or moderation. The Bush administration, however, wished to maximize the extent to which any such restraint was merely a *policy* choice, rather than a result of the existence of some legal obligation. With regard to the treatment of prisoners, for instance, the president proclaimed it in 2002 to be official policy to treat prisoners humanely.[53] Yet this was explicitly a *policy* choice rather than a legal requirement, and the administration reserved for itself the option of treating *some* high-value detainees differently if this was felt necessary[54]—as, of course, occurred.[55] Preserving maximal presidential flexibility was the watchword.

C. Novelty and Bargaining

The Bush administration's view of the law thus seemed to insist both that the war against *al Qaeda* and its affiliates presented an entirely novel situation *and* that the traditional bundle of largely unrestricted presidential war powers in actually fighting the enemy provided the appropriate tools with which to approach this new struggle. The president's complete discretion to attack enemy combatants wherever they might be found was drawn from conventional thinking derived from an era in which wars had clear front lines and easily identifiable participants, and generally took place "over there." On the other hand, his authority to treat prisoners however he felt most expeditious was, in effect, new—the result of circumstances that had not obtained in earlier conflicts, producing the arguable inapplicability of Geneva-based rules for prisoner treatment.

(1) The "New Normal" of Counterterrorist War

Whatever its legal implications, there has been widespread agreement that today's counterterrorist struggles *do* present a novel situation in some critical respects, and that they raise the specter that future armed conflicts we will face in the 21st century will tend to be more like this than what had come before. The Bush administration's ideas about precisely what rules should (and should not) apply in this emerging "new normal" of counterterrorist conflict were in many significant ways deeply controversial, of course, but there was little disagreement that we faced at least *some* novel challenges.

President Bush himself called his "global war on terrorism" a "war unlike any other," [56] and said that it called for "new thinking in the law of war."[57] Former Clinton administration Deputy Attorney General Philip Heymann has also acknowledged the novelty of this struggle, noting that the United States had not faced such a non-state enemy since the days of the Barbary pirates in the early 1800s.[58] Heymann's analogy, however, understates the problem, for the North African corsairs of that period were clearly a *foreign* threat that could be confronted thousands of miles away from American shores. By contrast, *al Qaeda* has clearly demonstrated the ability to attack the United States either at home *or* abroad. By May 2002, in fact—the point at which Jose Padilla (a.k.a. Muhajir Abdullah) was arrested in Chicago—*al Qaeda* was even understood to have acquired native-born American citizen recruits capable of moving entirely unobtrusively amongst other Americans. In this new war, therefore, it was not only the case that "the battlefield may be anywhere";[59] it also seemed to be that the enemy might turn out to be *anybody*.

These challenges presented unprecedented problems for security bureaucracies accustomed to operating within legal frameworks developed around a paradigm of international conflict in which the "normal" situation was a clash between regular armies raised and controlled by nation-states. Terrorists, however, did not "field military forces that we can grapple with in the open," and "are not content to operate against us abroad; they penetrate our country by stealth to kill us."[60] America did not face "a conventional war, because [this] is not a military conflict with a foreign state," but it was certainly a war nonetheless: "it has essential features of a war, indeed of a total war." [61] This war was "a conflict unlike any that this country has ever faced," and it "defie[d] all the usual norms of war."[62]

Administration lawyers contended that it would be ridiculous "[t]o pretend that rules written at the end of World War II," before the advent of global networks of non-territorial terrorist organizations such as *al Qaeda* and the proliferation of know-how about WMD, "are perfectly suitable for this new environment,"[63] but these officials were hardly the only ones to find traditional approaches radically inadequate. In Philip Bobbitt's characterization, for instance, the war with *al Qaeda*—which he emphasized was indeed, in the most important sense, a *real* war—demonstrated that

> the prevailing doctrines of international law are radically insufficient to regulate the efforts of states that must cope with global, networked terrorism, and with the related threats of weapons of mass destruction, genocide, and overwhelming civilian catastrophes. . . . [T]he entire system of the laws of war, which is predicated on definitions of warfare, on distinctions between the public and the private, on wars that have a beginning and an end, that are conducted on battlefields, that pit states against other states, is coming unraveled.[64]

Even some of the Bush administration's staunchest foreign critics seemed to recognize that U.S. officials found themselves in a situation that seemed devilishly hard to address by traditional methods. The Parliamentary Assembly of the Council of Europe, for instance, noted that the United States had concluded that "neither the classic instruments of criminal law and procedure nor the framework of the laws of war . . . have been apt to address the terrorist threat."[65] The Assembly decried some of the "new legal concepts" that the Americans developed in order to cope with this threat—in the process, it must be said, exaggerating both the novelty and the outlandishness of these steps[66]—but even it did not seem to question that post-9/11 counterterrorism faced notable new challenges.

In sum, the United States seemed to be facing an alarming and enormously challenging "new normal" of transnational conflict—a war in which the arena of combat was disturbingly *not* separate from, and indeed was largely coextensive and integrated with, civil society,[67] and in which traditional distinctions between "civilian" and "military" seemed to make little sense.[68] This new "paradigm of war amongst the people"[69] seemed to be replacing traditional conflict entirely. (The 21st century, though still young, has seen a notable lack of traditional wars between regular military forces reporting to territorial nation-states.) After 9/11, we seemed to face, in Mary Kaldor's words, a "new war" in which irregular, not localizable, and amorphous enemies with a global presence sought to shape local populations in their own image by terrorizing or killing *en masse*.[70]

(2) War Without End . . . ?

One of the most jarring and worrisome aspects of this "new normal" of counterterrorist struggle was the possibility that it would never clearly end. This was not, though it was sometimes thus portrayed by critics, a problem resulting simply from President Bush having described the conflict as a "war on terrorism," *as a phenomenon,* rather than a war against *al Qaeda* itself. At issue here was far more than mere semantics. Since our adversary was not a territorial nation-state possessing a regular, hierarchical military structure, but instead a loose, globe-spanning terrorist network and a protean web of like-minded *jihadist* affiliates united by ideals and objectives rather than by any kind of structure or institutional system, how was one to know when "victory" had been achieved? When could "military operations" be allowed to "conclude"? What did it mean to hold enemy combatants prisoner until the "end of hostilities"?

To be sure, it was hardly unusual in past wars for participants to have no idea, at the outset, how long any particular conflict would last. That essentially every war *would* have an end, however, was traditionally unquestioned. But the new paradigm of conflict seemed to undercut that assumption: it was distinctly possible that the counterterrorist war would end up being something akin to a *permanent* state of affairs. It might constitute, in other words, a "new normal" not merely by virtue of having replaced state-on-state warfare as the predominant type of transnational conflict in the modern world, but also, in fact, by emerging as the new *ground state* of the international security environment.

As Benjamin Wittes has noted, it soon transpired in the war against terrorism that "the spasmodic bursts of military power that characterized the earlier phase and looked most like traditional warfare" gave way to "something more elastic that takes place in slower motion" and began to look like "a permanent state of affairs"—in fact, a sort of "permanent state of emergency."[71] The issue of detainees was only the most obvious of the problems, but it illustrates the general challenge presented by this kind of conflict becoming the international community's new "normal" state.

A *jihadist* terrorist in captivity is not dangerous in the same sense as is a soldier belonging to the regular armed forces of an adversary state and captured in a traditional war. International law has long recognized that regular soldiers may be detained until the end of hostilities in order to preclude their return to combat in their country's armed forces. (In earlier and more innocent eras, in fact, this same objective was sometimes achieved through the trusting institution of parole: prisoners could be released on the strength of their oath not to return to combat. The fact that the institution of parole survived as long as it did suggests that such promises tended to be kept.) The need to keep such traditional prisoners disappeared when a truce was agreed, or their government surrendered, because at that point all elements of the opposing armed forces were expected to cease operations against each other—and, indeed, generally did.

The problem with *jihadist* terrorist prisoners, however, goes beyond merely the fact that it is not clear in modern counterterrorism conflicts when or whether "hostilities" can ever be declared over. As Wittes has observed, convinced *jihadist* detainees are dangerous "not merely as an arm of a particular military force but *in [their] individual capacity as well.*"[72] Their dangerousness would *not* necessarily disappear even if Osama bin Laden and all his lieutenants surrendered to U.S. federal marshals and some improbable truce were agreed upon, for that dangerousness lies not merely in such persons' institutional affiliation with *al Qaeda, per se,* but also in their *personal convictions* about the imperatives of deadly *jihad,* and such training as they may have acquired for its pursuit.

A serious war against fanatical terrorists, therefore, would seem to require some kind of "preventative incarcerations designed to keep extremely dangerous individuals from acting on their deeply held murderous beliefs and instincts."[73] The presence or absence of a state of "war," in fact, might even be said to depend upon nothing more or less than whether or not any such persons are alive and free from incarceration. If they remain true to their beliefs, such people could not be released into a pacified, post-terrorist world without almost automatically returning that world to something akin to a state of war once more. These are challenges for which even the Bush administration's initial war paradigm had difficulty providing easy answers.[74]

Ultimately, it may indeed be that the war against terrorism—and whatever steps we take in waging it—must be regarded as a permanent one. Some analysts have come to understand it this way. Henry Kissinger, for instance, regards this sort of modern conflict not as the "temporary interruption[ ]of a beneficent *status quo*" but as part of

> an inevitable transformation of the international order resulting from changes in the internal structure of many key participants, and from the democratization of politics, the globalization of economics, and the instantaneousness of communications. [75]

Philip Bobbitt, in fact, has articulated a grand theory of terrorism and its role in the modern world in which *al Qaeda*'s variety of global, theatrical, and mass-casualty-focused violence is a natural side-effect of sweeping developmental dynamics of modern governance—a phenomenon deriving and inseparable from the emergence of the contemporary *market state of consent* as a form of social organization to replace the more traditional, territorial nation-state. The market state of consent, in Bobbitt's description, is a democracy, but not *just* a democracy. It grounds its legitimacy as an organizational form in its ability to maximize the opportunities available to its civil society and individual citizens; this is its fundamental purpose. For Bobbitt, terrorism, in the distinctively modern form represented by *al Qaeda,* is "an incident of the underlying constitutional order" of states: a form of violence directly and unalterably opposed to the very *existence* of market states of consent.[76]

Modern terrorism, Bobbitt argues, is devoted to destroying, through mass terrorization by means of deliberately indiscriminate attacks upon civilians—who are targeted, as *al Qaeda* leaders such as Osama bin Laden and Abu Musab al-Zarkawi seem to have made clear, precisely *because* of their status as participants in the process of consent that produces democratic governments[77]—in ways designed to erode the very conditions that make democratic consent possible. Since protecting its citizens is the *raison d'être* of the market state of consent, it is the inescapable fate of such a state to war against such terrorists. These are, fundamentally, wars of *preclusion:* the objective of the market state is to prevent civilian populations from paying the sort of catastrophic costs that would in effect preclude the continued existence of a market state of consent.[78] Significantly, however, since such terrorism is an outgrowth of and reaction to the emergence of the market state as the latest organizational form of the global constitutional order, it follows from Bobbitt's logic that such wars are fated to be essentially endless: they will persist as long as does the market state itself.

One need not agree with all of Bobbitt's sweeping historical meta-analysis of modern terrorism, however, to appreciate that the "new normal" of modern counterterrorist warfare presents tremendous challenges both to traditional law-enforcement-based modes of handling terrorism *and* to the absolutist war paradigm initially offered by Bush administration attorneys. It is not surprising, therefore, to hear thoughtful voices coming to understand the seemingly permanent state of emergency elicited by the rise of modern mass-casualty terrorism as "a hybrid problem that requires its own rules" and which calls us to "a law-building project for something that ha[s] gone beyond war altogether," and which must involve the construction of "some kind of coherent law of terrorism, a body of law that could sustain the powers of presidential preemption before the courts and the public."[79]

Whatever the merits of the legal and policy logic that underlay the Bush administration's legal approach as a reaction to the urgent situation of crisis and looming further catastrophe in the immediate aftermath of the September 11 attacks, it is somewhat harder now to contend that a purist's "war paradigm" is, in its unadulterated form, the right answer for a democracy facing a conflict with terrorists that may never end. There is good reason—and no small amount of legal precedent—for permitting the president some very special and extraordinary powers in time of war, especially in the specific conduct of operations against the enemy. Indeed, there remain powerful reasons *not* to do otherwise with regard to traditional modes of state-on-state warfare and the immediate circumstances of catastrophic crisis. It is less obvious, however, that the administration's initial legal position is tenable as originally articulated as we continue our new war with a terrorist enemy who can literally be anywhere, and be almost anyone, *forever*.

John Yoo, one of the authors of the Bush administration's initial legal positions, has written that a candid approach to post-9/11 challenges requires admitting that "our old laws and policies did not address this new enemy, and that we need[ed] to start developing a new set of rules to confront it, and soon."[80] Today, it seems increasingly to be understood both that this is true *and* that the administration's wholesale importation of the war paradigm was not an entirely adequate answer—at least over the long term—if our current war against terrorism is to be sustainable.

The pure war paradigm was not, perhaps, as untenable as the law enforcement paradigm against which Yoo's work was so self-consciously a reaction, but *both* traditional modes of conceiving modern counterterrorism seem inadequate for a truly permanent state of war against such enemies. Accordingly, especially as the very successes of Bush administration counterterrorist policy helped ensure that no major follow-on attacks occurred in the United States—allowing the public's threat perceptions correspondingly to fade—some reaction and adjustment to the pure war paradigm was inevitable. It was not too long in coming.

(3) Evolving Practice

It has no doubt been infuriating to many of President Bush's fiercest critics that his successor has continued so many of the practices the Bush administration developed or expanded in order to confront the *al Qaeda* threat. This ratification by practice, quiet and almost embarrassed as it has proven, is worth examining further.

Seeking to distinguish himself from the unpopular 43rd president, Barack Obama promised a revolution in U.S. policies across the board, which would ensure that America would be "a very different place" under the Obama administration.[81] This was no less true in the counterterrorist realm than in any other. Obama spoke out on the campaign trail against the Bush administration's plan to use military commissions to try terrorist detainees. Immediately after his inauguration, he issued an executive order requiring humane treatment of all prisoners and ordering that their interrogations be conducted pursuant to the U.S. Army's Field Manual of September 2006, promised to close the Guantánamo facility within a year, and suspended all military commission activity.[82]

On the other hand, Obama enthusiastically embraced the Bush administration's policy of targeted killings against *al Qaeda* and its affiliates. In fact, the Obama administration has used drone aircraft strikes with *more* eagerness than its predecessor. According to press reports, between August 2008 and October 2009, U.S. Predator and Reaper aircraft firing Hellfire missiles or dropping Joint Direct Attack Munition (JDAM) guided bombs carried out some 70 such attacks in Northwestern Pakistan alone.[83] In 2007, President Bush had ordered only three drone strikes in Pakistan, a total that rose sharply to 34 in 2008, as intelligence information indicated *al Qaeda* to be trying to reconstitute its leadership in the largely unpatrolled badlands along that country's frontier with Afghanistan. President Obama embraced this tool eagerly, and in the first few months of 2009 alone, the United States conducted 16 strikes inside Pakistan. The new president reportedly ordered his first attacks upon against targets in North and South Waziristan within three days of taking office.[84] By mid-2011, U.S. drone strike campaigns were underway in *six* countries: Afghanistan, Iraq, Pakistan, Libya, Somalia, and Yemen.[85]

President Obama apparently also raised the ante in such targeted killings in September 2009, by eliminating a suspect of *al Qaeda*'s 2002 attack upon a hotel in the Kenyan port city of Mombasa, who was killed in a U.S. attack deep inside Somalia undertaken not with unmanned drone aircraft but actually with special forces commandos on the ground.[86] In 2009, the Obama administration with great fanfare canceled a Bush-era CIA program to send human "hit teams" to kill *al Qaeda* officials and other terrorist ringleaders overseas.[87] This ostentatiously post-Bush rectitude did not outlast the next opportunity for such a targeted killing, however, for Obama famously dispatched a commando team led by Navy SEALs—and reportedly including some CIA paramilitary officers as well—into the Pakistani town of Abbottabad to kill Osama bin Laden himself in early 2011.[88] (Ironically, CIA Director Leon Panetta, who had canceled the earlier "hit team" program, himself oversaw the successful bin Laden raid.[89])

At the time of writing, in fact, the Obama administration was stepping up its drone strike campaign still further, intensifying its use of such operations in Yemen[90]—including in attempts to kill a U.S. citizen, the American-born *jihadist* cleric Anwar al-Awlaki.[91] President Obama may prefer not to use the phrase "global war on terrorism" because he wishes to seem less bellicose than his predecessor, but he clearly agrees with George W. Bush that, in the most essential sense, the United States *is* at war, on a global basis, against *al Qaeda* and its affiliates.

The Obama administration also continued President Bush's internationally controversial policy of secret "renditions" of terrorist suspects to and between foreign jurisdictions. As part of his promises to revise heavy-handed U.S.

approaches to counterterrorism, the new president had set up an "Interrogation and Transfer Policy Task Force" with some fanfare after his inauguration. This task force seems to have found no adequate substitute for such renditions, however, and announced in August 2009 that the United States would continue to employ them.[92]

Though President Bush's program of electronic surveillance to look for, and intercept the communications of, suspected terrorists had been subject to bitter domestic criticism, President Obama also seems to have found it indispensable once he actually became responsible for America's security. In September 2009, his administration requested Congress to renew the legislative authorities that the Bush administration had previously obtained in order to bring the Foreign Intelligence Surveillance Act (FISA) more into line with the needs of counterterrorist surveillance in the Internet age. With a boldness that they themselves would surely have excoriated in President Bush, Obama administration officials graciously told legislators that they would be "willing to consider" adding privacy protections to U.S. electronic surveillance rules, but only if such modifications did not "undermine the effectiveness of these important authorities."[93]

Barack Obama's shift of position on electronic surveillance actually seems to have begun even during the course of the campaign, with his vote in support of giving immunity to telecommunications firms that had cooperated with Bush's secret NSA surveillance program.[94] Once in office, he continued to discover unanticipated reasonableness in his predecessor's actions. Following in the Bush administration's footsteps, Obama's new attorney general, Eric Holder, invoked the controversial "state secrets" privilege in October 2009, asking a federal court to dismiss a San Francisco lawsuit over warrantless wiretapping because proceeding with the litigation could compromise ongoing intelligence operations.[95] (At the time of writing, the Obama administration had also already distinguished itself by bringing Espionage Act charges against more "leakers" of classified information in its first three years than had the Bush administration in its eight—and more prosecutions, in fact, than all other U.S. administrations combined, including that of Richard M. Nixon.[96])

As early as June 2009, it was also clear that President Obama's plan to close Guantánamo was coming unraveled. He failed to persuade many foreign governments to take back their nationals detained at the Cuban base, and plans to bring Guantánamo prisoners into the United States created a firestorm of criticism even from the president's allies in the Democrat-controlled Congress. In April 2009, in fact, the new administration's solicitor-general admitted that it might still be necessary to hold *some* prisoners indefinitely.[97] By the new administration's first summer, it seemed quickly to be running out of options *other* than the Cuban base.[98]

Surely not by coincidence, this was about the time that Obama reversed his position of staunch opposition to the specially created military commissions before which the Bush administration had planned to try key terrorists. As one administration official put it somewhat sheepishly in May 2009, "[t]he more they [the lawyers] look at it, the more commissions don't look as bad as they did on [President Obama's first day in office on] Jan[uary] 20." Attorney General Holder publicly conceded that "[i]t may be difficult for some of those high-value detainees to be tried in a normal federal court,"[99] and military commissions seemed to present a possible solution. In early 2011, the Obama administration backtracked on its earlier promises to put self-proclaimed 9/11 mastermind Khalid Sheikh Mohammed (and four coconspirators) on trial in a civilian court in New York City. Instead, in a complete counterterrorist *volte face,* Attorney General Holder announced that these men would be tried by a military commission at Guantánamo Bay.[100]

To be sure, the Obama administration proposed some modifications to the procedures that would be used in the resuscitated military commissions, with Holder's legal team at OLC now declaring that defendants did have *some* constitutional rights,[101] but President Obama did indeed put these tribunals back in service.[102] Ironically, however, in part *because* of the constitutional rights that the lawyers now declared such detainees to possess—which included the right not to be convicted on the basis of information obtained from coercive interrogations—it also began to appear that the new administration might have to continue Bush's policy of detaining *some* prisoners indefinitely, perhaps even *without* military commission proceedings, under the president's broad post-9/11 authority to use force against America's enemies.[103] A few detainees might well prove too difficult to try, and yet too dangerous to release. These, it seemed, would still have to be detained until the "end of hostilities"—which is to say, perhaps forever.

Of course, the Obama administration still had trouble *admitting* that it had come back around to this core plank of the Bush "war paradigm." Indeed, U.S. officials seemed to be so scared of acquiring *new* prisoners that they refused to adopt rules for handling such situations, and openly declared themselves willing to *release* any new captives who could not either be tried in U.S. courts or transferred to some other country for (indefinite) detention.[104] Politically driven White House fears of repopulating Guantánamo may also have made the Obama administration more willing than Bush to simply *kill* suspected terrorists outright—as may have happened in Somalia, where U.S. officials reportedly used special operations troops to kill *al-Qaeda* suspect Saleh Ali Saleh Nabhan in 2009 because they did not know what to do with him if he were captured. (Corpses, after all, do not have to be kept in prison forever.) Nevertheless, a significant shift back in the direction of post-9/11

Bush-era approaches seems to have occurred, and some reports have suggested that the Obama administration may be using prisons in Afghanistan to handle new detainees without drawing attention to Guantánamo.[105]

One of the signature issues for critics of President Bush's counterterrorist policies had been his administration's willingness to use harshly coercive interrogation techniques—including the infamous technique of terrifying simulated drowning known as *waterboarding*—on a handful of senior *al Qaeda* figures who were believed able to provide critical information about ongoing terrorist plots. These techniques, it was commonly alleged in both U.S. and foreign media coverage, amounted to torture despite OLC's claims to the contrary. In his confirmation hearings, while still technically a private citizen, Eric Holder had himself declared that he felt such methods to be torture.

There are indications, however, that the U.S. government may yet be reserving itself some flexibility for the future, even in this regard. Dennis Blair, Obama's nominee for the post of director of national intelligence, pointedly refused, during his own confirmation hearings, to follow Holder in describing "waterboarding" as "torture."[106] Even one of the Bush administration's fiercest and most compelling critics over the "torture" issue—Senator John McCain—has conceded publicly that he himself might contemplate subjecting a suspect to such techniques in an extreme case. In a grave enough emergency, McCain averred, "[y]ou do what you have to do."[107] (Under President Obama, moreover, it was announced that the CIA would still remain involved in interrogating high-level terrorist prisoners, though the Agency would no longer lead the process.[108])

Notably, in fact, even Eric Holder, after becoming attorney general, seemed to steer a more nuanced and permissive course than one might have expected given the personal opinion he had expressed. Holder announced in August 2009 that he would name a special prosecutor to review whether CIA interrogators had broken the law (e.g., the federal torture statute) in their treatment of terrorist prisoners, but this much-publicized announcement was actually far more limited a step than it was apparently meant to seem.

In fact, Holder's announcement of this inquiry covered only agents who had *exceeded* the authority for harsh interrogations set forth in OLC's so-called "torture" memoranda. Those who *followed* these guidelines—observing their recommendations, for instance, in undertaking the repeated waterboarding of certain senior *al Qaeda* prisoners—did not appear to be in any legal jeopardy.[109] Nor did it seem very likely even that those who may have overstepped these extraordinarily permissive lines faced much chance of conviction.[110] After investigating approximately 100 cases, in fact, the Justice Department announced in July 2011 that it would open criminal investigations into only two incidents, each involving the death of a detainee while in U.S. custody.[111]

Meanwhile, U.S. officials continued to interrogate terrorist prisoners pursuant to the guidelines set forth in the Army Field Manual adopted under the Bush administration in 2006—waterboarding by that date having itself already been long since abandoned, as a policy choice, but some other coercive measures retained.[112] Obama's Justice Department also continued the Bush-era practice of invoking the state secrets privilege to obtain the dismissal of lawsuits involving allegations of CIA rendition and torture, as it succeeded in doing, for example, in February 2009, with a Ninth Circuit case involving a Guantánamo detainee.[113]

Conservatives might perhaps have described all these various developments as illustrating an initially naïve administration's learning curve on national security issues after actually arriving in office,[114] but the new president's allies on the political left were appalled. Law professor Joseph Marguiles, for instance, lamented that it was merely an "unfortunate myth" that Obama had "dramatically altered the detention policies of his predecessor."[115] For his part, *The New Republic's* Jeffrey Rosen simply declared that President Obama had "wimp[ed] out on torture."[116] Between these polar reactions, however, a more detached analyst might see U.S. counterterrorist policy as being in the process of *itself* settling into a new, and now apparently bipartisan, sort of "normal"—one quite different from how things had been in the more innocent years before September 11, 2001, but yet no Executive Branch playground of unchecked discretion either.

(4) In the Courts

Though it seems to have become the conventional wisdom that the Bush administration suffered major defeats before the U.S. Supreme Court with regard to its efforts to detain terrorist prisoners in legal limbo at Guantánamo and try them before military commissions, the truth is more complex. True, the Court did involve itself in these affairs in ways the Executive Branch opposed—and which, as we shall see, set up some very interesting dynamics that will shape how America continues to feel out for itself a legal regime for living in the "new normal" of counterterrorist war. It is often not noticed, however, the extent to which the courts have *agreed* with some of the most basic assumptions of the war paradigm that the Bush administration brought to the post-9/11 environment.

The *Hamdi* case,[117] for instance, endorsed the fundamental Bush administration assumption that the United States was indeed at war with *al Qaeda* and its affiliates, and that such terrorists could be detained until this war had concluded—whenever that happened to be. According to a five-justice majority, the power to detain enemy combatants was "so fundamental and accepted an incident to war as to be an exercise of the 'necessary and appropriate force' Congress has authorized the President to use." The president's power to detain enemy combatants, in fact, was even declared expressly to reach U.S. citizens.[118] The decision in the *Rasul* case[119] also rested upon this premise, both decisions revolving, in a sense, merely around the more *procedural* questions of whether and how the Executive Branch had to demonstrate that the detainees in question *were* in fact enemy combatants who might thus be locked away indefinitely. (*Hamdi* and *Rasul* also carefully stopped short of prohibiting trials of terrorist suspects before military commissions that did not employ the full range of procedural protections required in U.S. civilian trials.[120])

These Supreme Court decisions were thus cases—as Wittes has observed—that had "less bite than bark."[121] In fact, as John Yoo has chortled, they "confirmed the administration's basic legal approach to the war on terrorism" by making clear as a matter of law that war against *al Qaeda* is war indeed—and by implication "that the United States can [therefore] use all of the tools of war to fight this new kind of enemy."[122] The cases are perhaps best regarded as "split decisions,"[123] but Yoo is not wrong that they did uphold some of the most central assumptions of the Bush administration's war paradigm. (Nor was the administration without some legal success in lower court litigation related to the applicability of the Geneva Conventions to *al Qaeda* and Taliban prisoners, and in tearing down the notorious "wall" that had been erected in previous years between law enforcement activity and intelligence collection under the Foreign Intelligence Surveillance Act.[124])

(5) Bargaining in the Shadow of the Constitution

Nevertheless, it is in the very degree to which the Supreme Court cases on the Bush administration's detention program *were* "split decisions" that one finds the most interesting dynamics of these legal battles. Significantly, it seems also to be where one can find the most pregnant clues to where American counterterrorist law and policy may be going in the future.

The perennial challenge of preserving both liberty *and* national security in threatening times is usually approached as if these values existed in a zero-sum balance, such that having more of one necessarily implies having less of the other. This, of course, is to some extent a profoundly false dichotomy, for clearly having too much *in*security precludes the meaningful exercise of any liberty whatsoever. (For many purposes, therefore, it may be more useful to conceive of the situation as being one in which the government must simply preserve its citizenry's *rights*. Some rights—such as the right not to be blown to pieces by a terrorist bomb and the right to exercise political choice in a democracy free of terrorist intimidation—are ones that can perhaps only be vindicated, in challenging times, through a robust security posture. As a result, it is appropriate to balance their preservation against other rights.) Yet there remains a good deal of truth in the observation that there can be tension between liberty and security when it comes to modern counterterrorism.

Richard Posner, among others, has articulated this tension as reflecting an ongoing need for our society to find a balance between liberty and security. In general, he writes,

> [i]n times of danger, the weight of concerns for public safety increases relative to that of liberty concerns, and civil liberties are narrowed. In safer times, the balance shifts the other way and civil liberties are broadened. [125]

Accordingly, the scope of constitutional liberties is quite properly "less extensive at a time of serious terrorist threats and rapid proliferation of means of widespread destruction than at a time of felt safety."[126] For Posner, therefore,

> [t]he challenge to constitutional decision making in the era of modern terrorism is to restrike the balance between the interest in liberty from government restraint or interference and the interest in public safety, in recognition of the grave threat that terrorism poses to the nation's security. . . . The essential point is that, one way or another, law must adjust to necessity born of emergency.[127]

This conception of a dynamic balance—adjusting and readjusting itself to circumstances—is a compelling one, but in Judge Posner's articulation it may serve to hide an important insight into the challenges of modern counterterrorist war. He scoffs at civil libertarian concerns about according the president special powers in times of national emergency, arguing that contrary to such critics' views, the accretion of such powers is not a one-way ratchet. Every time liberties have been curtailed in time of crisis, Posner argues, they have subsequently been "fully restored."[128]

Yet this analysis may be too sanguine, at least as applied to the "new normal" of modern counterterrorism. It may be true that liberties have in the past been fully restored—and, indeed, eventually generally *expanded*—in the wake of America's past wars. But that historical pattern presupposes conflicts that actually *end*. Since it is not clear that there will actually *be* a conclusion to our present war on terrorism, however, Posner may in some sense be treating the concerns of civil libertarians too lightly.

It may be *conceivable* that we will at some point feel comfortable enough to return to a pre-9/11 security posture in every respect, but it is not very likely. Yet if our present war is to be, in effect, permanent, we may not be able to assume that the *status quo ante* will ever be "fully restored." Matters might be conceptually easier, and the legal and constitutional stakes actually *lower,* if the United States faced "only" a desperate conventional conflict against a state adversary. In a possibly never-ending struggle against a ghostly and potentially ubiquitous non-state terrorist enemy devoted to mass casualty attacks and eager to acquire weapons of mass destruction, however, it is our challenge to devise ways of meeting the threat that are sustainable—forever if need be—in a democracy under the rule of law. In our "new normal," it is not enough simply to allow the president to do whatever he wants for a brief time. The Bush administration's war paradigm was an understandable response to the horrifying exigencies of the 9/11 moment—and was perhaps not constitutionally "wrong" in the deepest sense, for the very reasons of dynamic balance about which Posner writes—but it must give way to something different, and new, if we wish to live indefinitely in the "new normal."

This is where the Supreme Court's approach to post-9/11 detainee litigation seems more interesting. Clearly, the Court did undertake to rewrite some of the legal understandings upon which the Bush administration had relied in developing its counterterrorist policy. In the the *Hamdi* case, it afforded a person detained as an unlawful enemy combatant the right to contest before a neutral decision maker the factual basis for the Executive Branch's determination that he actually *is* an enemy combatant.[129] *Rasul* rejected the administration's claim that the federal courts lacked jurisdiction to review statutory *habeas corpus* claims arising out of detentions at Guantánamo, while the *Boumediene* case[130] similarly held that *habeas corpus* review under the U.S. Constitution itself was also available even for designated enemy combatants held at Guantánamo—which was now found to be a *de facto* territory of the United States.

Together, *Rasul* and *Boumediene* therefore effectively threw out precedents set during the Haitian refugee detentions ordered by George H.W. Bush and Bill Clinton. For its part, *Hamdan* rejected the Bush administration's proposed mechanism for military commissions with which to try terrorist suspects, finding these specific procedures not to conform with the Uniform Code of Military Justice (UCMJ) and Common Article 3 of the Geneva Conventions—which the Court reinterpreted to apply to *al Qaeda*-type situations on the grounds that a conflict "not of an international character" simply meant one *not occurring between states,* rather than just an internal (i.e., civil) war.[131]

To this extent, therefore, the "split decisions" of the Supreme Court's post-9/11 detainee jurisprudence entailed some significant defeats for the Bush administration, which had sought unrestricted discretion with regard to the designation and potential prosecution of unlawful enemy combatants. Even while affirming some fundamental assumptions of the war paradigm, the Supreme Court was not willing to permit unrestricted presidential discretion in this regard.

Putting aside the merits or demerits of the specific legal reasoning the Supreme Court employed in reaching these conclusions, it must be said that from a *policy* perspective, at least, the Court's decisions had an undeniable logic rooted in the peculiar nature of our "new normal" of counterterrorist conflict—specifically, its factual ambiguity and yet potential permanence. It is certainly correct, as John Yoo has argued, that in contrast to a war carried out against the regular forces of a nation state, our present counterterrorist conflict is one in which there will necessarily now be great "uncertainty around detentions, as nationality alone cannot determine enemy status." In order to detain someone as an unlawful combatant in this war, "[t]here must be enough information to know that the individual has acted in association with *al Qaeda*."[132] Such determinations will likely be based in part upon intelligence information and in part upon complex fact patterns attendant to the circumstances of a prisoner's apprehension, and are likely often to be much more inferential and ambiguous than enemy combatant designations in traditional wars. (Indeed, combatants were traditionally *required* to distinguish themselves clearly from noncombatants—e.g., by wearing uniforms and carrying arms openly—if they wished to take advantage of the protections afforded by prisoner-of-war status.)

For Yoo, this heightened ambiguity—vis-à-vis the "old normal" of state-on-state conflict—is an argument for unfettered Executive Branch discretion, for only national security professionals can be expected to have the experience and institutional competence to make difficult judgment calls in such unlawful combatant cases.[133] Yet this argument could be turned precisely around. For Richard Posner, for instance, it is precisely this "greater uncertainty about membership in *al Qaeda* than about membership in a conventional military formation" that makes it important to *avoid* unfettered Executive Branch discretion: "[t]he danger of erroneously identifying an individual as an enemy of the United States is . . . much greater than in a conventional war," and "[t]his difference weighs in favor of allowing him to obtain, by means of *habeas corpus,* judicial review of the grounds of his detention." [134]

Posner's counterargument would be sharpened further if one acknowledges the potential *permanence* of "hostilities" in the wars of the "new normal." It is not just that there is a greater chance of an Executive Branch *mistake* in enemy combatant determinations—or perhaps even abuse, should officials faced with uncertainty err in draconian ways on the side of over inclusiveness, or should unscrupulous federal officers willfully employ these powers against non-terrorist undesirables. It is also that the consequences of a designation are enormous: in modern counterterrorism, as we have seen, an enemy combatant may perhaps *never* be released.

This factor of detention's potential *permanence* seems not to have escaped the Supreme Court, and indeed may have featured in its reasoning. In *Rasul,* for instance, one of the reasons the Court's majority found the old *Eisentrager* case not to apply was that, unlike in that litigation, the prisoners in *Rasul* claimed to be wholly innocent of wrongdoing (i.e., not in fact to be terrorists) and yet were facing "potentially indefinite detention."[135] For a detention *process* that might well continue in operation "forever," and whose prisoners cannot perhaps ever be freed, unfettered Executive Branch discretion seems less tenable an answer than it did in past wars. Even while affirming the president's power to detain enemy combatants essentially forever, therefore, the Court felt it important to create new legal requirements—imposing a review mechanism in order to help ensure that persons subject to such *de facto* disappearance *were* in fact enemy fighters.

More interesting still, perhaps, was how the Supreme Court did this, and what it did *not* do. Though *Boumediene* did deal with constitutional *habeas corpus* questions, most of the Court's detainee cases were decided on *statutory* grounds (e.g., interpreting the federal *habeas* statute, the Uniform Code of Military Justice [UCMJ], or treaty law in the form of the Geneva Conventions). For the most part, though its justices carefully carved out for themselves "a seat at the table" in this area of previously unchecked Executive Branch discretion,[136] the Court has refrained from basing most of its decisions upon constitutional law—that is, something that the president and Congress could not, between them, later amend and adjust if circumstances required.

Such amendment and adjustment, in fact is precisely what occurred in the Military Commissions Act (MCA) of 2006, which was passed in reaction to the Court's *Hamdan* decision—a case that was *itself* in part a response to the jurisdiction-stripping provisions of the Detainee Treatment Act (DTA) of 2005, a statute with which Congress had, in turn, tried to undo the *Rasul* decision.[137] As this example demonstrates, as long as the Court's post-9/11 jurisprudence remains principally statutory, there remains scope for an ongoing iterated game relationship between the judiciary and the political branches. Such conceptual and legal "space" allows the law to develop through dynamic tension, as the government, as a whole, struggles to refine appropriate ways to handle the challenges of the "new normal" over the long term.

This is not an unfamiliar process. Several years before 9/11 set these dynamics in motion with regard to detainee questions, this author argued the importance of understanding national security law through the prism of how coordinate branches of government *bargain in the shadow* of a possible constitutional confrontation and crisis. My specific focus at that time was the War Powers Resolution (WPR), and my thesis was that, to understand how national security law works in this area, the congressional-executive relationship must be analyzed "as it is lived over time 'in the shadow,' so to speak" of a possible constitutional impasse over war powers which *neither* political branch wishes to see, and which the judiciary was ill-equipped to referee.[138] The specifics of my explication revolved around war powers and confrontations between the two political branches over the details of the WPR's awkward statutory scheme and is less relevant here.[139] Its analytical framework, however, can help us understand what has been happening between all *three* branches on detainee law since September 2001—and how things may develop in the future.

John Yoo is right that Supreme Court cases such as *Rasul, Hamdi,* and *Hamdan* represent "an unprecedented insertion of the federal courts into military affairs," and perhaps also that the Court has with these decisions "displayed a lack of judicial restraint that would have shocked its predecessors."[140] He would probably thus agree with Benjamin Wittes that

> the Court's deepest impact to date has not lain in the substance of anything it has done but in its insistence on its own predominant role—the insistence that it has the final say. [141]

As a result of these cases, "the specter of a vastly different judicial posture in this area now haunts the executive branch"—that is, they face the possibility of what Wittes has called an entirely new "judicial power model" of court predominance in decisions related to war.[142]

For Yoo, the Supreme Court's self-insertion into this arena is simply "dangerous," bespeaking its Justices' improper activist "interfere[nce]" in seeking to "impose specific rules and override political judgments about military necessity." Such activism, in his eyes, foolishly assumes war to be something that can be handled with "the familiarity of the criminal justice system."[143] And in truth, of course, Yoo could yet be right: these dynamics may be far from having played themselves out.

Another way to view the Supreme Court's jurisprudence to date, however, is to see it as establishing—perhaps inadvertently—a powerful incentive structure for constructive congressional-executive "bargaining in the shadow" of the potential emergence of a worrisome "judicial power model" of court supremacy in war making. As long as the Court largely refrains from addressing post-9/11 challenges with the blunt and inflexible tool of constitutional precedent *but retains the theoretical option of doing so,* the political branches have powerful reasons to work together to develop sustainable approaches suited to the "new normal."

After all, national security decision making is generally an arena in which judges are uniquely *poorly* equipped to be stewards of the public interest. Judges have historically understood this, which is the reason that courts have traditionally proven so reluctant to second-guess the Executive Branch in matters of national security law, and why they have proven *particularly* loathe to intervene where both Congress *and* the president agree upon something.[144] The courts may also be, as Posner has argued, characteristically prone to errors in two different directions: either unduly to favor civil liberties concerns at the expense of security, or to defer too slavishly to the national security expertise of the Executive Branch, to the detriment of liberty.[145] (Wittes refers to this as erring "both by interfering with arguably necessary ugliness . . . and by blessing the most unholy of excesses."[146]) In contrast to accommodations between the political branches—e.g., in statutory schemes such as the MCA—judicial precedents in the national security arena, and especially constitutional precedents, cannot be modified easily, quickly, or perhaps even at all in response to changing factual circumstances, or in a process of policy development through trial and error.[147]

In light of all this—and precisely *because* of the unprecedented judicial activism it represents, and at more of which it hints—the Supreme Court's detainee case law would seem almost tailor-made to spur congressional-executive bargaining aimed both at devising sustainable approaches to the "new normal" *and* at precluding ham-fisted judicial interference in national security policy making. In its largely statutory holdings—affirming the basic parameters of the war paradigm but modifying its details in light of the ambiguities and likely permanence of our current counterterrorist war—the Court has arguably signaled the *kind* of solutions by which the Bush administration's initial approaches might be made sustainable over the long term. It has largely refrained, however, from preempting the field with sweeping and inflexible constitutional edicts on matters judges do not know well, leaving room for an ongoing process of "bargaining in the shadow of the constitution" as the political branches develop more new law for the perplexing challenges of our "new normal."

(6) What Next?

Will Congress and the Executive Branch take up this baton? Commentators with perspectives as diverse as Yoo and Wittes have complained at Congress' relative passivity. Yoo notes, for instance, that "so far Congress seems satisfied with staying silent and letting the President take the lead and bear the responsibility."[148] For his part, Wittes finds Congress gravely at fault for having abdicated its responsibilities in favor of the president and the courts, leaving post-9/11 legal issues to be handled through an executive-judicial dialogue he feels fundamentally incapable of producing workable long-term solutions.[149]

Such assessments are perhaps overly harsh. Any conclusion that Congress has *wholly* fled the field is belied by the complicated saga of detainee law with respect to military commissions—as it developed through the Detainee Treatment Act of 2005 and the Military Commissions Act of 2006—and by the ways in which FISA amendments have been used to partially "domesticate" the National Security Agency's post-9/11 electronic surveillance efforts.[150] Nevertheless, there is much truth in such criticisms. The president is inescapably involved in such matters, and the judiciary has shown an unprecedented willingness to involve itself, at least in the absence of congressional engagement. In general, Congress has been less engaged, and there is much more that it could yet do.

If indeed the Supreme Court has now set the table for an ongoing process of bargaining in the shadow of the constitution in developing a new Law of Terror, of course, it is not enough merely for there to exist the opportunity to develop sustainable approaches to the "new normal." Such opportunities must also be *taken*. Will our current president and Congress, however, be up to the job? So far, the signs are not too promising.

As we have seen, the Obama administration has been quietly ratifying many of the practices the Bush administration adopted in order to cope with post-9/11 challenges. It has, however, not liked to *admit* that it is doing so, and Obama officials have engaged in political theatrics—e.g., Eric Holder's decision to reinvestigate cases in which CIA officials may have *exceeded* the Bush administration legal authorities for harshly coercive interrogations—apparently designed to reinforce the public impression that Barack Obama is emphatically *not* George Bush. Having apparently tied much of its perceived legitimacy to repudiating the Bush legacy, the Obama administration seems quite *unwilling* to engage in the sort of open and honest debate about terrorism policy that a successful process of congressional-executive bargaining will likely require. To take up the baton of promoting vigorous counterterrorism policies and negotiating legal and institutional approaches that would, in effect, *permanently* move America into an adoption and adaptation of many Bush-era innovations seems to be exactly what the new White House wishes to *avoid* doing in any publicly accountable way.

Nor is it at all clear whether Congress will step up to the difficult and conceptually challenging work of building approaches for the long term. It was willing to be engaged enough to adjust statutory law in order to permit Obama's Department of Defense to withhold pictures of detainee abuse.

(This change permitted the Supreme Court recently to dismiss a case brought by the American Civil Liberties Union to compel such disclosure.)[151] Such tweaks, however, are small beer in comparison to the involvement that would be necessary in order to provide some kind of overarching statutory framework for modern counterterrorism. With Democrats still loathe to associate themselves with the Bush-era counterterrorist policies that they have in practice ratified, with "Tea Party"-era Republicans now keener on domestic spending issues than national security matters, with Osama bin Laden now dead at U.S. hands, and with a presidential election looming in 2012, serious interbranch bargaining will probably have to wait.

II. INTERNATIONAL LAW IN A NEW PARADIGM

The traditional framework of the Law of Armed Conflict (LOAC) revolves around the paradigm of state-on-state conflict carried out by regular military forces. The Geneva Conventions, the classic articulations of the LOAC, are agreements undertaken between signatories in order to reduce the brutality of their warring. As expressed, for instance, in the First Geneva Convention, the rules restricting conduct in warfare are intended to apply in "all cases of declared war or of any other armed conflict which may arise between two or more of the High Contracting Parties, even if the state of war is not recognized by one of them."[152]

The conceptual key to this approach is reciprocity: each nation-state that has agreed to become a High Contracting Party agrees to constrain its behavior in wartime, in the expectation that future opponents who are also High Contracting Parties will do likewise. The rules are generally not structured to apply in a conflict with a country that is *not* a High Contracting Party. Nor are most of Geneva's provisions on the treatment of prisoners, for instance, written to apply to persons who are not members of the regular armed forces of a High Contracting Party—that is, to persons who wear no identifiable uniforms and may not bear arms openly, and who do not *themselves* observe the laws of war.[153]

The conventions provide protections designed to mitigate some of the horrors of war for civilians who take no part in any fighting, devoting an entire convention to this end,[154] but they are notoriously "thin" when it comes to dealing with irregular *combatants* organized (if at all) on a non-state basis, and who do not follow the law themselves. The conventions are not necessarily voiceless when it comes to dealing with irregular, scofflaw combatants, for, as we have seen, the third article common to all of the original 1949 conventions provides basic standards of humane treatment—at least in a "conflict not of an international character," anyway—for "members of armed forces who have laid down their arms and those placed *hors de combat* by sickness, wounds, detention, or any other cause."[155] It is this "Common Article 3" that the U.S. Supreme Court found in its *Hamdan* case, over the objections of the Bush administration's Justice Department, to apply to the war against *al Qaeda*.

Nevertheless, the Geneva system was long felt to be empty enough of substantive content vis-à-vis irregular combatants that many countries felt it necessary to negotiate entirely new Additional Protocols to fill the gap. Additional Protocol I, for instance, "supplements" Geneva's treatment of war victims for "international armed conflicts" in which "peoples are fighting against colonial domination and alien occupation and against racist regimes in the exercise of their right of self-determination."[156] For its part, as noted earlier, Additional Protocol II sought to "develop and supplement" Common Article 3 in order to cover conflicts

> which take place in the territory of a High Contracting Party between its armed forces and dissident armed forces or other organized armed groups which, under responsible command, exercise such control over a part of its territory as to enable them to carry out sustained and concerted military operations and to implement this Protocol.[157]

All in all—particularly from an American perspective, for the United States rejected the 1977 additions—the traditional LOAC framework is not one well-equipped to provide much guidance in the war on terrorism. The Geneva Conventions and the standards of customary international law are structured for state-on-state conflicts between regular forces, and not for transnational struggles against non-state actors who are themselves contemptuous of the laws of war. To be sure, nothing in today's new wars suggests the fundamental *inapplicability* of the basic LOAC principles of restricting the legitimate use of force to conditions of military necessity, requiring proportionality in the employment of force, and observing the distinction between combatants and noncombatants. Nevertheless, large portions of the LOAC canon—and particularly its codified elements—have trouble speaking to modern conflict. State-on-state struggles were the "normal" situation for which the Geneva Conventions were designed, and irregular combatants, to the extent that they were contemplated at all, were relegated to the conceptual periphery of the system.

With respect to the provisions of the Additional Protocols, moreover, even these efforts to *update* the Geneva system would seem to be of only limited use even on their own terms. The 1977 protocols contemplated international armed conflicts occurring as part of the nationalist, anticolonial struggles of the time, or civil wars occurring between organized factional armies *within* a state. The idea of a global terrorist network fighting a war of religious *jihad* against essentially *all* states in the international system, however, was entirely unforeseen. What might have been assumed even in 1977 to be, at most, a type of conflict on the distant conceptual periphery of the LOAC has thus now become the most *common* type of international conflict in the world today. The "new normal" of international conflict in the 21st century is thus something largely beyond the ken of the traditional LOAC paradigm.

Nevertheless, the development of the former periphery of the LOAC into its center of gravity in the "new normal"—and the law's thinness of substantive content here by comparison to what it offers in traditional conflicts—does not make modern counterterrorist warfare entirely *lawless*. (That grim distinction should be reserved for the LOAC's *new* periphery, the dark and chaotic territories of "failed states" wracked by endemic conflict, in which no one even *tries* to observe the laws of war at all.) Rather, what is striking at least about the behavior of developed liberal democratic polities in modern counterterrorist conflicts—that is, about the behavior of those states which Philip Bobbitt might call "market states of consent"—is the degree to which they *do* attempt to minimize civilian casualties and to observe LOAC principles such as necessity, proportionality, and discrimination, and that they do so notwithstanding the fact that their opponents are non-territorial irregulars and themselves feel nothing but contempt for such norms.

It is true enough, but an incomplete analysis, to observe that the LOAC has in these regards been enlisted—at least since the drafting of Additional Protocol I in 1977—as a weapon of asymmetric conflict. Such "lawfare," as it has been called,[158] can indeed be a potent Lilliputian "weapon of the weak," tying stronger powers down with non-reciprocal rules that force them either to fight at an operational disadvantage against unscrupulous opponents or to suffer political and public relations defeats for lapsing into "illegal" activity in response to their enemies' own lawless brutalities. There is also, however, a deeper process that seems to be underway. As market states of consent institutionalize counterterrorist warfare, in fact, the law of war seems to be developing an intriguing new character as a *non*-reciprocal code of conduct—perhaps even to the point of building a new basis for its legitimacy, and reason for its observance, as an expression of the virtue ethics of civilized states. Let us explore this.

A. Evolving State Practice: The New Normal and Its Teething Pains

(1) Early Parallels—and Confusions

It is not quite true that there existed *no* precedent before 9/11 for transnational counterterrorist warfare. The *apartheid*-era Republic of South Africa and the breakaway British colony of Ian Smith's Rhodesia (modern Zimbabwe), for instance—as well as some European powers of the late-colonial period, as with Portugal over its possessions in present-day Angola and Mozambique—fought bitter cross-border wars against irregular guerrillas based in neighboring countries. There were differences between these "national liberation" and decolonization conflicts and our contemporary challenges, of course, not least in the fact that these governments' guerrilla opponents claimed to represent nationalist and territorially defined "peoples" with their ambition limited to replacing existing authorities in the territory in question and ruling it as a conventional nation state. Nonetheless, with the advantage of hindsight, one can see at least some anticipations of the post-9/11 world in these highly irregular, transnational shadow conflicts—a glimmering, perhaps, of the "new normal" with which the LOAC would have to deal in years to come.

The fact that the guerrilla opponents of those racist and/or colonial governments were regarded with sympathy by much of the emerging postcolonial international community, however—and that these irregulars' governmental opponents were seldom particularly scrupulous about observing LOAC principles themselves—helped obscure any potential lessons from these early episodes. One can see some signs of the "new normal" in this period, but postcolonial revolutionary politics led most observers to wish away the challenge such situations might pose to the future of international law vis-à-vis counterterrorism.

The 1977 Geneva Additional Protocols thus, in a sense, got things entirely backwards. The drafters of these instruments do not seem to have conceived their task as being that of developing ways to mitigate the horrors of war and protect the rule of law under trying and novel circumstances. Instead, they seem to have regarded the Protocols as an opportunity to engage in a now-classic campaign of "lawfare." A key purpose of the Protocols was to amend the rules in order to help *privilege* those who *rejected* legal constraints in the service of what the drafters felt to be a good cause.

"Peoples" who were "fighting against colonial domination and alien occupation and against racist regimes in the exercise of their right of self-determination"[159] were to be given Geneva-endorsed combatant status—making the politically correct point that despite their irregular tactics and unconcern for LOAC principles, such fighters were not brigands, terrorists, or other outlaws, but rather honorable warriors fighting for right and good. Such fighters were to be given legal advantages not enjoyed by combatants belonging to regular state forces. Article 44 of the First Additional Protocol, for instance, helpfully recognized that for such fighters, the exigencies of their struggle might permit them to dispense with the traditional requirement that a combatant clearly "distinguish himself" from noncombatants. Disguising oneself as a civilian, therefore, "shall not be considered as perfidious," except if engaged in by *state* forces: the rule was deliberately asymmetrical.

(The treaty claimed to make no change in "the generally accepted practice *of States* with respect to the wearing of the uniform by combatants.")[160] Any state that treated these fighters less generously, in fact, would be guilty of war crimes. In such respects, therefore, the 1977 agenda actually sided *against* the rule of law itself: it was designed to advance the cause of those who did not seem to care about such rules, it was to be used openly *against* the very states from which it demanded respect for the law, and it encouraged behavior that seemed likely to endanger civilians more than ever by legitimating guerrilla tactics of collocation and non-distinction that would put noncombatant populations increasingly in danger from state counterstrikes.

What this era of proto-precedents for our "new normal" therefore did *not* see was anything resembling a serious effort to devise a way for the law of war to handle *non*-reciprocity. No thought appears to have been given to the *real* challenges of war with non-state actors, such as how to respond effectively but in a moral and sustainable way to the lawlessness of irregular combatants. No effort was made to help the law adapt for survival in a threatening world that traditional approaches seemed incapable of handling. As a result, the colonial and racist regimes at which the 1977 effort was aimed continued to sneer at international law, and the international legal community passed up an opportunity to begin preparing itself for the 21st century "new normal" to come.

(2) The Israeli Analogy

The first country whose experience seems to stand as a fairly *direct* precedent for America's post-9/11 war is Israel. As Moshe Halbertal has observed,

> Since the early 1990s, the nature of the military conflict facing Israel has been dramatically shifting. What was mainly a clash between states and armies has turned into a clash between a state and paramilitary terror organizations, Hamas in the south and Hezbollah in the north. This new form of struggle is now called "asymmetrical war." It is defined by an attempt on the part of those groups to erase two basic features of war: the front and the uniform. [161]

Granted, Israel's opponents—or at least Hamas—remain to at least *some* degree nationalist (i.e., specifically Palestinian) and territorial in a traditional 1970s sort of way. Nevertheless, the salience of a supraterritorial Islamic fundamentalism in the Hamas and (especially) Hezbollah political programs, their embrace of indiscriminate anti-civilian terror, the degree to which they do not simply want to supersede the Israeli *government* but in fact wish to "eliminate"[162] Israel entirely—that is, its *polity and population*—and the continuing cross-border aspects both of their attacks and of Israel's responses, suggest closer parallels with America's post-9/11 challenges than past fights against "national liberation" movements.

It is certainly the case, at least, that U.S. officials after September 11, 2001, *felt* themselves to be following Israeli precedents in mounting vigorous responses against *al Qaeda* terrorists wherever they could be found. According to John Yoo, "[w]e (along with Israel) [we]re the first [government] to face a terrorist enemy intent on carrying out the catastrophic destruction of our nation."[163] It is not surprising, therefore, that the Bush administration felt itself to be "taking a page out of the Israeli terrorism playbook"[164] in response to this threat.

Some aspects of American post-9/11 counterterrorist policy in fact appear to have been inspired quite directly by Israel's tenacious and uncompromising responses to the "existential" threat presented first by Palestinian and then by more broadly Islamic terrorism. As noted earlier, the CIA reportedly started a program after 9/11, for instance, in which it was envisioned that specially trained teams of secret agents would be dispatched around the world to track down and kill *al Qaeda* personnel. This effort—the human counterpart to the Agency's use of armed drone aircraft to attack terrorist targets, but in this case "striking [from] two feet instead of 10,000 feet"[165]—was said to have been quite self-consciously inspired by Israel's successes around the world in finding and killing the Palestinian terrorists who had butchered the Israeli athletic team at the 1972 Summer Olympics in Munich.[166]

Interestingly, however, the International Court of Justice (ICJ) seems to have been trying to *resist* the idea that the Israeli experience offers any sort of a precedent for modern counterterrorist wars of the post-9/11 variety. In an advisory opinion in 2004, for instance, it addressed the question of the "security barrier" wall and fence line Israel has built along its borders against Palestinian terrorist attacks—declaring that, *as a matter of law,* the Israelis cannot justify this structure in terms of "self-defense" under Article 51 of the United Nations Charter. In this holding, the ICJ tried to distinguish Israel's situation from that of the U.S. conflict with *al Qaeda*—which the Court seems to have assumed *was* indeed a war of "self-defense" within the meaning of the Charter—arguing that Israel cannot invoke Article 51 because the threats against which it built its "wall" originate in territory (i.e., the West Bank) Israel *itself* controls. Accordingly, the Court declared, Article 51 is irrelevant and "self-defense" does not apply.[167]

This somewhat confused and confusing interpretation of "self-defense" demonstrates the Court's entrapment within a conception of conflict that remains fundamentally *territorial* in nature—and thus stuck in the twentieth century. As the ICJ would like to read the U.N. Charter, one can apparently indeed be at war with a non-state actor based outside one's borders. (The

Court did not criticize Israel's Article 51 argument for failing to allege a conflict with a *state*, but merely for the fact that Israel's *non-state* enemy was not based *outside* Israeli-controlled territory.) This is perhaps an important step forward for a legal system the core doctrines of which were built up around the now rather quaint paradigm of state-on-state conflict. But it may not be enough.

The ICJ's reading of Article 51 still seems to have nothing to say about conflict with a truly *non*territorial foe. It is precisely one of the perplexing novelties of the "new normal" that *borders* have little relevance in the global counterterrorist struggles of the 21st century. Yet the ICJ has apparently now tied its Article 51 jurisprudence to the idea that "self-defense" only applies when facing a threat that "originates" in a specific identifiable location external to the society that is thus threatened. Whatever one thinks of how the ICJ dealt specifically with Israel's situation, this theory provides no guidance for anyone facing a non-localizable threat capable of interpenetrating civilian society both in one's own territory and abroad.

Though, as noted, the ICJ seems to accept—based upon U.N. Security Council Resolutions 1368 and 1373[168]—that the U.S. struggle against *al Qaeda* is indeed a conflict in which "self-defense" applies, it is actually somewhat hard to see how this could be so under the Court's reasoning in the Israeli case. Did 9/11 give rise to an American right of "self-defense" *solely* because Osama bin Laden happened to base his organization in Afghanistan at the time? If *al Qaeda*'s leadership had snuck itself into suburban Detroit, or actually *remained* in present-day U.S.-occupied Afghanistan, would the U.S. right to self-defense evaporate? One can only be glad that the ICJ's mere advisory opinion—of which, in a formal sense, one can make as little as one wishes—technically has no binding value as case precedent, for it demonstrates that the ICJ still has unhelpfully little to say about warfare against modern terrorism of the *al Qaeda* variety. The Court seems unable to escape the paradigm of nation-state territoriality.

The ICJ's refusal to contemplate the existence of a non-territorial enemy and its fixation upon a narrowly territorial/jurisdictional notion of conflict is paralleled in a recent effort by the International Law Association's "Use of Force Committee" to argue that no "armed conflict" exists between the United States and *al Qaeda* anywhere *other* than Afghanistan and Iraq. By the Committee's reasoning, the existence of an armed conflict is apparently intrinsically territorially and jurisdictionally specific as a matter of law. Because sufficiently intense fighting of the traditional sort has not occurred elsewhere, therefore, an armed conflict exists only in Afghanistan and Iraq. Indeed, the committee has apparently concluded, a "global war on terrorism" is flatly impossible, because "[i]ntense intergroup armed fighting does not characterize the entire globe."[169] The Use of Force Committee thus also remains in the thrall of traditional territoriality, and conceptually unprepared for the very 21st century conflicts it was asked to analyze.

All in all, the community of professional international lawyers seems somewhat befuddled by the circumstances in which many countries now find themselves vis-à-vis *al Qaeda* and its affiliates, and unable to offer any particularly useful advice or guidance. Such conceptual abdication is not merely unhelpful; it may endanger the rule of law itself. If legal scholars pronounce a global war on terrorism to be a legal impossibility, those governments that feel themselves unquestionably to be in such a conflict—facing such things as embassy bombings in Kenya and Tanzania, hotel bombings in Bali, explosive speedboat attacks in Yemen, airliner plots over the Atlantic and Pacific, mass-casualty hijackings in the United States, train bombings in London and Madrid, and improvised explosive attacks in Iraq, Afghanistan, and Pakistan—will conclude, with apologies to Charles Dickens' Mr. Bumble, that the law must be an ass.

Nor is the international legal community distinguishing itself in grappling with the challenges of the actual *conduct* of modern counterterrorist warfare. Israel's military campaign in the winter of 2008–09 against Hamas in the Gaza Strip has come in for an enormous amount of international criticism, most prominently in the report prepared by a United Nations group under the leadership of South African jurist Richard Goldstone. This so-called Goldstone Report[170] bears close analysis.

It is beyond the scope of this paper to assess whether or not Israel was in fact guilty of systematic and deliberate LOAC violations during the Gaza conflict. It is enough, for present purposes, that whether or not Goldstone was actually right about Israel, he made his case remarkably unpersuasively—in large part because he seemed not to understand some important points about the challenges of modern counterterrorism. The Goldstone Report, in fact, illustrates some of the teething pains of the "new normal" by demonstrating some of the theoretical and practical difficulties attendant to trying to shoehorn modern counterterrorist conflicts into conceptual boxes derived from traditional warfare.

As with President George W. Bush's elaborate efforts to base U.S. government activity after 9/11 upon clearly articulated legal theories, one of the most interesting things about Israel's Gaza campaign is that its military authorities seem to have spent so much time and effort apparently trying to minimize civilian casualties and to *comply* with traditional LOAC principles of necessity, proportionality, and discrimination. To some extent, one might infer this from the actual casualty figures. If the Goldstone Report were right that the powerful and sophisticated Israeli military really *set out* indiscriminately to massacre Palestinian civilians in the crowded confines of Gaza's cramped urbanity, after all, one wonders how its forces could have managed to kill so *few* of them, or to have ended up (accidentally?) killing such a high proportion of Hamas militants.[171]

More specifically, however, Israel has detailed the many steps it says it took in order to minimize civilian casualties during the Gaza conflict. It claims to have aborted air strikes where the risk to civilians seemed too high, to have dropped leaflets warning of impending attacks, to have made warning telephone calls to Gazan civilians in advance of raids, to have declared daily humanitarian pauses in fighting, to have put military attorneys on full-time call in order to provide operational legal advice to operational commanders, and even to have allowed some Palestinians to complain directly to the Israeli Supreme Court.[172] If these claims are true, they would actually seem to go intriguingly *beyond* U.S. practice in Afghanistan and elsewhere. The Goldstone Report, however, concluded sweepingly not that Israel simply *failed* adequately to protect Palestinian civilians in Gaza, but that harming such civilians was actually Israel's *war aim.*

In discussing the "objectives and strategy" of the Israeli campaign, the Goldstone Report's reasoning followed a notably simplistic logic: Israel plans its campaigns carefully and has built elaborate institutions for providing legal advice to operational commanders, it enjoys state-of-the-art technology, and it does not claim to have made significant errors during the war. But many Gazan civilians nonetheless died, *ergo* Israel must have *meant* to kill them—and this is a war crime. This argument was fundamentally inferential, for Goldstone could apparently find no direct evidence of any Israeli *policy* of targeting civilians in this war.[173]

In a sense, this conclusion was flattering: in effect, the report assumed Israeli war making to be so hyper-competent that *any* civilian casualties *must* have been specifically intended. Under the circumstances of the Gaza conflict, his report concludes, the "incidents and patterns of events considered in this report," simply *had* to be "the result of deliberate planning and policy decisions."[174] This logic, however, is deeply flawed—bespeaking a failure of imagination on Goldstone's part in grappling with the real challenges of modern warfare against irregular opponents who shelter amongst, and are not easily distinguishable from, the civilian population, and who benefit politically from any civilian "collateral damage" that occurs as a result of their opponents' efforts to strike them.[175]

The extent to which civilian casualties might in fact be unavoidable in such a war, even with the most sophisticated intelligence and "surgical" strike capabilities and scrupulous efforts at LOAC compliance, appears never to have occurred to Goldstone. His report reads as if the Gaza war were a traditional conflict in which regular Hamas troops lined up against the Israeli Defense Forces (IDF) in open country, and there was no need for the Israelis ever to fire *anything* in the general direction of civilians in the urban mazes of the Gaza strip. In such circumstances, the simple inference that *any* civilian casualties were *prima facie* evidence of Israel's murderous intent might conceivably have been justified, but the conflict in Gaza looked nothing like that.

The Goldstone Report actually concedes that Palestinian fighters "were not always dressed in a way that distinguished them from civilians," and that there were "indications that Palestinian armed groups launched rockets from urban areas."[176] Nevertheless, the failure of his Hamas witnesses to admit doing these things with ill intent—and here it is worth remembering that Goldstone relied principally upon the testimony of Palestinians under Hamas supervision, the Israeli Defense Forces having refused to cooperate—led Goldstone to declare that there was "no evidence" that Hamas fighters mingled with civilians "with the intention" of "shielding themselves from attack," or that they launched attacks from urban areas "with the intention" of "shielding the rocket launchers form counterstrokes by the Israeli armed forces."[177]

Given Goldstone's eagerness to draw sweeping inferences about Israeli intentions in the absence of direct evidence, his refusal to infer anything about *Hamas'* intentions was odd, to say the least. In effect, Goldstone seems to have thought so little of Hamas' military competence that it did not bother him that its fighters launched unguided high-explosive rockets *at* Israeli civilian areas: nothing more sophisticated and discriminating could apparently be expected of Palestinians, so that conduct passed without comment. The only thing he seems to have considered at all was the fact that Hamas allegedly fired *from* Palestinian urban areas. Goldstone's handling of this awkward fact, however, suggests a more profound conceptual failure than can be explained merely by the anti-Israeli bias of which he is often accused. Quite apart from what evidence was (or was not) available to him, and what might have prompted Goldstone to pick one explanation over another, the report's phrasing indicates that the South African judge imagined only two possibilities. As the report conceived it, it would seem, Hamas either did nothing wrong or it wished to use civilians to shield its own fighters from attack. (Carefully avoiding a position on Hamas' culpability, and thus ruling out a finding on the latter point—because the use of human shields is a war crime—Goldstone effectively adopted the former position.)

It seems not to have occurred to Goldstone, however, that there is a third alternative—namely, that the self-professedly willing would-be religious martyrs of Hamas might have actually intended not specifically (or not merely) to *protect themselves* but in fact to *endanger* their fellow Palestinians, by provoking Israeli counterstrikes that would have the inevitable result of causing civilian deaths and thus "proving" to credulous foreign observers that Israel was, *ipso facto,* guilty of war crimes. The idea that this sort of war *unavoidably* causes at least some civilian deaths *even though* the regular state combatant tries to avoid them, and indeed that it may do so in part *because* the irregular combatant tries to encourage such bloodletting, seems to have been too big, too complicated, or too novel a notion to comprehend. As a result, one aspect of the real challenges of modern counterterrorism—and one potential facet of the Gaza conflict—is never addressed, and this conceptual oversight arguably leaves Goldstone's inquiry open to precisely the sort of manipulation of which such an insight might have warned him.

Similarly, as Moshe Halbertal has pointed out, Goldstone seems to have taken a rather blinkered view of Israel's targeting of the Hamas police force. Goldstone condemned this, but in fact such targeting is not *necessarily* problematic in this type of warfare. Whether or not Hamas police units or personnel were employed as combatants—and were therefore legitimate targets for the IDF—is really less a legal than an empirical question, though Goldstone seemed to treat attacks upon police as a *per se* war crime.[178] Goldstone envisioned at least the *possibility* that the Hamas police took part in fighting "as an organized force"—that is, that they fought *as police* units. Nevertheless, relying in part on declarations on a Hamas website, of all things, the report took essentially at face value Hamas officials' contention that the police in Gaza were just an ordinary "civilian law enforcement agency."[179]

Halbertal has aptly wondered whether the Goldstone Report missed the conceptual boat by ignoring the possibility that in a "semi-state" like Gaza, a civilian police force may be not just a traditional constabulary but also "a militia loyal to the movement or party" in charge, and just another way of "putting combatants on the payroll of the state." In places like Gaza, he noted, it is not *necessarily* the case that there is a clear functional like between combatants and "police."[180] Here again, assumptions about traditional wartime dichotomies—in this instance, the line between "civilian" and "military"—may have led Goldstone to misconceive the situation it was his mandate to analyze.

A related conceptual deficiency seems to have existed with regard to Goldstone's criticism of Israeli forces for attacking the "supporting infrastructure" of the Hamas forces. To Goldstone, conducting any such attacks was *prima facie* evidence of deliberately harming civilians: it showed Israel's intent to "transform civilians and civilian objects into legitimate targets."[181] There is no hint of any acknowledgement that if civilian infrastructure elements were used for the direct support of Hamas' irregular fighters, such facilities would actually *become* legitimate military targets. The report gives no sign of having considered that anything could have occurred in Gaza that was not consistent with the stereotypically crisp civilian/military dichotomies of traditional conventional war. It may have been politically comfortable to flatter the Palestinian polity by assuming that Hamas ran what was in all relevant respects a conventional state engaged in a traditional war, but it is far from clear that this was actually true. At the least, Goldstone's analysis does not seem to have addressed this empirical question, though its answer has sweeping implications for any LOAC analysis.

Where civilian harm occurred at Israeli hands, Goldstone's analysis effectively assumed three possibilities: the incidents were simple errors, they were the actions of "rogue elements" in the IDF, or they were the result of "a deliberate policy or planning" to target civilians *as civilians*.[182] There is no suggestion that he ever considered the possibility that conflict in the new age of counterterrorist war *necessarily* involves highly ambiguous fact patterns, an interpenetration of "military" and "civilian" personnel and facilities entirely unlike what traditional notions of warfare would lead one to expect, and a concomitant possibility of civilian casualties *notwithstanding* sophisticated targeting and scrupulous legal oversight by the state party confronting such irregular adversaries. (Nor, as noted, does the report seem to have considered the possibility of irregular combatants "drawing fouls" by *deliberately* endangering civilians in order to exploit the propaganda fallout from any civilian casualties resulting from counterstrikes by regular forces against irregular combatants carefully collocated with civilians.)

The closest the report gets to demonstrating an actual Israeli intent to attack civilian targets *per se* comes when Goldstone quotes comments made by Israelis in connection with *previous* conflicts that it was desirable to respond to terrorist attacks by using "disproportionate" force in order to help deter future terrorism. Such counterstrikes, these quotations suggest, can include targeting civilian infrastructure. What these quotes seem actually to describe, however, is some desire to undertake disproportionate counterattacks in Lebanon against Hezbollah military assets and the civilian infrastructure in Lebanon *that supported Hezbollah operations*.[183] It is not clear, therefore, in what sense these purported comments have anything to say even about Israel's earlier wars in Lebanon, much less its Gaza campaign.

Moreover, Goldstone concedes that the Israeli comments in question were not official doctrinal statements: two of the three were explicitly unofficial "writings" (i.e., apparently personal views) and the third was a comment (and perhaps also a personal view, though this is not clear) made by a serving Israeli general. Goldstone seemed entirely unconcerned, however, that he had found no evidence that any such sentiments reflected or influenced *official* Israeli policies *in Gaza* in any way whatsoever. Remarkably, in fact, his report declared that it "does not *have* to consider whether Israeli military officials [in Gaza] were [actually] influenced by these writings" because the facts Goldstone saw on the ground were *consistent* with targeting civilians.[184] He did not feel he *needed* any actual evidence of Israeli policies, in other words, because he already knew the answer.

Goldstone's fundamental, logically untenable inference—that because civilian casualties occurred in Gaza, Israel must therefore have intended them—was, therefore, all he thought was required in order to prove war crimes. The report's conceptual blindness was self-reinforcing: as the issue of certain Israelis' "writings" demonstrated, Goldstone's tendentious inference was not merely a *substitute* for actual evidence, but to some extent actually became an excuse not to *look* for any. All in all, therefore, Goldstone's U.N. mission seems to have been entirely conceptually unprepared for the realities of the "new normal."

(3) Doctrinal Conundrums

It would be unfair to suggest that no legal scholars have grappled with the challenges of modern counterterrorism from the perspective of international law. To outline a particularly interesting example—and one perhaps no less relevant for Israel than for the United States or indeed any other democratic polity facing an "existential" threat from terrorist groups—Philip Bobbitt has drawn characteristically elegant and far-reaching conclusions from his analysis of terrorism in the age of the market state.

If international law is to have relevance in an age in which mass-casualty terrorists seek to destroy the conditions that make it possible for the market state of consent to exist—and in which such terrorists seem increasingly likely to gain access to weapons of mass destruction (WMD) through a global market in which such technology is ever more commodified—Bobbitt feels international law needs to embrace a more permissive approach to "the practices of preemption and prevention associated with state practice in war."[185] The idea of being able to act in order to thwart an "imminent" attack, he believes, needs to be adjusted for these circumstances, in order to reflect the basic requirement that market states of consent need to be able to wage "wars of preclusion" in order to forestall the development of the kind of catastrophic civilian threats that would imperil the system of consent itself. As he sees it, preclusive war will necessarily become the distinctive type of warfare associated with the market state of consent.[186]

For the most part, however, the international legal community has resisted any suggestion that modern threats require any new understandings of a state's right to respond in self-defense to an "imminent" threat. This idea has traditionally been construed fairly narrowly, to cover such things as attacks in response to provocative massings of troops that suggest an immediately impending invasion, but not much more. In an era of potential WMD terrorism, however, some have argued that this may no longer be adequate. Yet a high-level panel appointed by the U.N. secretary-general seems to have rejected this idea, arguing against "rewriting or reinterpretation of Article 51" of the U.N. Charter. The panel was willing to do no more than endorse the idea that "if there are good arguments for preventative military action, with good evidence to support them, they should be put to the Security Council."[187]

To be sure, the panel's explanation of what should happen *after* a Security Council refusal to authorize preventative (as opposed to merely preemptive) war is intriguingly vague. It opined that if the council refuses to act, the petitioner would be able to "pursue other strategies, including persuasion, negotiation, deterrence and containment—and to visit again the military option."[188] It did not explain what it meant by this last phrase. Faced with Security Council inaction—e.g., as a result of a veto by one of the Council's permanent members—could the threatened country then feel free to respond "unilaterally" with preventative force once any remaining means of handling the problem had failed? Was the panel suggesting, in other words, a requirement simply to "check with the council first," or was it instead simply averring that no preventative action is *ever* authorized without Security Council approval? The panel's report seems to imply the latter interpretation, for it says that in the event of a council refusal to endorse preventative force, there will "by definition" be time in which to pursue less sanguinary solutions.[189] This suggests that it envisioned *no* action being permissible without council authorization.

If indeed the panel was of this view, however, it would seem to have followed all too many other traditional international lawyers in ducking the genuine challenges presented by the "new normal." For any future country that really feels itself to face an existential threat from a sworn mortal enemy's development of WMD, how persuasive are arguments likely to be that international legality requires that in the face of a single country's Security Council veto, for instance, it can take no action in self-defense until its adversaries have actually *obtained* nuclear, chemical, or biological weapons and are "imminently" preparing to deliver them? The panel argued that "the risk to the global order and the norm of non-intervention" is "simply too great" to permit unilateralism in the name of self-defense,[190] but it seems very unlikely that a government faced with potential annihilation and a paralyzed Security Council would share this view.

Despite the occasional counterexample such as Bobbitt or Ruth Wedgwood,[191] the examples of the High-Level Panel, the International Court of Justice's "wall" decision, the International Law Association's Use of Force Committee, and the Goldstone Report suggest that the center of gravity in the international legal community remains mired in traditional modes of understanding war exclusively through the prism of conventional state-on-state conflict. Such conceptual blinders obscure the realities of the "new normal" of counterterrorist conflict, and seem to be making coherent adaptation to its challenges more difficult.

This is worrisome in at least two respects. Most obviously, it leaves the legal community unable to provide much useful guidance to real-world decision makers trying to cope with modern terrorist challenges. As suggested earlier, moreover, because of this failing—and because the reaction of so many legal scholars seems to be to deny any *need* for innovations and to decry all adaptive efforts by states as being actual *violations* of the law—there seems to be a real danger that these problems will lead some to the conclusion that law *itself* has outlived its usefulness, or has indeed become counterproductive. It is not only with regard to the U.S. Constitution, after all, that Richard Posner might remind us that like any brittle thing, the law that will not bend may ultimately break.[192]

It is for this reason, for instance, that the traditional international legal community should acknowledge and worry much more about the advent of "lawfare"—that is, about the developing use of legal norms as a weapon of asymmetric conflict. The irregular combatant practitioners of such tactics self-evidently do not care that such approaches might profoundly destabilize the rule of law, and indeed even delegitimize the *idea* of law in international affairs. International lawyers, however, surely should. More than they need reflexive criticism, real-world state decision makers confronting modern terrorists need *help* in devising appropriate ways to address these challenges within a recognizable framework of legality. What they need perhaps least of all is sterile criticism unproductively entangled in a traditional paradigm of state-on-state conflict between regular armed forces that seems to have less and less relevance to current events.

It is certainly true that some international institutions seem to have begun to ratify at least some elements of modern state responses to the "new normal." In landmark resolutions passed after 9/11, for instance, the U.N. Security Council endorsed "the inherent right of individual or collective self-defense in accordance with the Charter" specifically in the context of 9/11. It declared that "such acts" as the New York and Washington attacks—"like any act[s] of international terrorism"—constitute a threat to international peace and security.[193] The council has also recognized "the need to combat by all means, in accordance with the Charter of the United Nations, threats to international peace and security caused by terrorist acts."[194] The member nations of NATO, moreover, have expressly recognized in 9/11 a situation implicating their collective right to self-defense against *al Qaeda*.[195] Some commentators have even argued that U.N. resolutions affirming support for post-2003 Iraqi reconstruction "can be taken as ratifications of the Coalition invasion," and that the example of NATO intervention in Kosovo without U.N. authorization shows that traditional ideas of mandatory U.N. authorization for the use of force are "becoming, as a matter of customary international law, a nullity."[196] Nevertheless, the most striking thing about the international community's response to the challenges of the "new normal" is how *little* has yet been articulated.

(4) Other State Practice

What can we learn, however, from actual *state practice* with regard to how the broader international community is feeling its way toward approaches capable of coping with the "new normal"? In assessing the weight of state practice vis-à-vis modern counterterrorist challenges, it makes sense to examine only the practice of states that have actually *confronted* such threats and which possessed at the time any meaningful capacity to respond to them in ways that might implicate LOAC principles. A state neither threatened nor capable of responding cannot contribute to our understanding of state practice in such matters. (Such a state might make assertions about what the law should be in the "new normal," but for purposes of understanding customary law, *state practice* can only coherently be judged by looking at those who possess the *option* of choosing alternative courses of action.)[197]

In this light, there are few examples to consider other than the American and Israeli examples we have already examined. Especially in view of the fierce *public* criticism that Bush-era American counterterrorist policies elicited abroad, however, no analysis of state practice should overlook the extent to which many governments around the world appear, in private, to have *cooperated* extensively with the United States. This raises interesting questions about the development of customary international law.

According to a report prepared by the Council of Europe, the governments of some 14 European nations—the United Kingdom, Italy, Germany, Sweden, Macedonia, Bosnia & Herzegovina, Turkey, Poland, Romania, Spain, Cyprus, Ireland, Portugal, and Greece—collaborated with the CIA in its global campaign of capturing, detaining, and transferring terrorist suspects. Their cooperation was said to range from various sorts of "active or passive" collusion all the way to actually hosting secret CIA detention facilities, as Poland and Romania were alleged to have done.[198] The CIA also allegedly flew well over 1,000 undeclared flights over European territory after 2001, partly in support of rendition operations.[199]

The Council of Europe report declared that some of its "member states have knowingly colluded with the United States" in renditions and other counterterrorist activity, including detaining suspects, participating in interrogations, using information from such interrogations, providing intelligence information to support these various CIA activities, and perhaps even themselves operating "secret detention centres."[200] Some countries—such as Sweden and Bosnia & Herzegovina—actually handed over suspects to the CIA for transport elsewhere.[201] Notably, many of these same governments seem in no way remorseful, apparently refusing to cooperate with the council's investigation.[202]

Both the leader of the Council of Europe's inquiry and that of a European Parliament investigatory committee have declared that it is very likely that government officials in all these countries knew about CIA "rendition" activity on their soil.[203] In Italy, Germany, Sweden, and Canada, investigations were begun into government officials' complicity in CIA renditions.[204] In Sweden, it was revealed that Swedish *ministers* had actually approved the apprehension of two Egyptian nationals and their release into CIA custody. A Canadian inquiry disclosed the involvement of Canadian intelligence officials in the rendition of a Syrian-born Canadian citizen seized in New York in 2002. Before CIA agents seized a radical Muslim imam suspected of terrorist activity off a street in Milan in February 2003, it has also been reported, the agency's station chief in Rome briefed Italian security officials on the operation and obtained their approval.[205] (Two successive heads of Italian military counterespionage were allegedly involved.[206])

By 2009, the British security service (MI-5) was under investigation for allegedly having colluded in the mistreatment of terrorist suspects by other countries, with members of Parliament asking awkward questions about "outsourcing" torture.[207] Foreign Secretary David Milliband also publicly admitted that U.S. officials had used UK airspace for some rendition flights, and that British officials had allowed their Indian Ocean naval base at Diego Garcia to be used for this purpose on two occasions.[208]

In fact, media reports have claimed that in "most" of the renditions carried out after September 2001, the security services of the foreign country had *themselves* apprehended the suspect and given him to the CIA.[209] Perhaps most dramatically, it has been said that "top intelligence officers" in each host country were involved in allowing the CIA to run secret detention centers—its notorious network reportedly consisting of a total of eight "black sites," the first of which was supposedly a facility established in Thailand in 2002—into which particularly high-value terrorist suspects disappeared for long periods of time, and where they were allegedly subjected to harsh interrogations.[210]

Given the murky and contested facts, it is hard to draw conclusions about state practice in these first years of the global war on terrorism. Nor, even if the facts could be more clearly established, is it likely to be at all clear the degree to which any such actions were accompanied by *opinio juris*—that is, the belief that the law required or permitted such behavior—in such a way that post-9/11 counterterrorist activity would help drive the development of new norms of customary international law.[211] Nevertheless, there are strong indications that whatever the legal scholars say, real-world decision makers have been exploring decidedly nontraditional ways to approach the security challenges of the "new normal." But where is all this going?

B. Law as Virtue Ethics

(1) Interiorization and Opacity

One of the hallmarks of conflict in the "new normal" of the post-9/11 world is the collapse of the Geneva ideal of reciprocity. With state-on-irregular conflicts having essentially entirely replaced state-on-state warfare, at least for now, as the predominant type of international conflict, the idea that states should follow the LOAC at least in part in hopes of reciprocity—that is, in the anticipation that their adversaries will do so in return—has largely disappeared. This significantly attenuates one of the foundational aspirations of the Geneva system: to ameliorate some of the brutality and suffering of war, for both combatants and noncombatant populations alike.

In the modern conflicts of the "new normal," there is no such reciprocity. Moreover, it is often a *war aim* of the irregular combatants to cause as *much* suffering as possible. Indeed, they may seek to maximize not only the suffering of combatants loyal to the *state* party, but also—and perhaps especially—the suffering of civilian populations. Indeed, terrorists may even deliberately endanger "friendly" civilian populations broadly sympathetic to their cause: in classic "lawfare" fashion, they can gain propaganda victories and recruit more combatants if operations by the *state* participant against irregular fighters produce significant civilian casualties.[212] One hopes and presumes that the *regular* combatant party will remain committed to LOAC principles of necessity, proportionality, and discrimination, to minimizing harm to civilians, and to as much of the Geneva corpus as can coherently be applied under such circumstances. But the law of war in this "new normal" emerges as a remarkably one-sided phenomenon.

The roiling controversies that have surrounded the Goldstone Report on Israel's Gaza war, moreover—coupled with the challenges of informational complexity and contextual contingency we have seen in combatant status determinations under U.S. law—suggest a further change: the *interiorization* of the law of armed conflict. It has "always" been the case that operational decision makers in time of war need to be cognizant of whatever restrictions the laws of war impose upon them. In more conventional state-on-state conflicts, this remained a comparatively manageable challenge. Today, however, the changing nature of conflict has placed unprecedented stresses upon the systems designed to handle these challenges.

Over the years, those countries most concerned with legal propriety in military operations have built up legal infrastructures for providing legal advice to commanders at various levels. In American practice, for instance, this has resulted in the emergence of a whole new discipline of "operational law," which trains military attorneys to "recognize, analyze, and resolve the problems they will encounter in the operational context"[213] when responsible for giving legal advice to commanders about what the law does and does not permit in war. It is comparatively easy for military lawyers to co-deploy in the field with senior officers, to sit on the boards that recommend targets for aerial bombing, and to advise on the treatment of enemy prisoners.

And they do. For years now, in U.S. practice, it has been required that military lawyers be available to provide law of war advice during all joint and combined operations, and they have been required to review all operational plans and orders in order to ensure consistency with U.S. statutory and international law.[214] U.S. lawyers, it is said, "have parachuted in with special operations forces in the 1989 invasion of Panama, flew with Army troops to Haiti in 1994[,] and were deployed by the hundreds in Kuwait and Saudi Arabia during the [1990] Gulf War, sleeping in the sand alongside troops in the field."[215]

In countries such as the United States, the United Kingdom, and Israel, this sort of operational legal advice is today quite routine. The Directorate of Legal Services for Britain's Royal Air Force, for instance, is charged with providing "advice and assistance during the operational planning process" and with advising deployed commanders on such things as the "rules of engagement, status of force issues[,] and targeting of military objectives."[216] The Israeli Military Advocate General's office is similarly responsible for tasks ranging from "verifying the legality of striking particular targets" to "considering the humanitarian aspects of conflict" and "assuring that the IDF's activities [are] commensurate with the provisions of international law"—including by advising on "how to distinguish between civilians and unlawful combatants."[217] For its part, the U.S. Army's *Operational Law Handbook* offers a reference guide for military attorneys, giving advice to commanders on a wide range of issues: from rules of engagement to the principles of necessity, proportionality, and discrimination; from reporting procedures for law of war violations to U.S. federal statutes governing military involvement in response to domestic terrorist attacks; and from prisoner interrogation practices to the standards for judging whether the use of force is authorized *at all*.[218]

Modern counterterrorist wars, however, present extreme challenges to such operational law systems, forcing upon them quite a radical decentralization of law-related decision making. The lack of a "front line" or of organized and uniformed enemy forces—and both the routine colocation of regular military units with members of the civilian population and that population's interpenetration with irregular enemy combatants—drive "operational law" decisions down to the very lowest levels of interaction between regular forces and the surrounding society, well below the point where specific *professional* legal advice can actually be had. In this environment, one turns to military lawyers when one can, but for individual soldiers on operations in the field, this is impossible much (or most) of the time, for any number of practical reasons. At the most fundamental level, therefore, *every* regular combatant must be his *own* legal advisor for countless day-to-day decisions of interaction with civilians and enemy combatants alike. Halbertal is right in describing contemporary counterterrorist conditions as having produced a "new kind of micro-war," in which "every soldier is a kind of commanding officer, a full moral and strategic agent."[219]

Significantly, at this most democratized individual level, the dynamics of operational law in the "new normal" have the effect of making the law of war look less like "law" *per se* than simply like morality. In modern war, "moral considerations have to be an essential part of military training," with legal rules becoming "part of the inner world of each soldier."[220] Ensuring that one's forces will follow LOAC principles thus becomes in large part an endeavor in *moral* training—and in the deliberate cultivation of habits and other routinized patterns of thought and reaction that operate almost at the level of instinct, far below the level of detailed analytical "lawyering." To some extent, therefore, the most important dynamics of the law of war, as they are lived in practice, are driven *inward:* into the development and maintenance of what is in effect an operational *moral code* at the level of individual combatants.

This is where the problems of the Goldstone Report suggest another lesson, for when the dynamics of legal constraint become so decentralized and interiorized, it can be devilishly hard for anyone on the "outside" to judge their operation in any meaningful way. This challenge of opacity is particularly acute in an environment in which operational decisions involve time-urgent judgment calls, made on the basis of immediate and evolving tactical circumstances and often fragmentary intelligence information, and where there may exist no clear boundary between "civilian" and "military" realms in any event. It will presumably always be possible to reach relatively clear and defensible conclusions about many of the most singular and egregious problems that arise in warfare. *Most* decisions in modern counterterrorist war, however, are likely to be highly resistant to after-the-fact analysis and second-guessing, particularly when undertaken by outsiders.

This seems to have been one of the reasons for the flaws in the Goldstone Report. The kind of information that would have *really* allowed Justice Goldstone to dissect Israeli intentions and practices in the Gaza conflict as a whole was not available to him—and not just because Israel refused to cooperate with a U.N. probe it viewed as being irremediably biased from the outset. Much of the information that Goldstone would have needed in order to develop a coherent analysis of Israel's specific actions in light of the complexities of that war was probably of a sort that he perhaps *could not* have gotten under almost any circumstances.

Much of the information Goldstone most needed was either for all practical purposes not really able to be reconstructed at all (e.g., detailed moment-by-moment understandings of the circumstances faced, individually, by considerable numbers of soldiers operating semi-independently on the ground) or it was of a sort that no combatant would likely divulge to an outsider in the first place (e.g., the details of operational intelligence reporting and intelligence-based analytical assessments). Even had Goldstone better understood the dilemmas of conflict in the "new normal," in other words, his analytical undertaking faced vast and potentially insurmountable evidentiary hurdles.

We should expect other wars of the "new normal" to be similarly resistant to exterior analysis. As an example, consider comments made by the U.N. Special Rapporteur on Extrajudicial Executions, Philip Alston, who voiced concerns in October 2009 that the U.S. practice of using unmanned aircraft to fire missiles and drop bombs on terrorist targets in Iraq, Afghanistan, Pakistan, and Somalia might violate international law. Alston did not say that these drone strikes *did* violate the law of war, however, merely that they *might*—and that it was therefore incumbent upon U.S. officials to provide the international community with full disclosure into the operational decision making of the CIA and military officials who carry out such missions. If the United States wished to reassure the international community that it was actually attacking enemy combatants rather than simply conducting "arbitrary extrajudicial executions," he indicated, it would have to come clean about the details of its operational decisions.[221]

In one sense, the technologies involved in the drone war may indeed permit quite exacting after-the-fact accountability, in that "everything an operator sees, hears, and reads is stored, and all decisions taken can be subject to a greater degree of analysis and evaluation after a mission than would be possible with [attacks conducted by] a manned platform."[222] Nevertheless, while drone combat may thus facilitate improved *internal* review of the "lessons-learned" variety, it is by no means likely that governments would be willing to open up this "everything" to inspection by outsiders.

According to press reports, as more unmanned aircraft have become available, targeting decisions for such CIA and military drone attacks have moved from efforts to find and kill specific high-ranking terrorist leaders to decision making based upon "signatures" of activity (a.k.a. "pattern of life") that suggest that individuals are enemy combatants.[223] This approach, of course, is intrinsically subjective, relying upon a complex and case-by-case mix of aerial surveillance, ground observation, informant reporting, electronic surveillance, the prior identification of terrorist-associated buildings or other facilities, and comparisons to patterns of behavior observed elsewhere in the observed locale over a considerable period of time.[224] Just what a "reasonable" targeting decision is under the circumstances is presumably very difficult to define, or for someone else to reconstruct and analyze "objectively" thereafter, even with access to all available intelligence, and it may be quite resistant to *ex ante* definition.[225]

Needless to say, the United States has shown no sign of being willing to open up its covert drone operations to U.N. legal observers, and U.S. officials keep their detailed targeting rules of engagement secret. And other aspects of modern counterterrorist activity, including day-to-day operational decision making by special operations forces or intelligence paramilitary operatives in the field, may well be even *more* structurally resistant to outsider second-guessing than is drone combat. Such exterior opacity is likely to be another hallmark of conflict in the "new normal."

Significantly, because these dynamics of interiorization and opacity are coupled with the collapse of the reciprocity ideal in modern counterterrorist conflict, it may be that the law of war is evolving into a form of virtue ethics. The LOAC is becoming, in effect, an explicitly one-sided code of conduct that has more to do with the moral *identity* of those who observe it—that is, what "kind" of people they are or what "kind" of country they represent—than it does with any specific notions of "legality" at all, and it is becoming a system compliance with which in day-to-day circumstances it is difficult to assess "from the outside." We may thus, in a sense, be witnessing the de*l-egalization* of law[226]: constraint in the conduct of war is becoming principally a matter of the identity politics of civilized nations, a self-conscious code of morality compliance which is undertaken in large part on each state's own recognizance.

(2) Back to the Future

As a result of this interiorized "moralization" of its substantive content, the law of war may be evolving back toward its origins. Modern international law has perhaps its earliest specifically legal origins in the writings of the Spanish theologian-lawyers Franciso de Vitoria (c.1492–1546) and Francisco

Suárez (1548–1617)—both of whom were notable in their time for arguments that the Spanish crown was obligated to treat recently "discovered" Native American peoples humanely.[227] Proceeding from the ancient Stoic-Christian view of mankind as a moral-legal unity anchored in natural law, they articulated a notion of international law as moral restraint that was *not* grounded in reciprocity. It was an obligation that bound the sovereign because of his status as a human being who was capable of virtue and therefore should be held morally to account.

As applied in the Americas, in fact, the law articulated by the Spanish School they are regarded as having founded was not even properly *international,* for it was set forth in an effort to constrain brutalities by the Spanish *conquistadors* in dealing with subject peoples in the New World. Both Suárez and Vitoria wrote of the duties of humanity after conquest,[228] and Vitoria described the moral challenges of the Americas lying principally in the sovereign's duties of humanity and fair dealing toward his vassals.[229] As a problem created by conquest and one that Vitoria felt could be solved by recognizing a sovereign prince's natural law obligations to care for his subjects,[230] therefore, the situation in the Americas was, properly speaking, not an "international law" but rather a "human rights" problem.[231] In a sense, it was, in an emerging legal discourse, an articulation of virtue ethics: a moral restraint upon the conduct of Christian princes precisely *because* they were Christian princes.

In fact, this virtue-ethical approach conceptually *preceded* the "international" aspects of these early articulations of international law. Spain's encounter with an emphatically different "Other" in the New World appears to have helped galvanize the development of *international* legalism of the Spanish School. The reasoning was straightforward: principles of moral conduct built on the authority of natural law that could serve to constrain the behavior of the King of Spain toward his own subjects could hardly fail also to constrain that sovereign in dealing with other monarchs.

Vitoria's extensive discussions of the ways in which sovereigns could, and could not, acquire just (i.e., legitimate) title to rule another people[232] provided the critical link. The conception of restraint upon a national sovereign let Vitoria hold the King of Spain accountable for mistreatment of New World peoples *and* underlay the conclusion sovereign states were bound, among themselves, to law-governed behaviour rooted in natural law.[233] Like Vitoria, Suárez posited a single set of universal norms governing the relations both of individuals within a state and of sovereigns toward others—most obviously, other states in a broader global community.[234] All humanity formed "a moral and political unity (as it were) enjoined by the natural precept of mutual love and mercy; a precept that applies to all, even to strangers of every nation."[235]

Similar virtue-ethical themes are prominent in the development of the international legal vision of the Dutch legal giant Hugo Grotius (1583–1645)—who is sometimes called the "father" of international law, at least by those unfamiliar with the Spanish School. It is not often understood, for instance, that the Grotian project was in some ways less a "legal" undertaking in the modern sense than a *legalized* articulation of the ancient Stoic project of teaching moral self-control—in this case to the Christian princes of early-modern Europe.

Grotius was powerfully influenced by his close family friend, the sixteenth century Dutch neo-Stoic philosopher Joest Lips (Lipsius), who brought Stoic thinking to the task of sending a message to Europe's current Christian rulers in order to instruct such "practicing statesmen" in how to act morally. The main thrust of Lipsius' work was to preach Stoic virtues and moral self-restraint to princes, to guide their conduct. This was not—until Grotius—given a particularly *legal* character, but Lipsian neo-Stoicism was virtue ethics for the prince: self-control and restraint grounded in right reason.[236] Grotius followed Lipsius in emphasizing the importance—though now as one of his most important groundings for specifically *legal* obligations—of

> the conformity of things with reason . . . in which moral goodness becomes the paramount object . . . [because] the first principles of nature commend us to right reason. [237]

Grotius' scheme for law, from which so much has since grown in Western international legal thought, thus revolved in large part around preaching "a doctrine of the limits virtue places upon expediency, even in that most bloody and desperate of activities, military conflict."[238]

In a sense, therefore, the interiorization of the modern LOAC as a sort of virtue ethics for liberal democracies under the rule of law—the moral operational code, as it were, for market states of consent even, or perhaps especially, in threatening times—thus brings international law back to its Spanish, Grotian, and even Stoic origins as a system to shape the behavior of the sovereign, even non-reciprocally, because of the *kind* of virtuous ruler he is. Through this lens, in other words, the law is about *who you are,* not what your adversary does or what particular body of codified rules declares itself most relevant.

Such a virtue-ethical vision of law could perhaps offer a way for international law to handle at least some of the challenges of the "new normal," insofar as it is a conception that is intrinsically *non*rigid. Just as observance of Buddhist precepts, for instance, is often said to differ from the Abrahamic conception in the Decalogue of divinely ordered legal commandments,[239] so virtue ethics as an approach to law is one capable of bending under stresses that might shatter a rigid *commandment* system. As it was long ago observed in the English Common Law tradition, "hard cases . . . are apt to introduce bad law."[240] Because "commandment" rules can neither bend nor easily proliferate in forms tailored to all possible circumstances, in confronting difficult or novel situations they can produce either lawless *lacunae* or new rules that poorly fit the more common run of "normal" cases.

As part of the practitioner's ongoing process of deepening awareness and moral development, however, a more virtue-ethical system is able to accommodate both one's departure from rigorous compliance in a moment of crisis or weakness and one's subsequent return to the path. Such an approach is not one of "bright-line rules." It is, instead, more a system of *standards*—just the sort of guiding but flexible understanding Judge Posner feels, in the domestic legal context, is most appropriate for issues of national security.[241] Perhaps, therefore, we should spend less time trying to fit contemporary practice into the binary judgment dichotomies to which lawyers are accustomed in domestic litigation, and more time exploring how to make the best of the bright-line-resistant, virtue-ethical system into which the law of war may be developing with regard to counterterrorist war.

From a conventional perspective, there is no doubt something troubling in such ideas, insofar as virtue-ethical international law in the modern context faces difficulties of exogenous accountability, and may be quite resistant to detailed intelligibility from the outside. The principal dynamics of such a system are *internal,* and its ethics are as much about *intentionality*—concerned, as it were, with where one's heart lies in taking action—as they are consequentialist. Ensuring specific outcomes, in other words, is arguably less important, or perhaps simply less achievable, than ensuring moral *effort* and right-mindedness in action.

A virtue-ethical reconceptualization of the LOAC would be a profound departure from traditional international legal conceptions, and would surely be perceived by some traditionalists as opening the door to hypocrisy and evasion, while yet closing the door to meaningful external oversight. Another worrisome aspect of a virtue-ethical approach to law is the degree to which it, almost by definition, would *fail* to restrain the unscrupulous. If the LOAC is increasingly becoming just the virtue ethics of civilized states, then *uncivilized* polities, as it were, would still be largely unreached by its strictures. Liberal democracies, in other words, may be the only states that could be entrusted with virtue ethics, for they may be the only ones likely actually to be constrained by it.

In fairness, of course, traditional approaches to international law *also* have great difficulty shaping the behavior of unprincipled scofflaws, so perhaps this contrast should not be overdrawn. Moreover, in the absence of effective enforcement mechanisms, traditional *commandment*-based approaches to legality actually function somewhat like virtue ethics anyway, though they generally have neither the honesty to admit this nor much ability to benefit from the conceptual and moral richness that comes from acknowledging that questions of proper conduct are not always ones usefully answerable by a binary choice between "legal" and "illegal." In truth, both traditional and virtue-ethical conceptions need—and lack—effective ways to deal with inveterate malefactors.

For all the questions that an explicitly virtue-ethical approach would doubtless raise, however, the example of the Spanish School and the Grotian project suggest that such ideas nonetheless have deep and compelling antecedents both in mankind's spiritual and philosophical traditions and in the corpus of modern Western international law. As we struggle to find ourselves a doctrinal foundation upon which to build approaches to the novelties of our troubling "new normal"—ways that will let us cope with contemporary terrorist challenges without abandoning the rule of law in its entirety—we should not too quickly dismiss the value of such ideas today.

In fact, it may be possible to glimpse the beginnings of a movement in this direction already underway, at least in U.S. circles. In its efforts to adapt soldiers to a post-cold war environment in which decentralized, low-to-medium intensity operations conducted in the midst of civilian populations have replaced cataclysmic "World War Three" scenarios, the U.S. military has for some years been exploring ways to cultivate improved self-aware moral agency among its members. Particularly in light of the failure of "nonlethal" technologies to live up to their billing in the early 1990s as near-miraculous tools with which to handle ambiguous and potentially combustible situations, it was realized that individual soldiers serving in places such as Somalia, Haiti, and Bosnia would have to be better trained to deal with battlespace ambiguity than "nuclear-age" military curricula had prepared them to be.[242]

Scenario-based training for soldiers in coping with complex situations presenting LOAC challenges has been an important part of these efforts, based upon the idea that whatever commanders and military lawyers might say in their delineation of rules of engagement (ROEs), soldiers' actions *after* the shooting starts will more commonly simply "follow those principles that repetitive or potent experiences have etched into their minds."[243] In a related development, however, there also seems to have been a much greater emphasis upon martial arts training—which, it was felt, could combine the acquisition of militarily useful skills (e.g., in close-quarters personal combat) with the cultivation of habits of mind conducive to moral restraint and self-control in conflict situations. The focus of this effort, as described by one of the creators of the U.S. Marine Corps' martial arts program, was to mold not just warriors but "*ethical* warriors." As he saw it, the aim was to give students "the capability to kill, balanced with the control and compassion to know when that's appropriate."[244]

To be sure, an earlier military attempt to integrate more explicitly moral and spiritual approaches to martial arts into the curriculum of U.S. Special Forces training—an effort that involved an aikido instructor teaching his art and meditation techniques to Green Berets—was discontinued.[245] Nevertheless, present-day U.S. military martial arts training focuses not only upon physical fitness and effective fighting techniques but also the psychophysiological discipline that facilitates self-possession and right conduct in escalation-of-force situations involving civilians in a potential combat environment—skills which are viewed as being fused together under the broad concept of military "professionalism."[246]

In this respect, therefore, one might regard the U.S. military as having come full circle, back to a strange and long-forgotten 1979 document published by the U.S. Army War College, the author of which predicted that soldiers would someday come to study martial arts "with the same ethical basis" as did the ancient Chinese warrior monks of Kung Fu legend. In this vision, future warriors would develop their "conscience . . . together with the ability to neutralize the opponent" so that their fighting techniques would never be "used as an instrument of indiscriminate war."[247] Today, perhaps, the Pentagon is starting to recognize—and, significantly, to *act* upon—Kenneth Anderson's insight that "it is honor, not law, that is the engine driving such adherence as exists to the laws of war."[248] If modern conflicts are indeed characterized by an increasing interiorization of the law of war, approaches to cultivating LOAC-compliant "reflexes" of military honor and professional rectitude may be at least as important in the future as the analytical interpositions of military operational lawyers.

III. CONCLUSION

This survey of the ways in which the international community—and in particular, the United States, the most important and influential player within it—has tried to cope with the challenges of modern counterterrorist war makes clear that the ongoing process of coming to grips with our emergent "new normal" is a complex one. It has been characterized by multiple dynamic tensions and long-running bargaining processes among key participants.

The development of responses to post-9/11 circumstances has not been a traditionally "legal" one, in the sense that it has not proceeded in a coherent way driven by doctrinal principles or authoritative articulations of the law. Participants in the global security system, in fact, have found traditional legal conceptions to be in important ways *inadequate* to the challenges of modern counterterrorism, and have been feeling their way toward new answers through complicated processes of exploration and innovation, trial and error, negotiation, and contestation.

In the United States, the government's initial answer to the inadequacies of traditional approaches to terrorism was to attempt the wholesale importation of a paradigm of absolutist war. This war paradigm was tailored to the circumstances of modern terrorism only in the sense that its proponents sought to cement in place a commanding presidential authority that, to the extent that it had sound doctrinal foundations in American law, still fitted only uncomfortably in the context of a struggle of potentially *permanent* duration against diffuse and ephemeral non-territorial irregulars moving stealthily among civilian populations both at home and abroad. This paradigm may have been a better answer to the peculiarities of the "new normal" of counterterrorism than the law enforcement paradigm it self-consciously replaced, but the unadulterated war model proved politically—and with a newly activist Supreme Court, also legally—unsustainable over the long term.

U.S. government practice over successive administrations of very different political complexions clearly demonstrates that much, though by no means all, of the "war" approach has indeed been ratified by practice, becoming part of an emerging, apparently bipartisan, counterterrorist doctrine. Intentionally or otherwise, moreover, the Supreme Court—by undertaking its *own* ambitious and unprecedented self-aggrandizing interjections into war making, and by making clear the potential for much more—has established conditions that may, in time, encourage and make possible a more serious process of congressional-executive accommodation. If we are lucky, such bargaining in the shadow of constitutional confrontation will, in time, indeed lead to the institutionalization of approaches that will allow America to cope with the "new normal" in ways sustainable over the very long term.

The *international* response to the advent of modern counterterrorism has proven less impressive and interesting, being still rather incoherent, and, in fact, perhaps also still dangerously inhibited by traditional—but now arguably obsolescent, or at least notably incomplete—assumptions about the nature of warfare. Whereas in domestic U.S. law and practice we see what may be the early stages of an emerging landscape in which elements of earlier, more doctrinally pure approaches have been hybridized and adopted, much of the international legal community remains deeply entangled in conceptions that blind it to the circumstances of our "new normal" and which may indeed risk making the law itself seem irrelevant.

The trajectory of the law of armed conflict under the pressure of modern developments suggests that it may be evolving in ways that will perhaps prove even more incompatible with traditional conceptions. It is not merely that the law will have to come to grips with conflicts lacking territorial boundaries, clear distinctions between "civilian" and "military," and a reasonable likelihood of never actually concluding; it is also that the law in this new environment is becoming both increasingly *non*reciprocal and sharply *interiorized*—and increasingly resistant to external assessment and accountability. There may be something to be said for reconceptualizing the law of armed conflict as the virtue ethics of civilized states, but from the perspective of traditional legal approaches there is something troubling and worrisome as well. The international community's struggle with the perplexities of law in the "new normal" is just beginning.

NOTES

1. *See* Benjamin Wittes, *Law and the Long War* (New York: Penguin Press, 2008).

2. *See* Jane Mayer, *The Dark Side* (New York: Anchor, 2009).

3. "U.S. Senate Select Committee on Intelligence & House Permanent Select Committee on Intelligence," *Joint Inquiry into Intelligence Community Activities Before and After the Terrorist Attacks of September 11, 2001,* S. Rept. No. 107–351, 107th Congress, 2d Sess. (December 2002) [hereinafter *Joint Inquiry Report*] at 283.

4. *Final Report of the National Commission on Terrorist Attacks Upon the United States* (New York: Norton, [undated]) [hereinafter *9/11 Commission Report*], at 111–14 & 126.

5. Mayer, *supra,* at 19 & 38.

6. *9/11 Commission Report, supra,* at 132.

7. *Joint Inquiry Report, supra,* at 283 (quoting Richard Clarke).

8. Mayer, *supra,* at 20 & 24.

9. *See,* e.g., Michael Scheuer, "A Fine Rendition," *New York Times* (March 11, 2005), at A23.

10. *Cited by* Wittes, *supra,* at 24–26.

11. Wittes, *supra,* at 40.

12. *See,* e.g., Ronald Wilson Reagan, Message to the Senate Transmitting a Protocol to the 1949 Geneva Conventions (January 29, 1987). Interestingly, President Reagan refused to submit Additional Protocol I for Senate ratification, in part because he felt it would be a setback to the cause of protecting civilians in wartime. By privileging irregular forces "even if they do not satisfy the traditional requirements to distinguish themselves from the civilian population and otherwise comply with the laws of war," his comments suggested, the proposed protocol could make things worse for

civilians. Encouraging such irregulars would "endanger civilians among whom terrorists and other irregulars attempt to conceal themselves." *Id.*, at 36.

13. Wittes, *supra*, at 29–30.

14. *See* Jack Goldsmith, *The Terror Presidency* (New York: Norton, 2009), at 36–37 (*citing* memorandum from Walter Dellinger, assistant attorney general, to Abner J. Mikva, counsel to the president, "Presidential Authority to Decline to Execute Unconstitutional Statutes" (November 2, 1994); memorandum from Walter Dellinger, assistant attorney general, to Alan J. Kreczko, special assistant to the president and legal advisor to the National Security Council, "Placing of United States Armed Forces under United Nations Operational or Tactical Control" (May 8, 1996).

15. In addition to the all-too-real attacks that had occurred, as Mayer has noted, there reportedly was also a biological attack false alarm at the White House itself, which jangled nerves and led some senior officials to worry for a time that they might have been fatally infected. After 9/11, the CIA also started reporting vast amounts of terrorism-related information directly to the president in his daily briefing. *See* Mayer, *supra*, at 4–5.

This "Threat Matrix"—the result, one suspects, of bureaucratic and political self-protection by CIA officials terrified of being accused of "missing" some hint that in fact presaged the *next* attack—made things seem even more threatening than they were, and did the president a disservice by rubbing his nose in every unsubstantiated oblique reference or vague rumor that could have indicated a possible terrorist interest in attacking the United States. This author had the privilege once of seeing an unredacted copy of one such document; it seemed to me both a basically useless and an unnecessarily inflammatory example of intelligence reporting.

16. *Quoted by* Richard A. Posner, *Not a Suicide Pact* (New York: Oxford University Press, 2006), at 158.

17. John Yoo, *War by Other Means* (New York: Atlantic Monthly Press, 2006), at 10.

18. Yoo, *supra*, at 3.

19. Mayer, *supra*, at 45.

20. Mayer, *supra*, at 46 & 62.

21. *See*, e.g., Daniel Klaidman, "Now We Know What the Battle Was About," *Newsweek* (December 18, 2008).

22. *See* Mayer, *supra*, at 66–67; *see also* Director of National Intelligence John Negroponte, letter to Dennis Hastert (May 17, 2006) (providing dates on which congressional leaders were briefed on terrorist surveillance program), *available at* <http://www.fas.org/irp/dni/dni051706.pdf>.

23. Assistant Attorney General Daniel Bryant, letter to Senator Richard Shelby (October 1, 2001) [hereinafter Bryant letter], at 6 (*quoting Lichter v. United States*, 334 U.S. 742, 782 (1948) & *Application of Yamashita*, 327 U.S. 1, 12 (1946)).

24. Bryant letter, *supra*, at 7 & 9 (emphasis added).

25. Neil A. Lewis & Eric Schmitt, "Lawyers Decided Bans on Torture Didn't Bind Bush," *New York Times* (June 8, 2004), at A1.

26. Dana Priest & R. Jeffrey Smith, "Memo Offered Justification for Use of Torture," *Washington Post* (June 8, 2004), at A1. It was reportedly suggested that defenses of necessity and self-defense could also defeat criminal liability in such instances.

27. *See* Goldsmith, *supra,* at 210.

28. Posner, *supra,* at 39. Posner does not argue this view himself, however, noting instead that "[w]e don't want the Constitution to be *just* an old piece of parchment." *Id.,* (emphasis in original). This author, however, was once told by an administration attorney in late 2002 that if *al Qaeda* combatants were discovered within the United States—say, in suburban Detroit—it would be a lawful exercise of the president's inherent constitutional power as commander in chief to attack them immediately with instruments of military force (e.g., a cruise missile or a SEAL team), just as one could in Afghanistan.

29. Yoo, *supra,* at 1432–43.

30. *See,* e.g., *Plyler v. Doe,* 457 U.S. 2020, 210–12 (1982) (citing *Shaughnessy v. Mezei,* 345 U.S. 206, 212 (1952) & *Wong Wing v. United States,* 163 U.S. 228, 238 (1896)) (discussing rights of aliens "within the territory of the United States"); *Johnson v. Eisentrager,* 339 U.S. 763, 783–85 (1950) (finding no support for idea that enemy aliens were entitled to 5th Amendment rights outside the sovereign territory of the United States); *United States v. Verdugo-Urquidez,* 494 U.S. 259, 267 & 271 (1990) (finding that 4th Amendment rights do not apply to aliens in foreign territory or international waters, and that foreign nationals only receive constitutional protections to extent that "they have come within the territory of the United States and developed substantial connections with the country").

31. *See,* e.g., *Cuban American Bar Ass'n v. Christopher,* 43 F.3d 1412, 1430 (11th Cir. 1995) (foreign nationals detained overseas "are without legal rights that are cognizable in the courts of the United States"); *Harbury v. Deutch,* 233 F.3d 596, 603–04 (D.C. Cir. 2000) (holding that aliens "not physically present in the United States, not tortured in a country in which the United States exercised *de facto* political control, and not abducted for trial in a United States court" have no 5th Amendment rights).

32. "Convention Against Torture and Other Cruel, Inhuman or Degrading Treatment or Punishment" [CAT], *available at* <http://www.hrweb.org/legal/cat.html>.

33. CAT, *supra,* at Art.2(1), Art.5(1), Art. 11, Art.12, Art.13, & Art.16(1). For that matter, while CAT's Article 3 seems to cover deportations *from* a state's jurisdiction to places where one might be tortured, the CAT did not on its face seem to cover "renditions" *between foreign jurisdictions* of captivity. *See* CAT Art.3(1).

34. *Sale v. Haitian Centers Council, Inc.,* 509 U.S. 155, 181–82 (1993).

35. *See* Convention Relating to the Status of Refugees (July 28, 1951), 189 UNTS150, 19 UST 6259, at Art.33(1).

36. *Sale,* 509 U.S., at 179–80.

37. G.A. Res. 2200A (XXI), 21 U.N. GAOR Supp. (No.16), at 52, U.N. Doc. A/6316 (1966), 999 UNTS 171, *entered into force* March 23, 1976 (hereinafter *ICCPR*).

38. *See,* e.g., *Congressional Record* (October 27, 1990), at S17491 (quoting resolution of ratification of CAT, at Part I(1)).

39. *Id.*, quoting resolution of ratification, at Part II(1)(a)(emphasis added); *Congressional Record* (April 2, 1992), at S4783 (reservations to ICCPR).

40. *Khaled A.F. Al Odah v. United States,* Case No. 02–5251 (D.C. Cir.) (Slip. Op., March 11, 2003) (emphasis added).

41. *See,* e.g., Geneva Convention to the Treatment of Prisoners of War (August 12, 1949), at Art.3(1).

42. Protocol Additional to the Geneva Conventions of 12 August 1949, and relating to the Protection of Victims of Non-International Armed Conflicts (June 7, 1977), at Art.1(1).

43. *See* Protocol Additional to the Geneva Conventions of 12 August 1949, and relating to the Protection of Victims of International Armed Conflicts (Protocol I) (June 8, 1977) [hereinafter Additional Protocol I], at Art.1(4).

44. *See* ICRC, Commentary on Article 3 of the Geneva Convention (III) Relative to the Treatment of Prisoners of War (August 12, 1949) [hereinafter *ICRC Commentary*] *available at* <http://www.icrc.org>, at 30–34.

45. *See ICRC Commentary*, *supra,* at 35–36 (discussing, *inter alia,* the existence of a "[p]arty in revolt" against a *de jure* government, "insurgents organized as a military and in possession of a part of the national territory," and insurgents who "have an organization purporting to have the characteristics of a State").

46. *See ICRC Commentary*, *supra,* at 37.

47. Protocol Additional to the Geneva Conventions of 12 August 1949, and relating to the Protection of Victims of International Armed Conflicts (Protocol I) (June 8, 1977), at Art.75(1); *see also id.*, at Art.45(3).

48. The United States was not the only country to refuse to accept the 1977 Additional Protocols, including the second one, dealing with internal conflicts. They were also not supported by Afghanistan, Iran, Israel, Malaysia, Myanmar, India, and Pakistan. *See* "Unleashing the laws of war," *The Economist* (August 15, 2009), at 53.

49. Yoo, *supra,* at 25.

50. Yoo, *supra,* at 36.

51. In 2004, the Bush administration withdrew the OLC's August 2002 guidance on harsh interrogation techniques, and subsequently issued a modified version. *See generally* Dana Priest, "CIA Puts Harsh Tactics on Hold," *Washington Post* (June 27, 2004), at A01; David Johnston & James Risen, "Aides Say Memo Backed Coercion for Qaeda Cases," *New York Times* (June 27, 2004). Much was made of the reissuance, but while the new document dealt with specific harsh techniques in more vague terms, it was not clear that the Justice Department's guidance had actually changed. *See* Douglas Jehl, "Report Warned C.I.A. on Tactics in Interrogation," *Washington Post* (November 9, 2005), at A1 & A16; *see also* Yoo, *supra,* at 169, 171, & 182–83 (criticizing replacement memorandum for having "basically the same" legal conclusions but making guidance less clear, and describing it as just an "exercise in political image-making"). *Cf.*, U.S. Department of Justice, Office of Legal Counsel, "Memorandum for John A. Rizzo, Senior Deputy General Counsel, Central Intelligence Agency" (May 10, 2005) [declassified version] (addressing permissible inter-

rogation techniques as a matter of statutory interpretation with regard to 18 U.S.C. § 2340A(a)).

52. Yoo, *supra*, from the introduction, at xii.

53. Richard W. Stevenson, "White House Says Prisoner Policy Set Humane Tone," *New York Times* (June 23, 2004), at A1.

54. Not by coincidence, the policy directive on "humane" treatment also did not apply to the CIA. *See* Eric Lichtlau, "Gonzales Says Humane-Policy Order Doesn't Bind C.I.A.," *New York Times* (January 19, 2005), at A17.

55. According to media reports, CIA interrogators seeking to elicit information about ongoing terrorist operations and planned future attacks used extremely harsh "waterboarding" techniques on two very senior *al Qaeda* prisoners an astonishing number of times. Abu Zubaida was apparently subjected to such simulated drowning 83 times in August 2002 alone, while Khalid Sheik Mohammed faced this treatment a total of 183 times. *See* Peter Finn et al., "CIA Report Calls Oversight of Early Interrogations Poor," *Washington Post* (August 25, 2009).

56. Mayer, *supra*, at 5.

57. Richard W. Stevenson, "White House Says Prisoner Policy Set Humane Tone," *New York Times* (June 23, 2004), at A1.

58. Jonathan Shaw, "The War & the Writ," *Harvard Magazine* (January-February 2009), at 24 (*quoting* Heymann).

59. Yoo, *supra*, at 8.

60. Posner, *supra*, at 6.

61. Wittes, *supra*, at 8 & 10.

62. Posner, *supra*, at 6.

63. Yoo, *supra*, at 22.

64. Philip Bobbitt, *Terror and Consent* (New York: Anchor, 2008), at 452 & 455.

65. Council of Europe, Parliamentary Assembly, Resolution 1507 (2006), "Alleged secret detentions and unlawful inter-state transfers of detainees involving Council of Europe member states" (June 27, 2006).

66. The Council's resolution specifically singled out "renditions" and the idea of an "enemy combatant"—by which it presumably meant an *unlawful* combatant—as being "previously unheard of in international law and stand[ing] contrary to the basic legal principles that prevail on our continent." *Id.* As noted earlier, however, renditions had been practiced for some years before 2001, and the idea of an unlawful combatant was inherent in the scheme set forth in the 1949 Geneva Conventions—an obvious *lacuna* that many countries sought to address with the Additional Protocols of 1977, which the United States did not ratify. (As described below, moreover, post-9/11 "renditions" undertaken by the CIA also frequently involved collusion or even outright participation by many of the very European governments whose representatives supported this resolution.)

67. *See* Lawrence Freedman, "The Transformation of Strategic Affairs," Adelphi Paper no.379 (London: IISS, 2006) (*quoted by* Bobbitt, *supra*, at 177).

68. *See* William S. Lind et al., "The Changing Face of War: Into the Fourth Generation," *Marine Corps Gazette* (October 1989), at 22 (*quoted by* Bobbitt, *supra,* at 153).

69. Rupert Smith, *The Utility of Force: The Art of War in the Modern World* (London: Allen Lane, 2005), at 26 (*quoted by* Bobbitt, *supra,* at 146–47).

70. *See* Kaija Virta, "The Way We War," *Helsinging Sanomat* (September 15, 1999) (recounting analysis by Mary Kaldor, *New and Old Wars: Organized Violence in a Global Era* (Stanford, CA: Stanford University Press, 1999)) (*quoted by* Bobbitt, *supra,* at 132).

71. Wittes, *supra,* at 12–13, 49, & 51.

72. Wittes, *supra,* at 161.

73. Wittes, *supra,* at 162.

74. In the first months of the "global war on terrorism" when *jihadist* captives began to accumulate from the campaign in Afghanistan, this author's own discussions with CIA lawyers and operations officials frequently came around to the concern that such persons might have to be held "forever." (One CIA official, in fact, joked about the need for one of his colleagues to start a detainee boarding house: we would have to keep prisoners in "Bob's basement.")

75. *Quoted by* Bobbitt, *supra,* at 178–79.

76. *See,* e.g., Bobbitt, *supra,* at 3, 9, 11–12, & 186.

77. Bobbitt, *supra,* at 81 & 185. Citing pronouncements made by both men, Bobbitt concludes that "because democracies are states of consent, every member of the society is [held by these terrorists as being] culpable for the state's actions and therefore every citizen is a legitimate target for violence." Such terrorist attacks are therefore, in a sense, an end in themselves: *al Qaeda* targets citizens "for their very existence as the constitutive participants in democracies." *Id.,* at 185.

78. *See* Bobbitt, *supra,* at 44–46, 137–38, 186, & 197.

79. Wittes, *supra,* at 54; *id.,* at 12–13 (calling for "more innovative, long-term legal approaches").

80. Yoo, *supra,* at 46–47.

81. "After the Dark Side," *The Economist* (April 25, 2009), at 40.

82. *See,* e.g., William Glaberson, "Obama Orders Halt to Prosecutions at Guantánamo ," *New York Times* (January 22, 2009); "Cross Purposes," *The Economist* (May 30, 2009), at 30; John J. Kruzel, "Obama Calls for Closing Guantánamo Detainee Facility," *AFPS* (January 22, 2009); "The Underside of War," *The Economist* (August 29, 2009), at 25, 26; "After the Dark Side," *supra; see also,* e.g., Executive Order of January 22, 2009, *available at* <www.whitehouse.gov/the_press_office/EnsuringLawfulInterrogations>.

83. *See* "U.S. Drone Strikes May Break International Law: UN," *AFP* (October 27, 2009).

84. Peter Bergen & Katherine Tiedemann, "The Drone Wars," *The New Republic* (June 3, 2009), at 22, 22–24.

85. Greg Jaffe & Karen DeYoung, "U.S. Drone Targets Two Leaders of Somali Group Allied with *al Qaeda,* Official Says," *Washington Post* (June 29, 2011).

86. *See* "The Long Arm of America," *The Economist* (September 30, 2009), at 60. President Obama also continued Bush administration policy by obtaining a waiver from the United Nations permitting him to send arms to the shaky coalition government threatened by *al Qaeda*-linked *jihadists* in Somalia—a country otherwise subjected to a U.N. arms embargo. *See* "How Different Is His Policy?" *The Economist* (July 18, 2009), at 43.

87. *See* Mark Mazetti & Scott Shane, "C.I.A. Had Plan to Assassinate Qaeda Leaders," *New York Times* (July 13, 2009).

88. *See*, e.g., "Osama bin Laden Is Dead," *CBS News* (May 1, 2011), *available at* <http://www.cbsnews.com/stories/2011/05/01/national/main20058777.shtml>.

89. *See*, e.g., Calvin Woodward, "Inside bin Laden's Lair with SEAL Team 6," *Army Times* (May 4, 2011).

90. *See*, e.g., Mark Mazetti, "U.S. Is Intensifying a Secret Campaign of Yemen Airstrikes," *New York Times* (June 8, 2001).

91. *See*, e.g., Mark Mazetti, "Drone Strike in Yemen Was Aimed at Awlaki," *New York Times* (May 6, 2001).

92. *See* David Johnston, "U.S. Says Rendition to Continue, but with More Oversight," *New York Times* (August 25, 2009).

93. Carrie Johnson and Ellen Nakashima, "White House Seeks Renewal of Surveillance Laws," *Washington Post* (September 16, 2009).

94. *Id.*

95. *See* Devlin Barrett, "Obama Administration: Toss Wiretap Lawsuit," *Associated Press* (October 31, 2009).

96. *See* "The Return of the Plumbers," *The Economist* (June 16, 2011).

97. "After the Dark Side," *supra.*

98. *See generally*, Peter Finn & Sandhya Somashekhar, "Obama Bows on Settling Detainees," *Washington Post* (June 12, 2009).

99. William Glaberson, "U.S. May Revive Guantánamo Military Courts," *New York Times* (May 2, 2009).

100. *See* Stephanie Condon, "KSM To Be Tried by Military Commission at Gitmo," *CBS News* (April 4, 2011).

101. David Johnston, "New Guidance Issues on Military Trials of Detainees," *New York Times* (June 29, 2009).

102. *See*, e.g., "Cross Purposes," *The Economist* (May 30, 2009), at 30.

103. *See*, e.g., "Better Safe than Sorry," *The Economist* (October 3, 2009), at 34, 34–35.

104. Craig Whitlock, "Admiral Says U.S. Has No Set Rules for Detaining Terrorists," *Washington Post* (June 29, 2011), at A10.

105. *See* David S. Cloud & Julian C. Barnes, "U.S. May Expand Use of Its Prison in Afghanistan," *Los Angeles Times* (March 21, 2010). In one recent instance, moreover, a prisoner was apparently held secretly on a U.S. Navy vessel on the high seas from April until early July 2011, while U.S. officials interrogated him. (He was ultimately indicted in New York, after having been secretly flown into the United States in order to bypass congressional objections to bringing terrorism suspects into the

country.) *See* Karen DeYoung, Greg Miller, & Craig Jaffe, "U.S. Indicts Somali on Terrorism Charges," *Washington Post* (July 5, 2011).

106. "Obama Spy Choice Won't Call Waterboarding Torture," *Reuters* (January 22, 2009).

107. Yoo, *supra,* at 173 (*quoting* McCain); *see also* Posner, *supra,* at 83. Furthermore, at least one Supreme Court Justice—albeit the conservative Antonin Scalia—has hinted that government officials who tortured a suspect in order to prevent something like a nuclear attack should be excused. Commenting on an episode with this plot line on the television series "24," Scalia asked: "Is any jury going to convict [the series' hero character] Jack Bauer? I don't think so." *See* "The Dark Pursuit of the Truth," *The Economist* (August 1, 2009), at 20, 20. Judge Richard Posner has similarly argued that while torture "should not be considered *legally* justified," it might yet be effectively tolerated in extreme cases as constituting "civil disobedience" *by the government* in service of a "moral duty to violate legal, including constitutional rights, when necessary to avoid catastrophic harm to the nation." Posner, *supra,* at 12 & 14; *id.,* at 85–86 & 154–55. (Posner has also argued that from a purely constitutional perspective, what even *counts* as torture may vary depending upon the gravity of the threat: "[w]hat shocks the conscience depends on circumstances. In life-and-death situations the use of even highly coercive methods of interrogation is unlikely to shock the conscience of most people, even thoughtful and humane ones." *Id.,* at 85.)

108. *See* David Johnston, "U.S. Says Rendition to Continue, but with More Oversight," *New York Times* (August 25, 2009).

109. "The Underside of War," *The Economist* (August 29, 2009), at 25.

110. Even before Holder's announcement, the specific cases in question had been reviewed by teams of career federal prosecutors, who declined to seek grand jury indictments. The earlier prosecutorial reviews, in 2008, had opted against prosecution on account of what were said to be fundamental problems with key witnesses and evidence. Holder reopened these cases based upon no more than a review by the department's office in charge of supervising professional ethics issues for practicing attorneys—an odd choice for judging the practice of professional spies, and one that smacked of political forum-shopping within a career bureaucracy, the regular organs of which had long since found these abuse cases too weak to pursue further. *See generally* Mark Mazzetti & Schott Shane, "C.I.A. Abuse Cases Detailed in Report on Detainees," *New York Times* (August 26, 2009); Anne E. Kornblut, "Obama Approves New Team to Question Terror Suspects," *Washington Post* (August 24, 2009); Jennifer Rubin, "Eric Holder's Anti-CIA Witch Hunt," *Weekly Standard* (September 7, 2009), at 7. It is also worth remembering that the United States Government *did* prosecute the perpetrators in some detainee abuse cases in which it was clear operatives had acted beyond legal authority. *See,* e.g., Sewell Chan, "Marine Sergeant to Face Court-Martial in Abuse," *Washington Post* (June 12, 2004), at A18.

111. "U.S. Justice Department to Investigate CIA Detainee Deaths" *VOA News* (July 1, 2011).

112. *See*, e.g., Wittes, *supra*, at 139 (noting that Attorney General Michael Mukasey appeared to have been of the view that waterboarding, while discontinued, was not outright impermissible).

113. "After the Dark Side," *supra*.

114. *See*, e.g., David Jackson, "Cheney: Obama Will Be a One-Term President," *USA Today* (January 18, 2011) (quoting former Vice President Dick Cheney about Obama that "I think he's learned that what we did was far more appropriate than he ever gave us credit for while he was a candidate. So I think he's learned from experience.").

115. Joseph Marguiles, "Barack Obama and Torture," letter to the editor, *The Economist* (August 15, 2009), at 13.

116. Jeffrey Rosen, "Truth or Dare," *New Republic* (May 20, 2009), at 7.

117. *Hamdi v. Rumsfeld*, 542 U.S. 507, 124 S.Ct. 2640 (2004).

118. *Hamdi, supra*, Slip. Op. No.03–6696, at 10–11.

119. *Rasul v. Bush*, 542 U.S. 466 (2004).

120. Wittes, *supra*, at 107.

121. Wittes, *supra*, at 106–07.

122. Yoo, *supra*, at 130 & 157.

123. *See* Kerrita McClaughlyn, "The Rights of Enemy Combatants," *Washington Lawyer* (November 2004), at 21 (discussing issue, and quoting Yoo).

124. The Bush administration apparently won a judge's agreement in the prosecution of U.S. citizen John Walker Lindh, for instance, that the Geneva Conventions did not apply to *al Qaeda* or its Taliban allies. *See*, e.g., Yoo, *supra*, at 133 (discussing case). The administration also persuaded the Foreign Intelligence Surveillance Court of Review to approve new "minimization procedures" for the handling of FISA information, to reaffirm that the president *does* have inherent constitutional authority to conduct warrantless electronic surveillance for foreign intelligence purposes, and to depart from a previous lower court case limiting such constitutional authority to cases in which the "primary" purpose of surveillance is intelligence gathering. *See In re: Sealed Case No. 02–001*, United States Foreign Intelligence Surveillance Court of Review (November 18, 2002), Slip. Op., at 13–14, 18, 27, 32–35, 48 & 56.

125. Posner, *supra*, at 9.

126. Posner, *supra*, at 10–11; *id.*, at 40 (stressing "the *dynamic* character of constitutional law—the fact that the scope of a constitutional right changes as the relative weights of liberty and safety change") (emphasis in original).

127. Posner, *supra*, at 31 & 158.

128. Posner, *supra*, at 44.

129. *Hamdi, supra*, Slip op., at 26.

130. *Boumediene v. Bush*, No. 06–1195 (June 12, 2008).

131. *See Hamdan, supra*, at 67–68.

132. Yoo, *supra*, at 131.

133. *See*, e.g., Yoo, *supra*, at 130–31.

134. Posner, *supra*, at 60; *id.*, at 64–65.

135. *Rasul, supra*, No.03–334, Slip op., at 17; *id.*, at 7–8.

136. Wittes, *supra,* at 15.

137. *See generally* Wittes, *supra,* at 66–69 & 139–48. In addition to setting up a more elaborate statutory scheme for military commissions, the MCA also narrowly defined the "grave breaches" of Geneva's Common Article 3 that would be subject to prosecution as war crimes under U.S. law, preserving as much flexibility as possible for the Executive Branch in light of *Hamdan*'s decision that Article 3 applied to *al Qaeda* and other unlawful combatant prisoners.

138. Christopher A. Ford, "War Powers as We Live Them: Congressional-Executive Bargaining Under the Shadow of the War Powers Resolution," *Journal of Law and Politics,* vol. xi, no.4 (Fall 1995), at 609, 619–20.

139. *See,* e.g., Ford, *supra,* at 707 ("The very undesirability of strict compliance with [the WPR's] terms and the contentiousness of its validity help establish the boundaries of war powers policy debate, and provide both sides with powerful incentives to avoid a formal constitutional showdown. At the same time, the ambiguity of its [the Resolution's] ability to self-execute is exactly what *permits* this debate by leaving conceptual space in which the statute's commands neither obviously apply nor fail to do so.")

140. Yoo, *supra,* at 130 & 237–38.

141. Wittes, *supra,* at 109.

142. Wittes, *supra,* at 15 & 109.

143. Yoo, *supra,* from the introduction at xi, & at 237–38.

144. *See,* e.g., Posner, *supra,* at 9–10, 35, & 37.

145. Posner, *supra,* at 150.

146. Wittes, *supra,* at 121.

147. *See* Wittes, *supra,* at 145 (comparing statutory remedies favorably to judicial case law as a means for handling counterterrorism challenges); Posner, *supra,* at 21 (same). In Wittes' characterization, such improvisational flexibility is critical in this area because terrorism law exists on a slippery slope—but one the slipperiness of which runs in two opposite directions. In counterterrorism law, there are "two distinct bottoms" one must avoid: "a government capable of torture with impunity, the very essence of tyranny," and "a government incapacitated from expeditiously taking those steps necessary to protect the public from a catastrophic attack." Wittes, *supra,* at 4.

148. Yoo, *supra,* at 155.

149. *See* Wittes, *supra,* at 7–8, 10, 13–14, & 48.

150. *See,* e.g., the discussion in Wittes, *supra,* at 245–46.

151. *See,* e.g., "Court Sides with Government in Detainee Photo Case," *Associated Press* (November 30, 2009).

152. Geneva Convention (I) for the Amelioration of the Condition of the Wounded and Sick in Armed Forces in the Field (12 August 1949), at Art.2.

153. Geneva Convention (III) relative to the Treatment of Prisoners of War (12 August 1949), at Art.4.

154. Geneva Convention (IV) relative to the Protection of Civilian Persons in Time of War (12 August 1949).

155. *See,* e.g., Geneva Convention (II) for the Amelioration of the Condition of Wounded, Sick and Shipwrecked Members of Armed Forces at Sea (12 August 1949), at Art.3.

156. Additional Protocol I, *supra,* at Art.1(4).

157. Protocol Additional to the Geneva Conventions of 12 August 1949, and relating to the Protection of Victims of Non-International Armed Conflicts (Protocol II) (June 8, 1977), at Art.1(1).

158. *See,* e.g., David Rivkin & Lee A. Casey, "Lawfare," *Wall Street Journal* (February 23, 2007).

159. Additional Protocol I, *supra,* at Art.1(4).

160. *Id.,* at Art.44(3) & (7) (emphasis added).

161. Moshe Halbertal, "The Goldstone Illusion," *New Republic* (November 18, 2009), at 22.

162. *See,* e.g., Charter of the Islamic Resistance (Hamas) (1988), *available at* <http://middleeast.about.com/od/palestinepalestinians/a/me080106b.htm>.

163. Yoo, *supra,* from the introduction, at xii.

164. Yoo, *supra,* at 67.

165. Joby Warrick & Ben Pershing, "CIA Had Program to Kill Al-Qaeda Leaders," *Washington Post* (July 14, 2009) (quoting unnamed U.S. intelligence official).

166. *See* Siobhan Gorman, "CIA Had Secret Al Qaeda Plan," *Wall Street Journal* (July 13, 2009. This plan to use human killers, however, reportedly never actually became operational. *See generally,* e.g., Pamela Hess & Adam Goldman, "AP Source: Tenet Canceled Secret CIA Hit Teams" (July 15, 2006); Carrie Johnson & Joby Warrick, "Bush Anti-Terror Policies Get Reluctant Revisit," *Washington Post* (July 13, 2009).

167. International Court of Justice, "Legal Consequences of the Construction of a Wall in the Occupied Palestinian Territory" (July 9, 2004), at Paragraph 139.

168. *See* U.N. Security Council, S/RES/1368 (September 12, 2001); U.N. Security Council, S/RES/1373 (September 28, 2001).

169. *See* Mary Ellen O'Connell, "Defining Armed Conflict," *Journal of Conflict & Security Law,* vol.13, no.3, at 393–400.

170. U.N. Fact Finding Mission on the Gaza Conflict, "Human Rights in Palestine and Other Occupied Arab Territories," A/HRC/12/48 (September 15, 2009) [hereinafter Goldstone Report].

171. According to the Israeli human rights organization B'Tselem, only some 1,387 persons were killed in Gaza, in a ratio of about one Hamas militant to every three civilians. Given that, as Moshe Halbertal calculates, the ratio of militants to the general population of the Gaza Strip may have been something like 1 to 150, one wonders how Israel could possibly have *failed* in its supposed objective of indiscriminately killing civilians by actually harming so few and by (accidentally?) hitting such a high proportion of Hamas fighters. *See* Halbertal, *supra,* at 26.

172. *See,* e.g., "Israel in the Dock," *The Economist* (September 19, 2009), at 57, 57.

173. Though Goldstone has subsequently recanted some of his report's most important conclusions—conceding publicly that "[i]f I had known then what I know now, the Goldstone Report would have been a different document"—he still admits this much. As he put it in April 2011, "[t]he allegations of intentionality by Israel were based on the deaths of and injuries to civilians in situations where our fact-finding mission had no evidence on which to draw any other reasonable conclusion." Richard J. Goldstone, "Reconsidering the Goldstone Report on Israel and War Crimes," *Washington Post* (April 1, 2011).

174. *See* Goldstone Report, *supra,* at 21, Paragraph 61; *id.,* at 324–28, ¶ 1174–88.

175. This does not mean, of course, that the report did not recount some specific incidents—albeit ones not particularly indicative of general objectives—of troubling actions by some Israeli forces. As even Goldstone's thoughtful critics have conceded, such incidents, some of which tragically occur in any war, deserve investigation. *See, e.g.,* Halbertal, *supra,* at 27.

176. Goldstone Report, *supra,* at 147, at ¶ 480–81.

177. *Id.*

178. *See* Halbertal, *supra,* at 23.

179. *See* Goldstone Report, *supra,* at 12, ¶ 34, at 126–277, ¶ 412–15.

180. Halbertal, *supra,* at 23.

181. Goldstone Report, *supra,* at 21, ¶ 62.

182. Goldstone Report, *supra,* at 324, ¶ 1175.

183. Goldstone Report, *supra,* at 329–31, ¶ 1189–95.

184. Goldstone Report, *supra,* at 329–31, ¶ 1189–95 (emphasis added).

185. Bobbitt, *supra,* at 306.

186. *See* Bobbitt, *supra,* at 138, 181, & 435.

187. *See* Note by the Secretary-General, A/59/565 (December 2, 2004) [hereinafter Panel Report], at ¶ 189–92.

188. Panel Report, *supra,* at ¶ 190.

189. *Id.*

190. Panel Report, *supra,* at ¶ 191.

191. *See, e.g.,* Ruth Wedgwood, in "Defending and Advancing Freedom: A Symposium," *Commentary* 120, no.4 (November 2005), at 40 (*quoted by* Bobbitt, *supra,* at 435).

192. *See* Posner *supra,* at 1 ("Like any brittle thing, a Constitution that will not bend will break.").

193. U.N. Security Council, S/RES/1368 (September 12, 2001).

194. U.N. Security Council, S/RES/1373 (September 28, 2001). Resolution 1373 also acted in an unprecedented quasi-"legislative" way by using the Security Council's power under Chapter VII of the U.N. Charter to *require* all states to prohibit terrorist financing—thus setting an innovative international legal precedent that was subsequently also used vis-à-vis WMD trafficking. *See* U.N. Security Council, S/RES/1540 (April 28, 2004).

195. *See, e.g.,* North Atlantic Treaty Organization, "NATO Update" (October 2, 2001), *available at* <http://www.nato.int/docu/update/2001/1001/e1002a.htm>.

196. Bobbitt, *supra,* at 454.

197. In this respect, in fact, John Yoo has argued that U.S. practice should matter the *most* in assessing contemporary developments in the law of war. As the country with the most powerful military machine on the planet, and still the only country with truly global interests and reach, he contends, the United States should be considered the principal shaper of customary international practice in these regards. *See* Yoo, *supra,* at 37.

198. Dan Bilefsky, "Report Faults Europe in C.I.A. Detainee 'Web,'" *New York Times* (June 8, 2006), at A8.

199. Dan Bilefsky, "European Inquiry Says C.I.A. Flew 1,000 Flights in Secret," *International Herald Tribune* (April 27, 2006), at A12; ["EU Endorses Damning Report on CIA," *BBC News* (February 14, 2007).

200. *See* Council of Europe, Parliamentary Assembly, Resolution 1507 (2006), "Alleged Secret Detentions and Unlawful Inter-State Transfers of Detainees Involving Council of Europe Member States" (June 27, 2006) [hereinafter Council of Europe Report] at Paragraph 9–10 & 14.

201. Bilefsky, "European Inquiry Says C.I.A. Flew 1,000 Flights in Secret," *supra.*

202. *See* Council of Europe Report, *supra,* at Paragraph 11; "EU Endorses Damning Report on CIA," *supra.*

203. Bilefsky, "European Inquiry Says C.I.A. Flew 1,000 Flights in Secret," *supra;* "Report Rendered," *The Economist* (June 10, 2006), at 49.

204. Nat Hantoff, "Ending Torture Outsourcing," *Washington Times* (April 11, 2005), at 19.

205. Dana Priest, "Italy Knew About Plan To Grab Suspect," *Washington Post* (June 30, 2005), at A1, A18.

206. Stephen Grey & Elisabetta Povoledo, "2 Italians Seized in '03 Kidnapping of Imam in Milan," *New York Times* (July 6, 2006), at A1 & A6.

207. *See,* e.g., "Extraction," *The Economist* (July 11, 2009), at 56; "The Dark Pursuit of the Truth," *The Economist* (August 1, 2009), at 20, 21.

208. *See* "In Full: Milliband Rendition Statement," *BBC News* (February 21, 2008).

209. Priest, "Italy Knew About Plan To Grab Suspect," *supra.*

210. Dana Priest, "Debate Is Growing Within Agency About Legality and Morality of Overseas System Set Up After 9/11," *Washington Post* (November 2, 2005), at A1; Peter Finn et al., "CIA Report Calls Oversight of Early Interrogations Poor," *Washington Post* (August 25, 2009); Dana Priest, "CIA Holds Terror Suspects in Secret Prisons," *Washington Post* (November 2, 2005). Media reports also suggested that Diego Garcia had for a time also been used as a secret CIA detention site, though British officials denied it. *See* Dana Priest & Barton Gellman, "U.S. Decries Abuse but Defends Interrogations," *Washington Post* (December 26, 2002), at A01. In September 2006, President Bush announced the existence of secret detention centers, though he did not reveal where they were or had been. *See* Nedra Pickler, "Bush Acknowledges Secret CIA Prisons," *Associated Press* (September 6, 2007);

R. Jeffrey Smith & Michael Fletcher, "Bush Says Detainees Will Be Tried," *Washington Post* (September 7, 2006), at A01.

211. It does not tell us much that these governments' alleged collaboration with U.S. policy occurred in secret. The fact that in at least one case—an Italian magistrate's arrest of the two senior Italian officials involved—such collaboration has raised *domestic* legal questions does not necessarily speak to the question of the status of this state practice vis-à-vis *international* law. The fact it was foreseeable that such activities would be *politically* combustible if revealed, moreover—and that they might also have elicited retaliation from terrorists—provided ample reason for secrecy unrelated to any issue of assumed international legality or illegality.

212. In Iraq, foreign *al Qaeda* fighters seem to have hurt popular support for their war against the Americans by *themselves* slaughtering innocent Iraqis in bombing attacks—as a result of which terrorist collocation with civilians became an operational liability as homegrown militias turned against "the Arabs" in disgust and allied themselves with U.S. forces. In Afghanistan, by contrast, the Taliban has engaged in less wholesale civilian butchery, so its fighters' collocation with civilians remains politically useful: Coalition air strikes that cause civilian casualties have become a point of purported grievance on the part of the government of Hamid Karzai and a rallying cry for anti-American agitation at home and abroad.

213. U.S. Army, *Operational Law Handbook* (Charlottesville, Virginia: Judge Advocate General's Legal Center and School, 2007), from the Preface.

214. *See,* e.g., Lt. Col. H. Wayne Elliott, "Military Lawyers Go to War," *Army* (April 1993), at I–47, I–48.

215. Esther Schrader, "War, on Advice of Counsel," *Los Angeles Times* (February 15, 2002), at 1; *see also,* Steven Keeva, "Lawyers in the War Room," *ABA Journal* (December 1991), at 52.

216. *See* Royal Air Force, Directorate of Legal Services website (October 8, 2008), *available at* <http://www.raf.mod.uk/legalservices/>.

217. *See* Israeli Defense Forces, Military Advocate General's Corps website (undated), <http://www.law.idf.il/589-en/Patzar.aspx>.

218. *See Operational Law Handbook, supra,* at Chapters 1, 3, 5, & 17.

219. Halbertal, *supra,* at 25.

220. *Id.*

221. *See* "U.S. Drone Strikes May Break International Law: UN," *AFP* (October 27, 2009).

222. Paul Mcleary, Sharon Weinberger, & Angus Batey, "Fly and Smite," *Aviation Week & Space Technology* (July/August 2011), at 40, 42.

223. *See,* e.g., Greg Miller, "Increased Drone Strikes in Pakistan Killing Few High-value Militants," *Washington Post* (February 21, 2011).

224. *See,* e.g., David S. Cloud, "Anatomy of a Tragic Error," *The Week* (April 29, 2011).

225. *See,* e.g., Miller, *supra.*

226. To some extent, it might be that a kind of delegalization is already underway. It is sometimes overlooked the degree to which even many criticisms of Bush-era

policies were not specifically *legal* in character. Instead, they often tended to be consequentialist—focusing upon instrumental and political considerations such as the worry that detention and interrogation policies were creating a *political* backlash overseas and otherwise harming America's image. The bitter critique of Bush policy offered by liberal eminence Arthur Schlesinger, Jr., for instance, focused less on legality *per se* than upon reputational harm: he attacked Bush for doing terrible "damage to the American reputation in the world." Quoted in Mayer, *supra,* at 8. In another example, Senator John McCain's compelling public and legislative opposition to harsh CIA interrogation techniques often stressed not their legal impropriety but instead the effect of such revelations "on America's image in the world." The *image* of Americans using torture, he said, "is killing us around the world." *See* Dana Priest & Robin Wright, "Cheney Fights for Detainee Policy," *Washington Post* (November 7, 2005), at A1 & A10; Carrie Johnson & Joby Warrick, "Bush Anti-Terror Policies Get Reluctant Revisit," *Washington Post* (July 13, 2009). Even the Pentagon worried about such things. When Defense Department officials issued new guidance for interrogations in the U.S. Army Field Manual of 2006, senior officials explained it to the press not in *legal* terms but in *political* terms: "you have to look at what you lose diplomatically." Eric Schmitt, "Pentagon Rethinking Manual with Interrogation Methods," *New York Times* (June 14, 2006), at A19.

Indeed, such a focus upon political or other *consequences* apparently prevailed even among government lawyers—who might have been expected to put *legal* analysis first. Uniformed military lawyers reportedly resisted President Bush's determination that *al Qaeda* and Taliban prisoners fell outside the Geneva Conventions principally on consequentialist grounds related to reciprocity—worrying that such a ruling might make future adversaries more likely to abuse U.S. servicemen. *See* Yoo, *supra,* at 34–35; Neil A. Lewis, "Military's Opposition to Harsh Interrogation Is Outlined," *New York Times* (July 28, 2005), at A21. Even U.S. State Department attorneys—presumably experts on international law—were said to have based their opposition to OLC legal theories about Taliban-era Afghanistan being a failed state less on legal analyses debunking the Justice Department's views than on *consequentialist* arguments about the parade of horrible results that might flow from Afghanistan's disappearance from a web of international agreements unrelated to terrorism. *See* Yoo, *supra,* at 26–29, 34 & 39.

227. *See generally,* e.g., Mark Weston Janis, "Religion and International Law," *ASIL Insights* (November 2002); Sanderson Beck, "Vitoria and Suárez," *available at* <http://san.beck.org/GPJ13-InternationalLaw.html#1>.

228. *See,* e.g., James Brown Scott, *Francisco Vitoria and His Law of Nations* (Oxford: Clarendon Press, 1934), at 77–78 (discussing the Dominican friar Bartolomé de las Casas).

229. Scott, *supra,* at 80.

230. Quoted in Scott, *supra,* at 80–81.

231. *Cf.* Scott, *supra,* at 98 (noting that "we may not suppose that he [Vitoria] had in mind the creation of the law of nations").

232. *See* Franciscus de Victoria, *On the Indians Recently Discovered* (John Pawley Bate, trans.) [hereinafter Vitoria, *On the Indians*], § I, at xi (reprinted in Scott, *supra,* at Appendix A), § I, at vi–xiv, § II, at xvi–xxxiv; *see also generally,* Scott, *supra,* at 116–36.

233. Judge Rosalyn Higgins's speech on the occasion of the presentation of the Francisco de Vitoria Medal to the International Court of Justice (April 5, 2006).

234. *See* Sergio Villa, "The Spanish School of the New Law of Nations", in *International Review of the Red Cross,* no.290 (September-October 1992).

235. Francisco Suárez, *On Laws,* bk.II, ch.XIX, § 9, in *Selections from Three Works of Francisco Suárez, S.J.* (Gwladys L. Williams, Ammi Brown, & John Waldron, eds.) (Oxford: Clarendon Press, 1944), at 348.

236. *See generally,* Christopher A. Ford, "Preaching Propriety to Princes: Grotius, Lipsius, and Neo-Stoic International Law," *Case Western Reserve Journal of International Law,* vol.28, no.2 (Spring 1996), at 313, 321–22, 327–29, & 336.

237. Hugo Grotius, *De Jure Belli ac Pacis Libri Tres* (Francis W. Kelsey trans. 1925), Paragraph 2, at 51 (*quoted by* Ford, "Neo-Stoic International Law," *supra,* at 343).

238. Ford, "Neo-Stoic International Law," *supra,* at 357. (Grotius even believed the prince should often show "moderation" by refraining from doing even what the law permitted. *Id.,* at 357–58.)

The Grotian-Stoic conception of restraint even in the conduct of war actually precedes the modern concept of a "civilian"—a type of person that it is one of the cardinal aims of modern LOAC rules to protect in time of conflict—which only began to develop in the early modern period. When used to mean a noncombatant person, the word "civilian" is itself, in English usage, a product only of the mid-nineteenth century. *See generally,* Leo Braudy, *From Chivalry to Terrorism: War and the Changing Nature of Masculinity* (New York: Random House, 2005), at 128–29 & 459.

239. *Compare,* e.g., David Loy, *The Great Awakening: A Buddhist Social Theory* (Boston: Wisdom Press, 2003), at 37 & 131 (noting that Buddhist precepts are not legal *commandments* to be followed rigidly and automatically, but standards valuable for their effect in guiding and encouraging "personal development and spiritual progress") *with* The Bible, Exodus 20:3–17 (setting forth commandments) and *id.,* Deuteronomy 10:4 & Exodus 34:28 (discussing the "Ten Commandments").

240. *Winterbottom v. Wright* (1842) 10 M&W 109, (1842) 152 ER 402.

241. In his view, "cases involving a clash between liberty and safety cannot yet be governed by rules." *Id.,* at 34. For Posner's discussion of the distinction between *standards* and *rules, see* Posner, *supra,* at 33–34.

242. Joseph R. Svinth, "Martial Arts Meets the New Age: Combatives in the Early Twenty-First Century American Military," in *Martial Arts in the Modern World* (Thomas A. Green & Joseph R. Svinth, eds.) (Westport, CT: Praeger, 2003), at 262, 265.

243. Maj. Mark S. Martins, "Rules of Engagement for Land Forces: A Matter of Training, Not Lawyering," *Military Law Review,* vol. 143 (Winter 1994), at 1, 4.

244. Andrea Stone, "Martial Arts To Create New Breed of Marines," *USA Today* (March 8, 2001) (*quoting* Lt. Col. George Bristol, USMC) (emphasis added). In this

sense, the U.S. Marines might seem to be trying to replicate some aspects of the psychology observed by the historian François Billaçois in seventeenth century French duelists, or in the culture of the stereotypical medieval Japanese samurai, both of whom were said to be able to display "aggression without hostility." *See* Braudy, *supra*, at 156. Without also cultivating "the mental and character discipline to regulate and control" the violent physical techniques involved, the Marines' Bristol averred, "you basically produce a thug." Stone, *supra*. This distinction is presumably very important from the perspective of LOAC compliance.

245. *See*, e.g., Richard Strozzi Heckler, *In Search of the Warrior Spirit* (Berkeley: North Atlantic Books, 1992).

246. *See*, e.g., Cpl. Zachary J. Nola, "Deployed Marines Learning Professionalism Through MCMAP [Marine Corps Martial Arts Program]" (January 1, 2010), *available at* <http://www.marines.mil/unit/iimef/2ndmeb/Pages/DeployedMarinesLearningProfessionalismthroughMCMAP.aspx>.

247. Jim Channon, *The First Earth Battalion: Ideas and Ideals for Soldiers Everywhere* (Carlisle, PA: U.S. Army War College, 1979) (quoted by Svinth, *supra*, at 264).

248. David Rieff, "The Humanitarian Illusion," *The New Republic* (March 16, 1998) (quoting Kenneth Anderson).

Chapter 10

Some Conclusions and Thoughts for the Future

Amichai Cohen

The events of September 11, 2001, together with the consequent realization of just how acutely the world confronts global terrorism, generated ripples of change in all liberal democracies. No government could ignore the dangers posed by terrorism; no society could continue to behave as though the threat of terrorist activities did not exist. The changes that followed the realization that terrorism forms part of life were evident in politics, society, and culture. As the papers in this volume describe, many of these changes affected the constitutional legal regime of decision making in matters relating to national security.

In these concluding pages, I offer a framework for the analysis of those changes. It builds on the results and conclusion of studies presented in this volume, and suggests some of the challenges likely to intrigue scholars in the near future.

I. COUNTERTERRORISM MEASURES AND NATIONAL SECURITY

One conclusion shared by almost all contributors to this volume is that counterterror measures cannot be analyzed in a void. Their adoption necessarily affects entire areas of life that are not directly concerned with the measure itself. Hence, as John Shenefield has shown, for example, the adoption of counterterror measures deeply affected the way in which the Foreign Intelligence Surveillance (FISA) mechanism (allowing supervised use of electronic surveillance) was used within the United States in general. This effect was evident in other areas of law: Amichai Cohen shows how decisions of courts in counterterror measures were affected by the impact of these decisions on other areas of law. Steven David's analysis cautions that the use of the policy of targeted killings of terrorist can easily turn into a general policy of solving political differences by using lethal force. Finally, as Christopher Ford relates, the emerging doctrine of counterterrorism required the Congress and the Executive branches reconsider their powers vis-à-vis each other, and to constitute an arrangement that would enable both to act.

Hence, it seems clear that there is no "counterterrorism" doctrine that can be viewed in isolation, detached from its effects on other spheres of political and legal action. Papers in this volume focused on the relationship between counterterrorism and the general framework of national security decision making.

II. THE MEANING OF NATIONAL SECURITY

"National security" has always been a notoriously imprecise term, meaning different things to different people.[1] National security can be defined along a spectrum, beginning with a broad definition and ending with a narrow one.

In its broadest definition it extends to threats to the quality of life emanating from state and non-state actors alike.[2] These include: threats to the environment; global climate change; disease pandemics; transboundary pollution; drug trafficking; and computer viruses and hacking. Since problems of that scale defy solution at the national level, even in the most powerful of states, many observers advocate that old concepts of "national security" be replaced by a multilayered network of "international security" paradigms, more in tune with the realities of increased interdependence in world affairs.[3]

It would have been foolish to try and cover within the covers of a single volume the entire spectrum of matters relating to national security in this broadest definition. Hence, we deliberately limited our discussions to the narrower sense of national security, when it refers primarily to the circumstances actually or potentially warranting the state's exercise of military force. Even its narrowest definition, of course, national security embraces an exceptionally wide variety of interests, needs and priorities. This volume focuses on the connections between these interests and law, as examined through the prism of states' struggle with irregular non-state actors—specifically, terrorist organizations.

III. WHAT CONSTITUTES NATIONAL SECURITY LAW?[4]

The waxing or waning salience of national security, in its narrow sense, affects law in two major ways. One is in its effect upon the division of powers between the different branches of government—or government and international organizations—responsible for decision making in matters of national security and the use of force. (This is *the internal law of national security.*) The second sense in which national security affects legal matters concerns how national security is balanced against human rights. (One might call this *the external law of national security.*)

A. Internal National Security Law

The internal law of national security encompasses four basic dimensions, which may be referred to as the hierarchical, the functional, the spatial, and the temporal.

Briefly summarized, the *hierarchical* dimension is concerned with the following questions:

- What is the constitutionally ordained chain of national command with respect to national security issues?
- Does there exist a decision-making hierarchy within the civilian government?
- Which minister or official is designated responsible for transmitting government instructions to the security agencies?

Functional questions include:

- Which agencies of government are responsible, individually or collectively, for national security activities other than the transmission of government instructions to the military (such as officially declaring the nation to be at war, or in a situation that warrants the resort to emergency decrees and/or the imposition of martial law)?
- Which mechanisms and measures are available to the legislature and judiciary for the purposes of monitoring executive decisions and the oversight of executive action in matters relevant to national security?
- What provisions, if any, exist for resolving differences of opinion within and between branches of government over national security issues?

Spatial questions ask:

- To what extent has the content and tone of the national security legal framework been affected by territorial change, such as the geographical expansion or contraction of areas over which state agencies, and especially the military, exercise control?
- Is the same legal framework applied to all regions under state control, or do there exist, concomitantly, separate legal "regimes," one operative in the core area of the homeland and another in regions under military administration?
- Do there exist legal constraints on the geographical deployment of the armed forces, either within the state's borders or beyond then?

Temporal questions ask:

- What provisions (if any) does the legal framework make for state-sponsored violations of liberal democratic principles at moments of extreme threat to the survival of the constitutional order and/or the state?
- Are legal controls placed on the exercise of "emergency powers" and their extension?
- Do provisions exist to ensure the speedy restoration of whatever civil liberties may have been suspended during the state of emergency?

In many liberal democracies there have always been heated discussions regarding the appropriate balance in all of these areas. Each country, in the course of its history, has arrived at different solutions regarding the actual balance in each area, and these balances are periodically adjusted or changed with changing circumstances. Though there are similarities between states in this regards, it is hard to identity any hard and fast rules. It seems that during the second half of the twentieth century most liberal democracies attained some form of civilian control over the military (the issue lying at the heart of the *hierarchical* dimension), witnessed some involvement of parliaments in decisions of national security (a primary concern of the *functional* dimension), placed limitations on the use of military powers at home (the *spatial* dimension), and set up a specific regime of emergency powers for times of emergencies (the *temporal* dimension).

B. External national security law

Law also deals with the manner in which national security is balanced against other considerations. These include human rights, environmental issues, zoning requirements, etc. In most liberal democracies, national security considerations have traditionally overcome other considerations. However, in the second half of the 20th century this situation too has been changing. National courts, and especially international tribunals, were willing to collide with governments in efforts to protect human rights even in cases where this required the government to be flexible in addressing national security requirements.

C. International Law and National Security

Further developments were apparent in the area of international law. After decades of stagnation, principally caused by the East-West divide of the Cold War, which stalled development in the area of international cooperation in national security matters, the last decade of the twentieth century witnessed a massive realignment. The most important symptom was the creation and strengthening of various mechanisms designed to impose international and humanitarian obligations on states. There included the strengthening of international cooperation in the use of force (as visible in the First Gulf War in 1991, the NATO campaign against Serbia in 1999) and the creation of various international tribunals, which attributed individual criminal liability against violators of international obligations (e.g., the International Criminal Tribunal for Former Yugoslavia, the International Criminal Tribunal for Rwanda, the Special Court for Sierra Leone, and the International Criminal Court). As a result, the importance of the international law of armed conflicts, and of international human rights norms, increased.

IV. COUNTERTERRORISM AND CHANGES IN NATIONAL SECURITY LAW

Various chapters in this book show how modern campaigns against terrorism have changed many of the attributes of the national security legal regime, both internal and external. In the *internal* sphere, within the United States, the change from a paradigm of law enforcement to one of war making discussed by Christopher Ford involved institutional changes too. The Executive Branch gained more power, and, at least initially, tried to evade congressional control and oversight. Amichai Cohen shows how courts tried to maintain some of their authority in the face of so assertive an executive, and to rebalance the power of different branches. Thus the constitutional *functional* paradigm has changed. Regarding the *spatial* issues, modern democracies' wars against terrorism included some use of armed forces in domestic areas, a clear break with tradition, disputes over just what laws applied in semi-foreign jurisdictions such as Guantánamo Bay, and the use of new methods of war abroad, such as the "targeted killings" discussed by Steven David.

Some of the most important changes have concerned the *temporal* dimension of national security law. Some states declared themselves to be in some kind of emergency regime, for instance—either an actual state of emergency or a "war" triggering special wartime authorities—and passed or invoked laws that allowed governments to take radical measures in the counterterror campaign.

These changes in law were also reflected in the *external* aspect of national security. All over the world, states curtailed the rights of citizens and noncitizens alike. John Shenefield's discussion of the FISA is but one example of this process, showing how governments sought to alter the delicate balance between concern for national security and consideration for human rights. As Christopher Ford depicts, after a while, some of the new measures adopted in this regard (such as harsh interrogation techniques) were abandoned, but others remained part of the legal fabric of liberal democracies—albeit often with adjustments (e.g., the imposition of judicial *habeas corpus* review for detentions, the use of modified military commissions to try terrorist suspects, or the "domestication" of presidential electronic surveillance authority in a modified form pursuant to congressional enactment).

It is important to note that the changes in domestic law and politics were not detached from those taking place in international law. First, it became clear that international law and international cooperation act in dual roles. On the one hand, international human rights laws have traditionally imposed external obligations on states that have pushed in directions counter to some of the measures which states have sought to use in their "war on terrorism." On the other hand, however, it seems that international law has also been used here by all sides as a political tool in a much larger clash over legitimacy:

- Most states—though not uniformly, as Juan Gómez reminds us—have tended to take the position that their struggles against terrorists enabled them to act under the laws of armed conflict (i.e., in a "war" mode) and not under the obligations of human rights law (i.e., in a "law enforcement" mode). In this way, they were able to use international law in order to *lessen* their obligations. Instead of the strict limitations imposed by domestic and international human rights requirements, states declared that they were only limited by the flexible and lenient requirements of the laws of armed conflict.
- As Jeremy Rabkin and Elizabeth Samson point out, invocations of international legal norms and the conduct of international legal inquiries have sometimes been used—or been seen to be used—as tools in broader struggles over the objectives (e.g., decolonization or Palestinian statehood) for which combatants have also engaged in hostilities. (As Ariel Zemach points out, moreover, not all efforts to use legal norms in such struggles have the effect intended by their advocates.)
- The United Nations Security Council became an important factor in the "war on terror," helping states to legitimize steps they wished to take to impose limitations on individuals and organizations.

This apparent change in the role of international law required actors to revise some of their previously held beliefs and concepts of international law. International law is not always a limiting factor on the behavior of states, but rather can sometimes be a legitimizing and empowering mechanism for one side or the other.

All these changes have created a chaotic state of law regarding counterterrorism and national security. The court cases, some of them detailed in Amichai Cohen's discussion, tell only part of the story. In almost every liberal democracy there are deliberations and confusion regarding the proper limits to counterterror measures. This area of national security law, in other words, remains very much a work in progress. Some of the most pertinent current questions are as follows below.

On the *internal* issues of national security:

- Traditionally, it was the Executive Branch that had the power of initiative and default control in armed conflict. This makes sense in large-scale wars, which are either fought abroad or in such desperate domestic circumstances of invasion that there is little reason not to privilege executive efficiency. The "war against terrorism," however, even if it is a war, is a new kind of war. It is a small war, part of which takes place at home, and over a long period of time. How much power should really be given to the Executive over the Legislative Branch? How much supervision should the Legislative Branch have over counterterrorism?
- Courts have traditionally been on the sidelines of national security law, especially when there is a war going on. Courts and judges were not supposed to become involved in matters about which they possess little understanding or professional training, and in situations in which the existence of the state is at stake. Counterterrorism measures, however, aim at adversaries who are not generally to be met openly on a battlefield and who are frequently all but indistinguishable from civilians. With their extreme reliance on methods that require restrictions on individual liberties and their indefinite duration, counterterrorist campaigns necessarily are of interest to the courts. What should be the extent of judicial review of counterterror activities? Likewise, should emergency regimes be used in order to combat terrorism, or should the "regular" security constitutional system be adapted to the changing realities of international terrorism?

On the *external* issues of national security:

- Counterterrorism measures usually entail some limitations on individual rights, such as privacy, free speech, and movement. How much should individual rights (e.g., of terrorist suspects) give way to counterterrorism measures intended to protect the lives of innocent civilians against terror attacks?
- International law has been considered a source of influence on domestic practices. The conventional wisdom at the end of the 20th century, sup-

ported by the experience of post-Soviet Europe, was that international law could serve as a vehicle for the promotion of individual liberties and rights. Yet counterterror measures, as explained above, require international lawyers to reconsider their positions. The calls for "revisions of international law" in order to allow states more flexibility in the fight against terrorism, together with the double-edged role that international law plays when both limiting and legitimizing the actions of belligerents in such struggles, all create puzzles that may not be solvable without further development of international law.

All these questions still await resolution. This volume offers only glimpses into some possible avenues for future solutions.

Regarding the institutional or functional questions, Christopher Ford's analysis suggests that states have the ability to adapt, with time, to the exigencies of the need to fight terrorism, developing new methods and adjusting older ones to the peculiarities of this idiosyncratic form of "warfare." Amichai Cohen delineated the possible areas in which courts have hitherto intervened, and would most probably intervene in the near future. But what if such adjustments do not turn out to be enough to resolve the issues and difficulties presented? Possibly, there should further shifts in our understanding of how law operates with regards to counter terrorism measures.

In his contribution to this volume, Yuval Shany presented one possible way forward when suggesting that international institutions be entrusted with oversight responsibilities over states. However, Elizabeth Samson's analysis of the Goldstone Report cautions against the extreme use of such external international mechanisms of control, and Jeremy Rabkin's chapter warns against ceding too much interpretative discretion to institutions that may not understand the actual dilemmas states face in counterterrorism struggles. Indeed, it seems that the correct role of international law in these matters should be further developed and researched.

As we have seen, international law is not of course the sole question on the table, and certainly cannot be the only linchpin of a solution. Thought should thus be devoted to possible changes in the roles of different domestic institutions and branches, to redefining individual rights, and to the role of courts in preserving this system.

This too is a goal that lies beyond the scope of the present work. The future task of researchers in law, political science, history, and philosophy is to develop answers to the questions it raises. With luck, however, this volume will help scholars and policy experts move a bit further in drawing the boundaries of issues and questions that should be discussed.

NOTES

1. Arnold Wolfers, "National Security as an Ambiguous Symbol," in *Discord and Collaboration: Essays on International Politics*, (A. Wolfers ed.) (Baltimore: Johns Hopkins University Press, 1962), at 147–65.

2. Jessica Mathews, "Redefining Security," *Foreign Affairs*, vol. 68 (1989), at 162–77.

3. Dan Caldwell & Robert E. Williams, *Seeking Security in an Insecure World* (Lanham, MA: Rowman, 2006).

4. This typology is based in part on Amichai Cohen and Stuart A. Cohen, *Israel's National Security Law: Political Dynamics and Historical Developments* (London, Routledge, 2011), at Chapter 1.

Index

About the Authors

Amichai Cohen is a senior lecturer at the Ono Academic College in Israel, specializing in international law and national security law. Dr. Cohen holds degrees from the Hebrew University in Jerusalem (LL.B.) and the Yale Law School (LL.M. & J.S.D.). He is also a research fellow at the Israel Democracy Institute. His most recent book is: *Israel's National Security Law: Political Dynamics and Historical Development* (with Stuart A. Cohen, Routledge, 2011).

Steven R. David is a professor of international relations and vice dean for Undergraduate Education at the Johns Hopkins University (JHU), specializing in international politics and security issues. With a B.A. in political science from Union College, an M.A. in East Asian studies from Stanford University, and both an M.A. and Ph.D. from Harvard University, Professor David became a full professor in 1991. He has chaired JHU's Political Science Department, and served as associate dean for Academic Affairs, special assistant to the dean of the Krieger School of Arts and Sciences, vice dean for Centers and Programs, and director of Jewish Studies at Johns Hopkins. He was named vice dean for Undergraduate Education in 2010.

Christopher A. Ford is a Senior Fellow at Hudson Institute in Washington, D.C. He previously served as U.S. special representative for nuclear nonproliferation, principal deputy assistant secretary of state, and general counsel to the U.S. Senate Select Committee on Intelligence. He holds the rank of Lieutenant Commander as an intelligence officer in the U.S. Navy Reserve. A contributing editor for *The New Atlantis* magazine and an ordained Buddhist lay chaplain, Dr. Ford runs and writes for the *New Paradigms Forum* website (www.NewParadigmsForum.com). He holds degrees from Harvard University (A.B.), Oxford University (D.Phil. as a Rhodes Scholar), and the Yale Law School (J.D.). His publications include *The Mind of Empire: China's History and Modern Foreign Relations* (University Press of Kentucky, 2010) and *The Admirals' Advantage: U.S. Navy Operational Intelligence in World War II and the Cold War* (Naval Institute, 2005).

Jeremy Rabkin is a professor at the George Mason School of Law, where he teaches courses on public international law, the law of war and American constitutional history. Before coming to George Mason in 2007, he was professor in the Department of Government at Cornell University. He serves on the board of directors of the U.S. Institute of Peace (a federal advisory agency) and of the Center for Individual Rights (a private advocacy organization). He holds a Ph.D. in political science from Harvard University and a B.A. from Cornell University. His most recent book is *Law Without Nations? Why Constitutional Government Requires Sovereign States* (Princeton University Press, 2007).

Juan Carlos Gómez Ramírez holds the rank of colonel in the Colombia Air Force, in which he serves on active duty. Col. Gómez has also served as a visiting professor at the U.S. National Defense University's Center for Hemispheric Defense Studies. From January 2005 until April 2009, he served as director of the Human Rights and International Humanitarian Law Office in the Colombian Ministry of Defense.

Elizabeth Samson is a Visiting Fellow at Hudson Institute, a Washington, D.C.-based nonpartisan policy research organization dedicated to innovative research and analysis that promotes global security, prosperity, and freedom. She holds a J.D. degree from Fordham Law School in New York and an LL.M. degree in international and European law from the University of Amsterdam, Netherlands.

Yuval Shany is Hersch Lauterpacht Chair in Public International Law on the Faculty of Law at the Hebrew University of Jerusalem. Professor Shany also serves as a board member of the International Law Forum at the Hebrew University, a director in the Project on International Courts and Tribunals (PICT), a member of the steering committee of the DOMAC project (assessing the impact of international courts on domestic criminal procedures in mass atrocity cases) and as a Senior Research Fellow at the Israel Democracy Institute.

John H. Shenefield is a former senior partner in the law firm of Morgan, Lewis & Bockius LLP. He served in the United States Department of Justice as assistant attorney general in charge of the Antitrust Division in 1977–79, and then as the associate attorney general of the United States in 1979–81. In addition, he was the chairman of the President's National Commission for the Review of Antitrust Laws and Procedures (1978–79). In these capacities, Mr. Shenefield had considerable responsibilities related to national security law, including playing a role in the presidential findings process for covert actions, helping develop the bill that became the Intelligence Oversight Act of 1980, and overseeing some of the electronic surveillance applications under the then-new Foreign Intelligence Surveillance Act (FISA). He is the coauthor (with Dr. Irwin M. Stelzer) of *The Antitrust Laws: A Primer*, whose fourth edition was published in 2001 by the American Enterprise Institute. Mr. Shenefield has taught at the University of Richmond and the Georgetown law schools, and has written articles on a variety of antitrust topics.

Ariel Zemach is a lecturer at the faculty of law of the Ono Academic College. He holds degrees from Columbia University (J.S.D. & LL.M.) and the Hebrew University. He has written widely on subjects related to international law, especially with regard to applications of the law of war and international criminal law to events occurring within occupied territories.

CPSIA information can be obtained at www.ICGtesting.com
Printed in the USA
BVOW042350151211

278297BV00002B/2/P